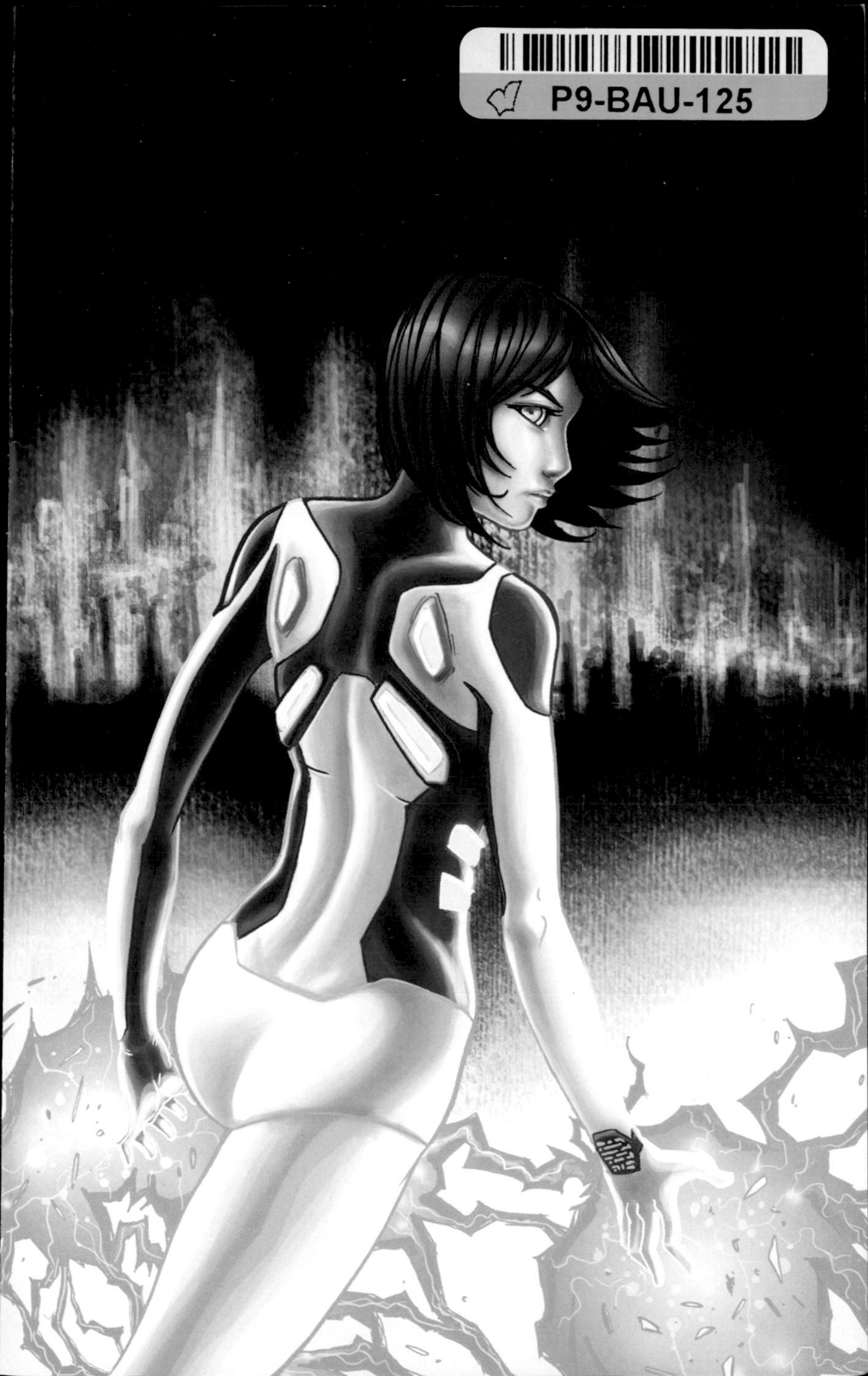

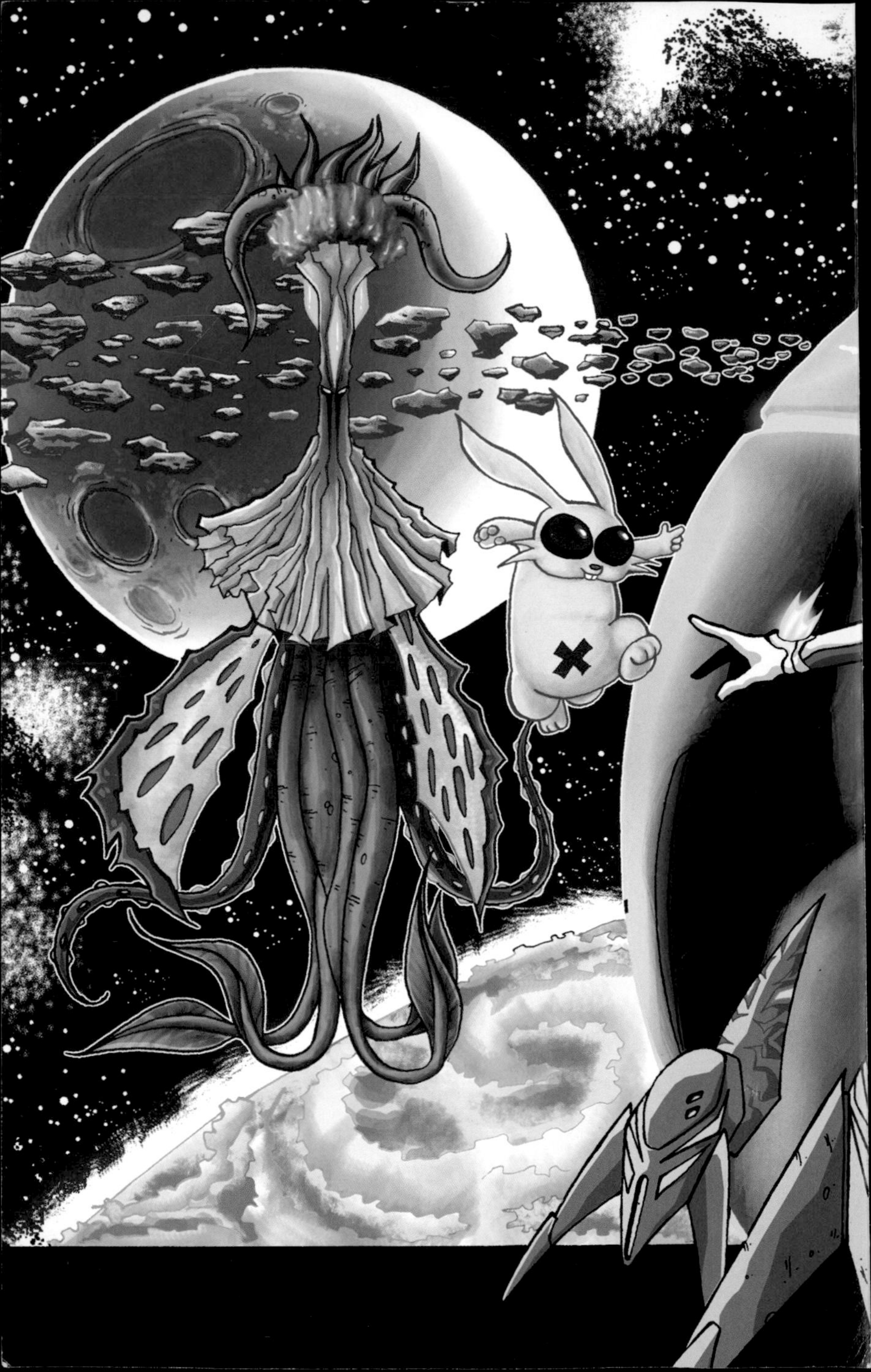

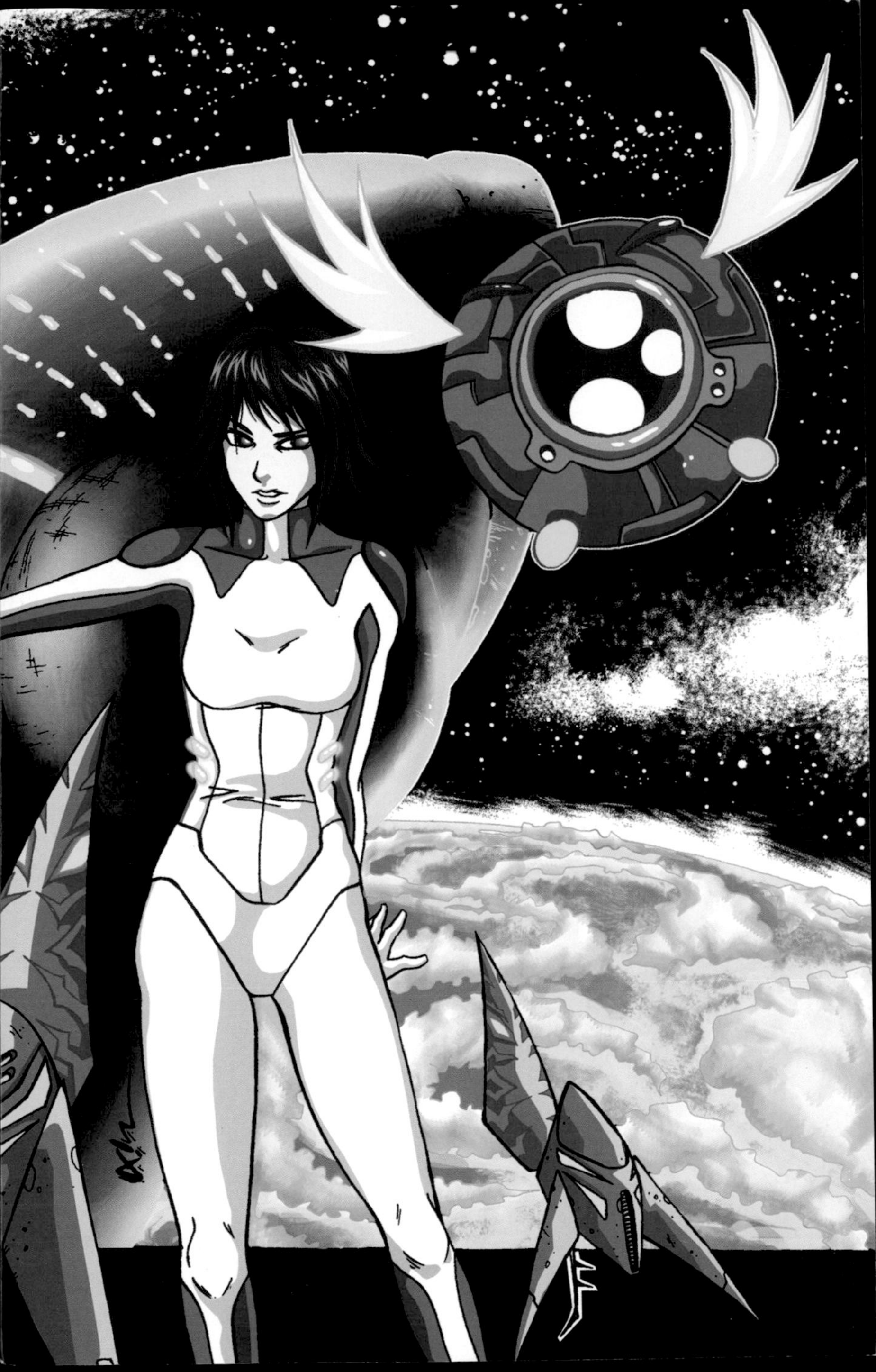

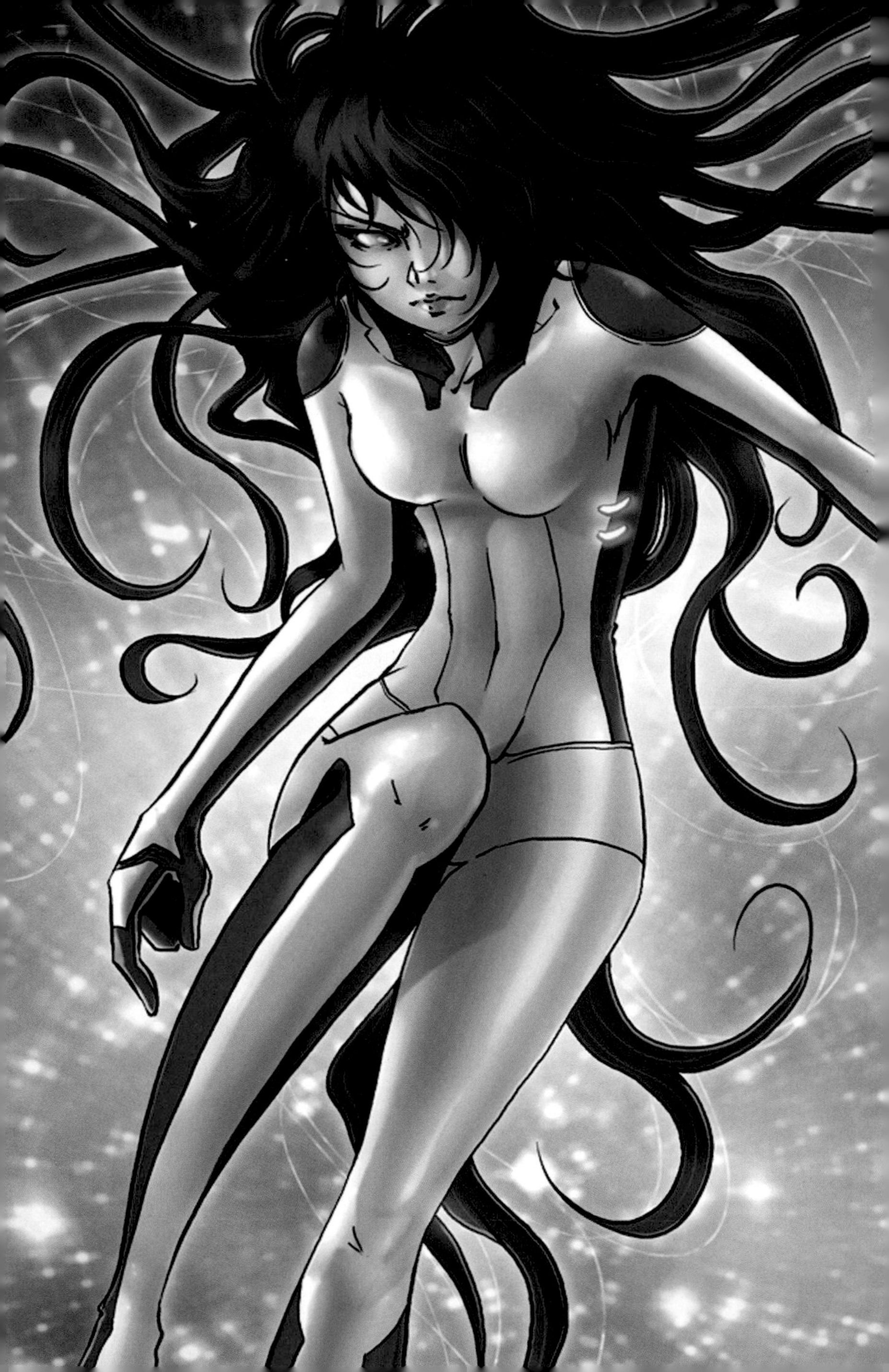

eV Vol.1
Created by Roger Mincheff
Written by James Farr
Art by Alfa Robbi and Papillon Studio

Lettering - Lucas Rivera
Cover Illustration - Emma Vieceli and Annette Kwok
Cover Design - Louis Csontos

Editor - Bryce P. Coleman
Digital Imaging Manager - Chris Buford
Pre-Production Supervisor - Erika Terriquez
Production Manager - Elisabeth Brizzi
Managing Editor - Vy Nguyen
Creative Director - Anne Marie Horne
Editor-in-Chief - Rob Tokar
Publisher - Mike Kiley
President and C.O.O. - John Parker
C.E.O. and Chief Creative Officer - Stuart Levy

A **TOKYOPOP** Manga

TOKYOPOP and 🐾 are trademarks or registered trademarks of TOKYOPOP Inc.

TOKYOPOP Inc.
5900 Wilshire Blvd. Suite 2000
Los Angeles, CA 90036

E-mail: info@TOKYOPOP.com
Come visit us online at www.TOKYOPOP.com

ISBN: 978-1-4278-0714-4

First TOKYOPOP printing: April 2008
10 9 8 7 6 5 4 3 2 1
Printed in the USA

VOL. 1

CREATED BY
Roger Mincheff

WRITTEN BY
James Farr

ART BY
Alfa Robbi and Papillion Studio

HAMBURG // LONDON // LOS ANGELES // TOKYO

For Spacedog Entertainment:

Created by - Roger Mincheff
Written by - James Farr
Art by - Papillon Studio
Pencils - Alfa Robbi
Inks - Anang Setyawan
Tones - Han & Bowo
Cover Illustration - Emma Vieceli and Annette Kwok
Editors for Spacedog - Mark Kauffman and David Wohl
Project Manager - Lauren Perry
Art Director for Spacedog - Chris Moreno
Pin up art - Emma Vieceli, Alfa Robbi and Annette Kwok

eV website created by James Farr
Visit the website at: www.ev-book.com

Special Thanks to: Susan Aberbach, Richard Mincheff and Ana Maria Lopez

SPACEDÖG

Roger Mincheff - President & Chief Executive Officer
Lauren Perry - Executive Editor
Mark Kauffman - Creative Executive
Heather Noonan - Marketing Director
Meredith Bunche - Director, Account Management
David Wohl - Consulting Editor
Michael Yong - Production Manager
Chris Moreno - Art Director
Dave Baxter - Commerce Specialist

Vol.1
Table of Contents

FORWARD

THIS ALL STARTED WITH A PHONE CALL. AND NOT UNLIKE THE PHONE CALL FEATURED IN THE OPENING PAGES OF THIS BOOK, IT WOULD ENTAIL A TREMENDOUS AMOUNT OF WORK.

eV WAS A CONCEPT CREATED BY ROGER MINCHEFF, AND LATER PITCHED TO ME AS AN OPEN-ENDED FRANCHISE. CUTE GIRL. OUTER SPACE. EARTH'S SOLE POLITICAL REPRESENTATIVE. IT WAS UP TO ME TO FILL IN THE BLANKS AND DELIVER WHAT WOULD BECOME THIS VERY BOOK. AS A RABID DISCIPLE OF SCIENCE FICTION, COMIC BOOKS AND CUTE GIRLS, I WAS AN EASY SELL. AND SO BEGAN THE PROCESS OF BUILDING -- WHAT WOULD EVENTUALLY BE -- eV'S DENSELY POPULATED UNIVERSE.

UP UNTIL THEN, MY WRITING CAREER HAD BEEN LARGELY CONFINED TO THE WEB, WHERE ZOMBIES, MUMMIES AND GIANT PREHISTORIC CRUSTACEANS DELIVERED MY LINES WITHOUT COMPLAINT. AT THE TIME, THE LEAP TO PRINT WAS AN IMPOSSIBLE DREAM -- ONE OF THOSE GOALS THAT FLOATS IN THE ETHER, JUST A LITTLE TOO IMPROBABLE TO REACH FOR. FORTUNATELY, IT REACHED FOR ME INSTEAD.

OVER THE NEXT TWO YEARS, I SET ABOUT CREATING A CAST OF PERSONALITIES TO INHABIT THESE PAGES, REFINING THEM LITTLE BY LITTLE, AND CARVING AWAY ANYTHING THAT DIDN'T FEEL -- IN A WORD -- AWESOME. THANKS TO A BRILLIANT EDITING STAFF, AND THE TOP SHELF CREATURE DESIGNS OF ALFA ROBBI, I'D SAY WE'VE PRODUCED A PRETTY INSANELY GREAT BUNCH OF CHARACTERS. AFTER ALL, WHEN YOU'RE WRITING, YOUR CHARACTERS ARE YOUR CO-WORKERS. SO THEY MAY AS WELL BE A BLAST TO HANG OUT WITH, RIGHT?

THAT SAID, IT'S BEEN A PLEASURE TO SPEND SOME TIME WITH EVIE AND HER FRIENDS. SHE'S EVOLVED GRADUALLY ALONG THE WAY, DEFYING HER INEXPERIENCE, MASTERING HER FEARS AND FINALLY GAINING THE CONFIDENCE TO CONQUER A STRANGE NEW WORLD.

I'M STILL NOT SURE WHO BENEFITED MORE FROM THE EXPERIENCE.

JAMES FARR
TULSA, OK.
DECEMBER, 2007

CHAPTER 01

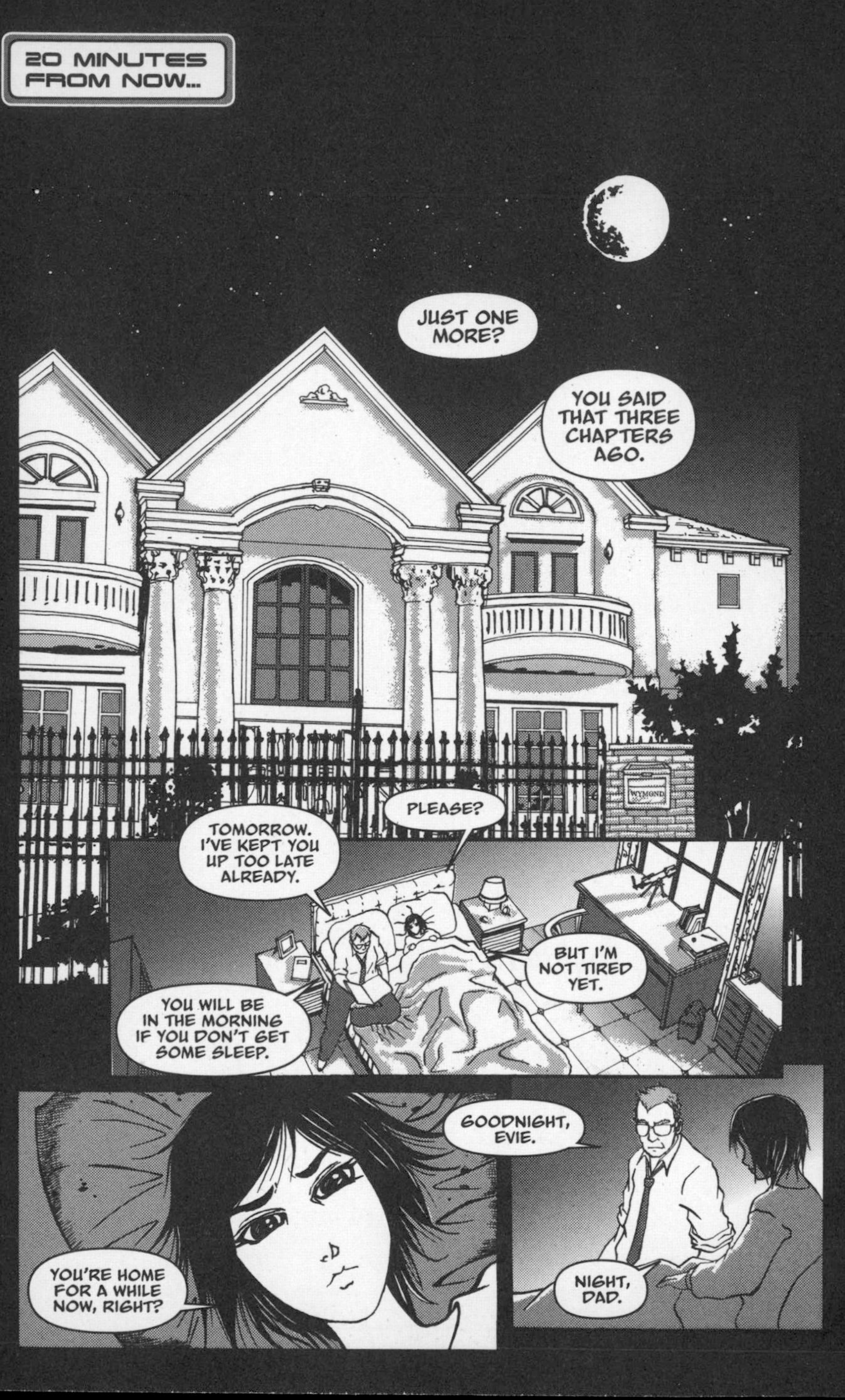
20 MINUTES FROM NOW...
JUST ONE MORE?
YOU SAID THAT THREE CHAPTERS AGO.
WYMOND
TOMORROW. I'VE KEPT YOU UP TOO LATE ALREADY.
PLEASE?
BUT I'M NOT TIRED YET.
YOU WILL BE IN THE MORNING IF YOU DON'T GET SOME SLEEP.
YOU'RE HOME FOR A WHILE NOW, RIGHT?
GOODNIGHT, EVIE.
NIGHT, DAD.

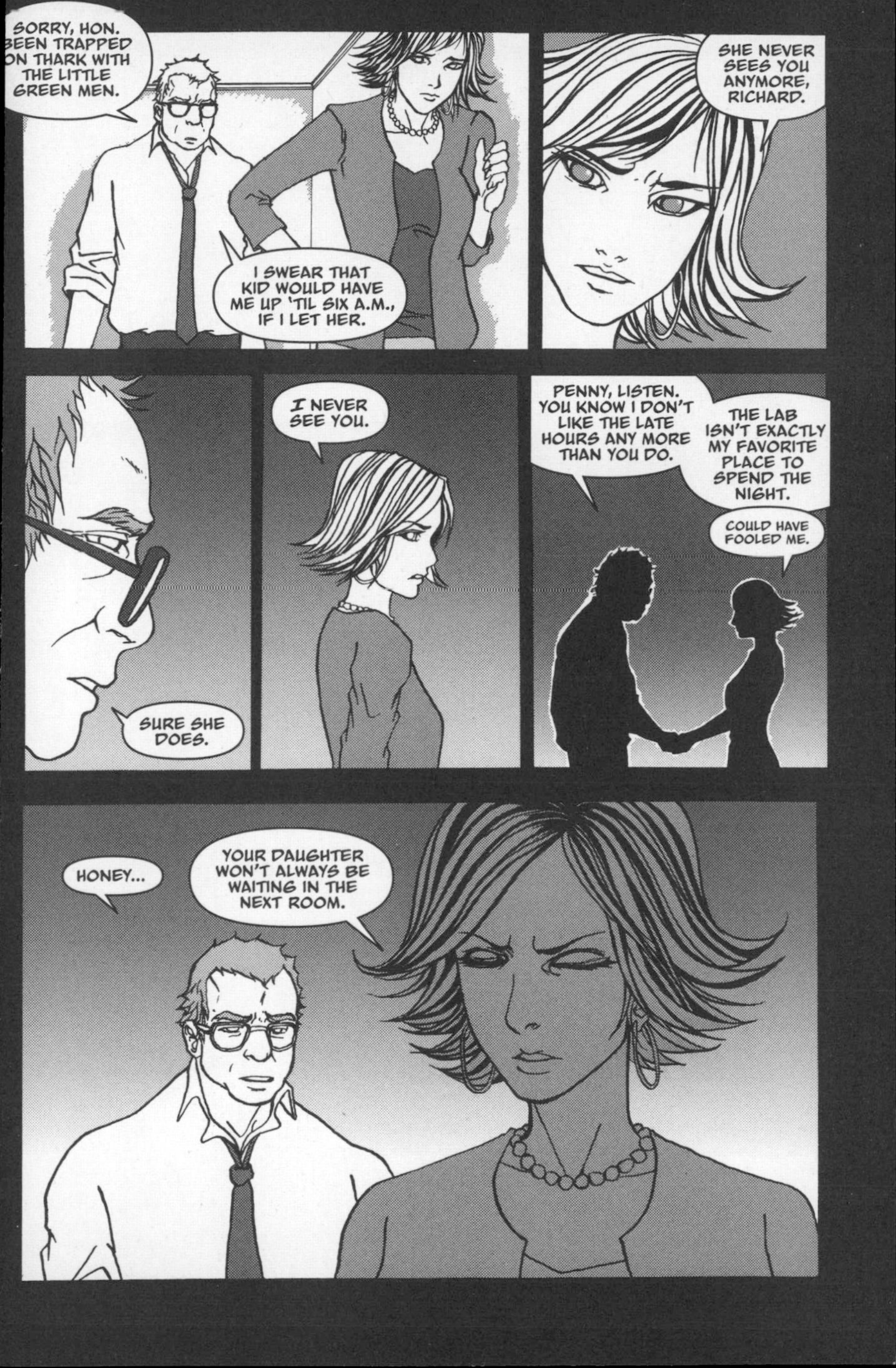
SORRY, HON. BEEN TRAPPED ON THARK WITH THE LITTLE GREEN MEN.
I SWEAR THAT KID WOULD HAVE ME UP 'TIL SIX A.M., IF I LET HER.
SHE NEVER SEES YOU ANYMORE, RICHARD.
SURE SHE DOES.
I NEVER SEE YOU.
PENNY, LISTEN. YOU KNOW I DON'T LIKE THE LATE HOURS ANY MORE THAN YOU DO.
THE LAB ISN'T EXACTLY MY FAVORITE PLACE TO SPEND THE NIGHT.
COULD HAVE FOOLED ME.
HONEY...
YOUR DAUGHTER WON'T ALWAYS BE WAITING IN THE NEXT ROOM.

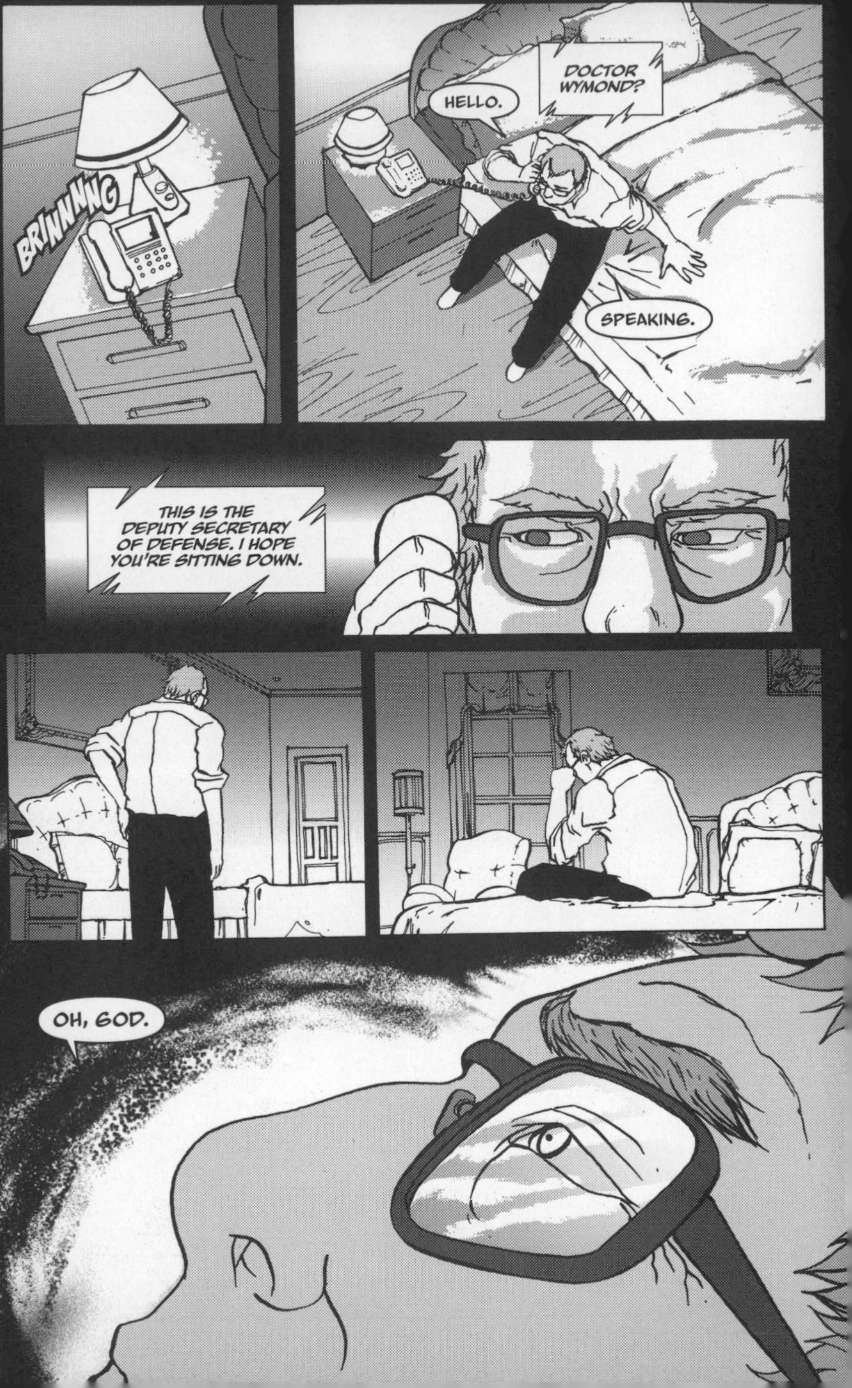
BRINNNNG
HELLO.
DOCTOR WYMOND?
SPEAKING.
THIS IS THE DEPUTY SECRETARY OF DEFENSE. I HOPE YOU'RE SITTING DOWN.
OH, GOD.

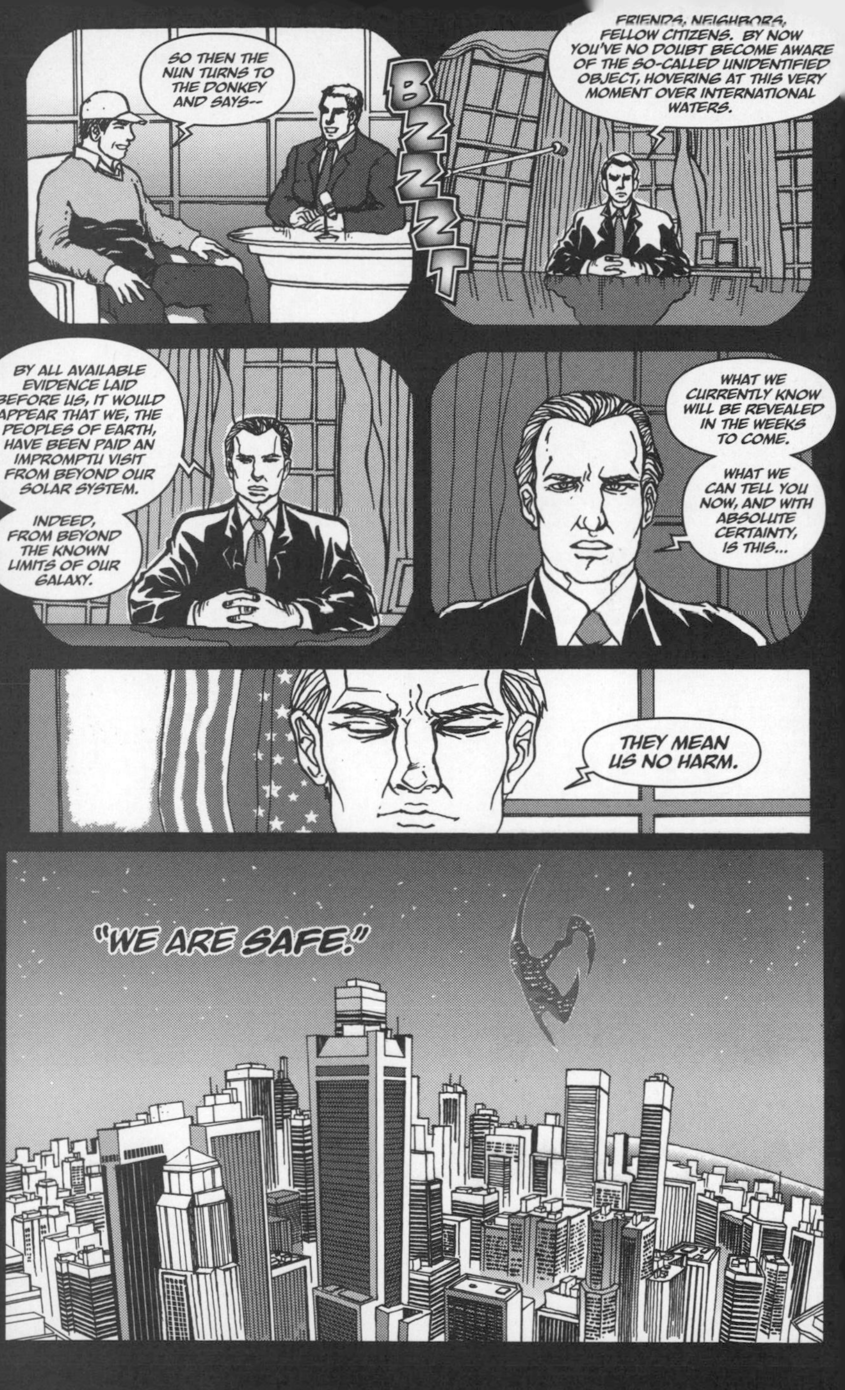
SO THEN THE NUN TURNS TO THE DONKEY AND SAYS--
BZZZZT
FRIENDS, NEIGHBORS, FELLOW CITIZENS. BY NOW YOU'VE NO DOUBT BECOME AWARE OF THE SO-CALLED UNIDENTIFIED OBJECT, HOVERING AT THIS VERY MOMENT OVER INTERNATIONAL WATERS.
BY ALL AVAILABLE EVIDENCE LAID BEFORE US, IT WOULD APPEAR THAT WE, THE PEOPLES OF EARTH, HAVE BEEN PAID AN IMPROMPTU VISIT FROM BEYOND OUR SOLAR SYSTEM.
INDEED, FROM BEYOND THE KNOWN LIMITS OF OUR GALAXY.
WHAT WE CURRENTLY KNOW WILL BE REVEALED IN THE WEEKS TO COME.
WHAT WE CAN TELL YOU NOW, AND WITH ABSOLUTE CERTAINTY, IS THIS...
THEY MEAN US NO HARM.
"WE ARE SAFE."

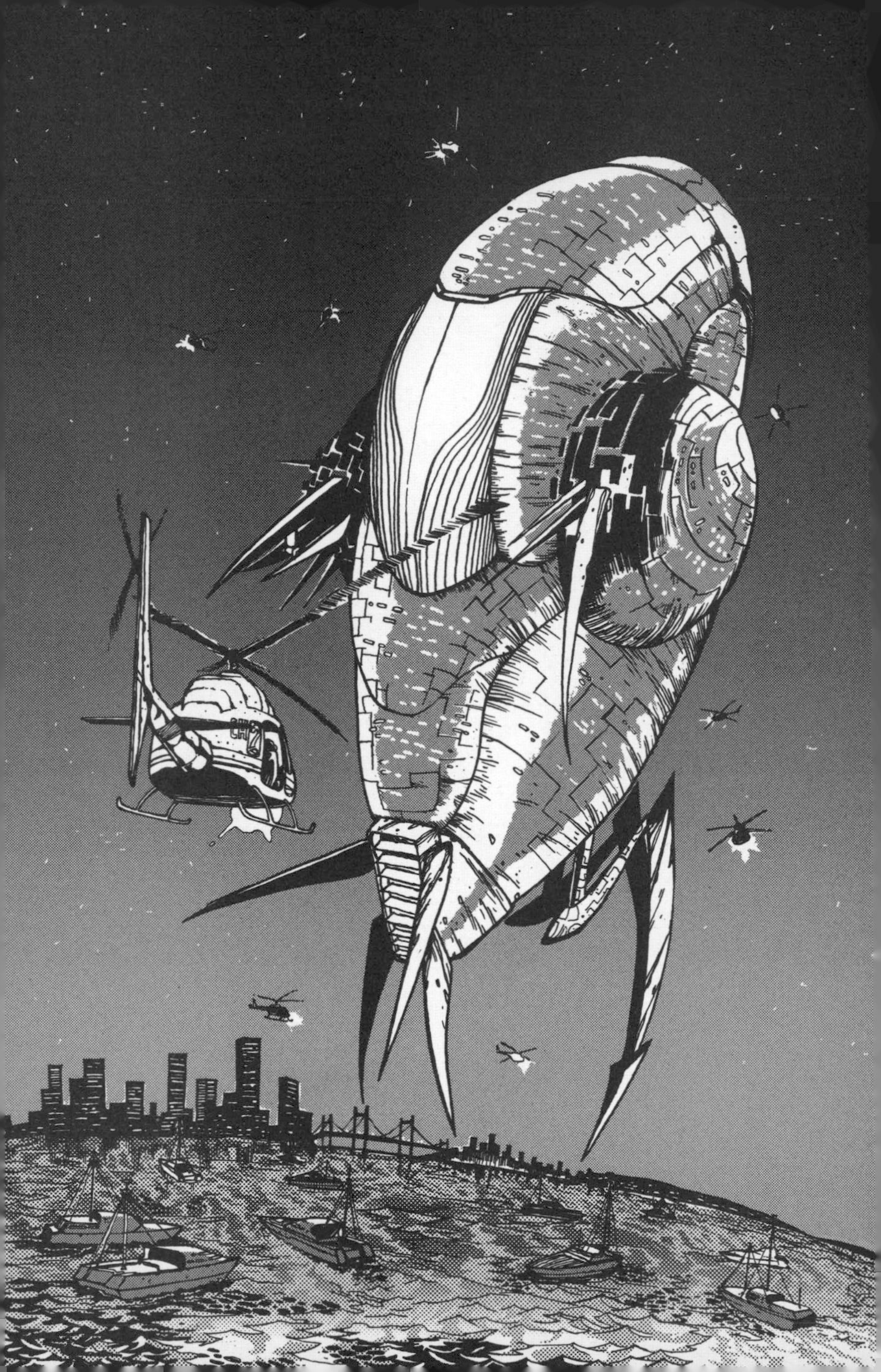
CH 7

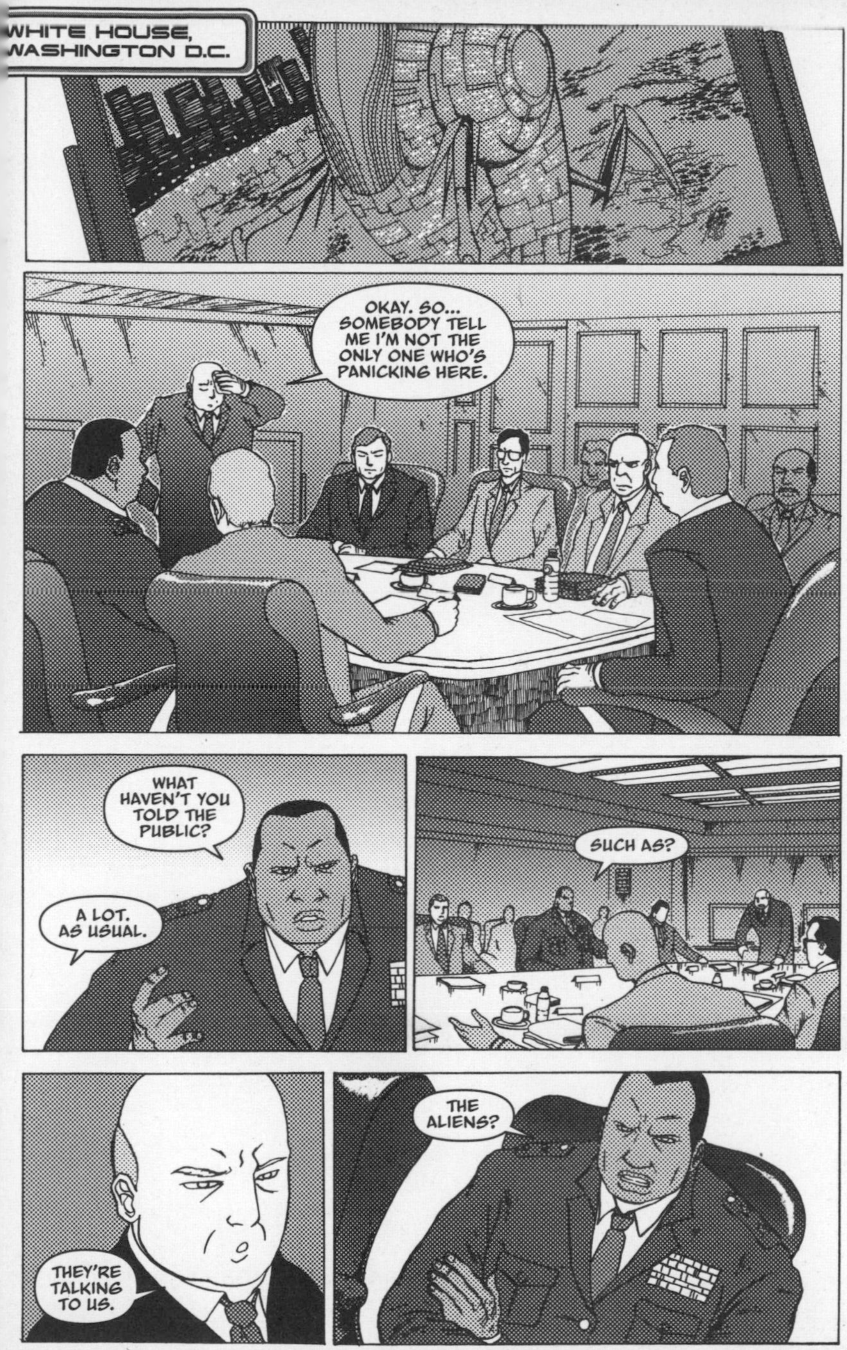
WHITE HOUSE,
WASHINGTON D.C.
OKAY. SO... SOMEBODY TELL ME I'M NOT THE ONLY ONE WHO'S PANICKING HERE.
WHAT HAVEN'T YOU TOLD THE PUBLIC?
A LOT. AS USUAL.
SUCH AS?
THEY'RE TALKING TO US.
THE ALIENS?

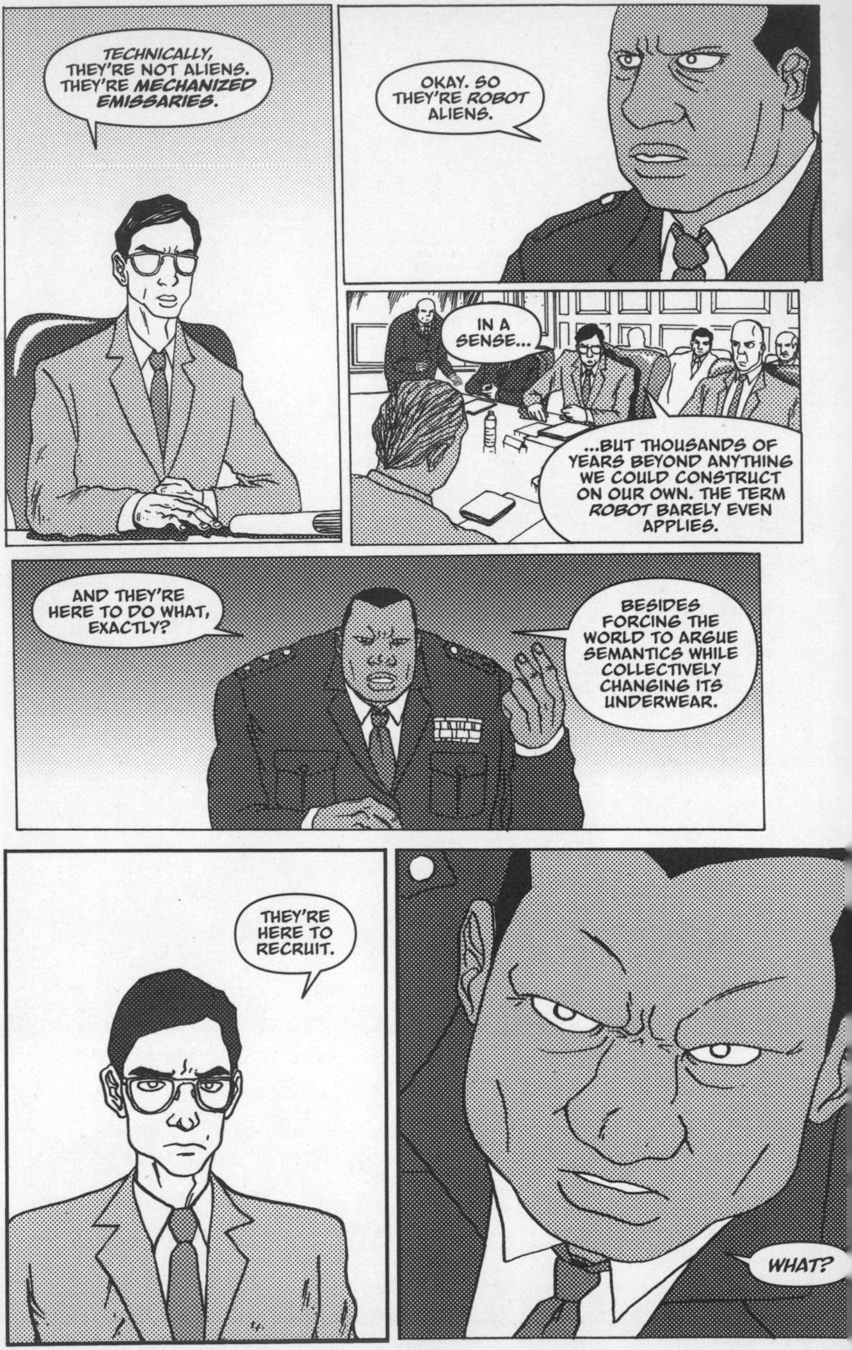
TECHNICALLY, THEY'RE NOT ALIENS. THEY'RE *MECHANIZED EMISSARIES*.
OKAY. SO THEY'RE *ROBOT* ALIENS.
IN A SENSE...
...BUT THOUSANDS OF YEARS BEYOND ANYTHING WE COULD CONSTRUCT ON OUR OWN. THE TERM *ROBOT* BARELY EVEN APPLIES.
AND THEY'RE HERE TO DO WHAT, EXACTLY?
BESIDES FORCING THE WORLD TO ARGUE SEMANTICS WHILE COLLECTIVELY CHANGING ITS UNDERWEAR.
THEY'RE HERE TO RECRUIT.
WHAT?

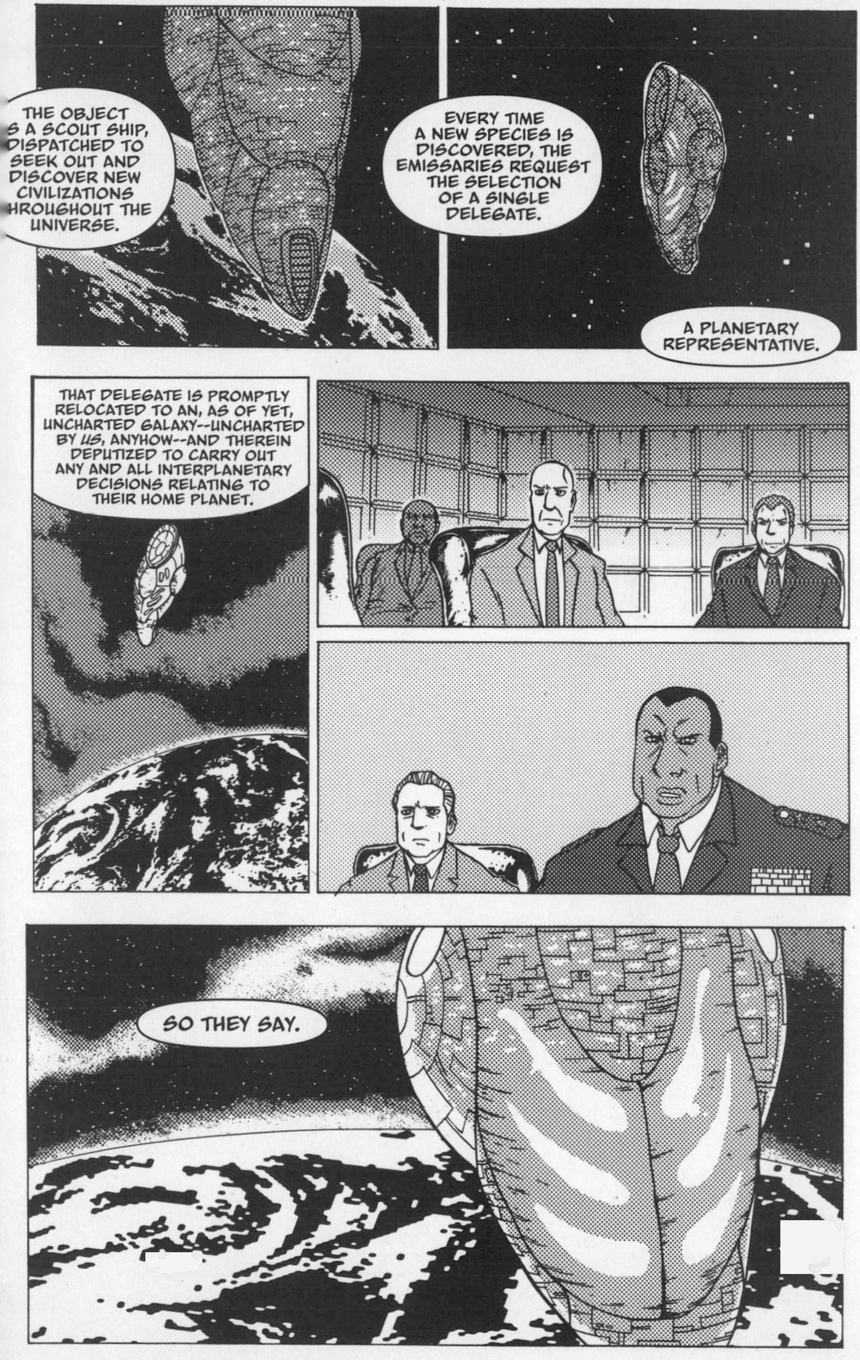
THE OBJECT S A SCOUT SHIP, DISPATCHED TO SEEK OUT AND DISCOVER NEW CIVILIZATIONS HROUGHOUT THE UNIVERSE.
EVERY TIME A NEW SPECIES IS DISCOVERED, THE EMISSARIES REQUEST THE SELECTION OF A SINGLE DELEGATE.
A PLANETARY REPRESENTATIVE.
THAT DELEGATE IS PROMPTLY RELOCATED TO AN, AS OF YET, UNCHARTED GALAXY--UNCHARTED BY *US*, ANYHOW--AND THEREIN DEPUTIZED TO CARRY OUT ANY AND ALL INTERPLANETARY DECISIONS RELATING TO THEIR HOME PLANET.
SO THEY SAY.

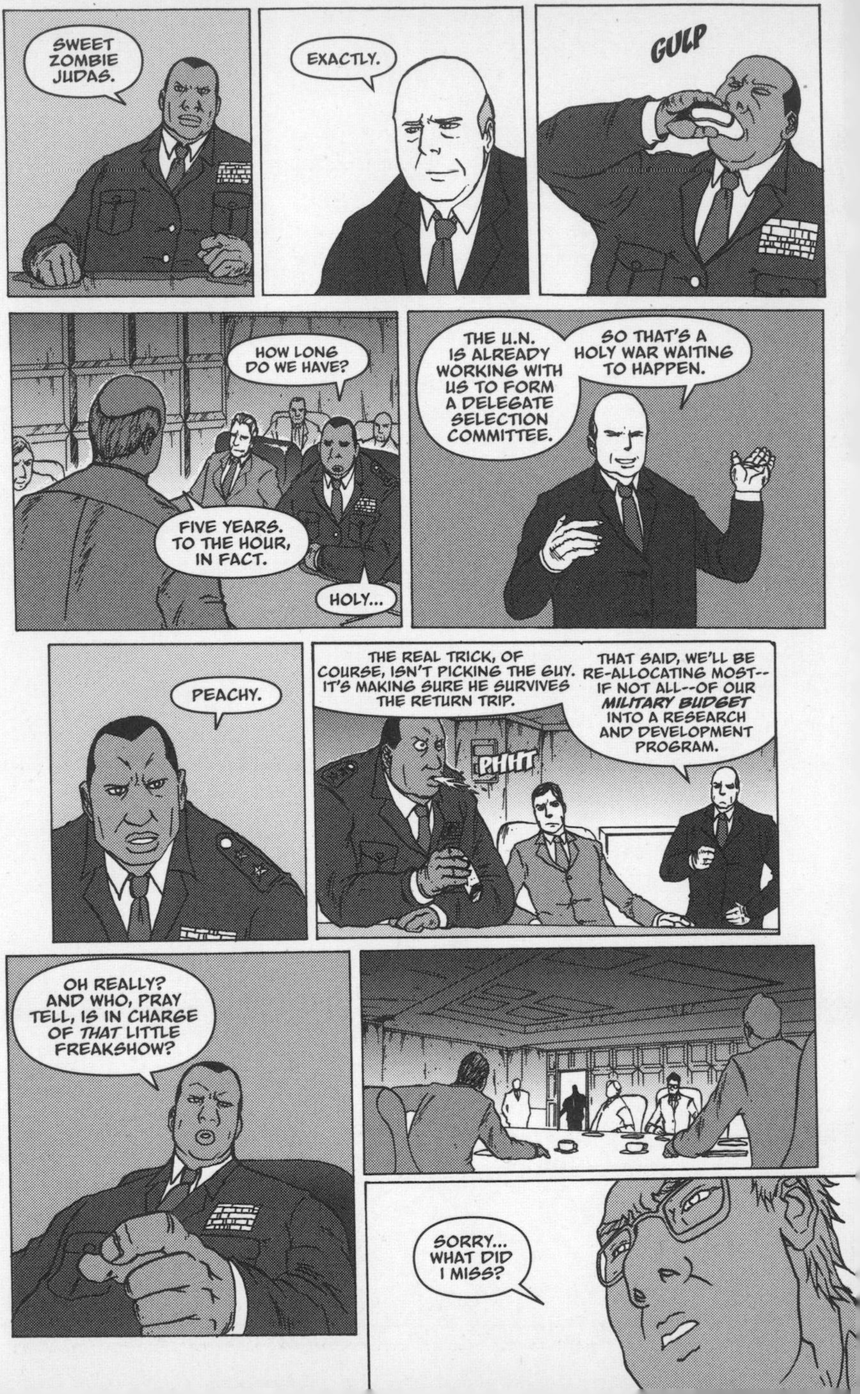
SWEET ZOMBIE JUDAS.
EXACTLY.
GULP
HOW LONG DO WE HAVE?
FIVE YEARS. TO THE HOUR, IN FACT.
HOLY...
THE U.N. IS ALREADY WORKING WITH US TO FORM A DELEGATE SELECTION COMMITTEE.
SO THAT'S A HOLY WAR WAITING TO HAPPEN.
PEACHY.
THE REAL TRICK, OF COURSE, ISN'T PICKING THE GUY. IT'S MAKING SURE HE SURVIVES THE RETURN TRIP.
THAT SAID, WE'LL BE RE-ALLOCATING MOST--IF NOT ALL--OF OUR *MILITARY BUDGET* INTO A RESEARCH AND DEVELOPMENT PROGRAM.
PHHT
OH REALLY? AND WHO, PRAY TELL, IS IN CHARGE OF *THAT* LITTLE FREAKSHOW?
SORRY... WHAT DID I MISS?

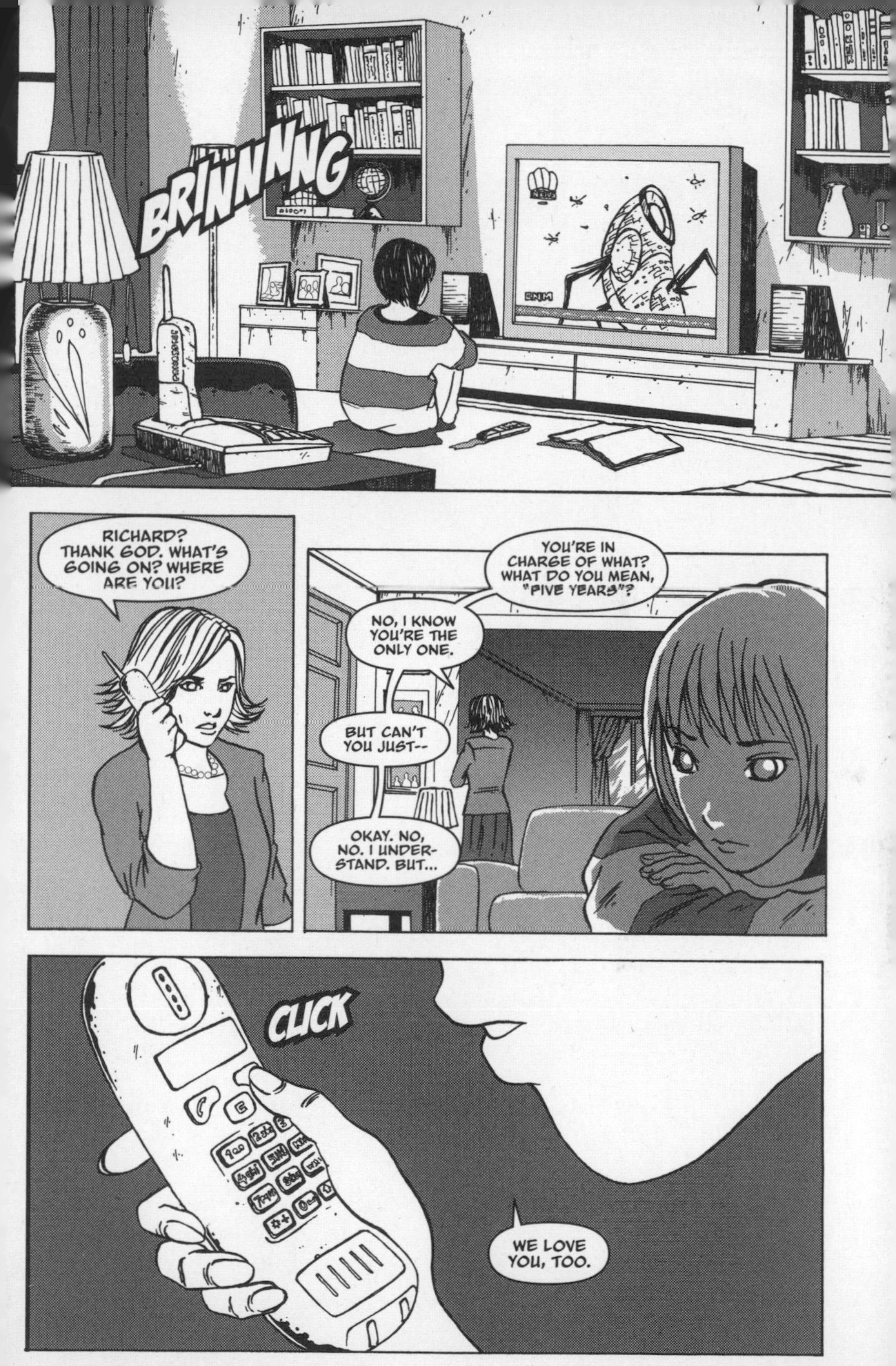
BRINNNNG
RICHARD? THANK GOD. WHAT'S GOING ON? WHERE ARE YOU?
YOU'RE IN CHARGE OF WHAT? WHAT DO YOU MEAN, "FIVE YEARS"?
NO, I KNOW YOU'RE THE ONLY ONE.
BUT CAN'T YOU JUST--
OKAY. NO, NO. I UNDERSTAND. BUT...
CLICK
WE LOVE YOU, TOO.

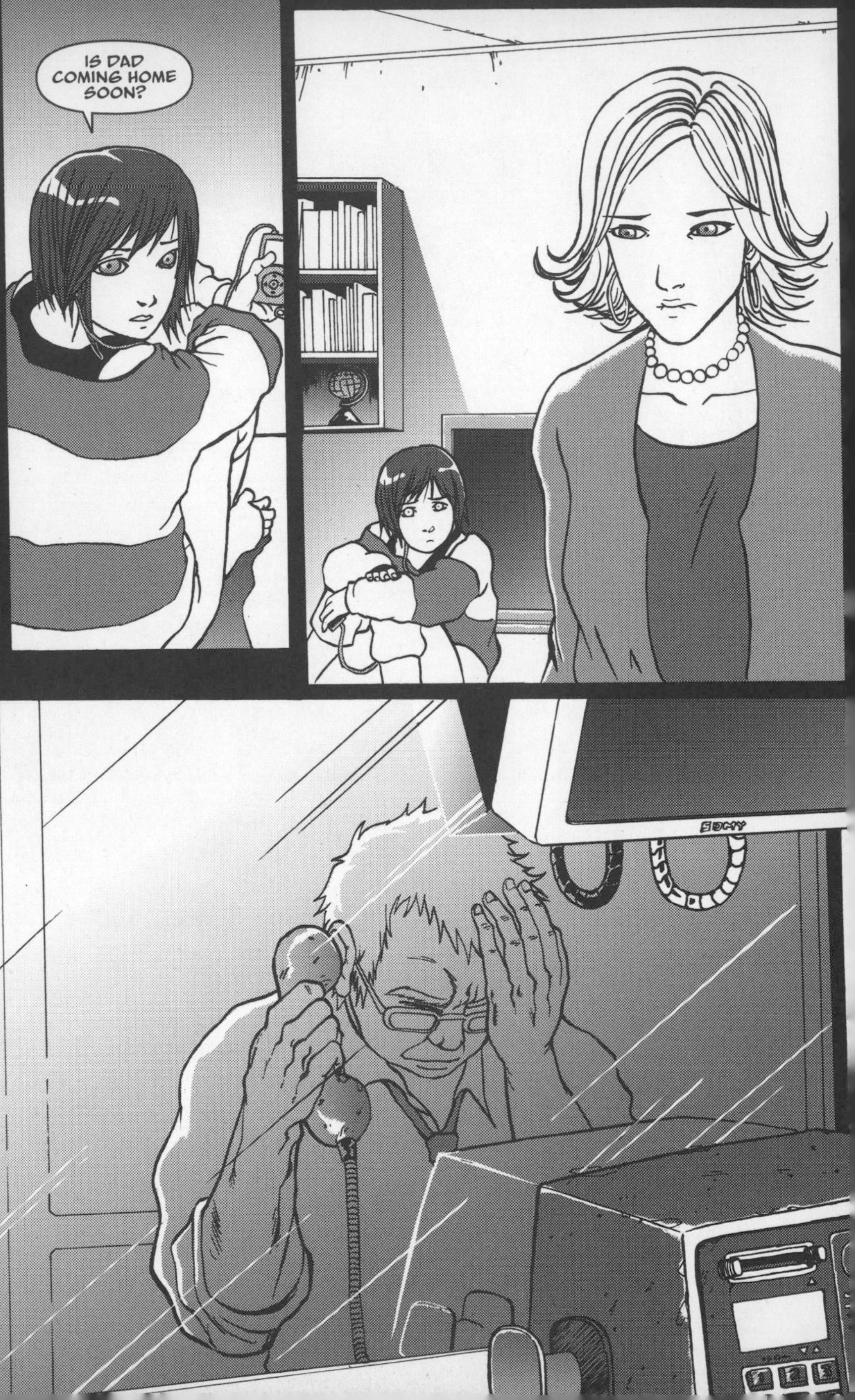
IS DAD COMING HOME SOON?
SONY

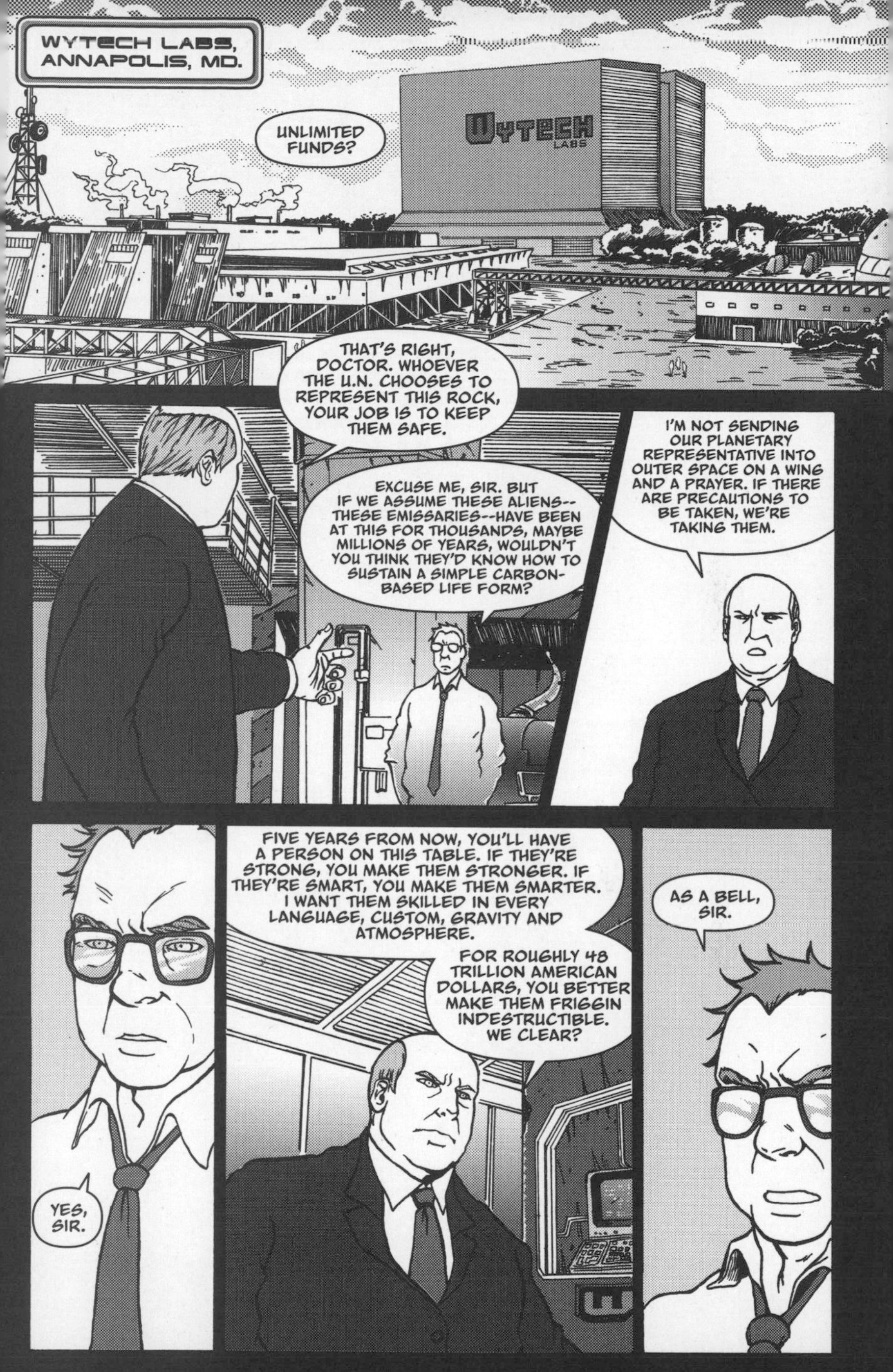
WYTECH LABS, ANNAPOLIS, MD.
UNLIMITED FUNDS?
WYTECH LABS
THAT'S RIGHT, DOCTOR. WHOEVER THE U.N. CHOOSES TO REPRESENT THIS ROCK, YOUR JOB IS TO KEEP THEM SAFE.
EXCUSE ME, SIR. BUT IF WE ASSUME THESE ALIENS--THESE EMISSARIES--HAVE BEEN AT THIS FOR THOUSANDS, MAYBE MILLIONS OF YEARS, WOULDN'T YOU THINK THEY'D KNOW HOW TO SUSTAIN A SIMPLE CARBON-BASED LIFE FORM?
I'M NOT SENDING OUR PLANETARY REPRESENTATIVE INTO OUTER SPACE ON A WING AND A PRAYER. IF THERE ARE PRECAUTIONS TO BE TAKEN, WE'RE TAKING THEM.
YES, SIR.
FIVE YEARS FROM NOW, YOU'LL HAVE A PERSON ON THIS TABLE. IF THEY'RE STRONG, YOU MAKE THEM STRONGER. IF THEY'RE SMART, YOU MAKE THEM SMARTER. I WANT THEM SKILLED IN EVERY LANGUAGE, CUSTOM, GRAVITY AND ATMOSPHERE.
FOR ROUGHLY 48 TRILLION AMERICAN DOLLARS, YOU BETTER MAKE THEM FRIGGIN INDESTRUCTIBLE. WE CLEAR?
AS A BELL, SIR.

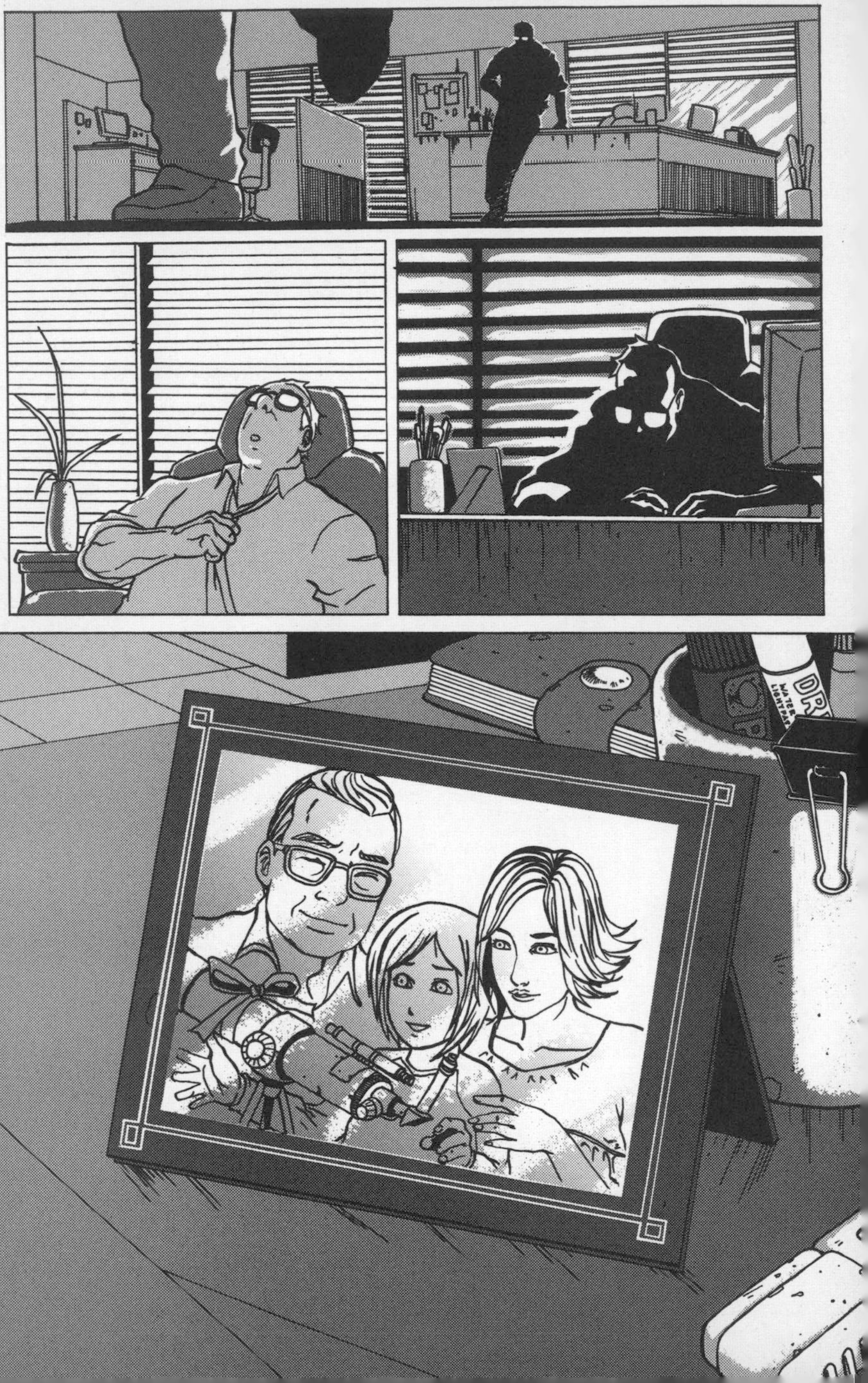

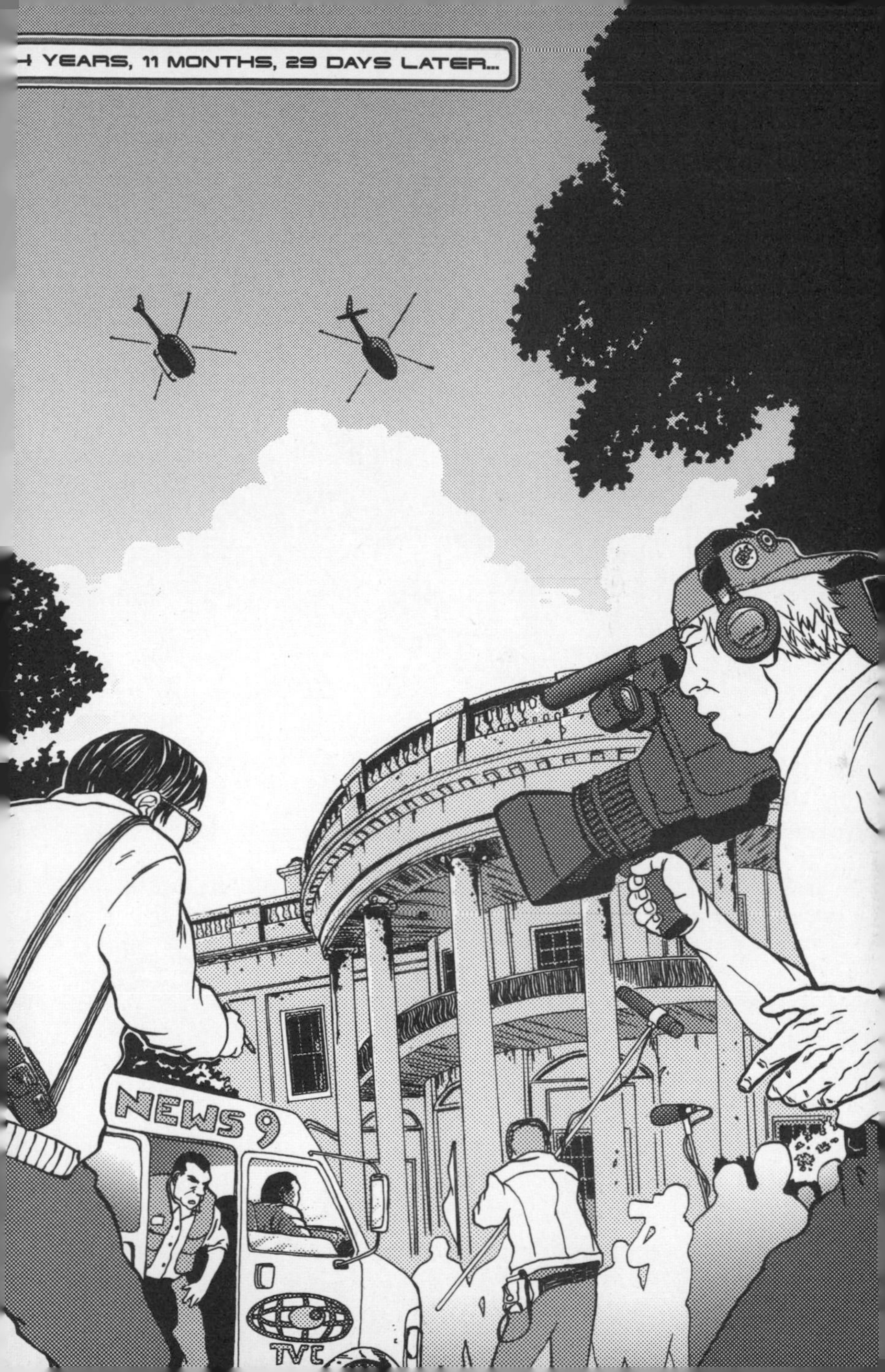
YEARS, 11 MONTHS, 29 DAYS LATER...
NEWS 9
TVC

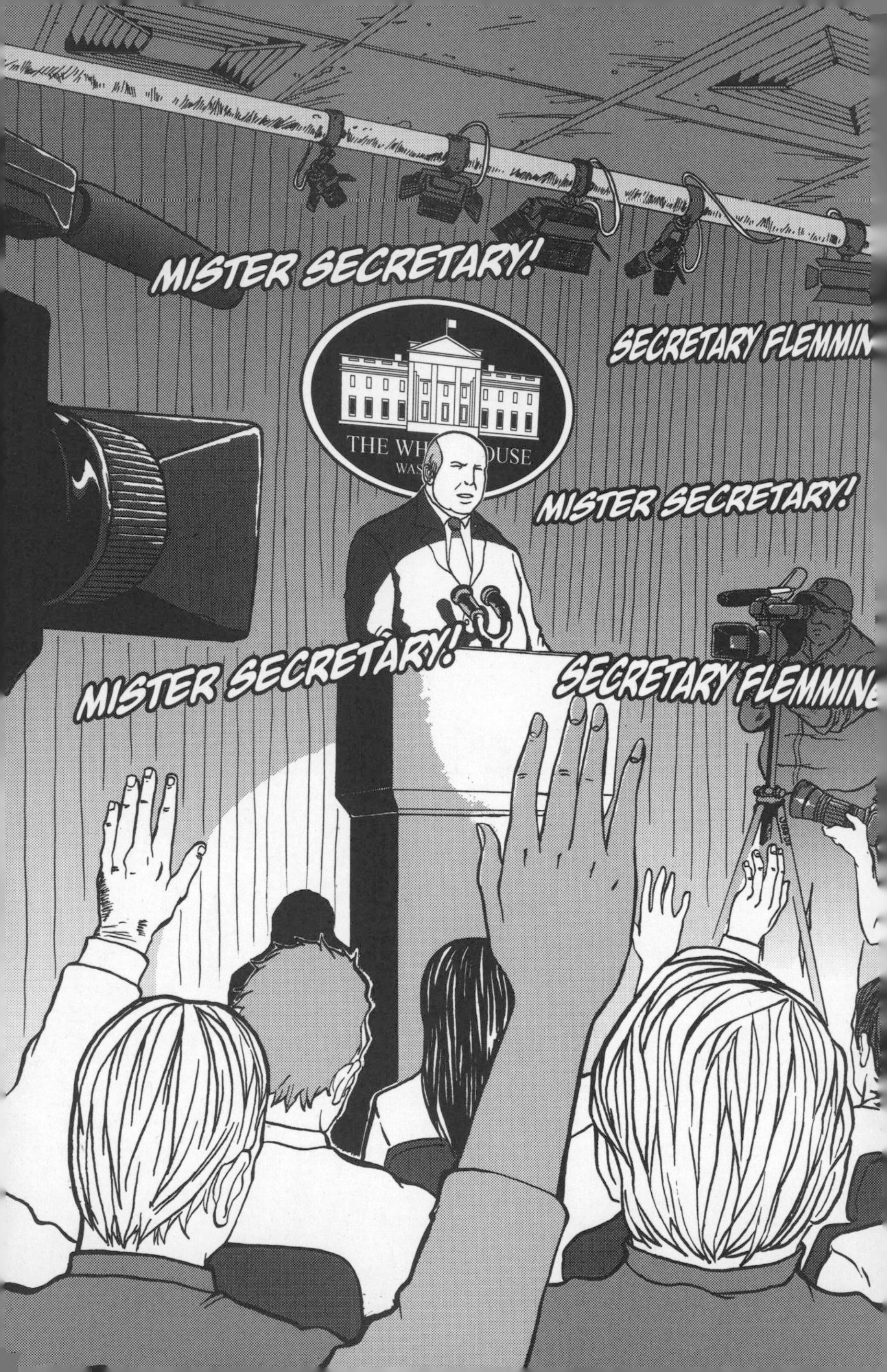
MISTER SECRETARY!
SECRETARY FLEMMIN
MISTER SECRETARY!
MISTER SECRETARY!
SECRETARY FLEMMIN

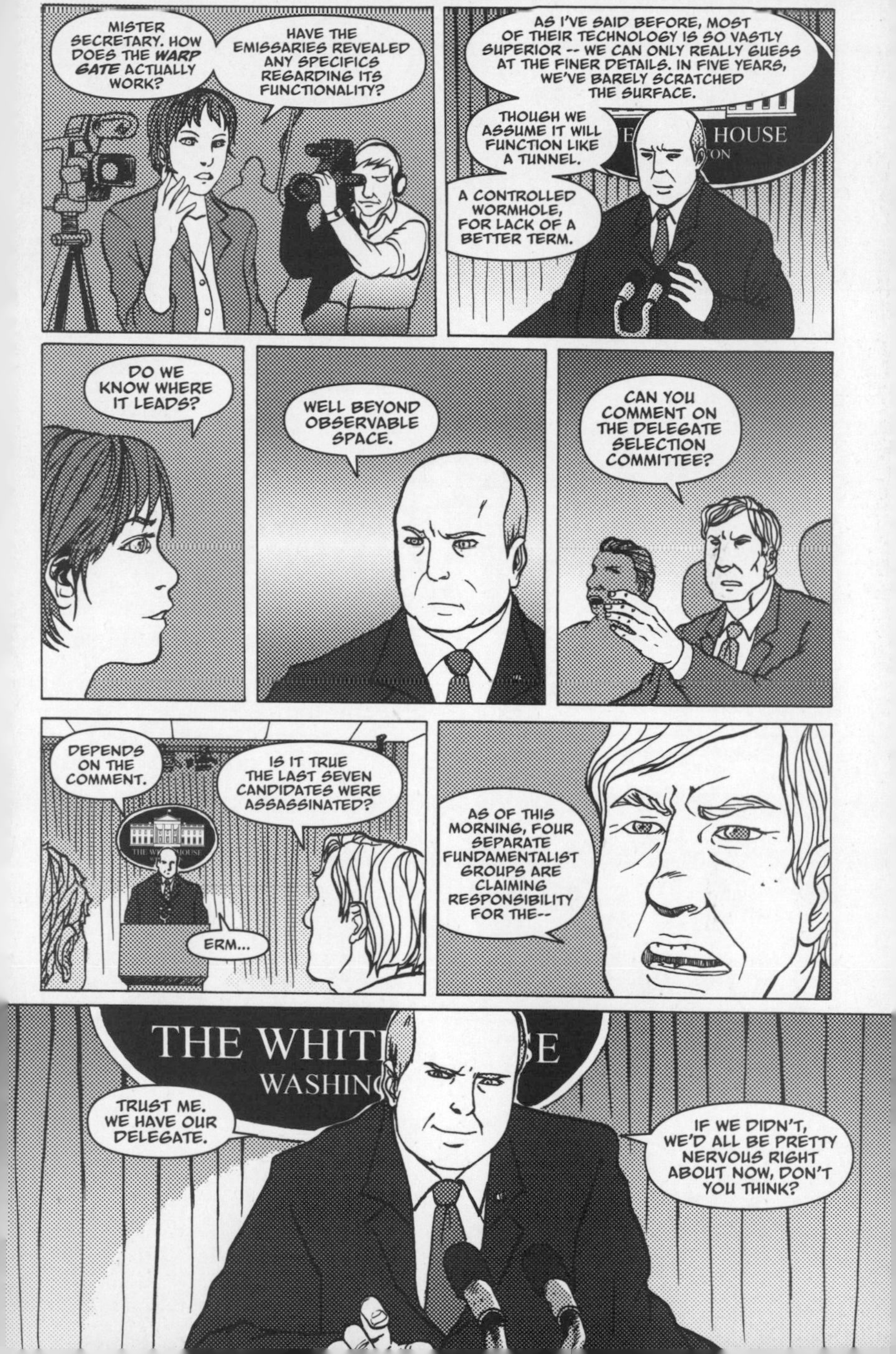
MISTER SECRETARY. HOW DOES THE *WARP GATE* ACTUALLY WORK?
HAVE THE EMISSARIES REVEALED ANY SPECIFICS REGARDING ITS FUNCTIONALITY?
AS I'VE SAID BEFORE, MOST OF THEIR TECHNOLOGY IS SO VASTLY SUPERIOR -- WE CAN ONLY REALLY GUESS AT THE FINER DETAILS. IN FIVE YEARS, WE'VE BARELY SCRATCHED THE SURFACE.
THOUGH WE ASSUME IT WILL FUNCTION LIKE A TUNNEL.
A CONTROLLED WORMHOLE, FOR LACK OF A BETTER TERM.
DO WE KNOW WHERE IT LEADS?
WELL BEYOND OBSERVABLE SPACE.
CAN YOU COMMENT ON THE DELEGATE SELECTION COMMITTEE?
DEPENDS ON THE COMMENT.
IS IT TRUE THE LAST SEVEN CANDIDATES WERE ASSASSINATED?
ERM...
AS OF THIS MORNING, FOUR SEPARATE FUNDAMENTALIST GROUPS ARE CLAIMING RESPONSIBILITY FOR THE--
THE WHIT SE
WASHIN
TRUST ME. WE HAVE OUR DELEGATE.
IF WE DIDN'T, WE'D ALL BE PRETTY NERVOUS RIGHT ABOUT NOW, DON'T YOU THINK?

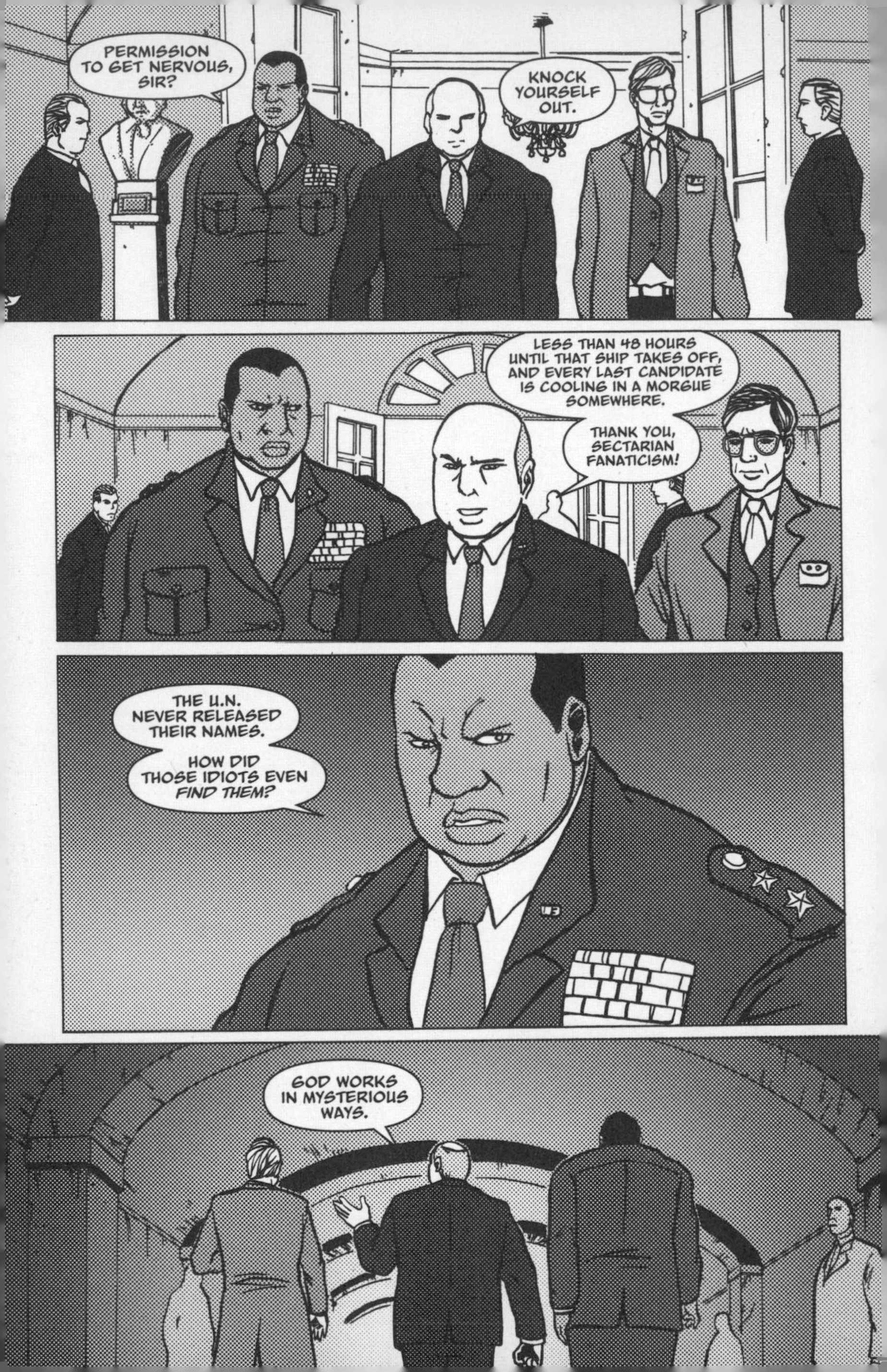
PERMISSION TO GET NERVOUS, SIR?
KNOCK YOURSELF OUT.
LESS THAN 48 HOURS UNTIL THAT SHIP TAKES OFF, AND EVERY LAST CANDIDATE IS COOLING IN A MORGUE SOMEWHERE.
THANK YOU, SECTARIAN FANATICISM!
THE U.N. NEVER RELEASED THEIR NAMES.
HOW DID THOSE IDIOTS EVEN FIND THEM?
GOD WORKS IN MYSTERIOUS WAYS.

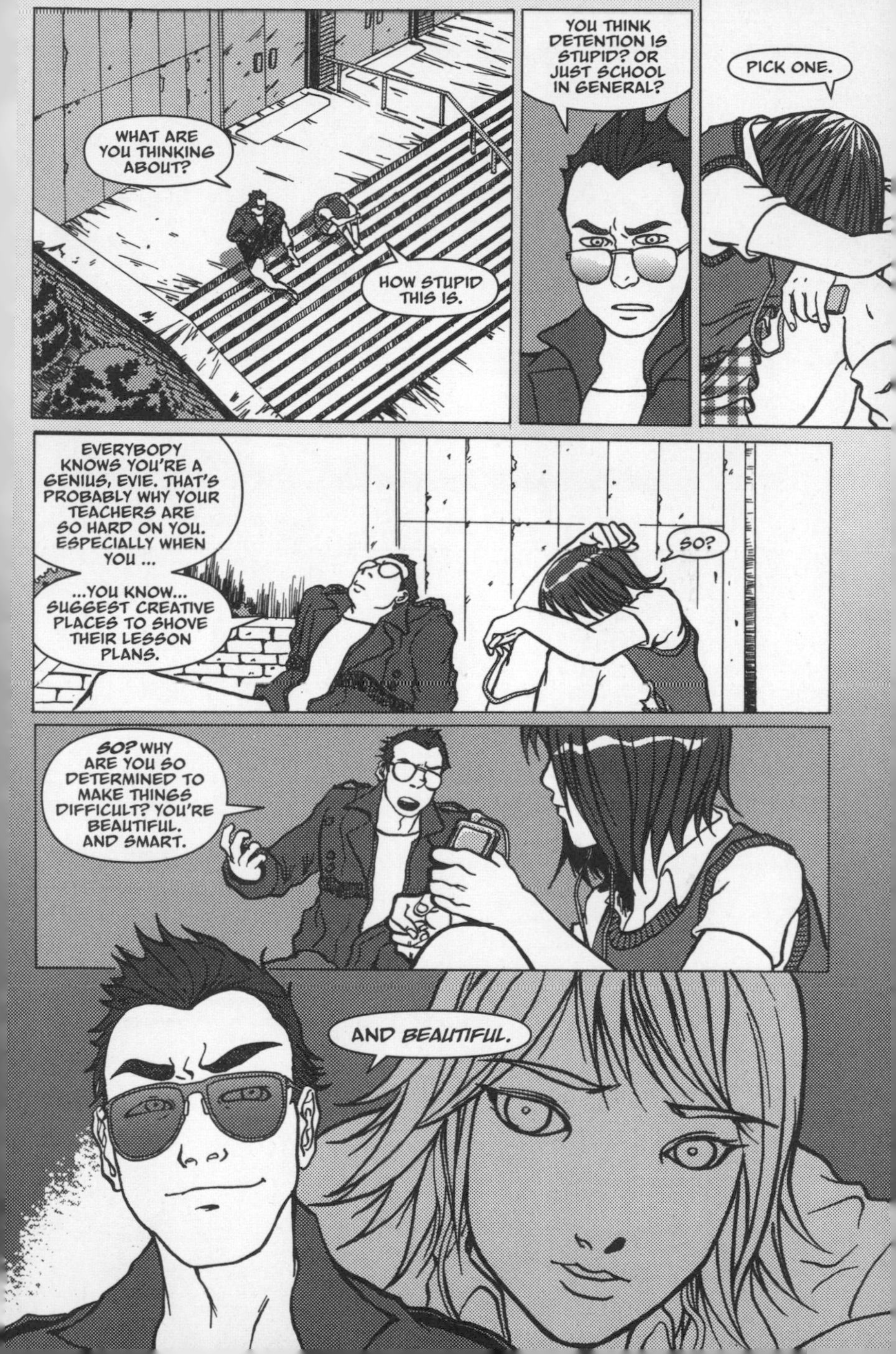
WHAT ARE YOU THINKING ABOUT?
HOW STUPID THIS IS.
YOU THINK DETENTION IS STUPID? OR JUST SCHOOL IN GENERAL?
PICK ONE.
EVERYBODY KNOWS YOU'RE A GENIUS, EVIE. THAT'S PROBABLY WHY YOUR TEACHERS ARE SO HARD ON YOU. ESPECIALLY WHEN YOU ...
...YOU KNOW... SUGGEST CREATIVE PLACES TO SHOVE THEIR LESSON PLANS.
SO?
SO? WHY ARE YOU SO DETERMINED TO MAKE THINGS DIFFICULT? YOU'RE BEAUTIFUL. AND SMART.
AND BEAUTIFUL.

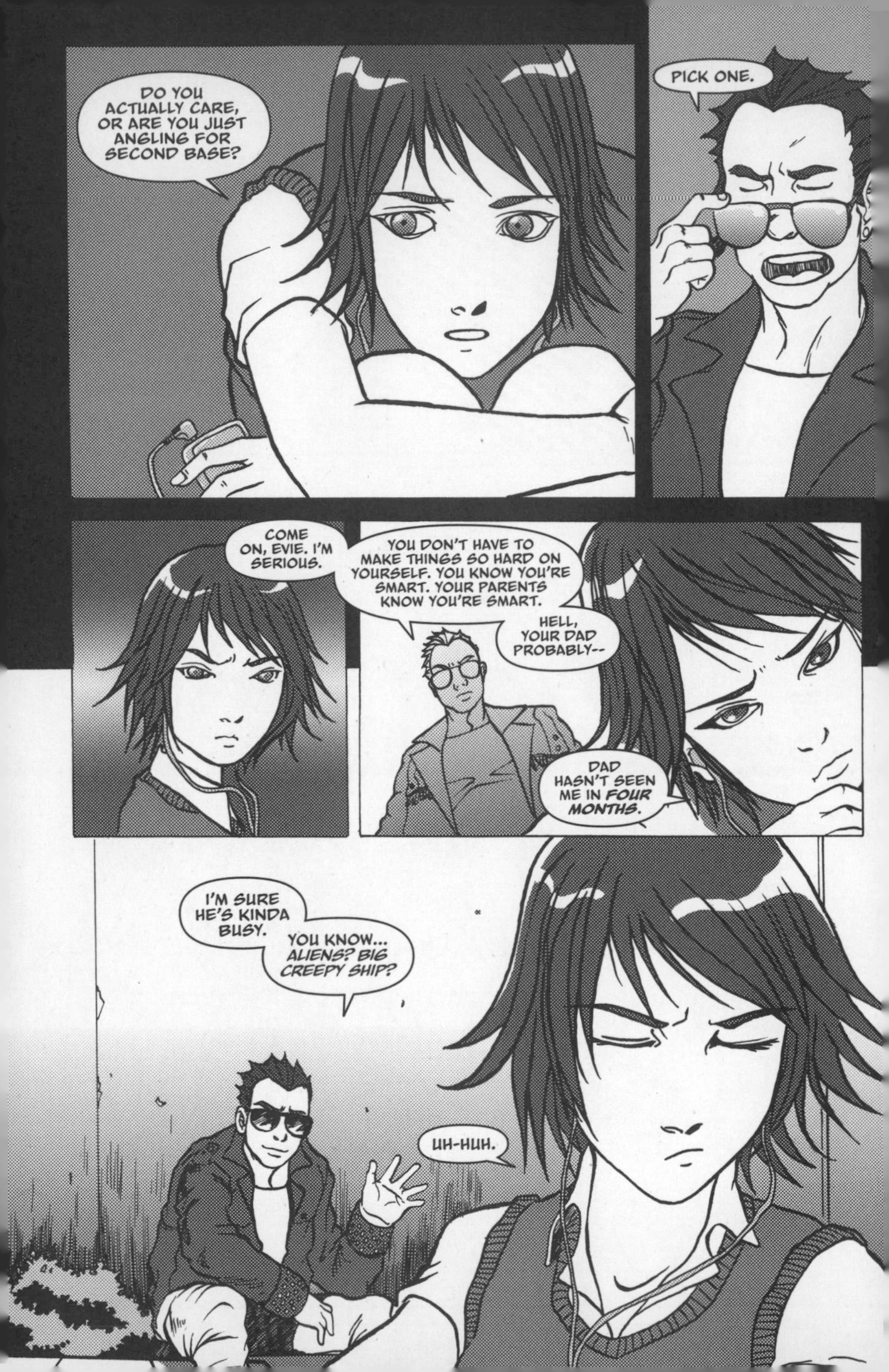
DO YOU ACTUALLY CARE, OR ARE YOU JUST ANGLING FOR SECOND BASE?
PICK ONE.
COME ON, EVIE. I'M SERIOUS.
YOU DON'T HAVE TO MAKE THINGS SO HARD ON YOURSELF. YOU KNOW YOU'RE SMART. YOUR PARENTS KNOW YOU'RE SMART.
HELL, YOUR DAD PROBABLY--
DAD HASN'T SEEN ME IN *FOUR MONTHS*.
I'M SURE HE'S KINDA BUSY.
YOU KNOW... *ALIENS? BIG CREEPY SHIP?*
UH-HUH.

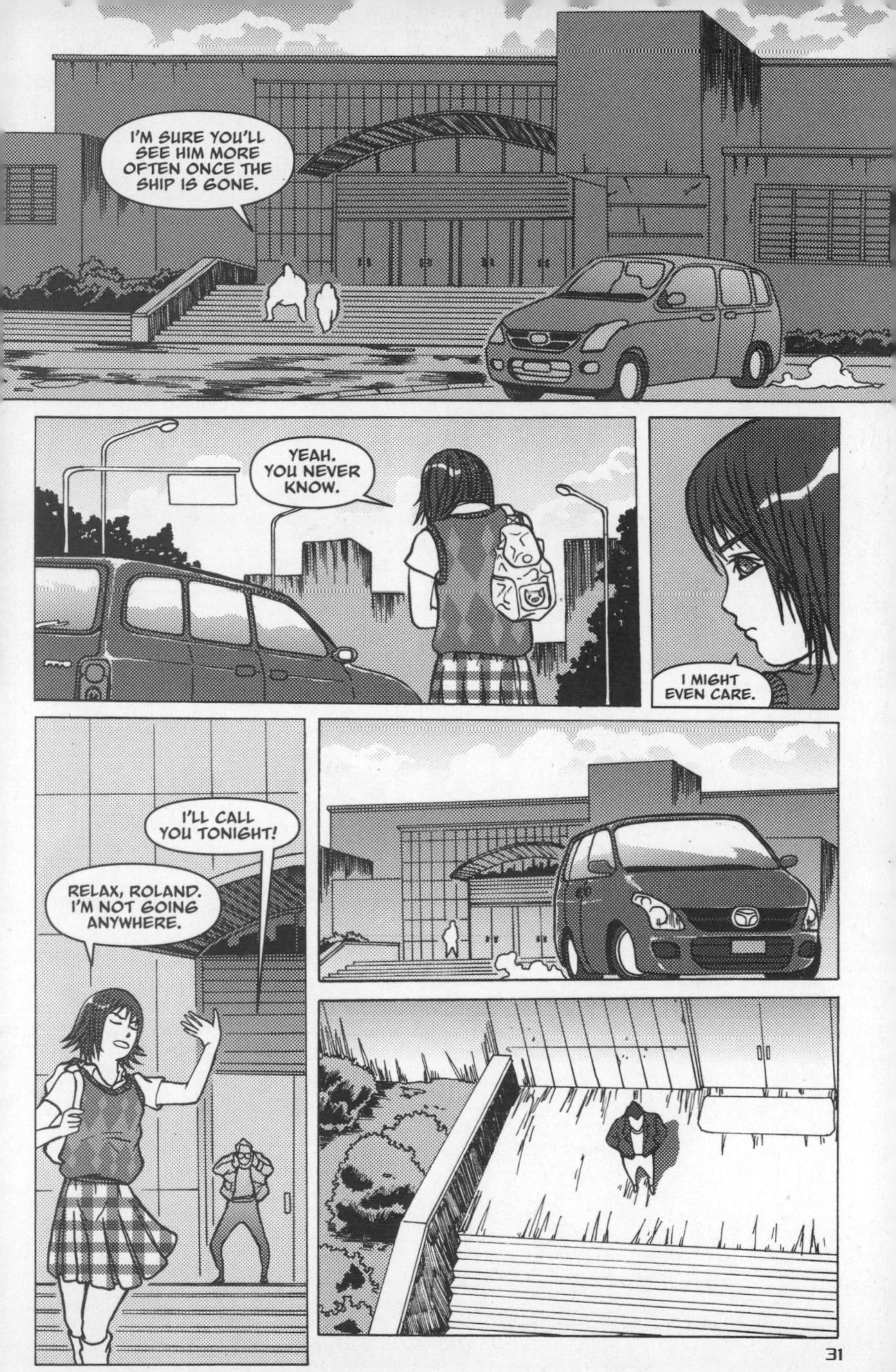
I'M SURE YOU'LL SEE HIM MORE OFTEN ONCE THE SHIP IS GONE.
YEAH. YOU NEVER KNOW.
I MIGHT EVEN CARE.
I'LL CALL YOU TONIGHT!
RELAX, ROLAND. I'M NOT GOING ANYWHERE.

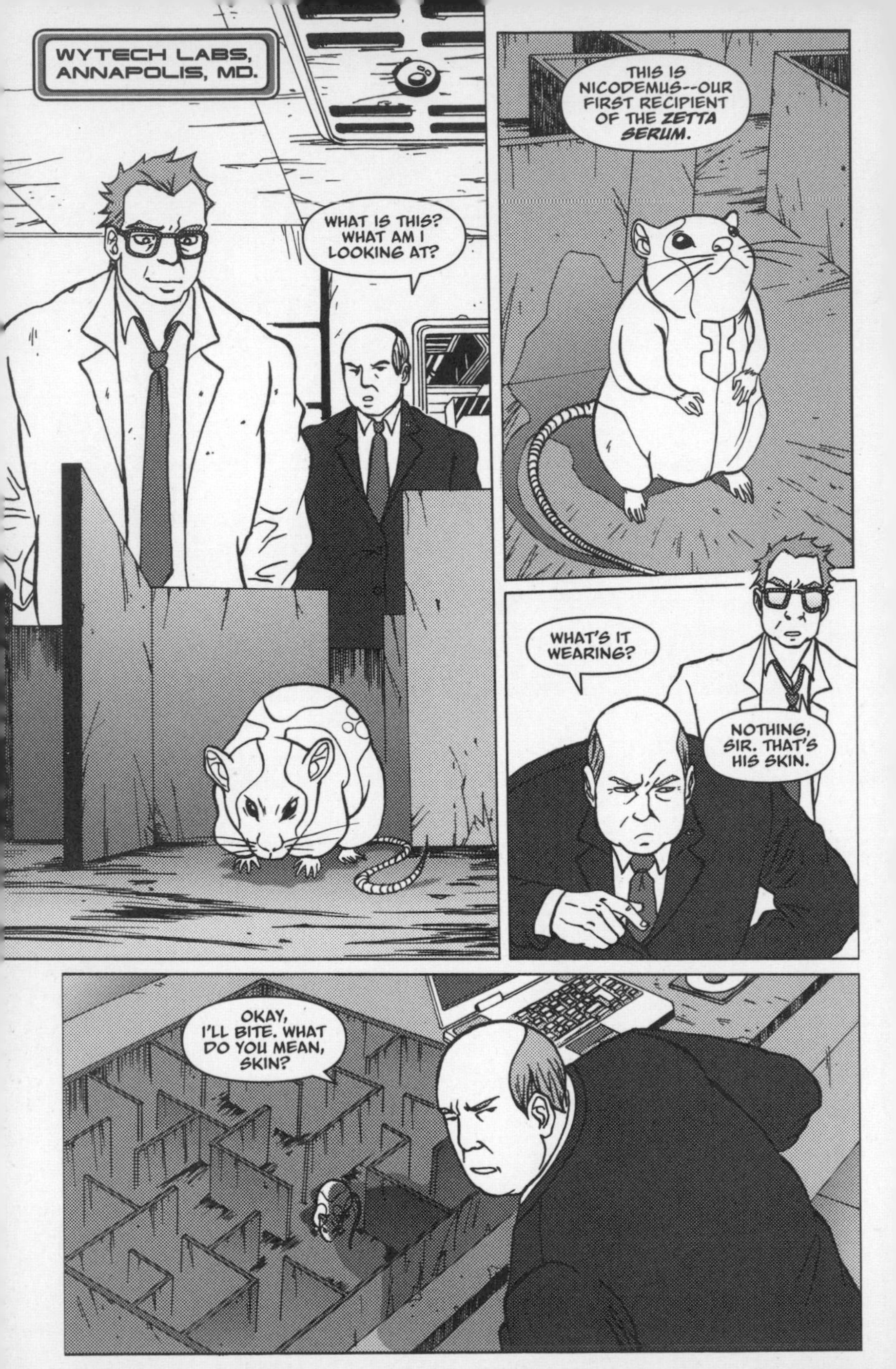
WYTECH LABS, ANNAPOLIS, MD.
WHAT IS THIS? WHAT AM I LOOKING AT?
THIS IS NICODEMUS--OUR FIRST RECIPIENT OF THE *ZETTA SERUM*.
WHAT'S IT WEARING?
NOTHING, SIR. THAT'S HIS SKIN.
OKAY, I'LL BITE. WHAT DO YOU MEAN, SKIN?

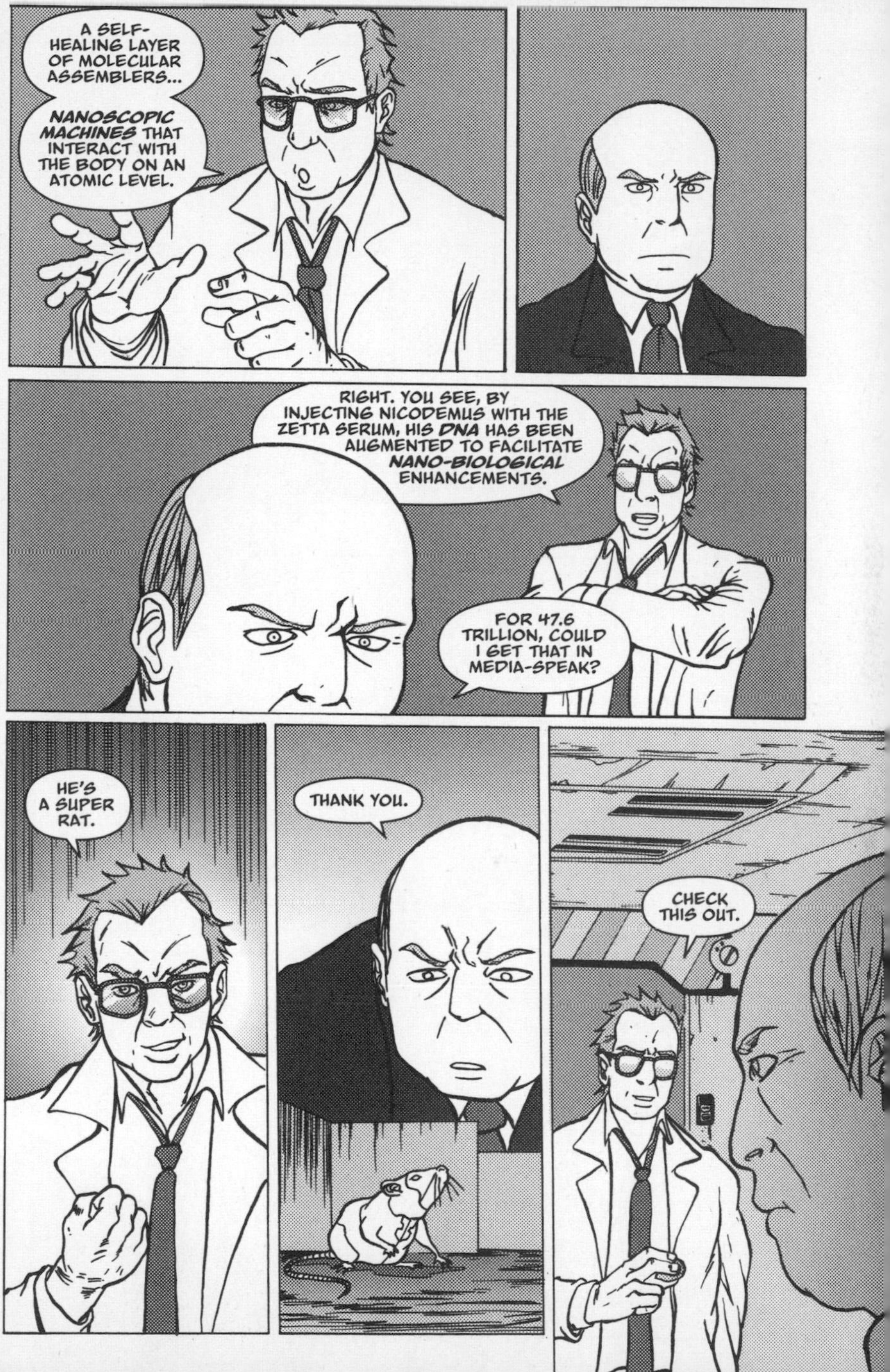
A SELF-HEALING LAYER OF MOLECULAR ASSEMBLERS...
NANOSCOPIC MACHINES THAT INTERACT WITH THE BODY ON AN ATOMIC LEVEL.
RIGHT. YOU SEE, BY INJECTING NICODEMUS WITH THE ZETTA SERUM, HIS *DNA* HAS BEEN AUGMENTED TO FACILITATE *NANO-BIOLOGICAL* ENHANCEMENTS.
FOR 47.6 TRILLION, COULD I GET THAT IN MEDIA-SPEAK?
HE'S A SUPER RAT.
THANK YOU.
CHECK THIS OUT.

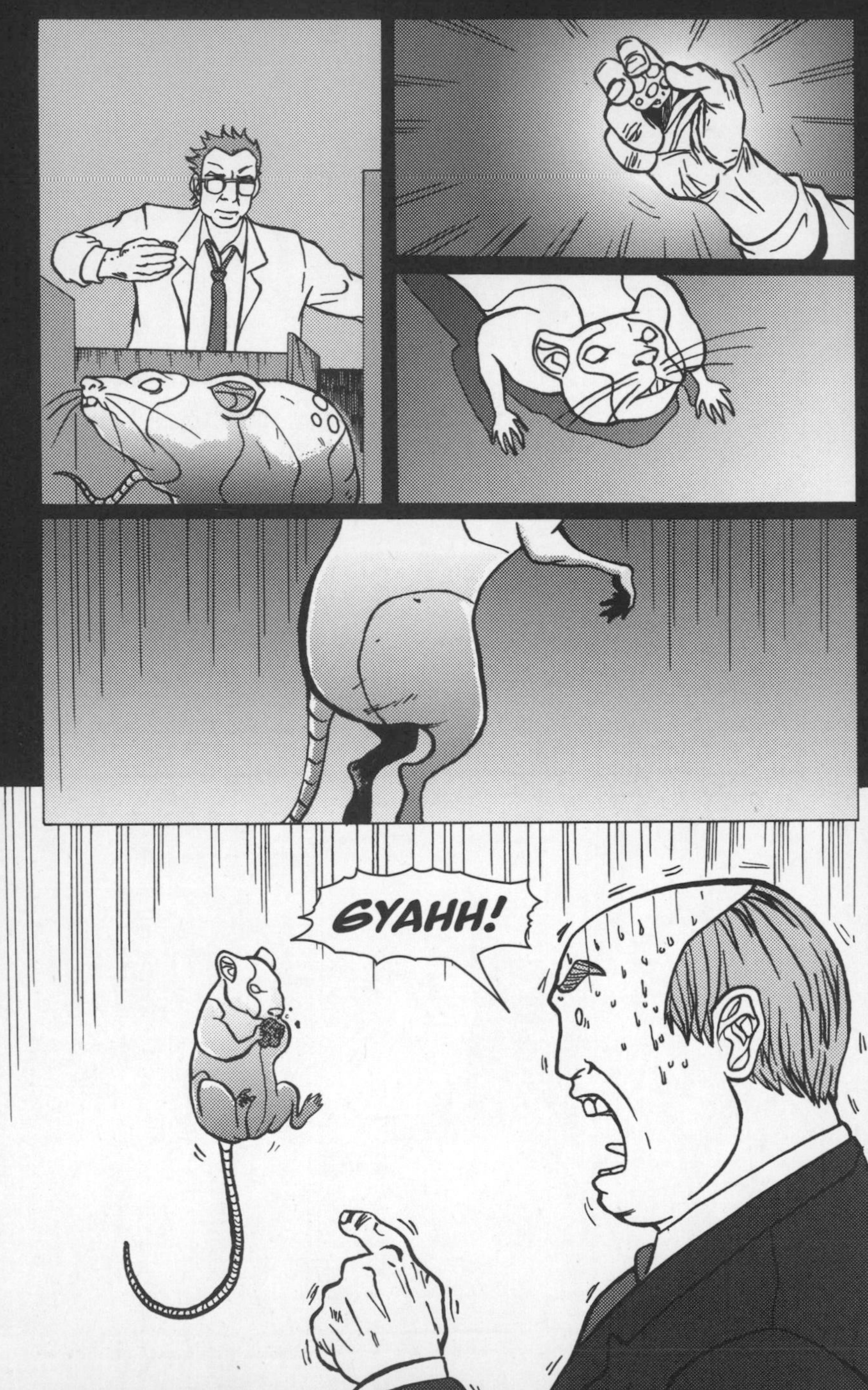
GYAHH!

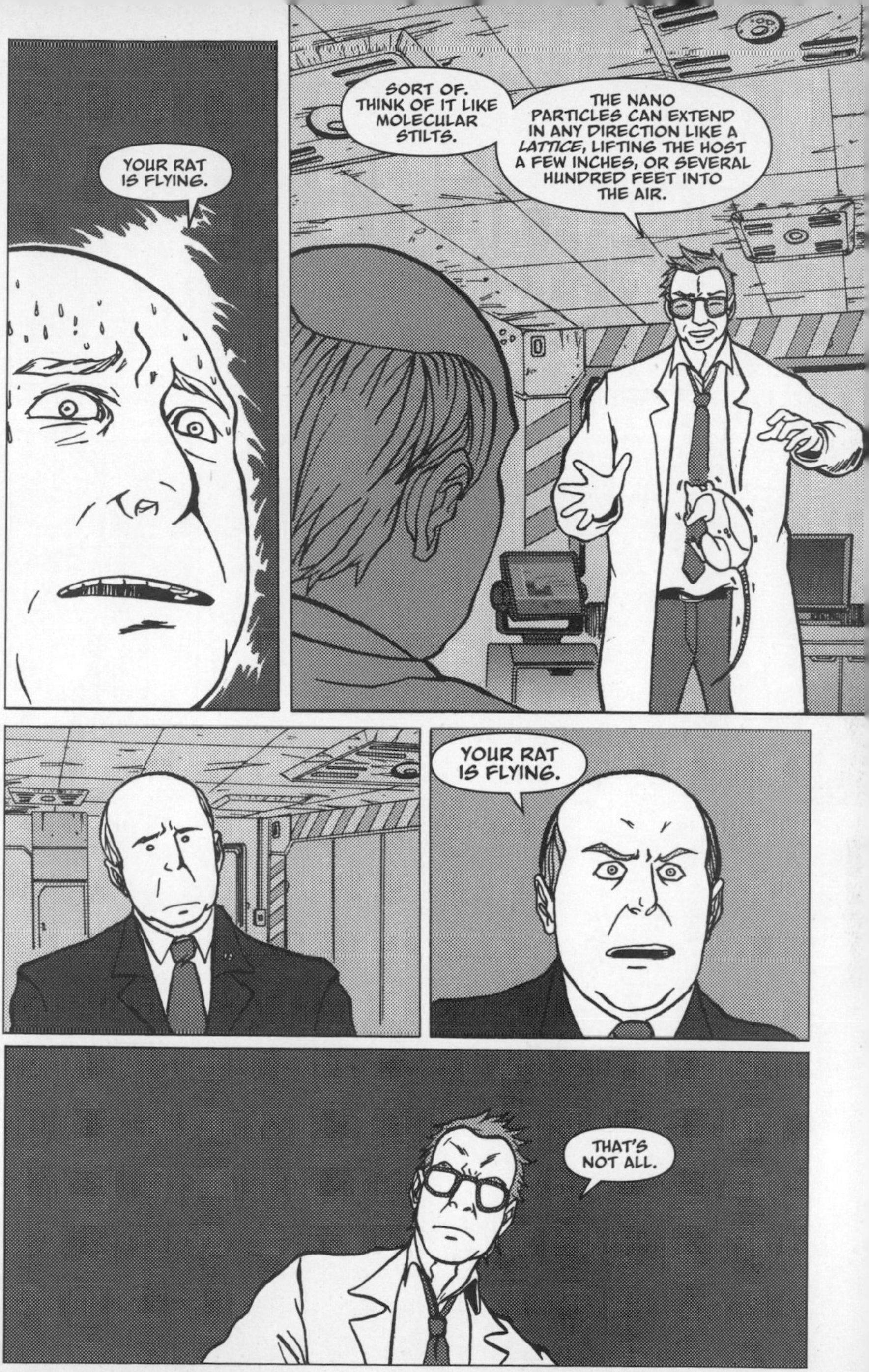
YOUR RAT IS FLYING.
SORT OF. THINK OF IT LIKE MOLECULAR STILTS.
THE NANO PARTICLES CAN EXTEND IN ANY DIRECTION LIKE A *LATTICE*, LIFTING THE HOST A FEW INCHES, OR SEVERAL HUNDRED FEET INTO THE AIR.
YOUR RAT IS FLYING.
THAT'S NOT ALL.

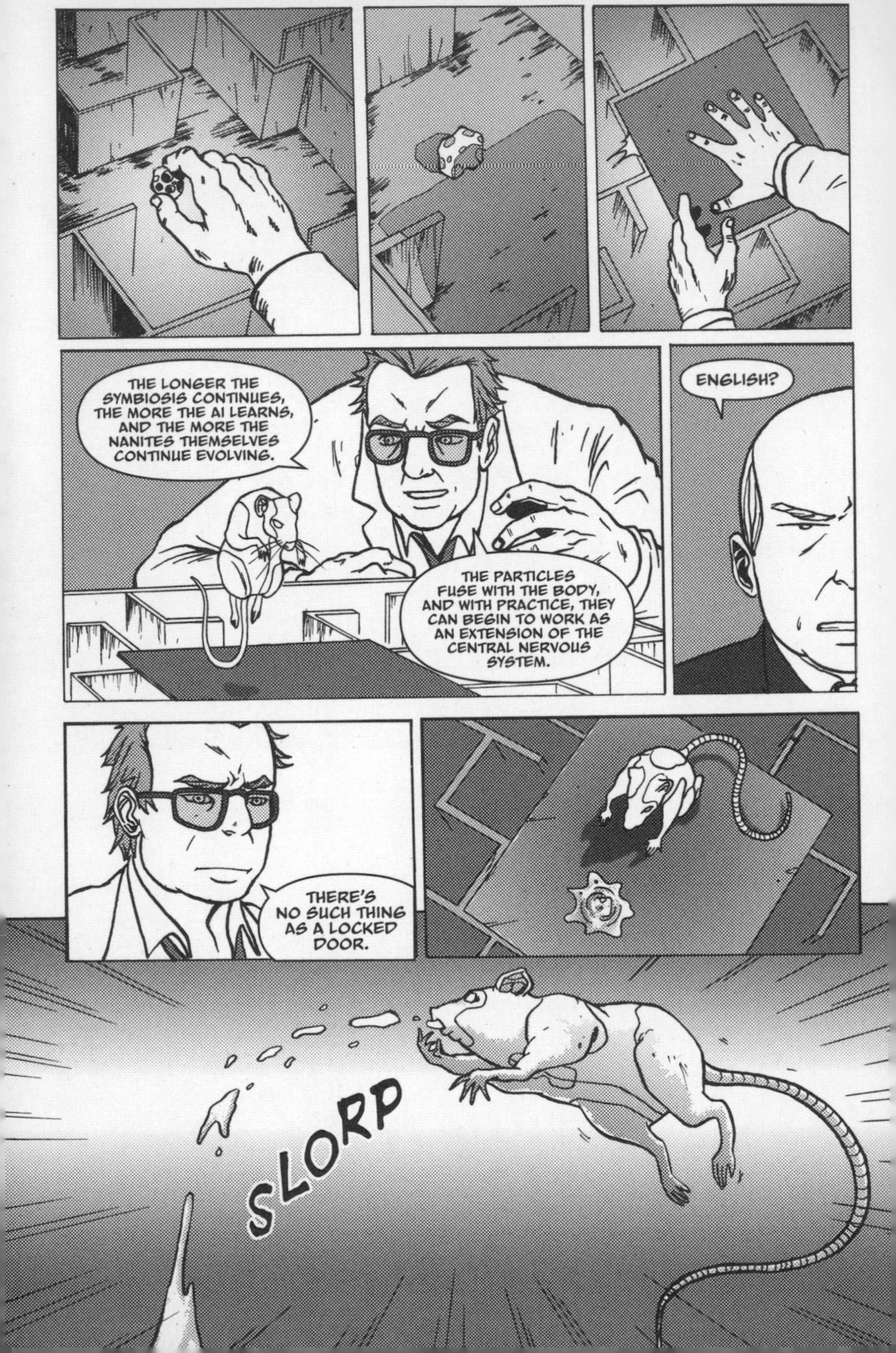
THE LONGER THE SYMBIOSIS CONTINUES, THE MORE THE AI LEARNS, AND THE MORE THE NANITES THEMSELVES CONTINUE EVOLVING.
THE PARTICLES FUSE WITH THE BODY, AND WITH PRACTICE, THEY CAN BEGIN TO WORK AS AN EXTENSION OF THE CENTRAL NERVOUS SYSTEM.
ENGLISH?
THERE'S NO SUCH THING AS A LOCKED DOOR.
SLORP

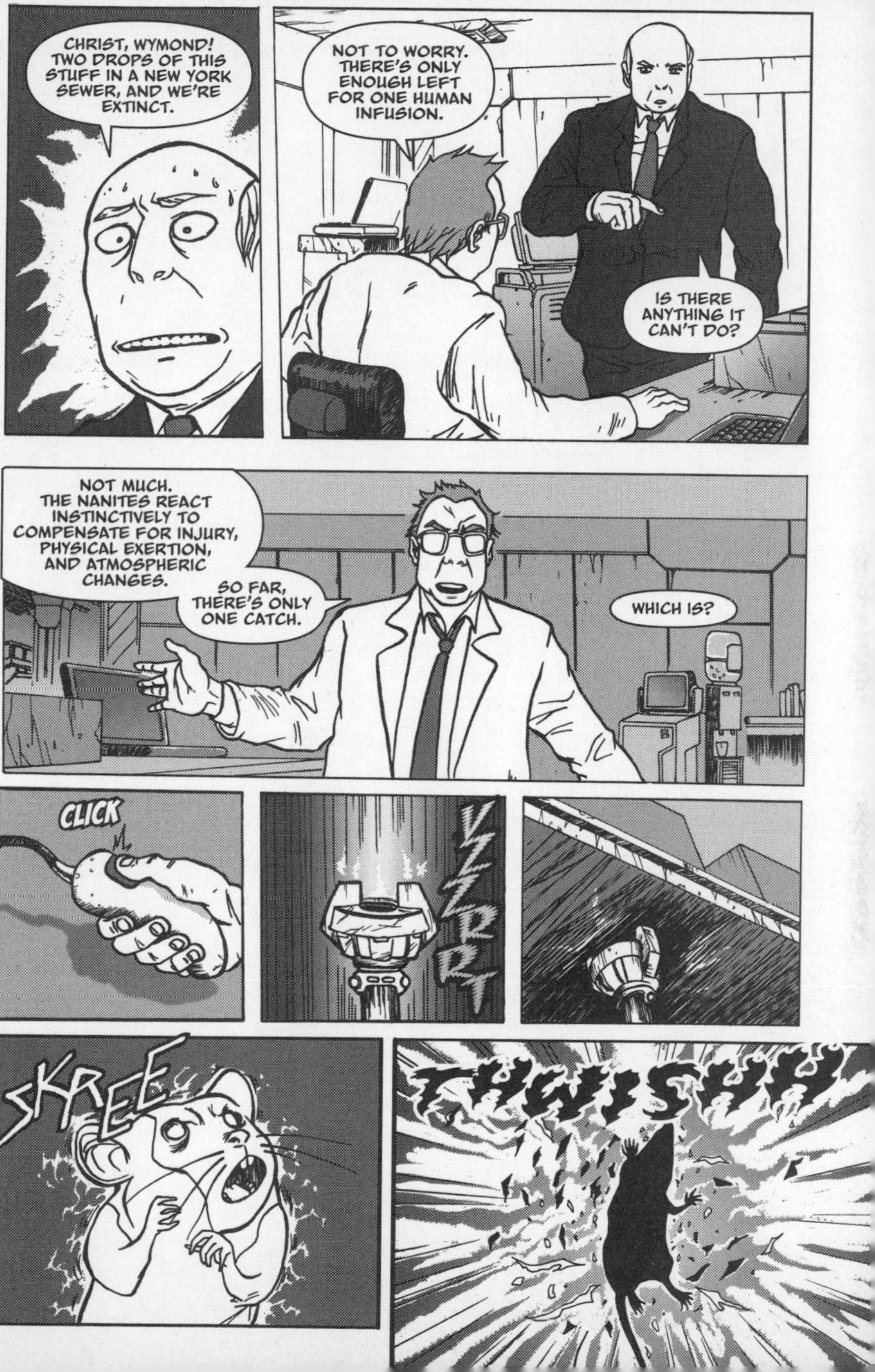
CHRIST, WYMOND! TWO DROPS OF THIS STUFF IN A NEW YORK SEWER, AND WE'RE EXTINCT.
NOT TO WORRY. THERE'S ONLY ENOUGH LEFT FOR ONE HUMAN INFUSION.
IS THERE ANYTHING IT CAN'T DO?
NOT MUCH. THE NANITES REACT INSTINCTIVELY TO COMPENSATE FOR INJURY, PHYSICAL EXERTION, AND ATMOSPHERIC CHANGES.
SO FAR, THERE'S ONLY ONE CATCH.
WHICH IS?
CLICK
VZZRRT
SKREE
THWISHH

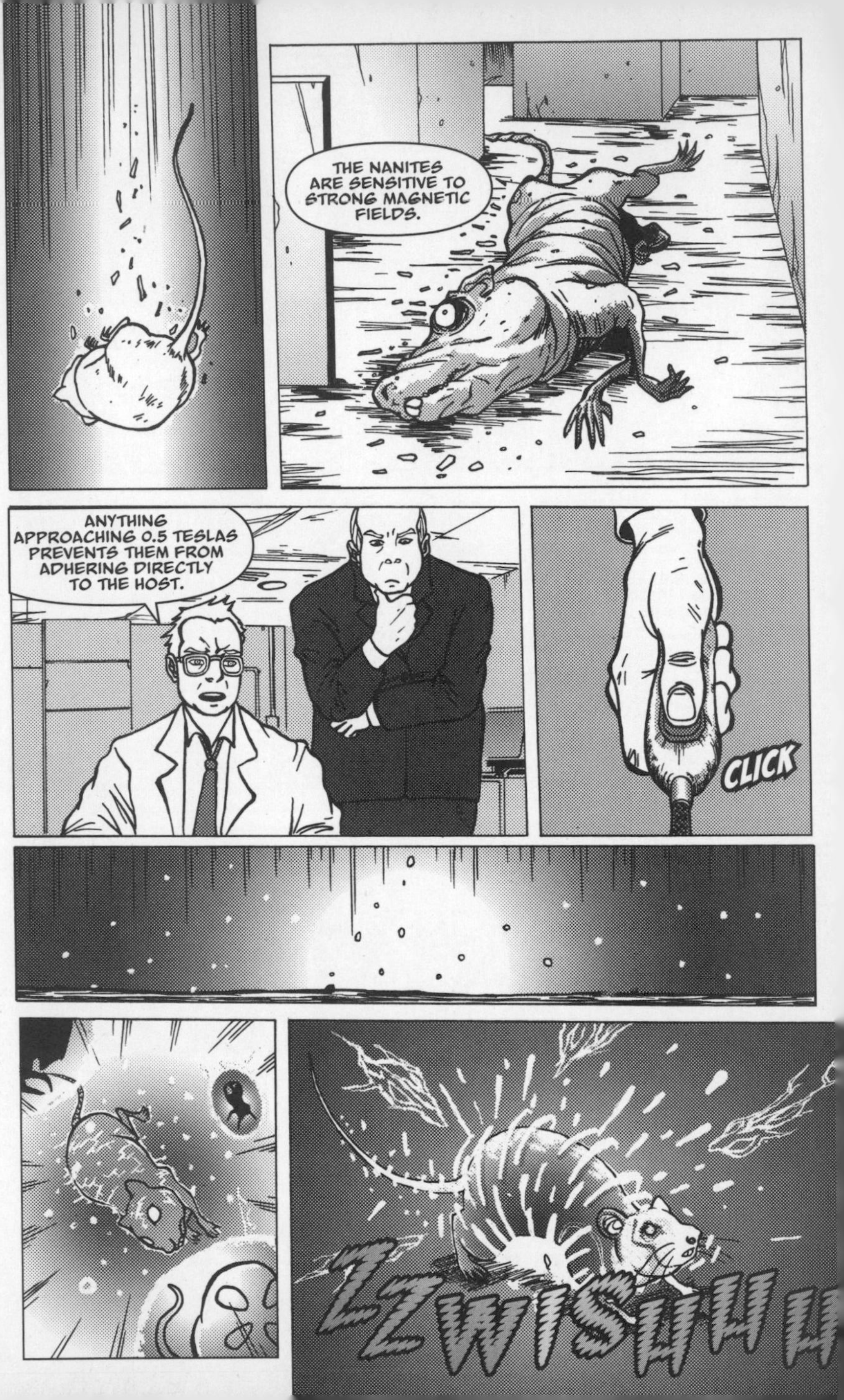
THE NANITES ARE SENSITIVE TO STRONG MAGNETIC FIELDS.
ANYTHING APPROACHING 0.5 TESLAS PREVENTS THEM FROM ADHERING DIRECTLY TO THE HOST.
CLICK
ZZWISHH

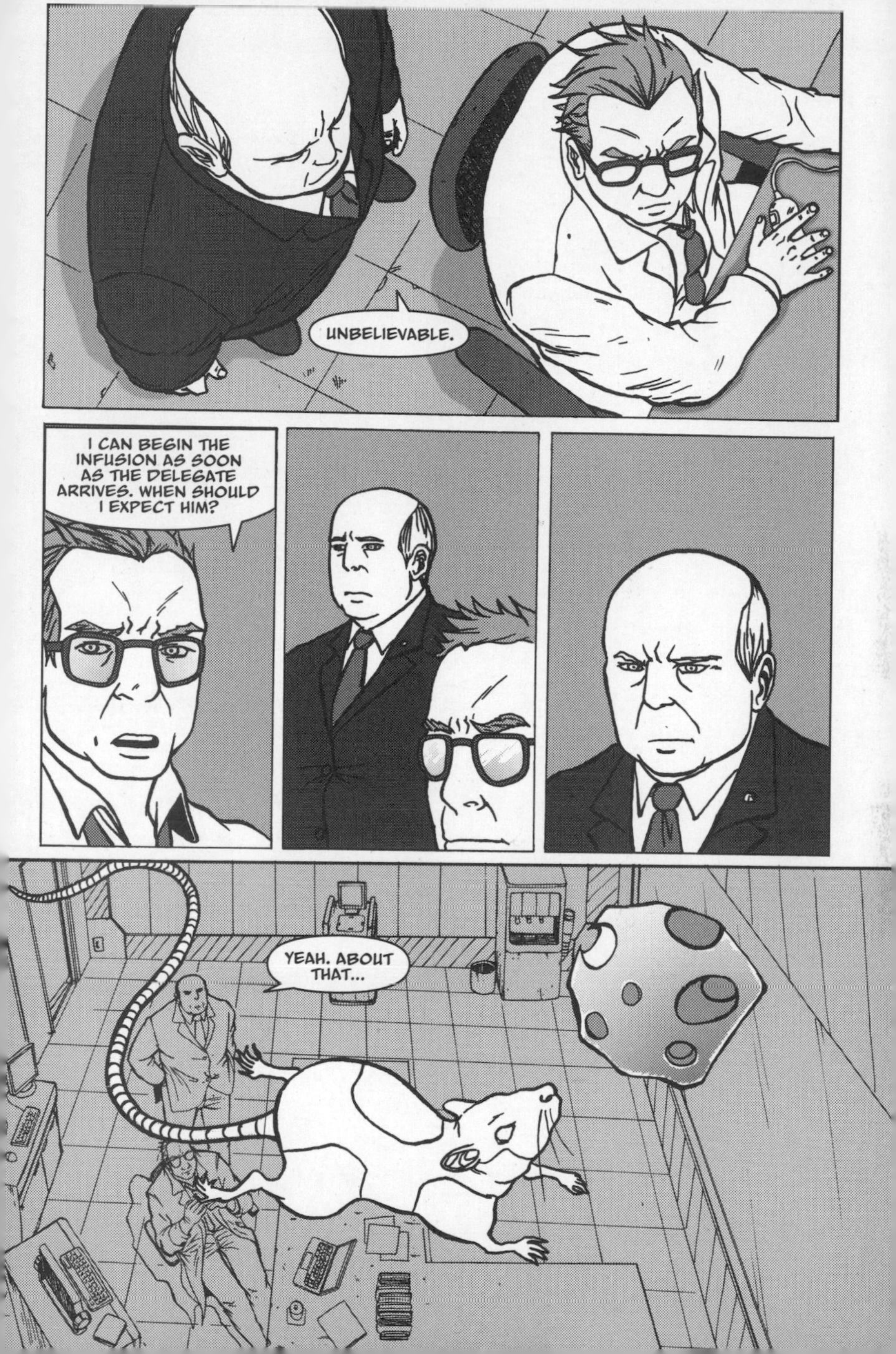
UNBELIEVABLE.
I CAN BEGIN THE INFUSION AS SOON AS THE DELEGATE ARRIVES. WHEN SHOULD I EXPECT HIM?
YEAH. ABOUT THAT...

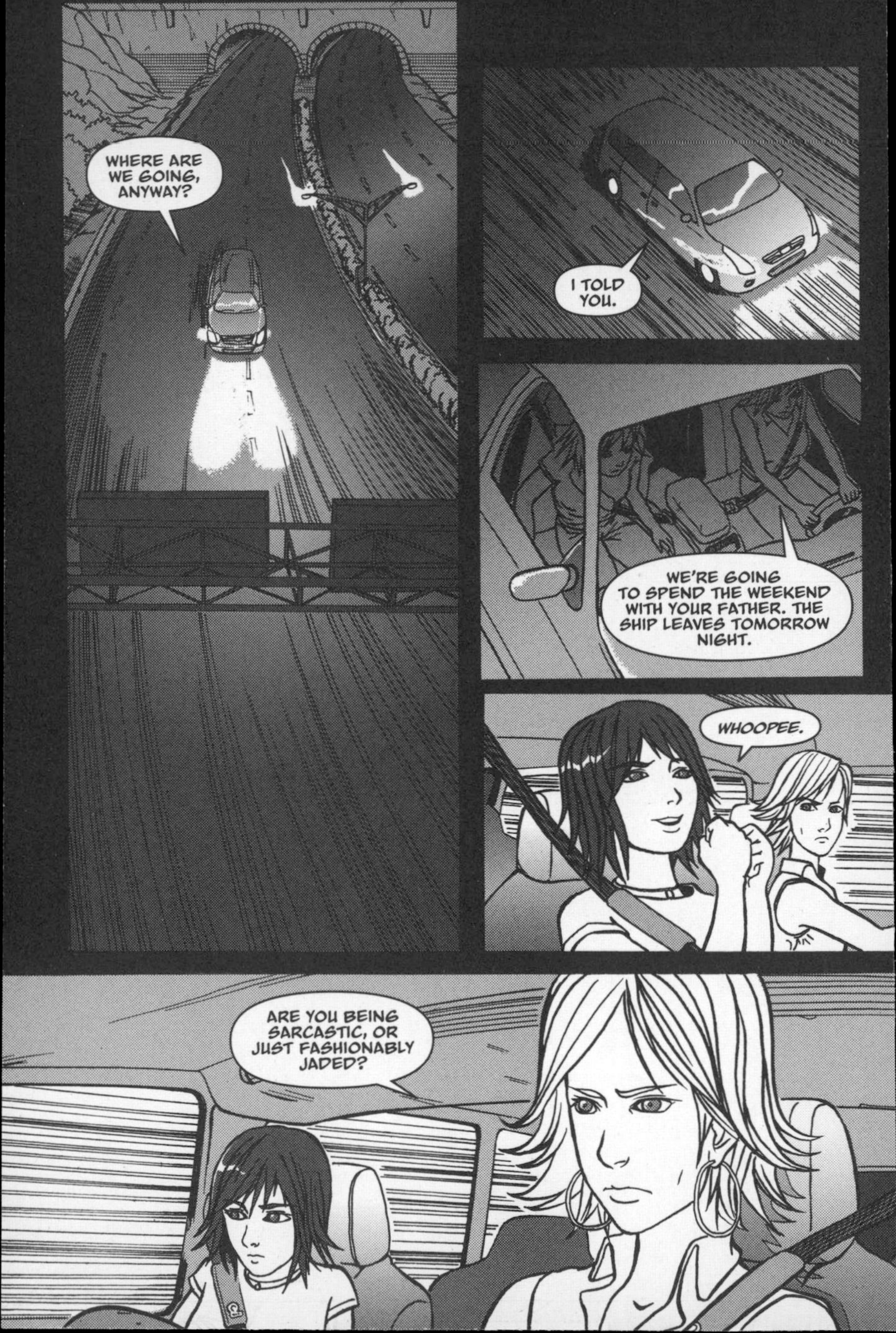
WHERE ARE WE GOING, ANYWAY?
I TOLD YOU.
WE'RE GOING TO SPEND THE WEEKEND WITH YOUR FATHER. THE SHIP LEAVES TOMORROW NIGHT.
WHOOPEE.
ARE YOU BEING SARCASTIC, OR JUST FASHIONABLY JADED?

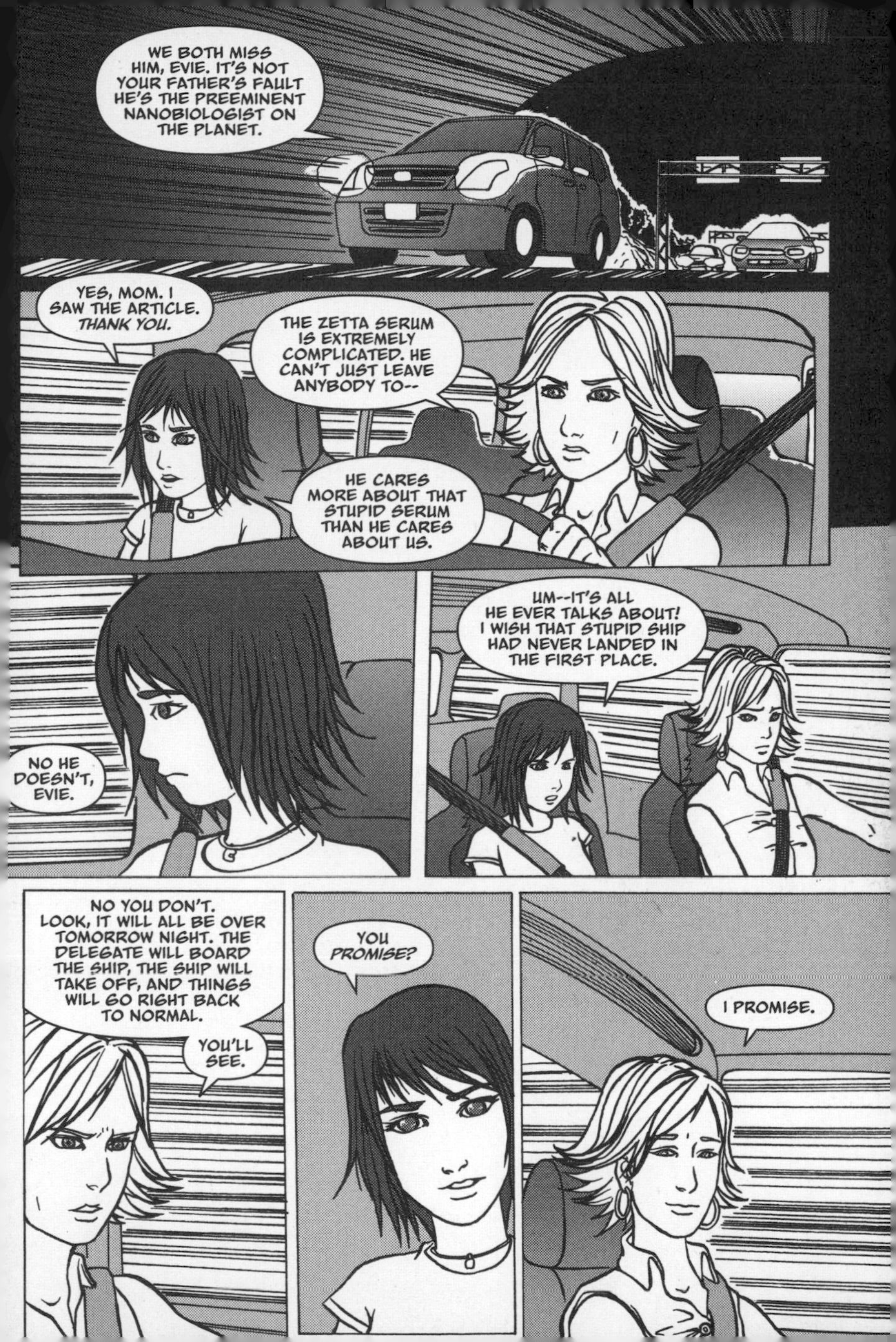
WE BOTH MISS HIM, EVIE. IT'S NOT YOUR FATHER'S FAULT HE'S THE PREEMINENT NANOBIOLOGIST ON THE PLANET.
YES, MOM. I SAW THE ARTICLE. *THANK YOU.*
THE ZETTA SERUM IS EXTREMELY COMPLICATED. HE CAN'T JUST LEAVE ANYBODY TO--
HE CARES MORE ABOUT THAT STUPID SERUM THAN HE CARES ABOUT US.
NO HE DOESN'T, EVIE.
UM--IT'S ALL HE EVER TALKS ABOUT! I WISH THAT STUPID SHIP HAD NEVER LANDED IN THE FIRST PLACE.
NO YOU DON'T. LOOK, IT WILL ALL BE OVER TOMORROW NIGHT. THE DELEGATE WILL BOARD THE SHIP, THE SHIP WILL TAKE OFF, AND THINGS WILL GO RIGHT BACK TO NORMAL.
YOU'LL SEE.
YOU *PROMISE?*
I PROMISE.

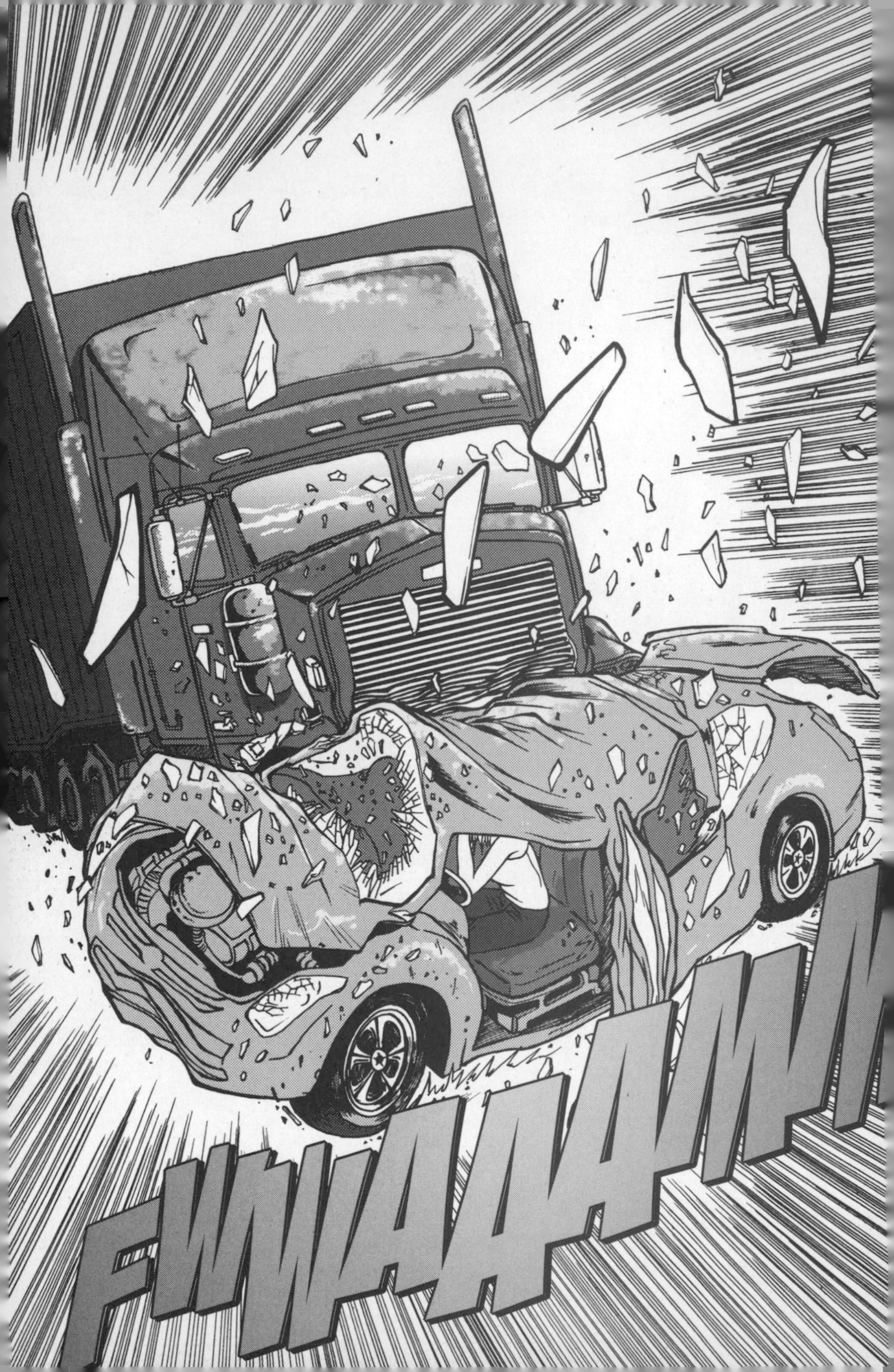
FWAAAMM

CHAPTER 02

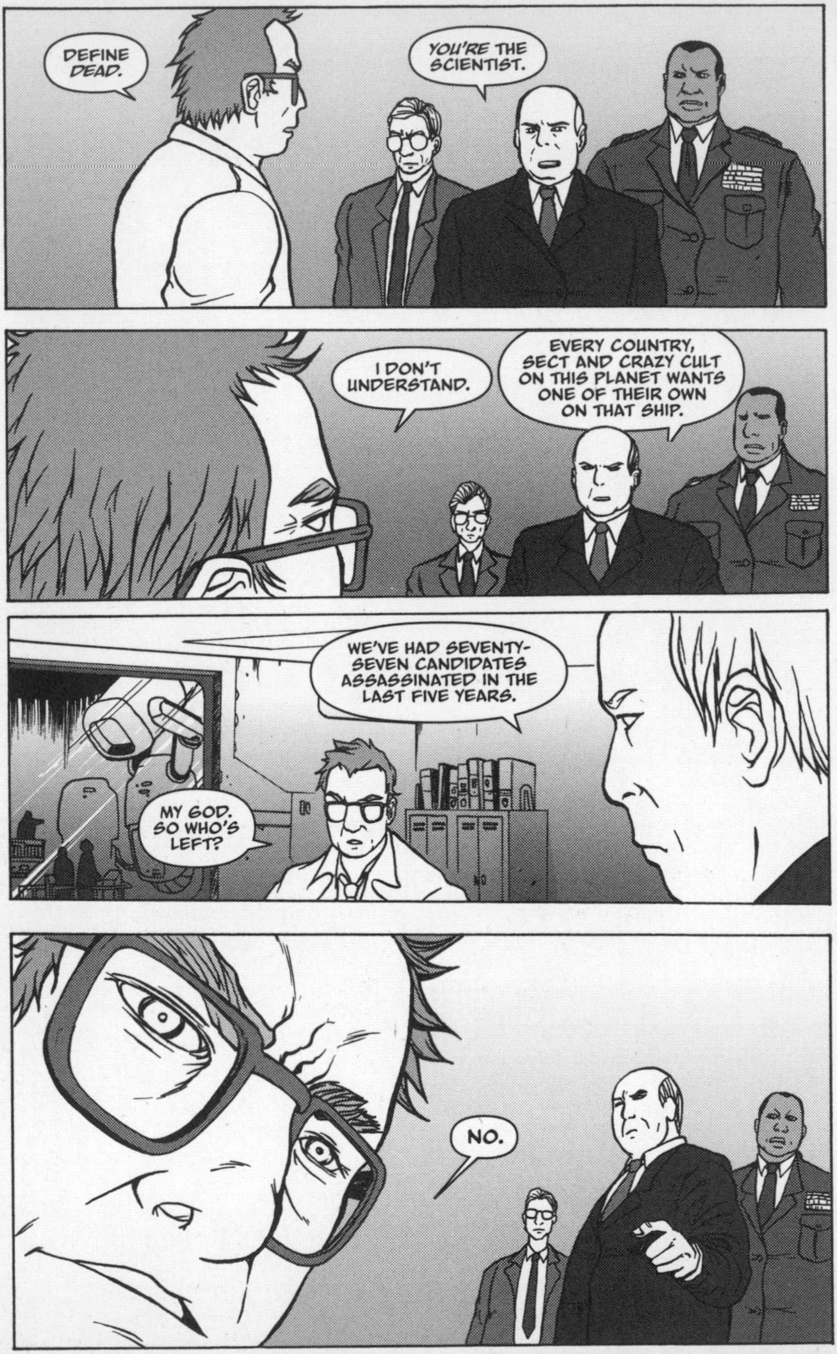
DEFINE DEAD.
YOU'RE THE SCIENTIST.
I DON'T UNDERSTAND.
EVERY COUNTRY, SECT AND CRAZY CULT ON THIS PLANET WANTS ONE OF THEIR OWN ON THAT SHIP.
WE'VE HAD SEVENTY-SEVEN CANDIDATES ASSASSINATED IN THE LAST FIVE YEARS.
MY GOD. SO WHO'S LEFT?
NO.

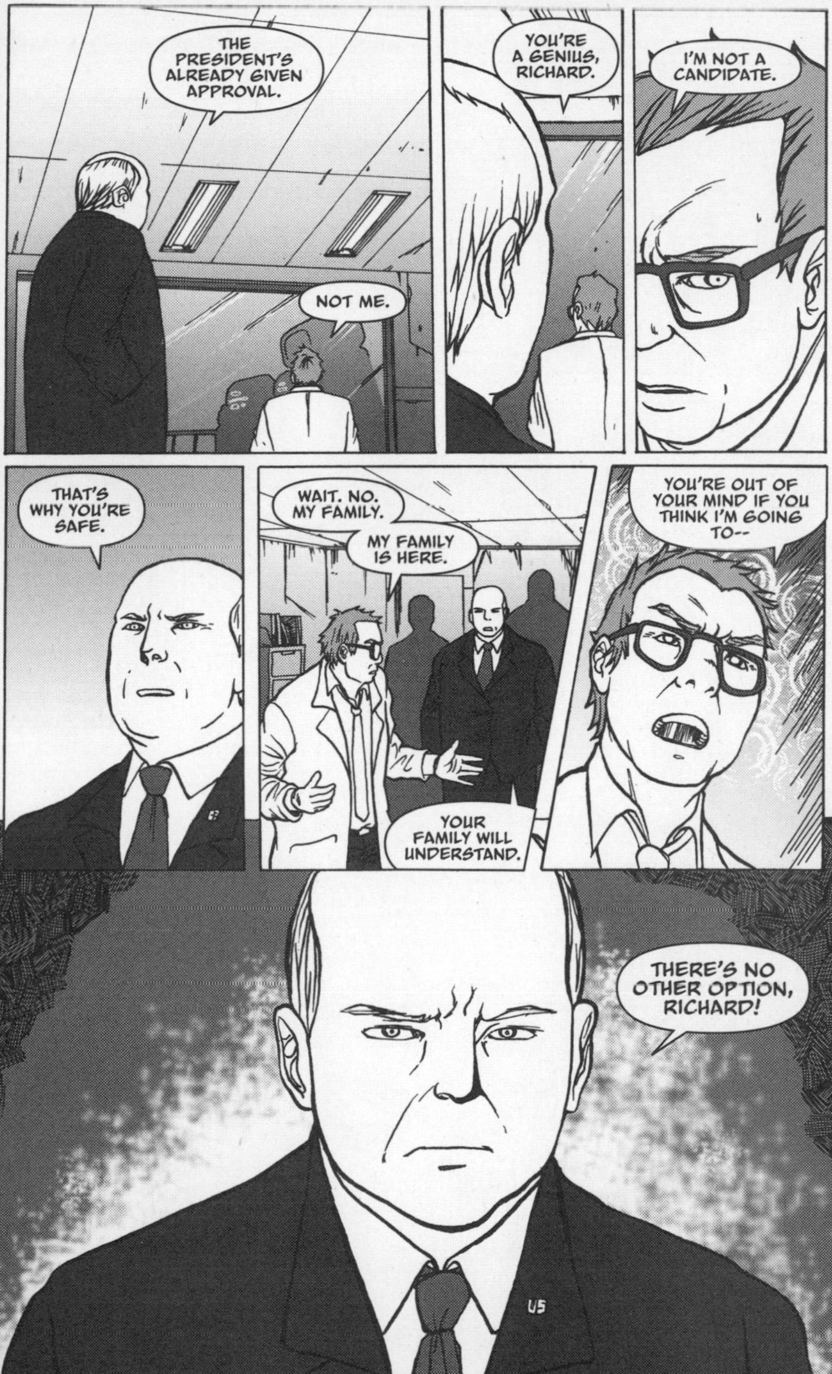
THE PRESIDENT'S ALREADY GIVEN APPROVAL.
NOT ME.
YOU'RE A GENIUS, RICHARD.
I'M NOT A CANDIDATE.
THAT'S WHY YOU'RE SAFE.
WAIT. NO. MY FAMILY.
MY FAMILY IS HERE.
YOUR FAMILY WILL UNDERSTAND.
YOU'RE OUT OF YOUR MIND IF YOU THINK I'M GOING TO--
THERE'S NO OTHER OPTION, RICHARD!
US

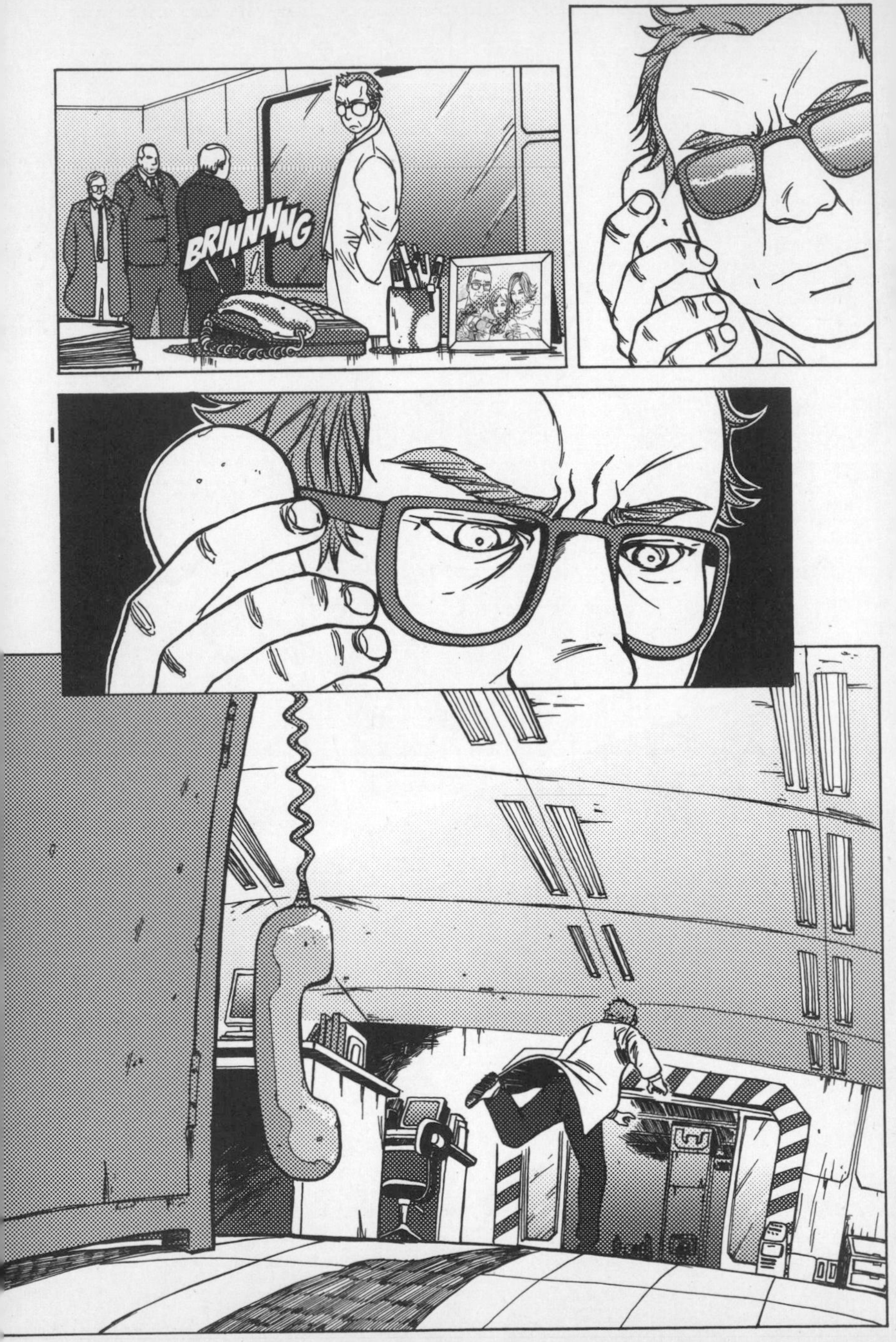
BRINNNNG

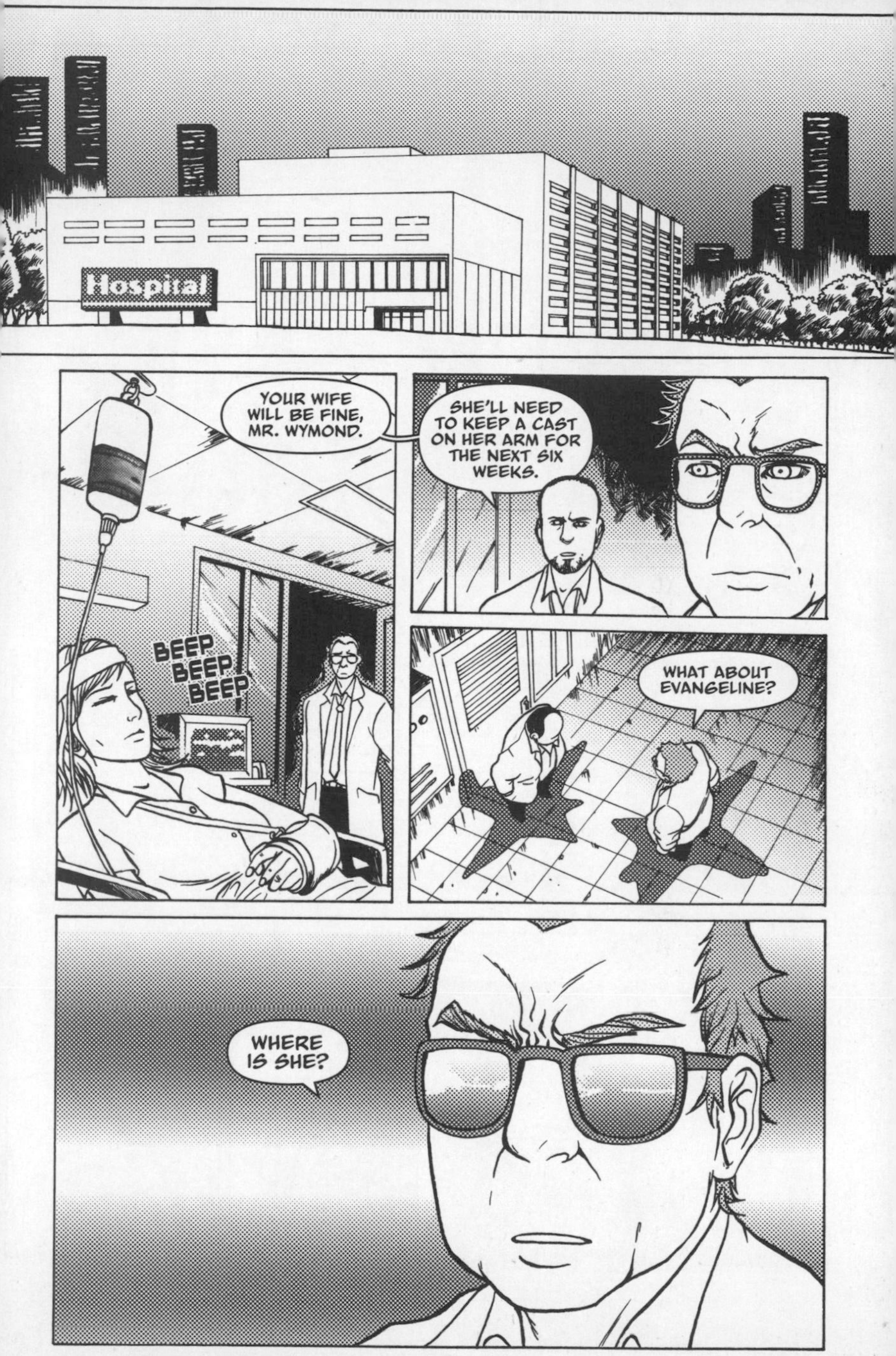
Hospital
YOUR WIFE WILL BE FINE, MR. WYMOND.
SHE'LL NEED TO KEEP A CAST ON HER ARM FOR THE NEXT SIX WEEKS.
BEEP BEEP BEEP
WHAT ABOUT EVANGELINE?
WHERE IS SHE?

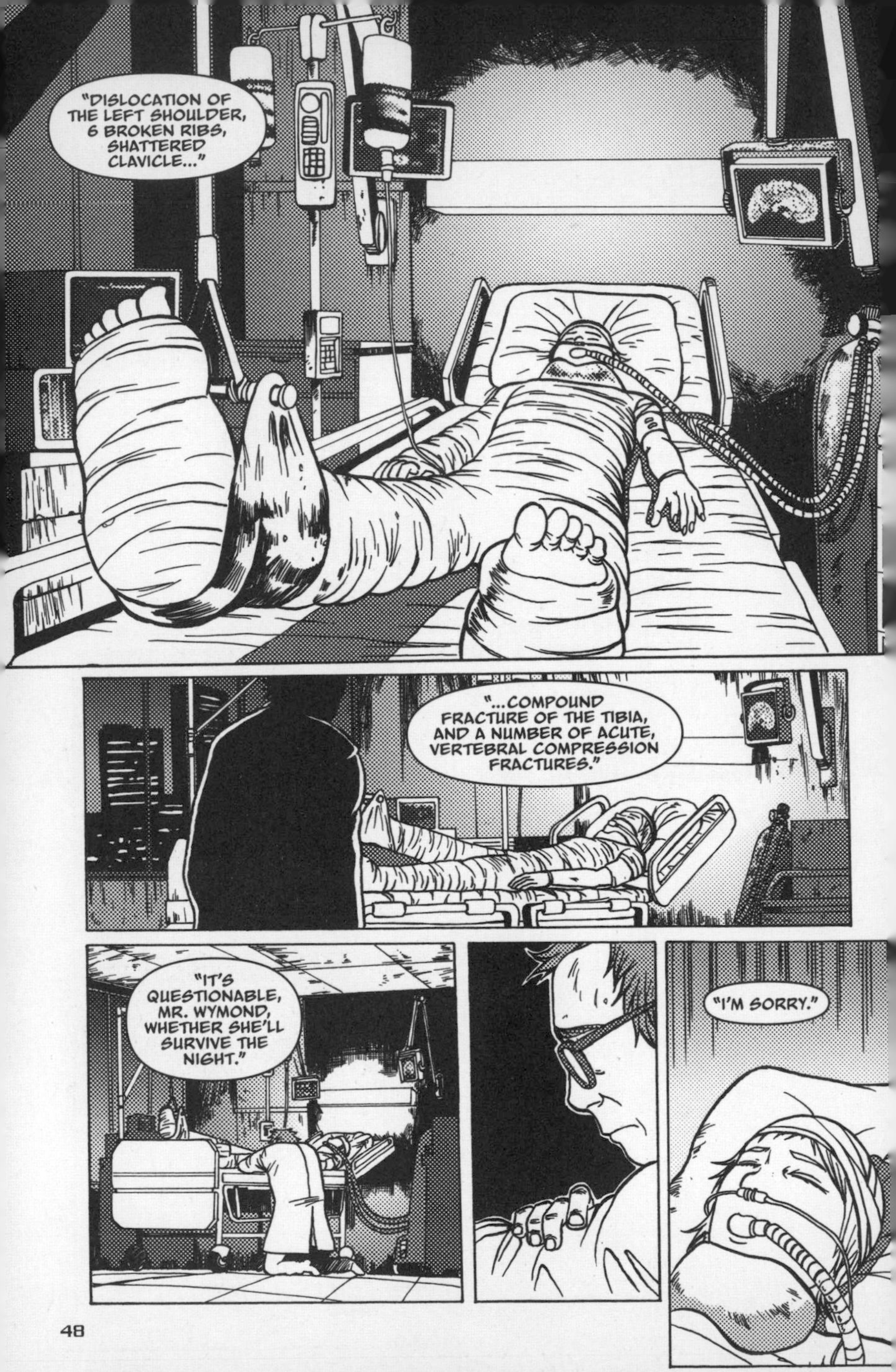
"DISLOCATION OF THE LEFT SHOULDER, 6 BROKEN RIBS, SHATTERED CLAVICLE..."
"...COMPOUND FRACTURE OF THE TIBIA, AND A NUMBER OF ACUTE, VERTEBRAL COMPRESSION FRACTURES."
"IT'S QUESTIONABLE, MR. WYMOND, WHETHER SHE'LL SURVIVE THE NIGHT."
"I'M SORRY."

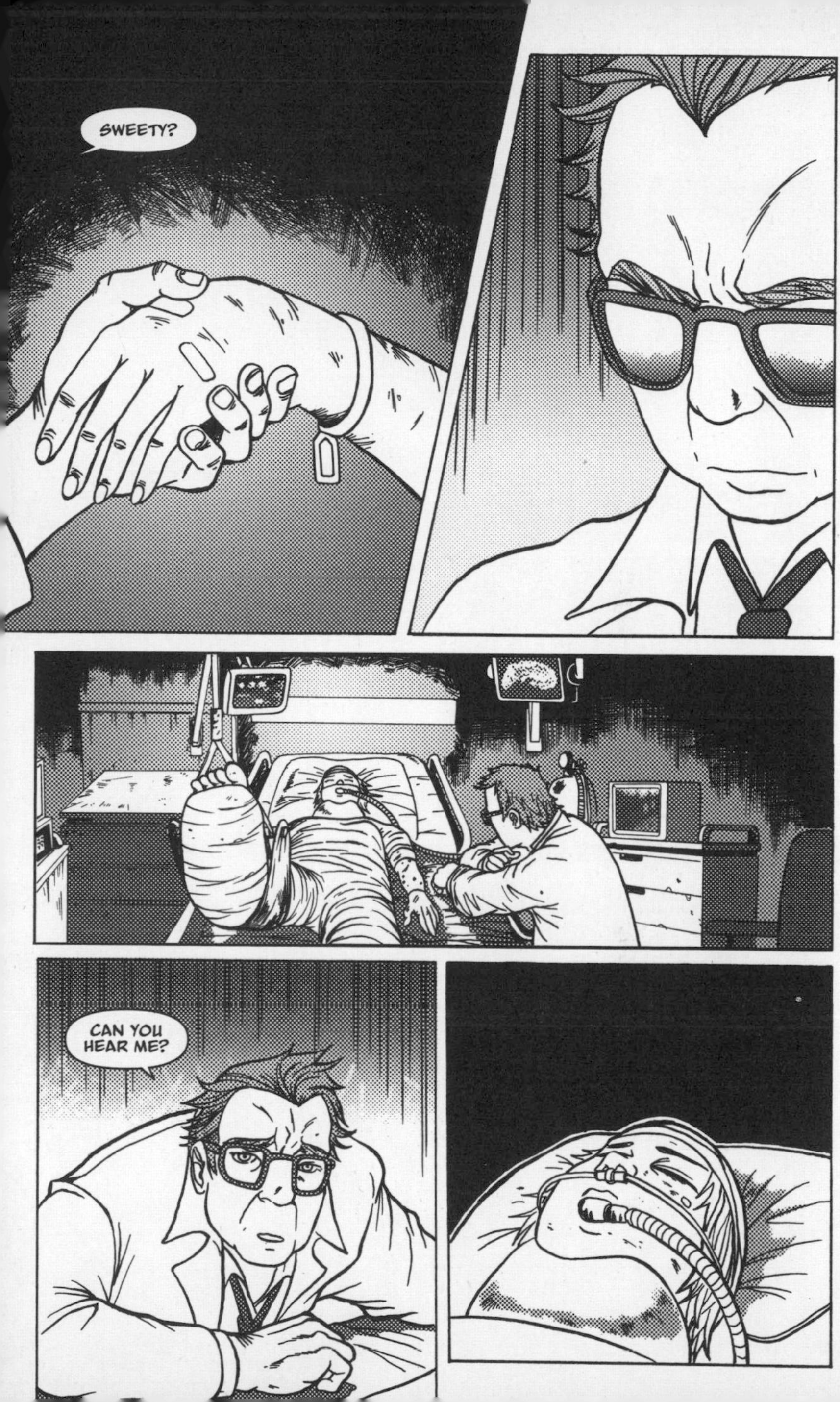
SWEETY?
CAN YOU HEAR ME?

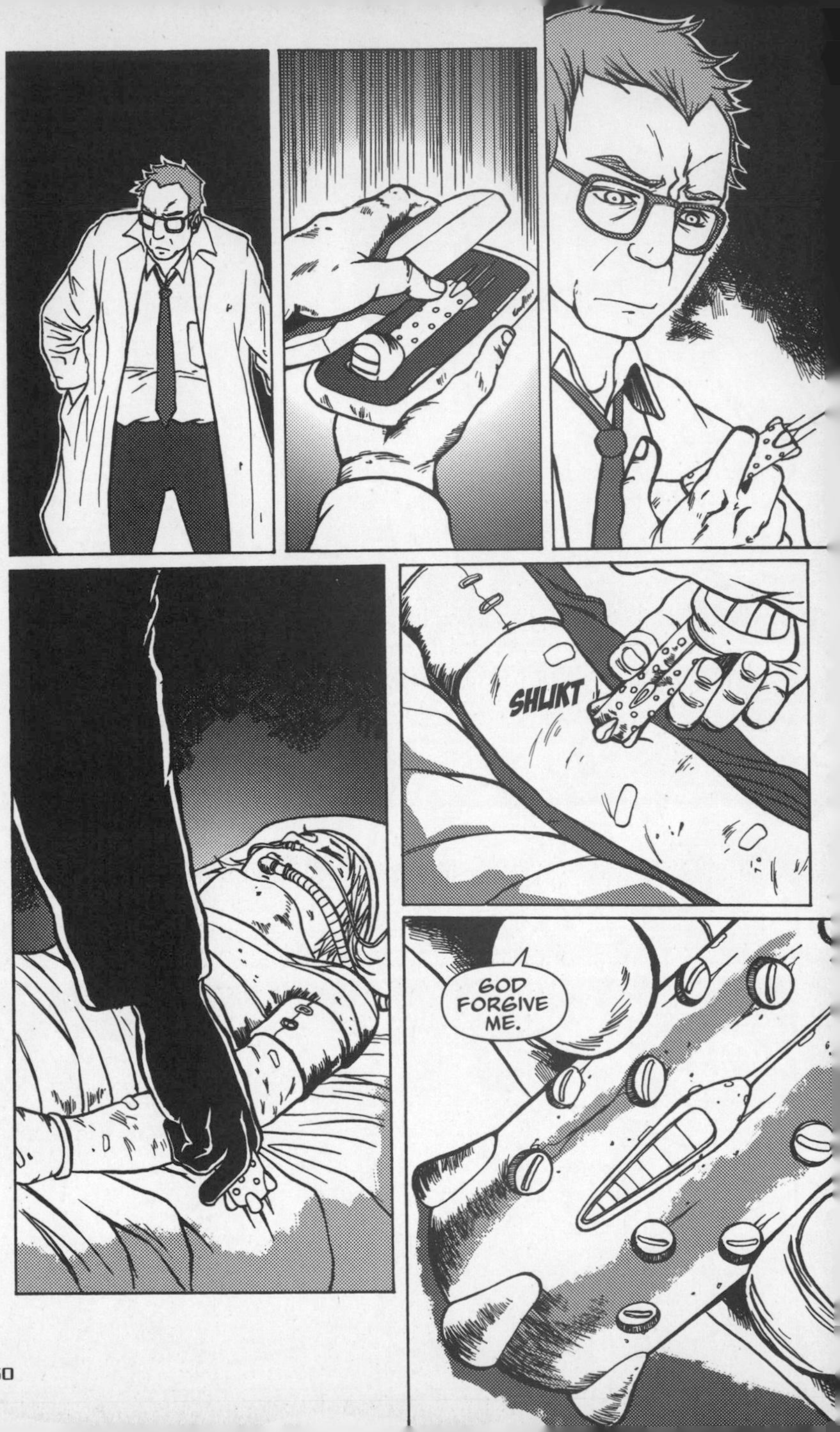
SHUKT
GOD FORGIVE ME.

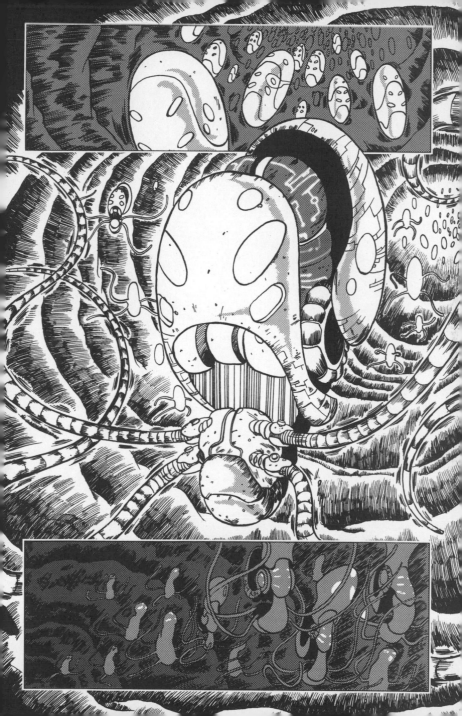

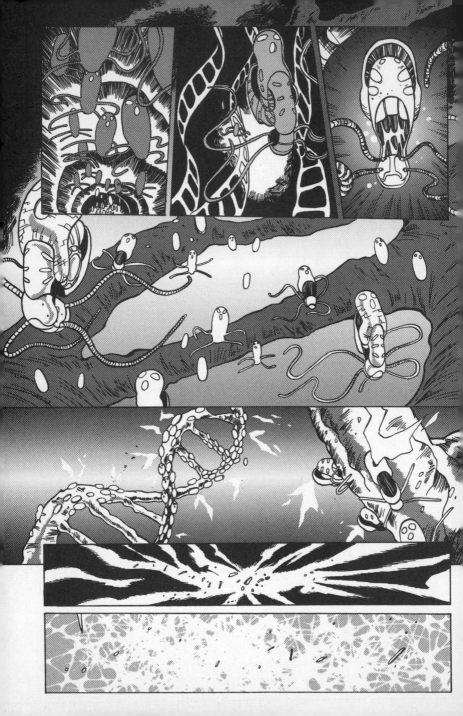

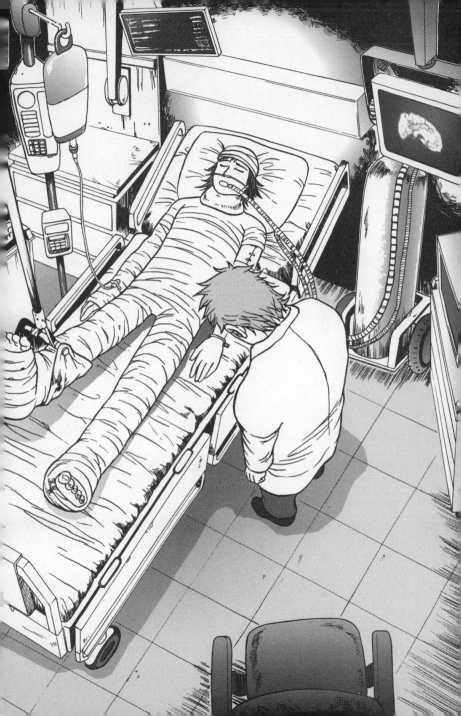

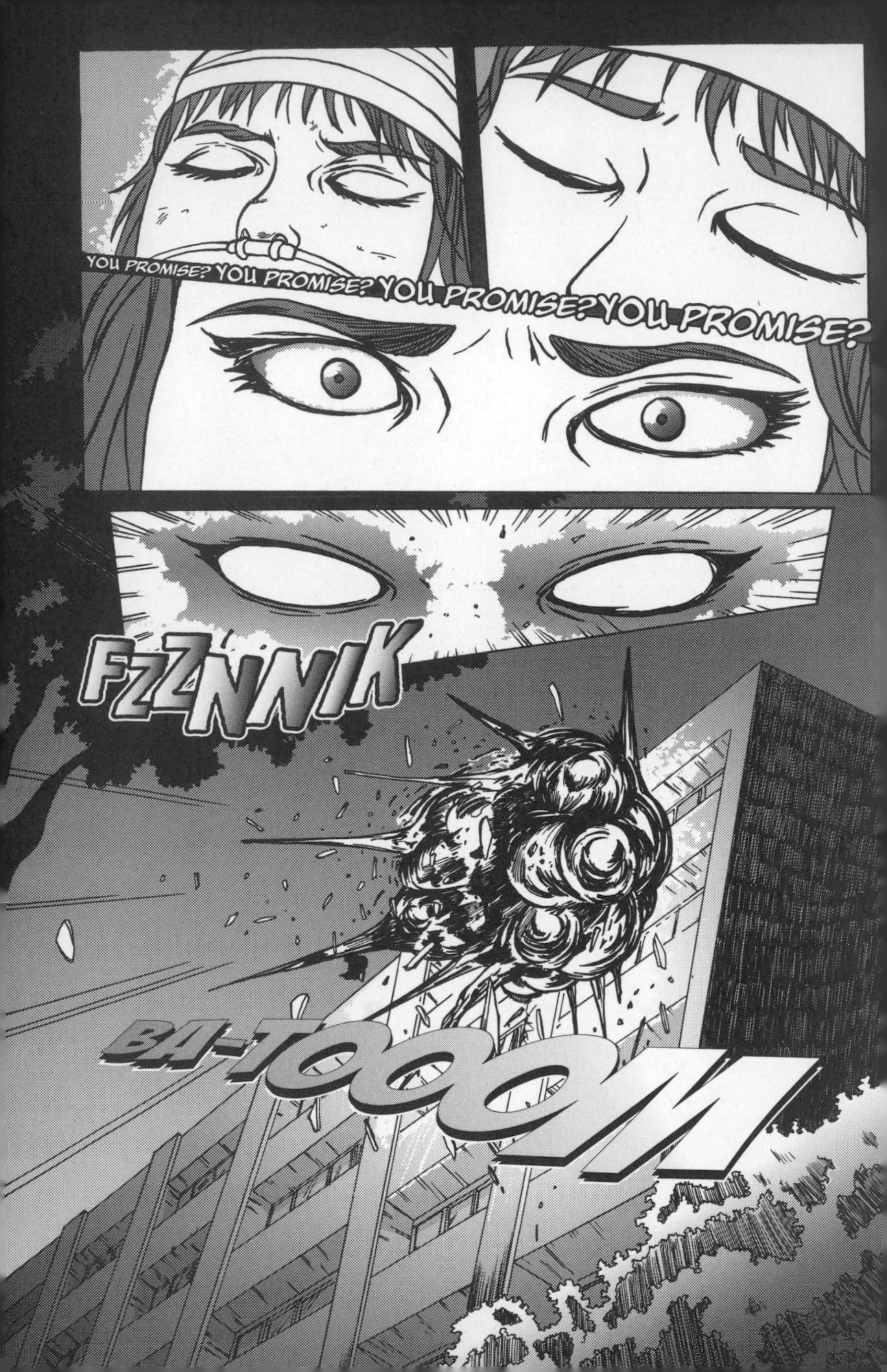
YOU PROMISE? YOU PROMISE? YOU PROMISE? YOU PROMISE?
FZZNNIK
BA-TOOOM

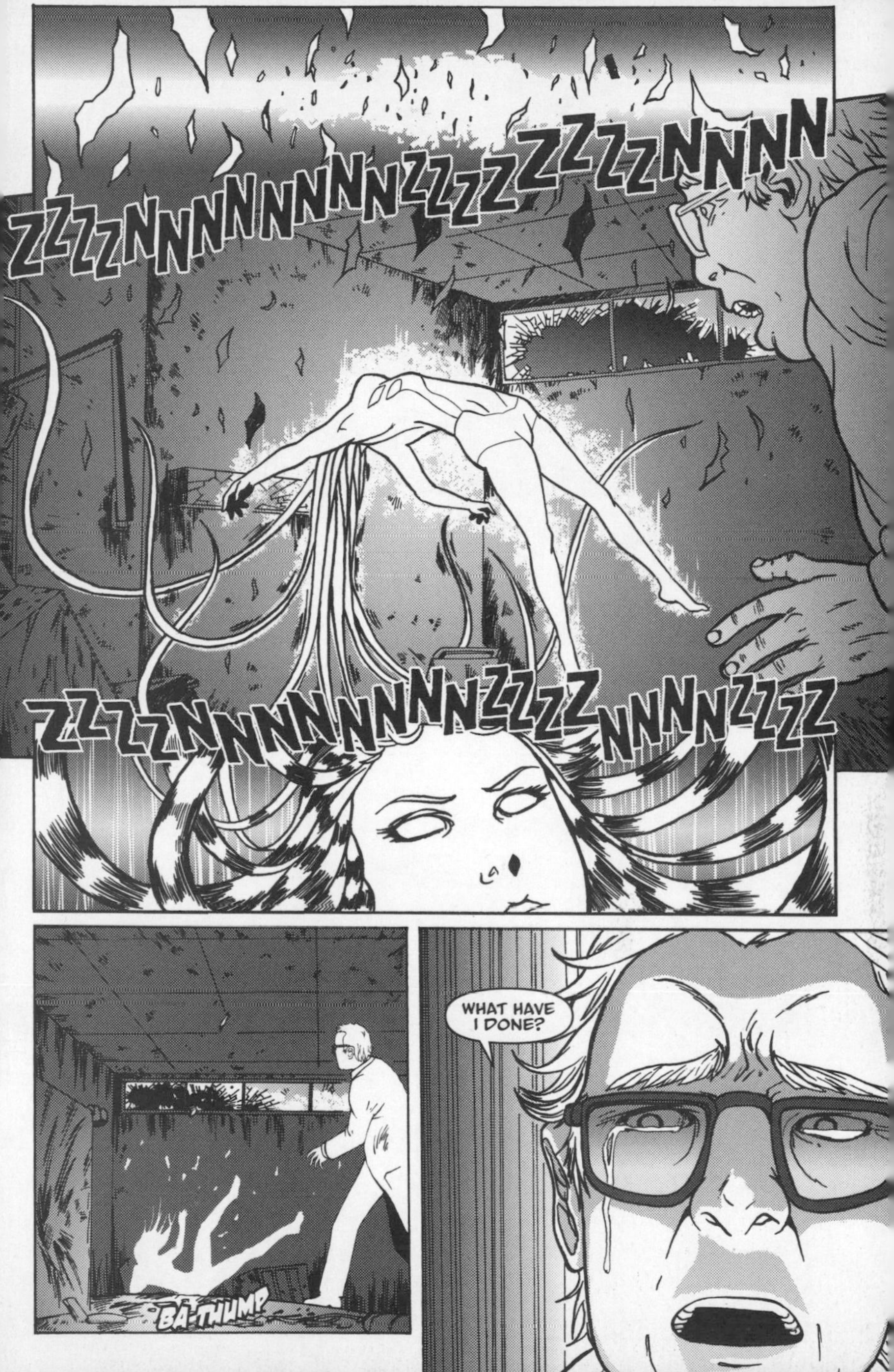
ZZZZNNNNNNNNZZZZZZZZZZNNNN
ZZZZNNNNNNNNZZZZNNNNZZZZ
BA-THUMP
WHAT HAVE I DONE?

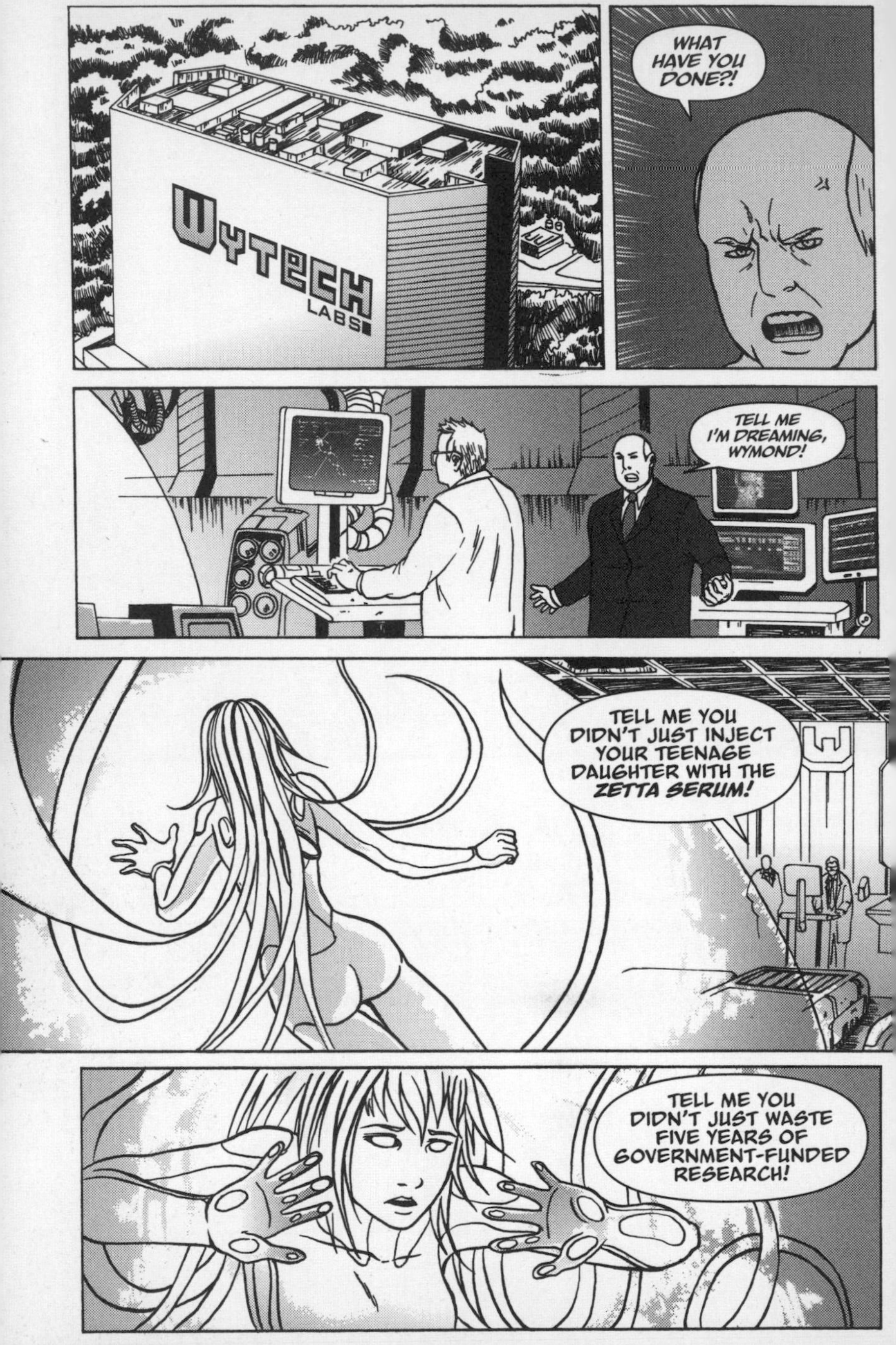
WYTECH LABS
WHAT HAVE YOU DONE?!
TELL ME I'M DREAMING, WYMOND!
TELL ME YOU DIDN'T JUST INJECT YOUR TEENAGE DAUGHTER WITH THE ZETTA SERUM!
TELL ME YOU DIDN'T JUST WASTE FIVE YEARS OF GOVERNMENT-FUNDED RESEARCH!

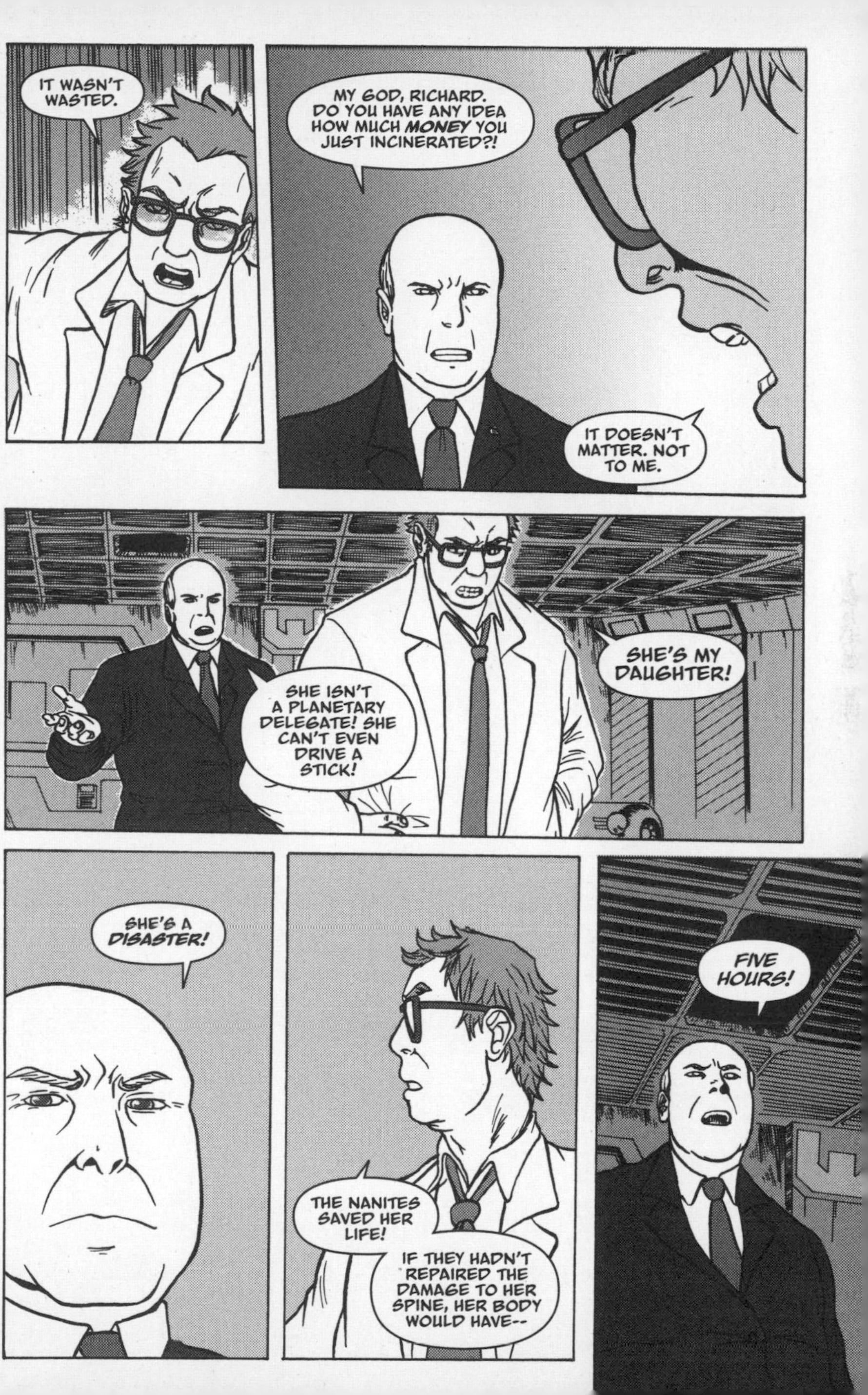
IT WASN'T WASTED.
MY GOD, RICHARD. DO YOU HAVE ANY IDEA HOW MUCH MONEY YOU JUST INCINERATED?!
IT DOESN'T MATTER. NOT TO ME.
SHE ISN'T A PLANETARY DELEGATE! SHE CAN'T EVEN DRIVE A STICK!
SHE'S MY DAUGHTER!
SHE'S A DISASTER!
THE NANITES SAVED HER LIFE!
IF THEY HADN'T REPAIRED THE DAMAGE TO HER SPINE, HER BODY WOULD HAVE--
FIVE HOURS!

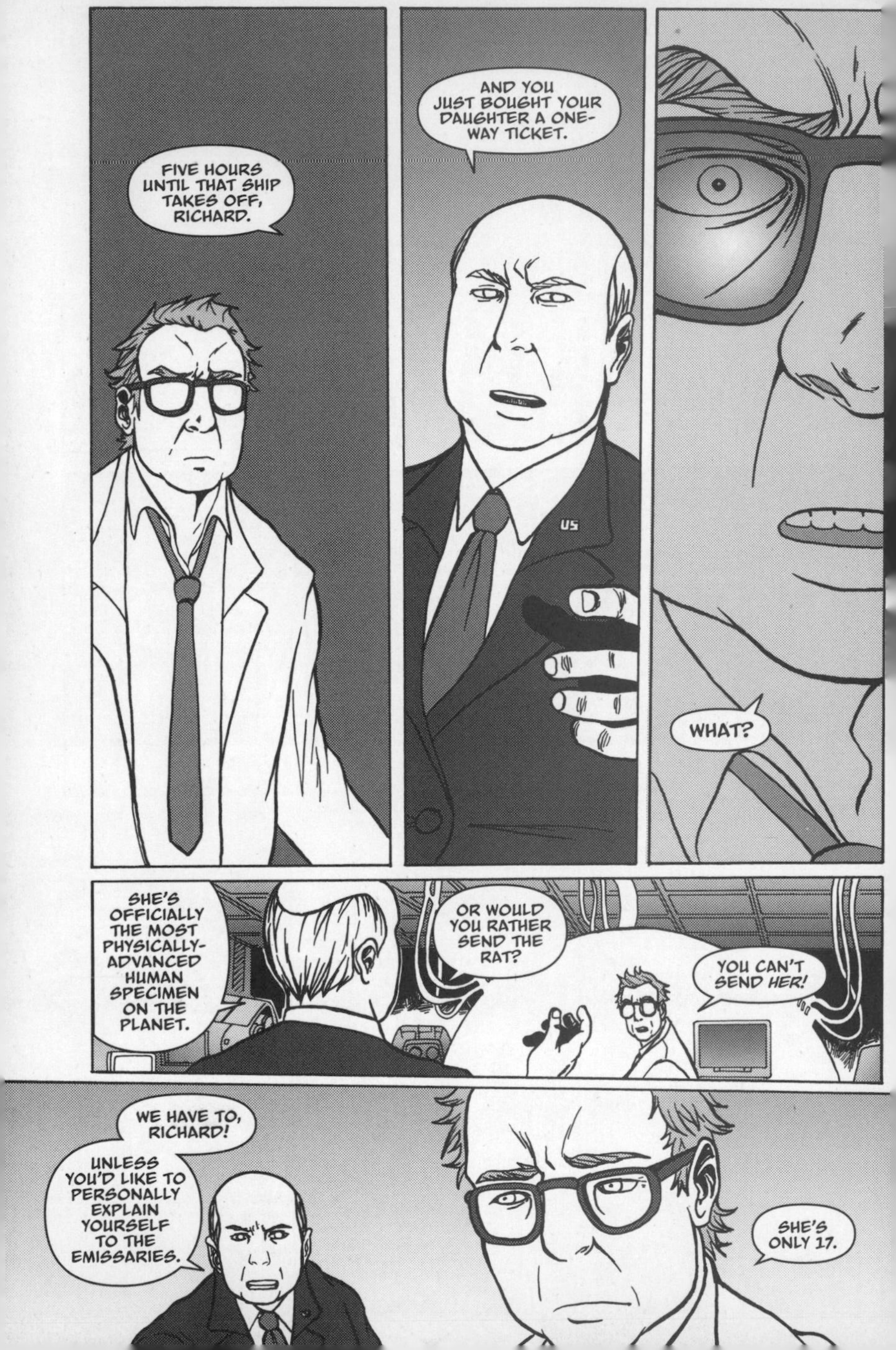
FIVE HOURS UNTIL THAT SHIP TAKES OFF, RICHARD.
AND YOU JUST BOUGHT YOUR DAUGHTER A ONE-WAY TICKET.
US
WHAT?
SHE'S OFFICIALLY THE MOST PHYSICALLY-ADVANCED HUMAN SPECIMEN ON THE PLANET.
OR WOULD YOU RATHER SEND THE RAT?
YOU CAN'T SEND HER!
WE HAVE TO, RICHARD!
UNLESS YOU'D LIKE TO PERSONALLY EXPLAIN YOURSELF TO THE EMISSARIES.
SHE'S ONLY 17.

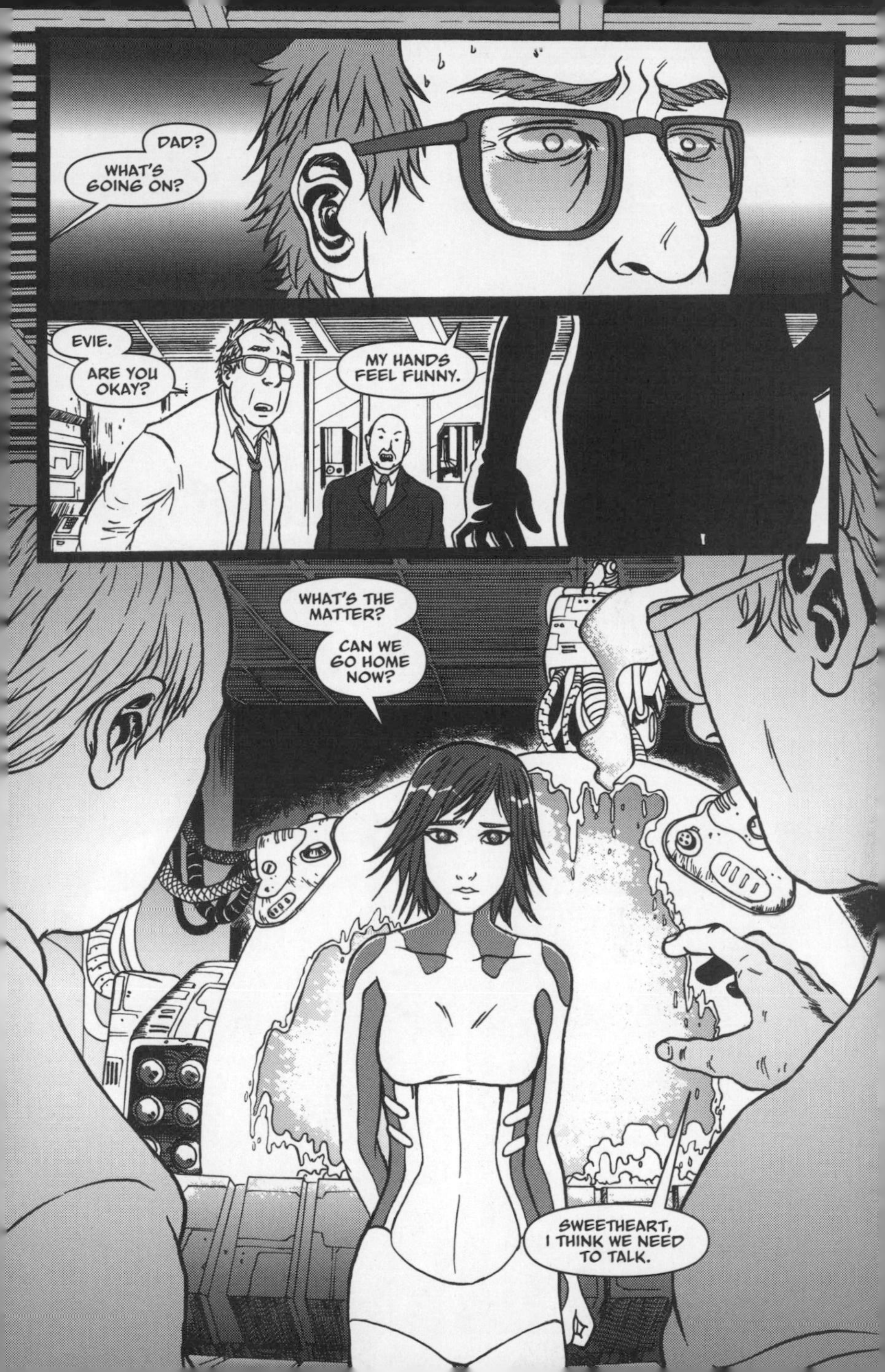
DAD?
WHAT'S GOING ON?
EVIE.
ARE YOU OKAY?
MY HANDS FEEL FUNNY.
WHAT'S THE MATTER?
CAN WE GO HOME NOW?
SWEETHEART, I THINK WE NEED TO TALK.

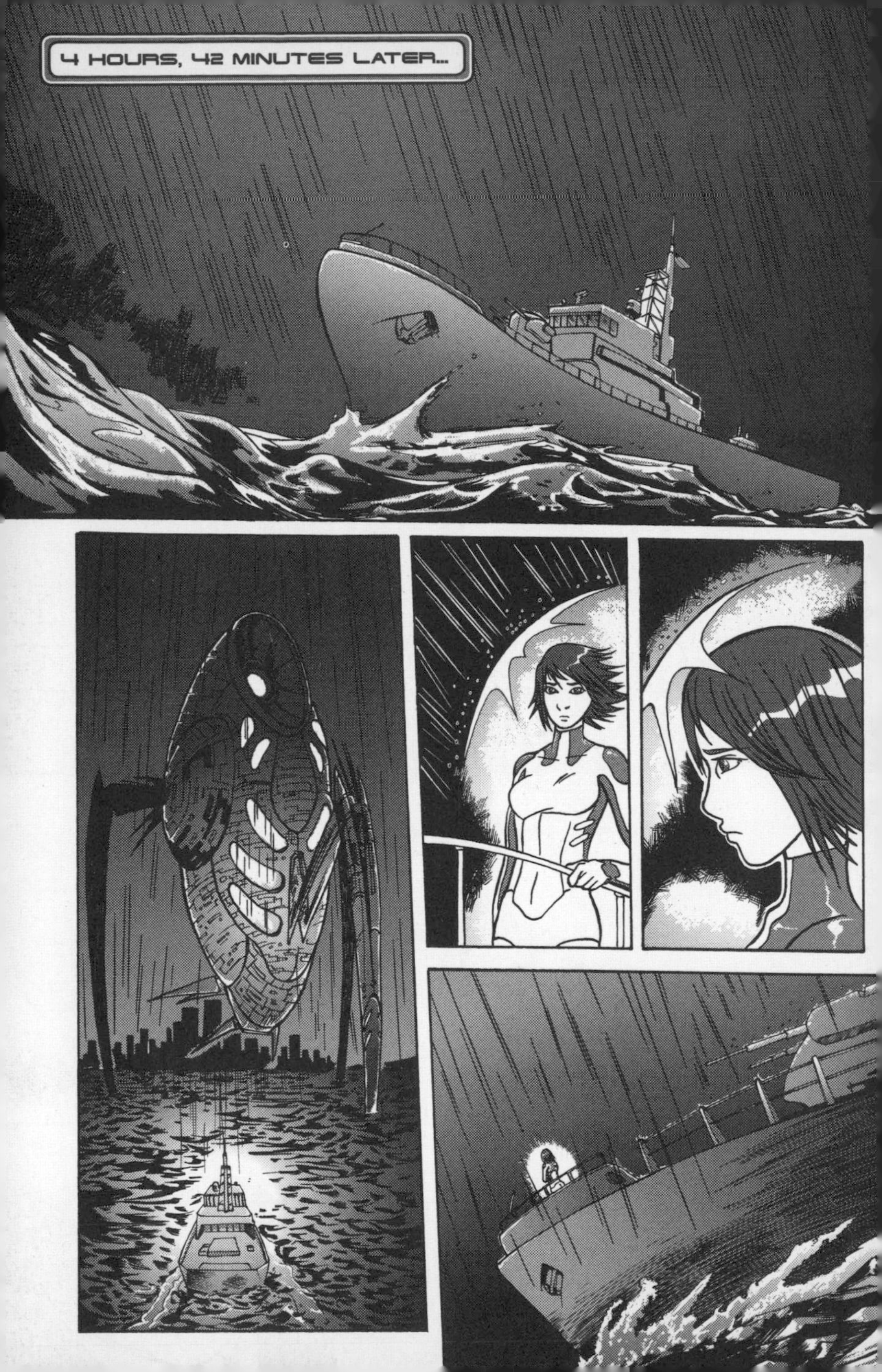
4 HOURS, 42 MINUTES LATER...

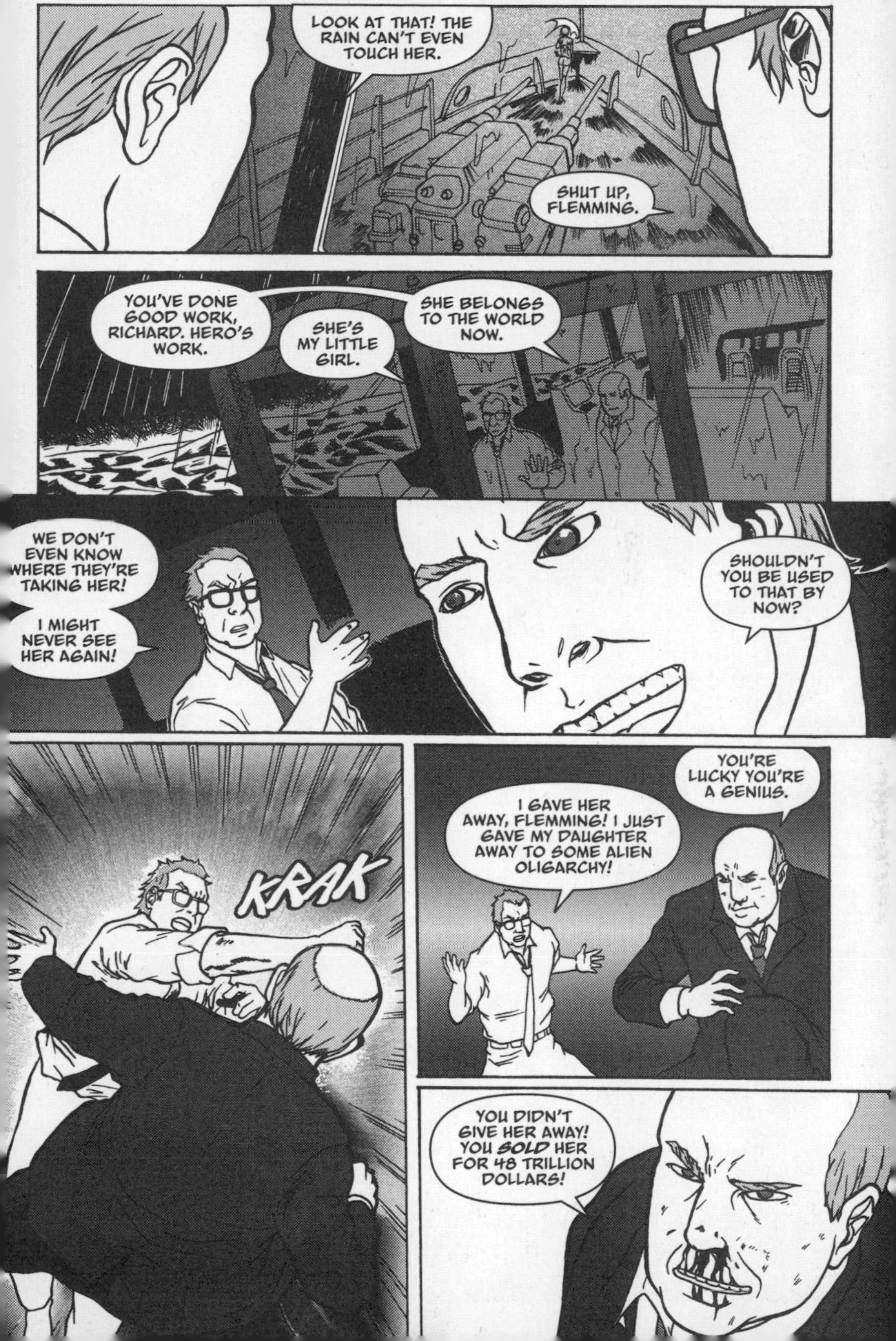
LOOK AT THAT! THE RAIN CAN'T EVEN TOUCH HER.
SHUT UP, FLEMMING.
YOU'VE DONE GOOD WORK, RICHARD. HERO'S WORK.
SHE'S MY LITTLE GIRL.
SHE BELONGS TO THE WORLD NOW.
WE DON'T EVEN KNOW WHERE THEY'RE TAKING HER!
I MIGHT NEVER SEE HER AGAIN!
SHOULDN'T YOU BE USED TO THAT BY NOW?
KRAK
YOU'RE LUCKY YOU'RE A GENIUS.
I GAVE HER AWAY, FLEMMING! I JUST GAVE MY DAUGHTER AWAY TO SOME ALIEN OLIGARCHY!
YOU DIDN'T GIVE HER AWAY! YOU *SOLD* HER FOR 48 TRILLION DOLLARS!

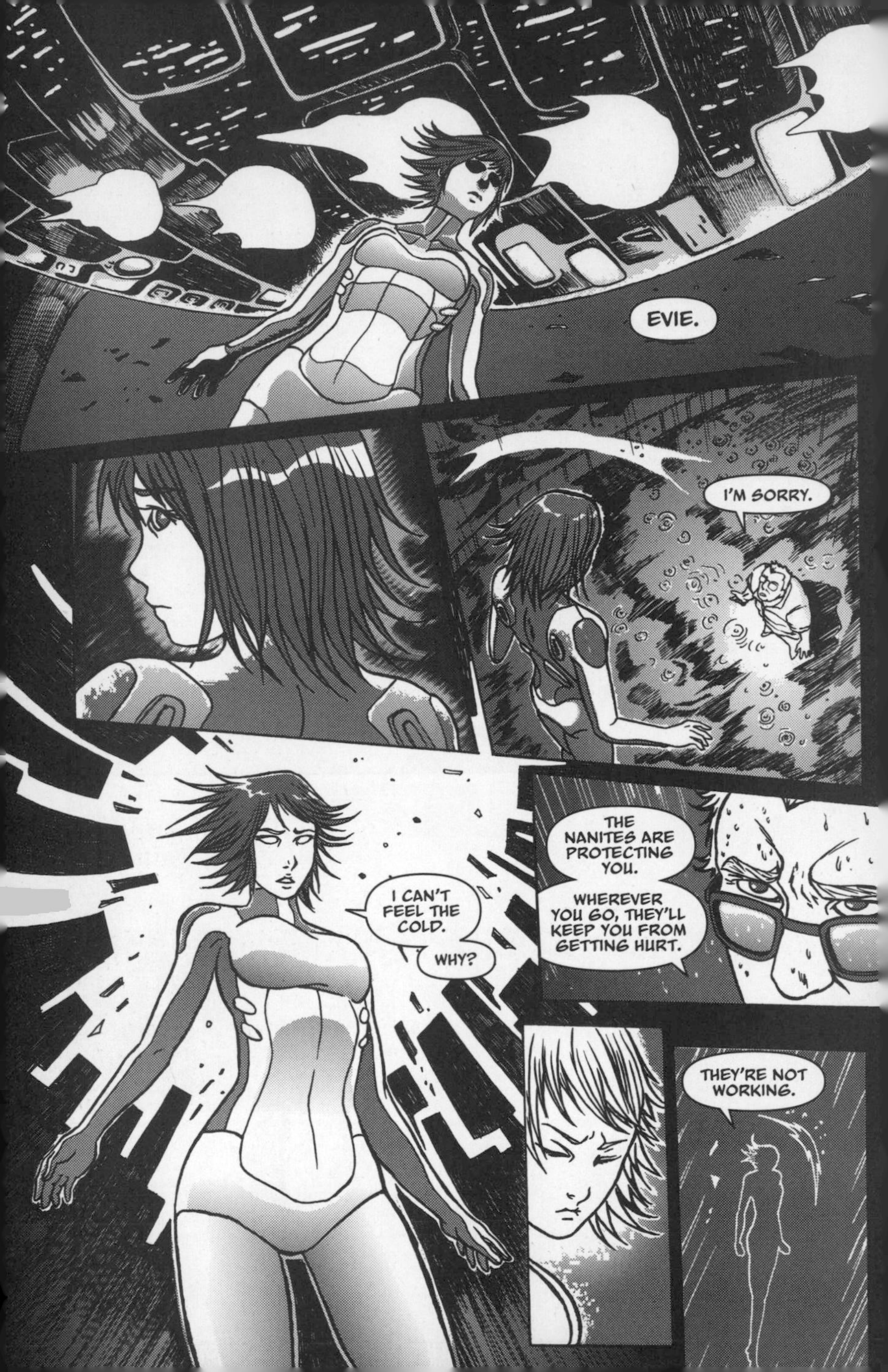
EVIE.
I'M SORRY.
I CAN'T FEEL THE COLD.
WHY?
THE NANITES ARE PROTECTING YOU.
WHEREVER YOU GO, THEY'LL KEEP YOU FROM GETTING HURT.
THEY'RE NOT WORKING.

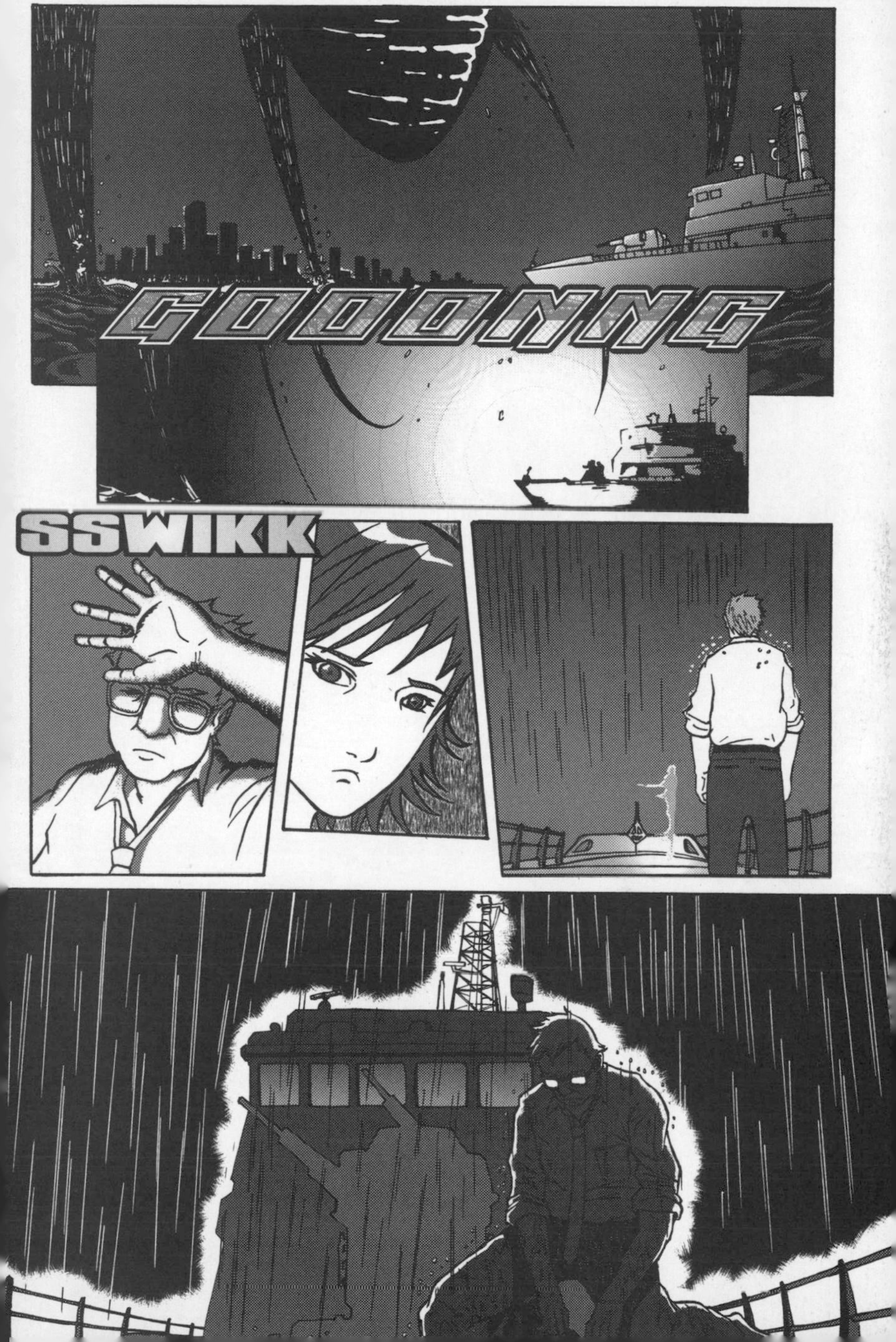
GOOONNG
SSWIKK

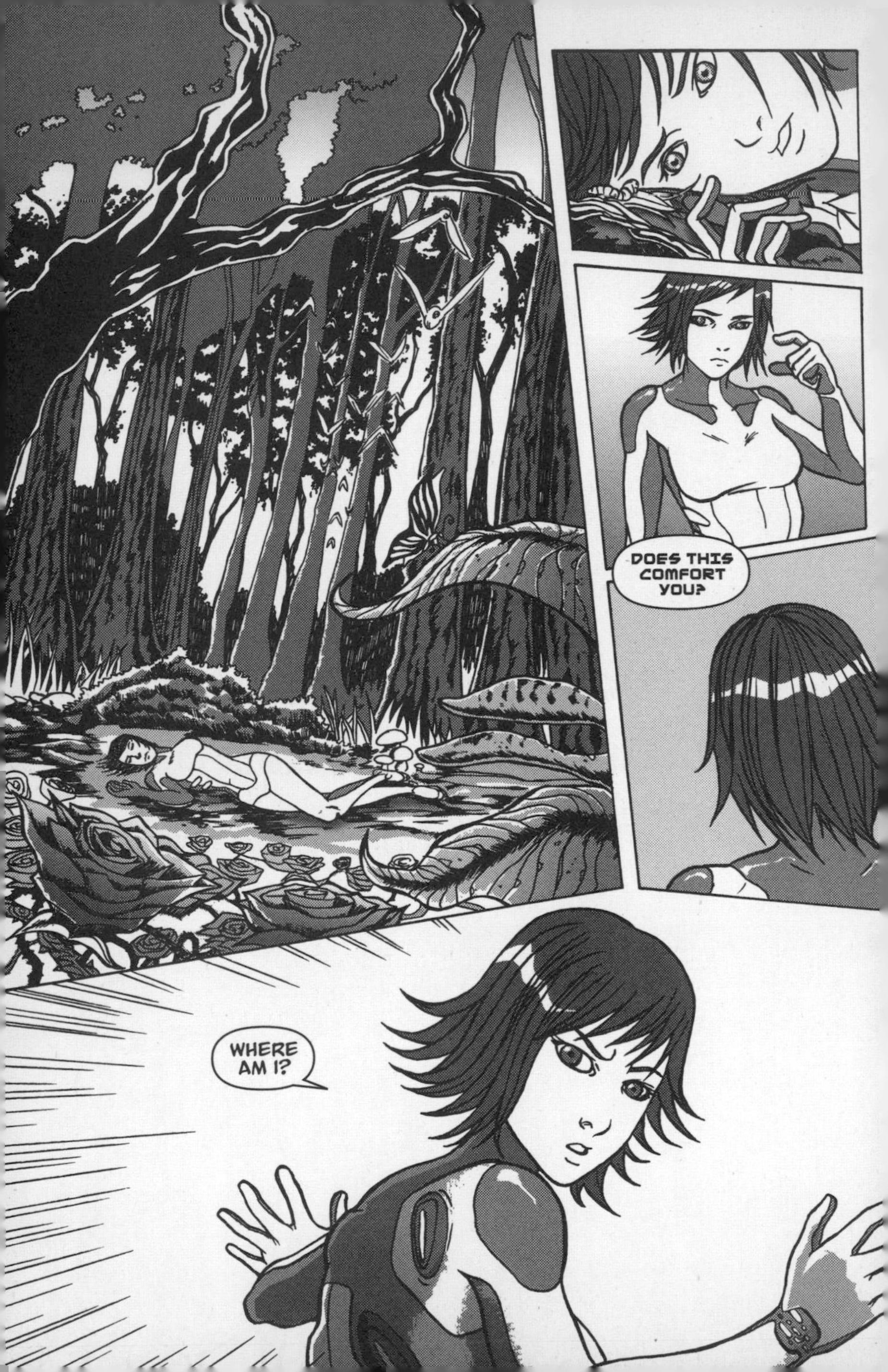
DOES THIS COMFORT YOU?
WHERE AM I?

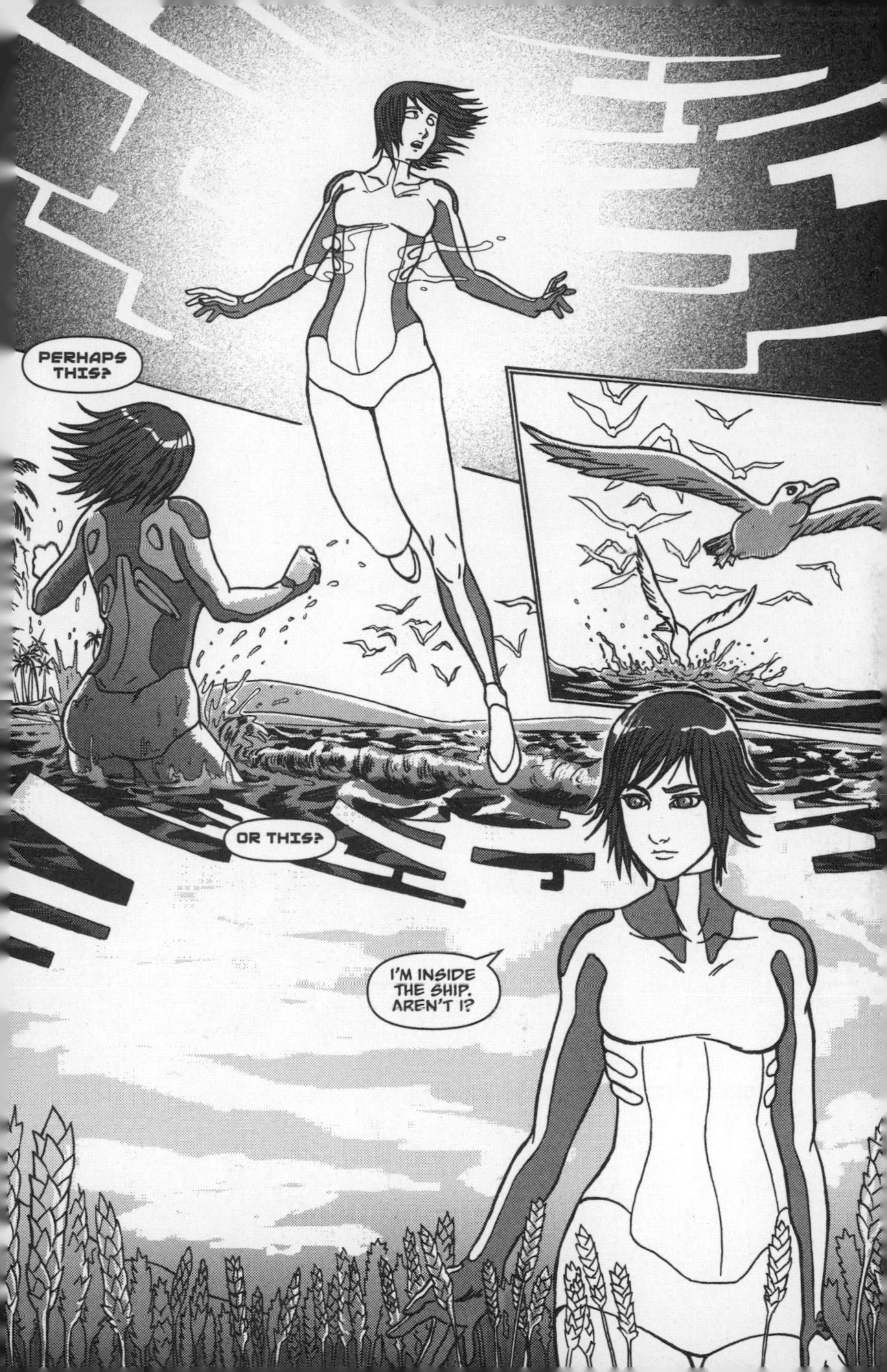
PERHAPS THIS?
OR THIS?
I'M INSIDE THE SHIP. AREN'T I?

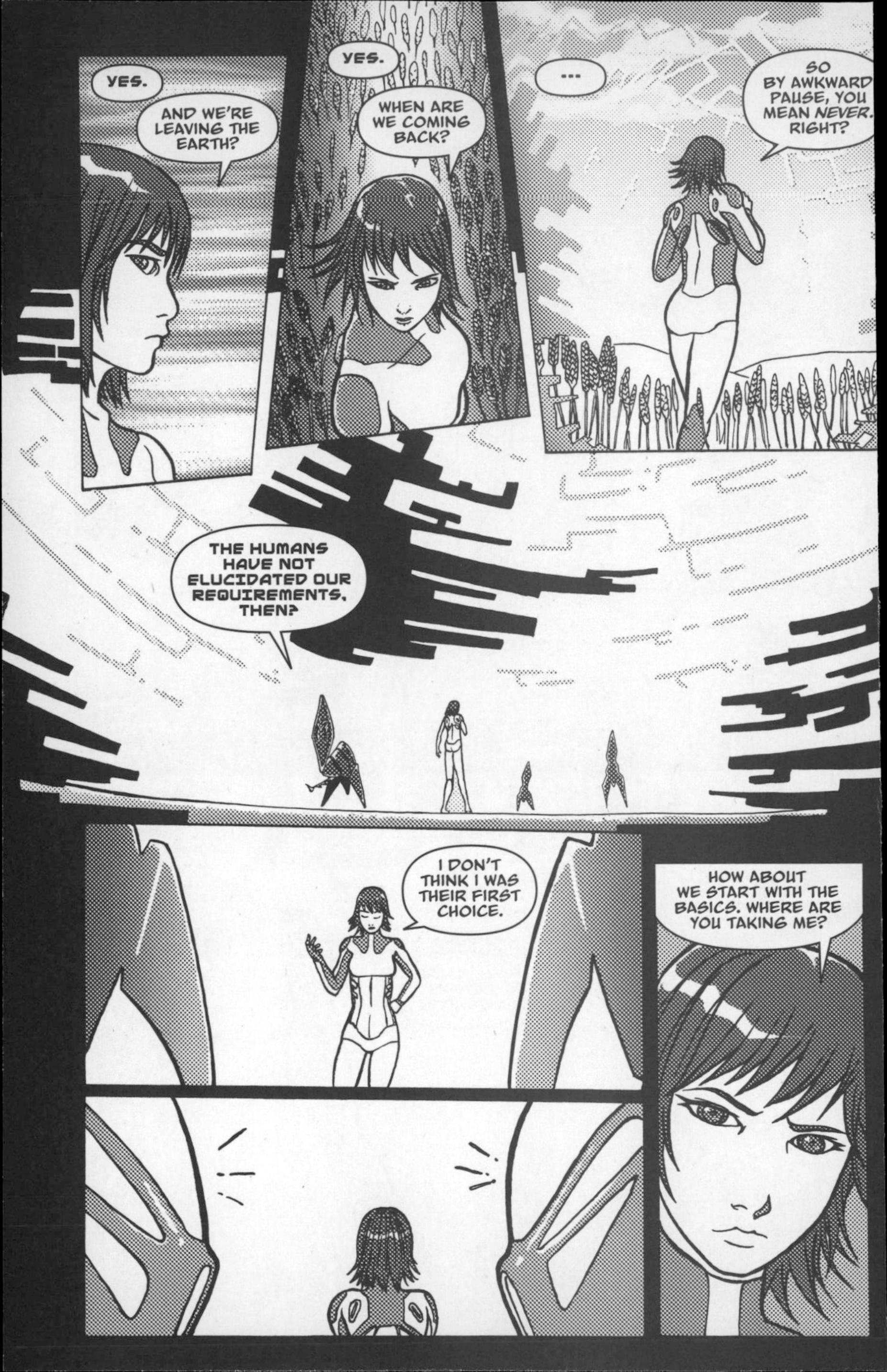
YES.
AND WE'RE LEAVING THE EARTH?
YES.
WHEN ARE WE COMING BACK?
...
SO BY AWKWARD PAUSE, YOU MEAN *NEVER*. RIGHT?
THE HUMANS HAVE NOT ELUCIDATED OUR REQUIREMENTS, THEN?
I DON'T THINK I WAS THEIR FIRST CHOICE.
HOW ABOUT WE START WITH THE BASICS. WHERE ARE YOU TAKING ME?

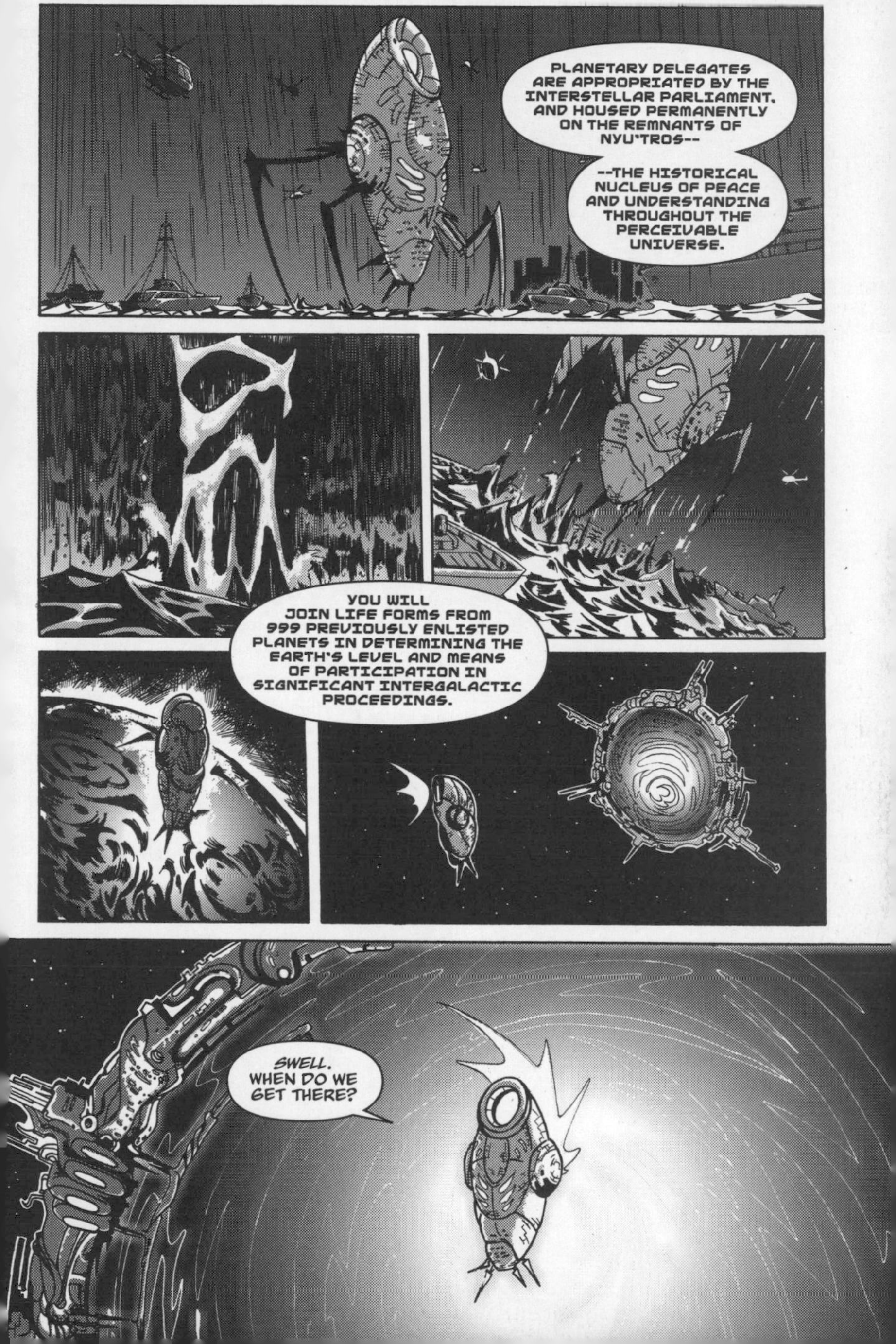
PLANETARY DELEGATES ARE APPROPRIATED BY THE INTERSTELLAR PARLIAMENT, AND HOUSED PERMANENTLY ON THE REMNANTS OF NYU'TROS--
--THE HISTORICAL NUCLEUS OF PEACE AND UNDERSTANDING THROUGHOUT THE PERCEIVABLE UNIVERSE.
YOU WILL JOIN LIFE FORMS FROM 999 PREVIOUSLY ENLISTED PLANETS IN DETERMINING THE EARTH'S LEVEL AND MEANS OF PARTICIPATION IN SIGNIFICANT INTERGALACTIC PROCEEDINGS.
SWELL. WHEN DO WE GET THERE?

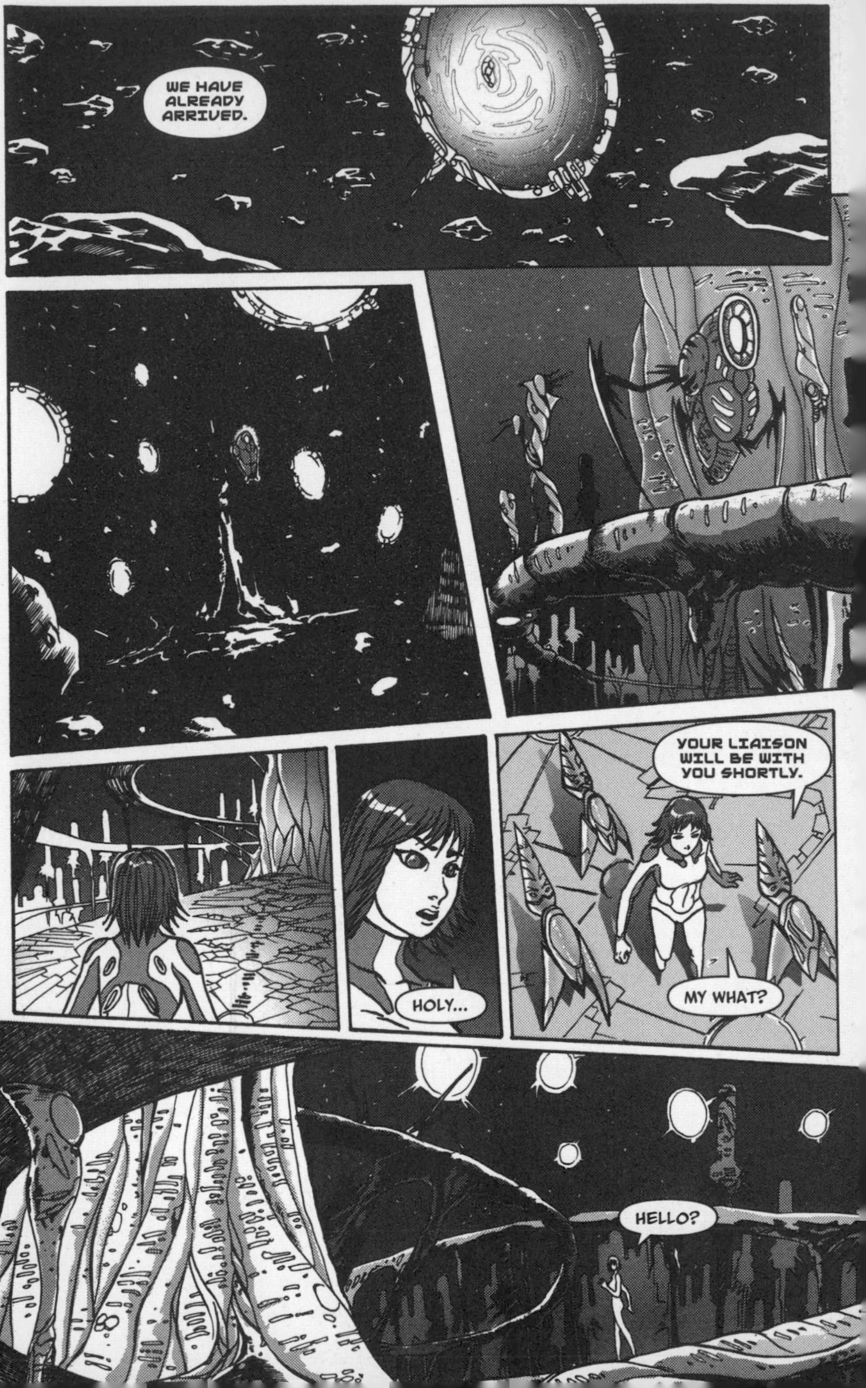
WE HAVE ALREADY ARRIVED.
HOLY...
YOUR LIAISON WILL BE WITH YOU SHORTLY.
MY WHAT?
HELLO?

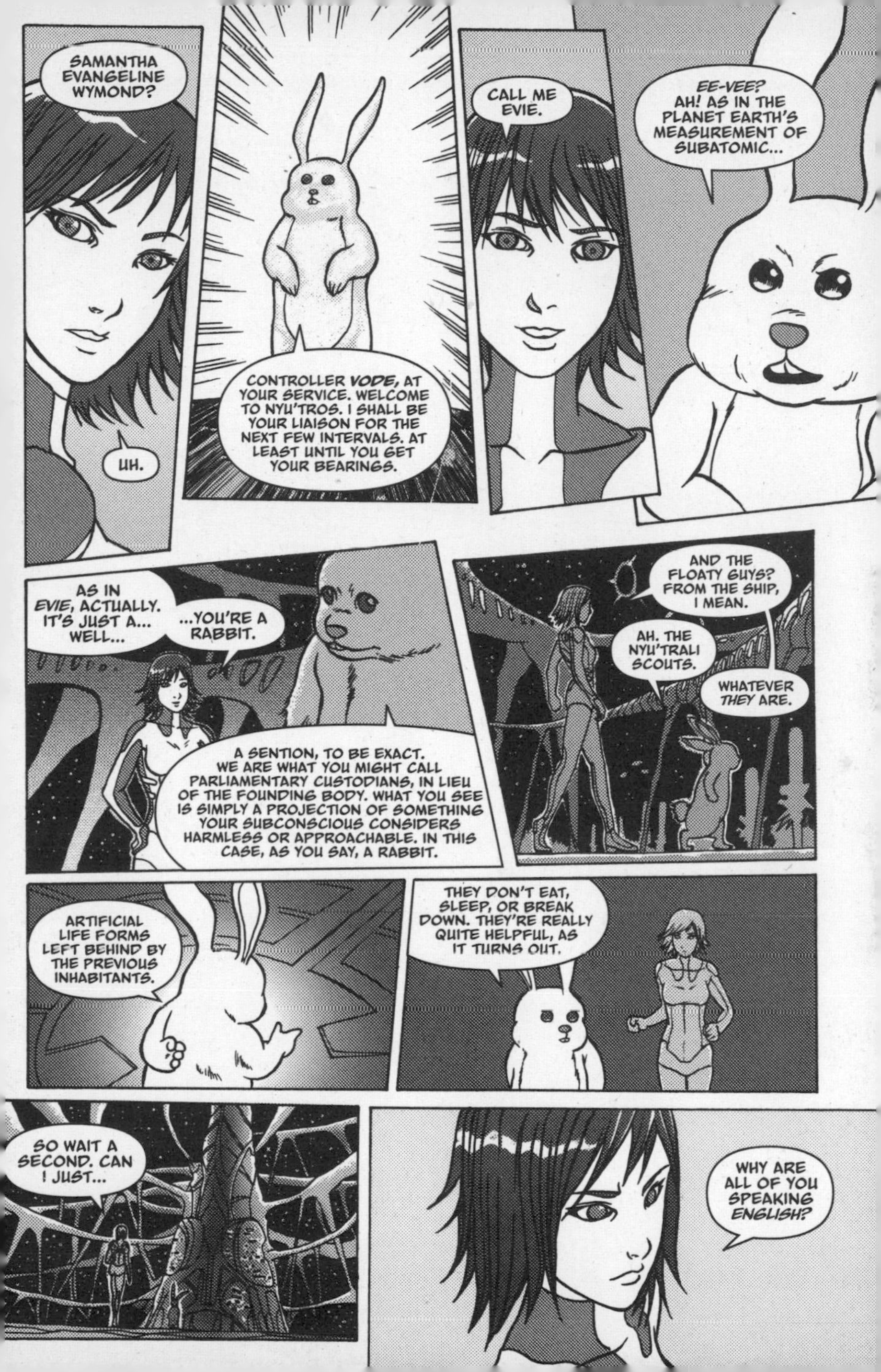

SAMANTHA EVANGELINE WYMOND?
UH.
CONTROLLER *VODE*, AT YOUR SERVICE. WELCOME TO NYU'TROS. I SHALL BE YOUR LIAISON FOR THE NEXT FEW INTERVALS. AT LEAST UNTIL YOU GET YOUR BEARINGS.
CALL ME EVIE.
EE-VEE? AH! AS IN THE PLANET EARTH'S MEASUREMENT OF SUBATOMIC...
AS IN *EVIE*, ACTUALLY. IT'S JUST A... WELL...
...YOU'RE A RABBIT.
A SENTION, TO BE EXACT. WE ARE WHAT YOU MIGHT CALL PARLIAMENTARY CUSTODIANS, IN LIEU OF THE FOUNDING BODY. WHAT YOU SEE IS SIMPLY A PROJECTION OF SOMETHING YOUR SUBCONSCIOUS CONSIDERS HARMLESS OR APPROACHABLE. IN THIS CASE, AS YOU SAY, A RABBIT.
AND THE FLOATY GUYS? FROM THE SHIP, I MEAN.
AH. THE NYU'TRALI SCOUTS.
WHATEVER *THEY* ARE.
ARTIFICIAL LIFE FORMS LEFT BEHIND BY THE PREVIOUS INHABITANTS.
THEY DON'T EAT, SLEEP, OR BREAK DOWN. THEY'RE REALLY QUITE HELPFUL, AS IT TURNS OUT.
SO WAIT A SECOND. CAN I JUST...
WHY ARE ALL OF YOU SPEAKING ENGLISH?

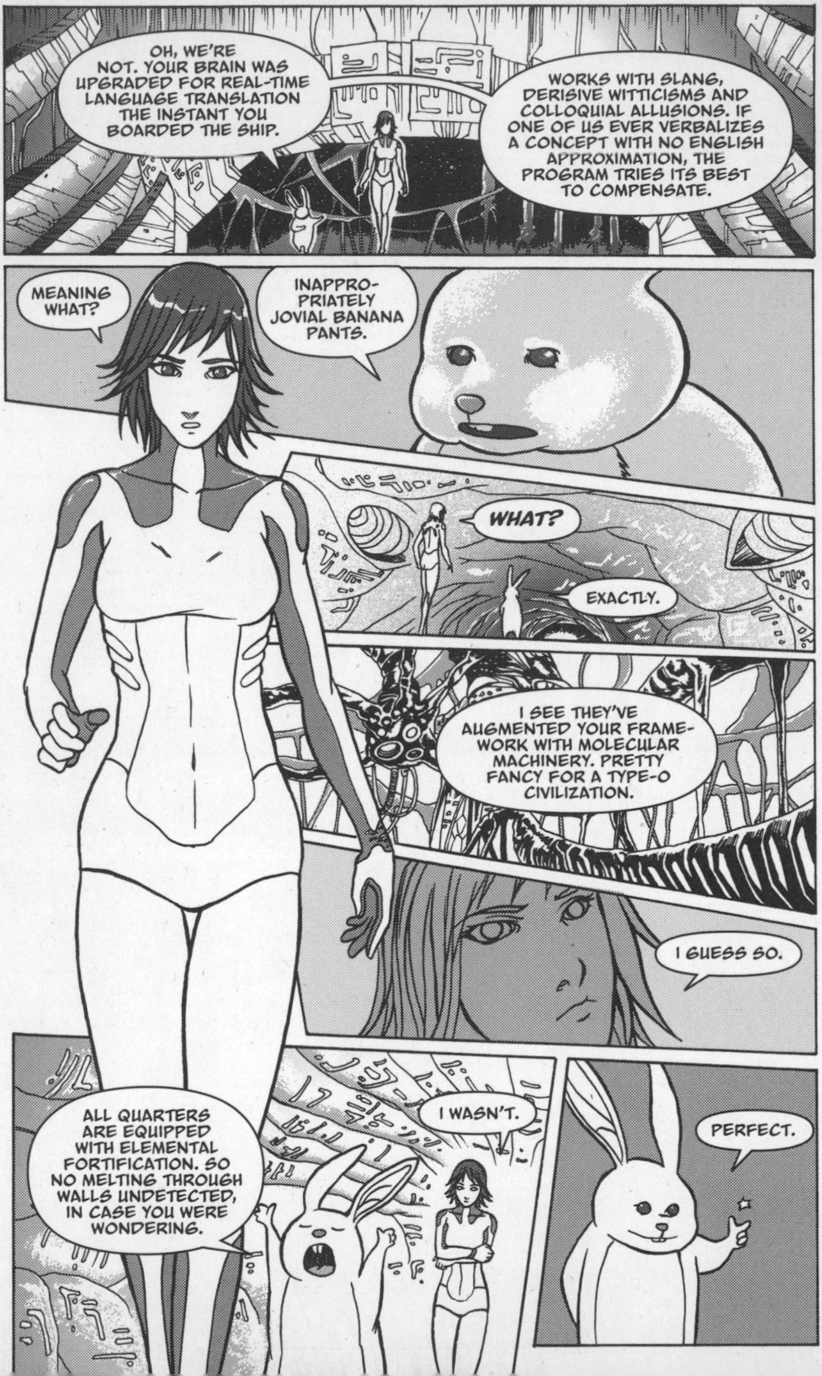
OH, WE'RE NOT. YOUR BRAIN WAS UPGRADED FOR REAL-TIME LANGUAGE TRANSLATION THE INSTANT YOU BOARDED THE SHIP.
WORKS WITH SLANG, DERISIVE WITTICISMS AND COLLOQUIAL ALLUSIONS. IF ONE OF US EVER VERBALIZES A CONCEPT WITH NO ENGLISH APPROXIMATION, THE PROGRAM TRIES ITS BEST TO COMPENSATE.
MEANING WHAT?
INAPPRO-PRIATELY JOVIAL BANANA PANTS.
WHAT?
EXACTLY.
I SEE THEY'VE AUGMENTED YOUR FRAME-WORK WITH MOLECULAR MACHINERY. PRETTY FANCY FOR A TYPE-O CIVILIZATION.
I GUESS SO.
ALL QUARTERS ARE EQUIPPED WITH ELEMENTAL FORTIFICATION. SO NO MELTING THROUGH WALLS UNDETECTED, IN CASE YOU WERE WONDERING.
I WASN'T.
PERFECT.

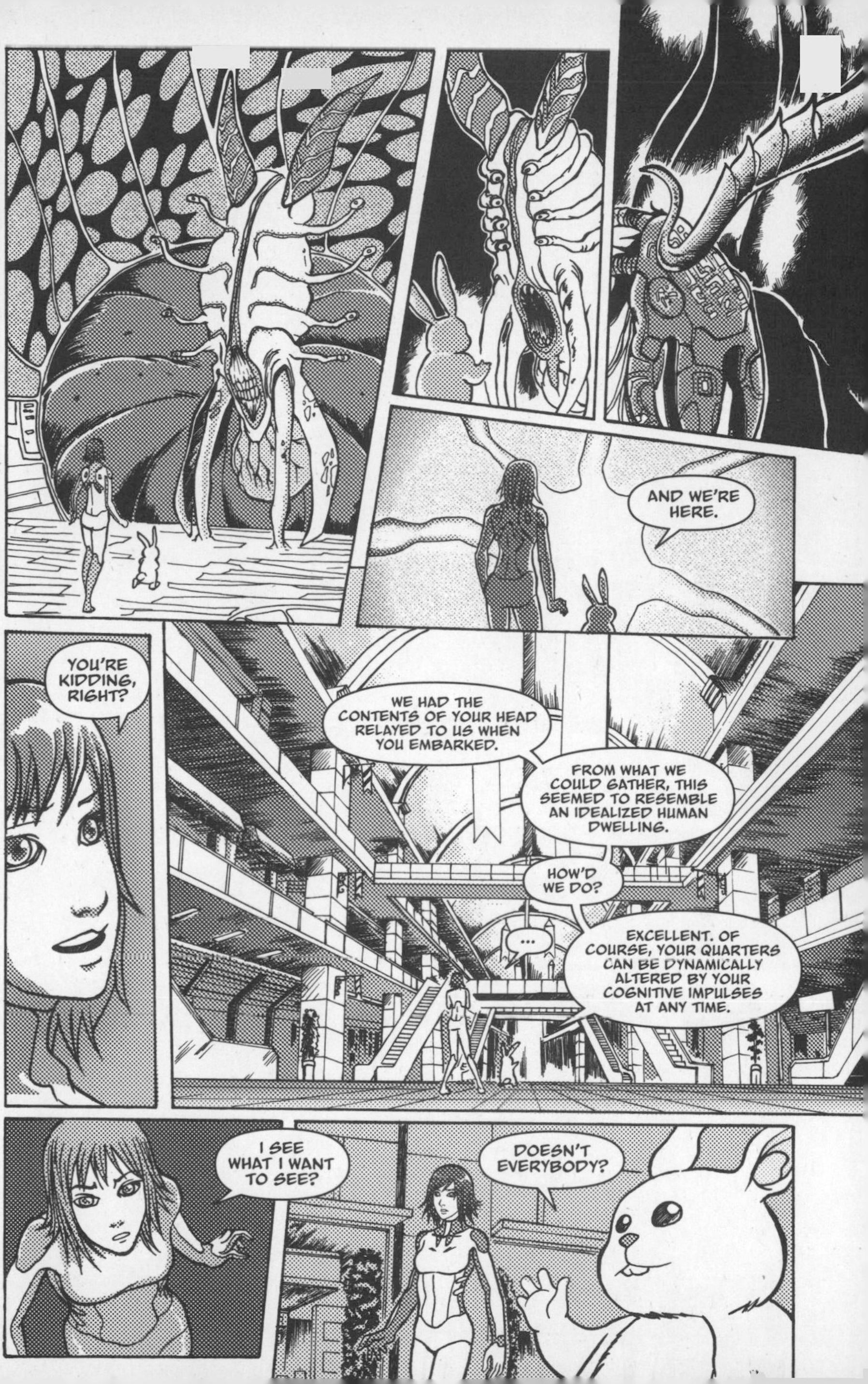
AND WE'RE HERE.
YOU'RE KIDDING, RIGHT?
WE HAD THE CONTENTS OF YOUR HEAD RELAYED TO US WHEN YOU EMBARKED.
FROM WHAT WE COULD GATHER, THIS SEEMED TO RESEMBLE AN IDEALIZED HUMAN DWELLING.
HOW'D WE DO?
...
EXCELLENT. OF COURSE, YOUR QUARTERS CAN BE DYNAMICALLY ALTERED BY YOUR COGNITIVE IMPULSES AT ANY TIME.
I SEE WHAT I WANT TO SEE?
DOESN'T EVERYBODY?

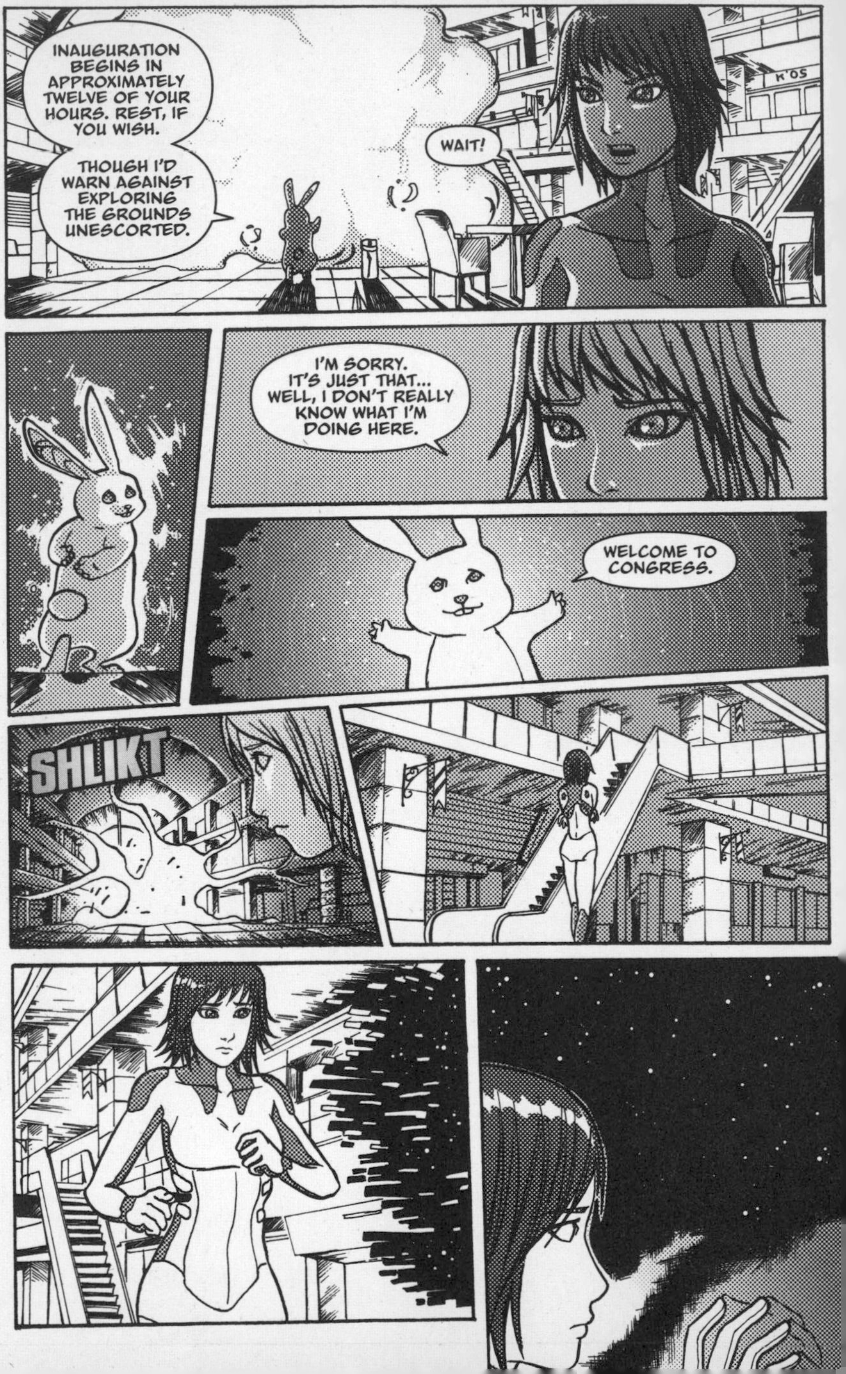
INAUGURATION BEGINS IN APPROXIMATELY TWELVE OF YOUR HOURS. REST, IF YOU WISH.
THOUGH I'D WARN AGAINST EXPLORING THE GROUNDS UNESCORTED.
K'05
WAIT!
I'M SORRY. IT'S JUST THAT... WELL, I DON'T REALLY KNOW WHAT I'M DOING HERE.
WELCOME TO CONGRESS.
SHLIKT

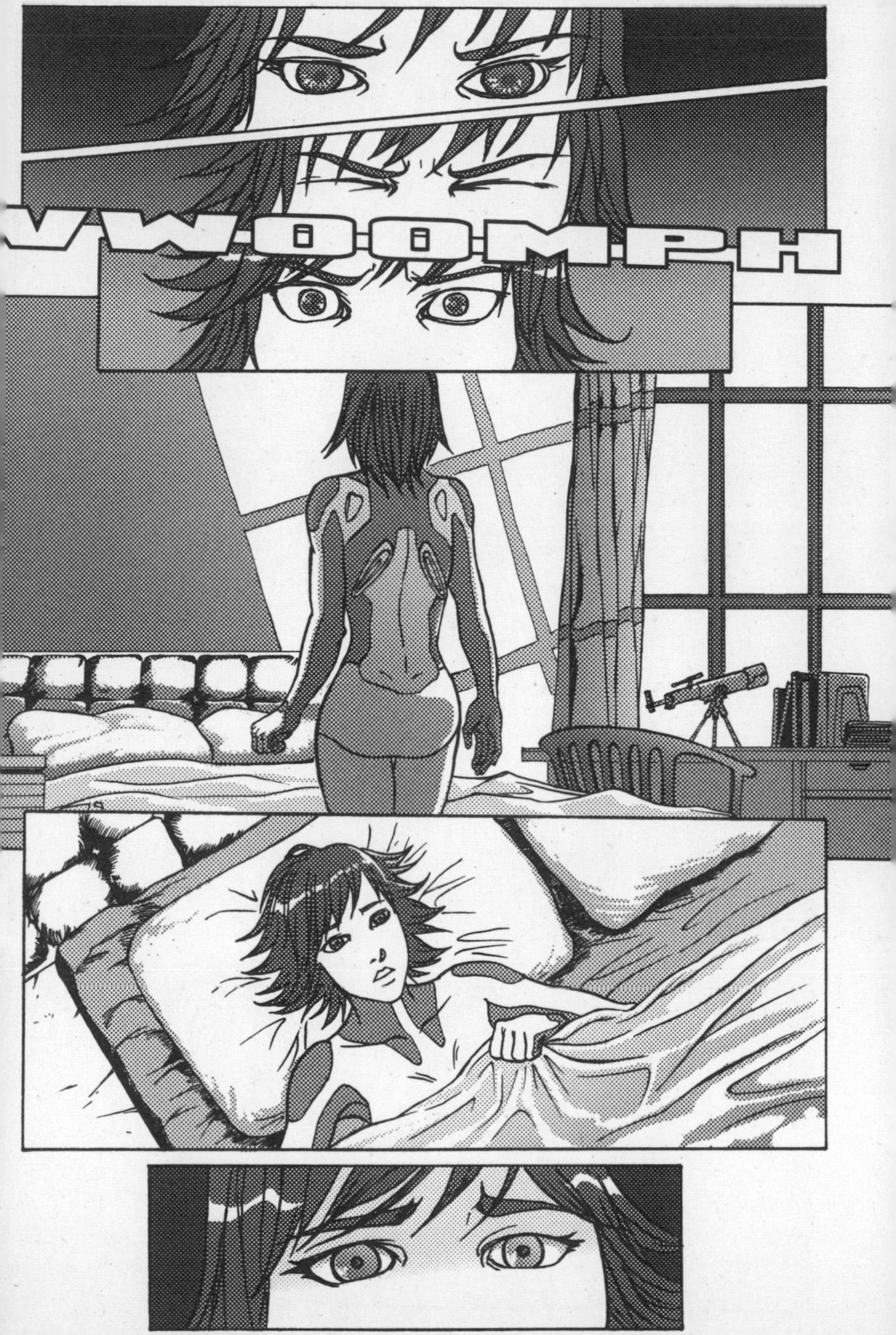
VWOOMPH

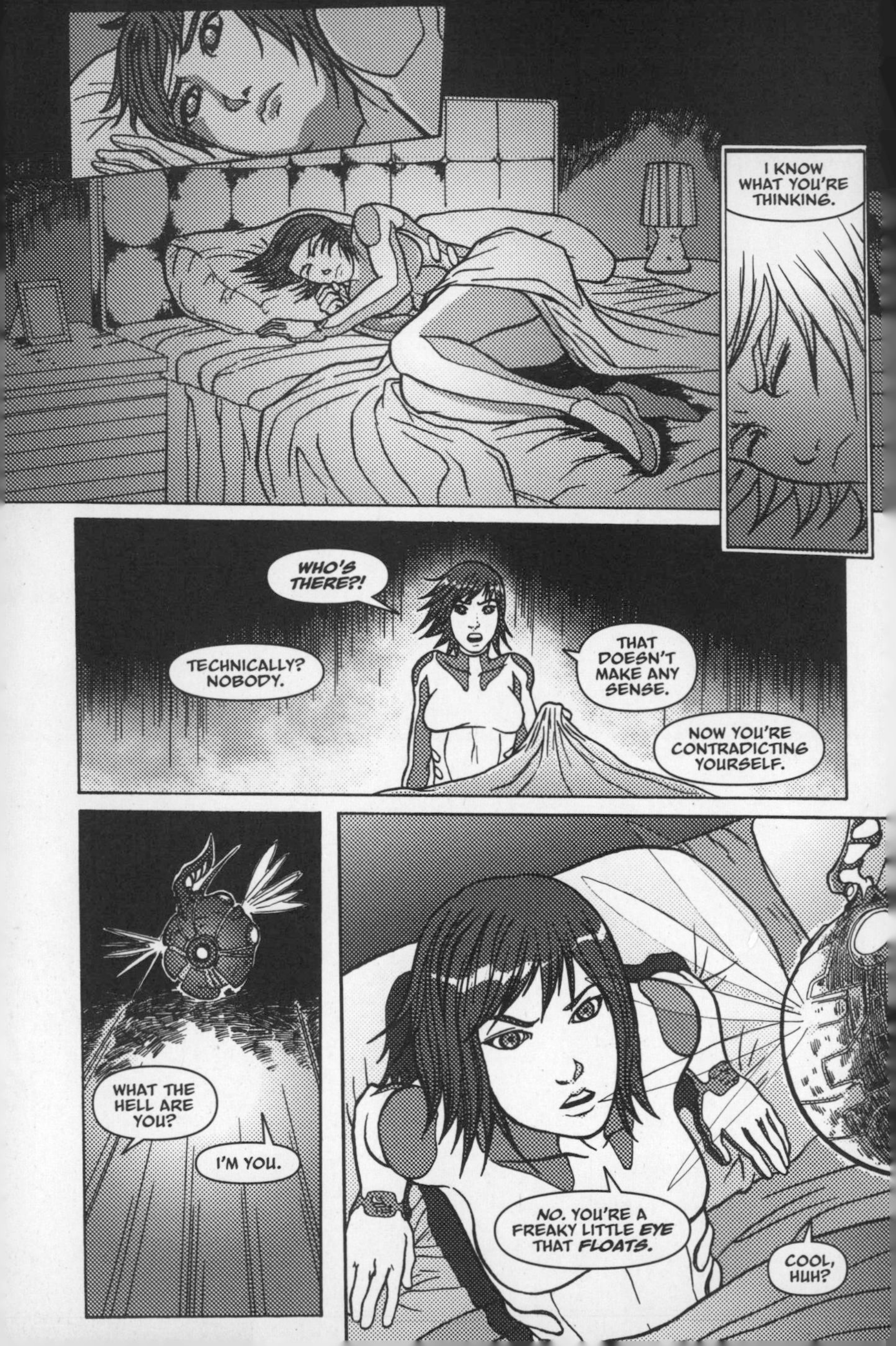
I KNOW WHAT YOU'RE THINKING.
WHO'S THERE?!
TECHNICALLY? NOBODY.
THAT DOESN'T MAKE ANY SENSE.
NOW YOU'RE CONTRADICTING YOURSELF.
WHAT THE HELL ARE YOU?
I'M YOU.
NO. YOU'RE A FREAKY LITTLE EYE THAT FLOATS.
COOL, HUH?

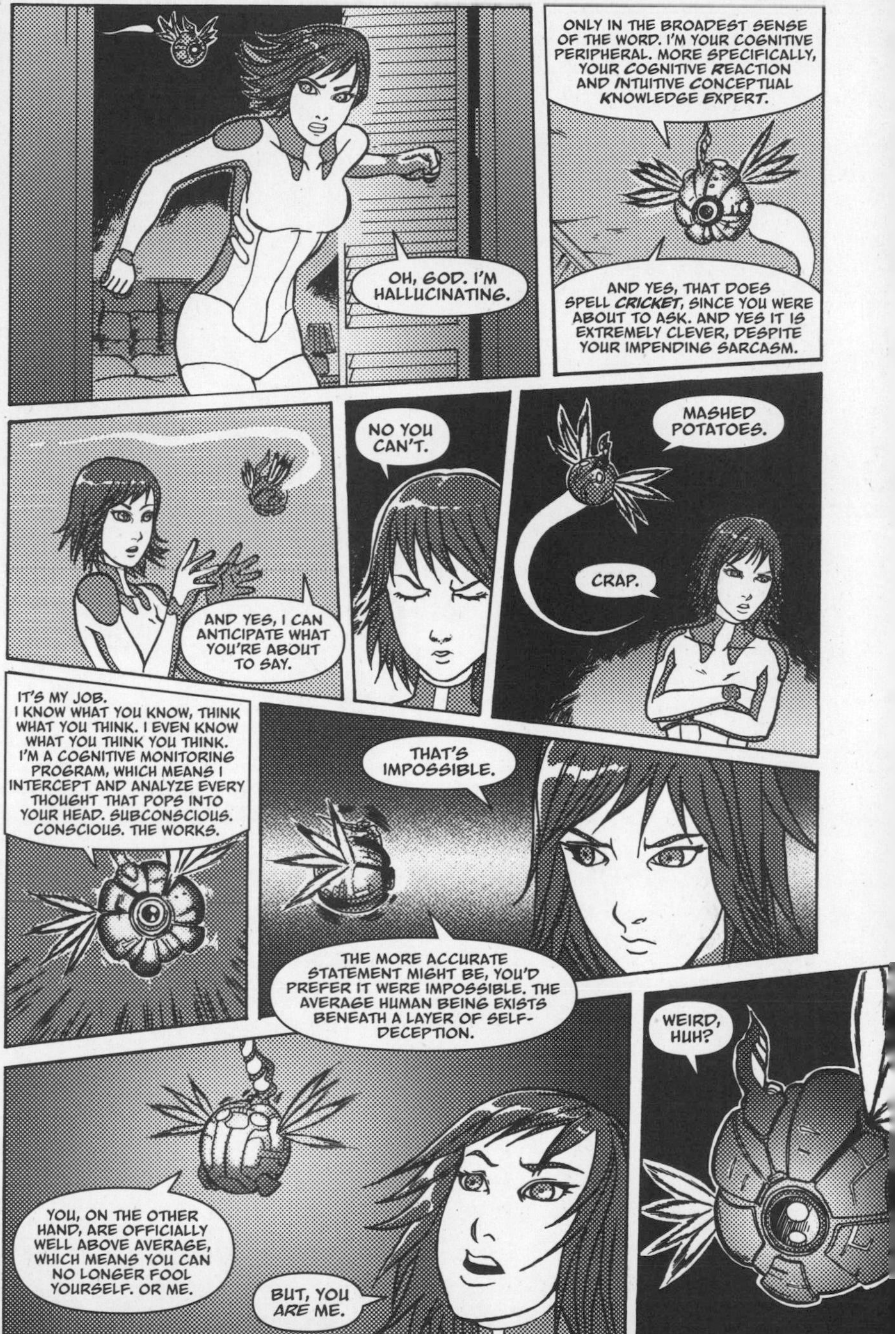
OH, GOD. I'M HALLUCINATING.
ONLY IN THE BROADEST SENSE OF THE WORD. I'M YOUR COGNITIVE PERIPHERAL. MORE SPECIFICALLY, YOUR COGNITIVE REACTION AND INTUITIVE CONCEPTUAL KNOWLEDGE EXPERT.
AND YES, THAT DOES SPELL CRICKET, SINCE YOU WERE ABOUT TO ASK. AND YES IT IS EXTREMELY CLEVER, DESPITE YOUR IMPENDING SARCASM.
AND YES, I CAN ANTICIPATE WHAT YOU'RE ABOUT TO SAY.
NO YOU CAN'T.
MASHED POTATOES.
CRAP.
IT'S MY JOB. I KNOW WHAT YOU KNOW, THINK WHAT YOU THINK. I EVEN KNOW WHAT YOU THINK YOU THINK. I'M A COGNITIVE MONITORING PROGRAM, WHICH MEANS I INTERCEPT AND ANALYZE EVERY THOUGHT THAT POPS INTO YOUR HEAD. SUBCONSCIOUS. CONSCIOUS. THE WORKS.
THAT'S IMPOSSIBLE.
THE MORE ACCURATE STATEMENT MIGHT BE, YOU'D PREFER IT WERE IMPOSSIBLE. THE AVERAGE HUMAN BEING EXISTS BENEATH A LAYER OF SELF-DECEPTION.
YOU, ON THE OTHER HAND, ARE OFFICIALLY WELL ABOVE AVERAGE, WHICH MEANS YOU CAN NO LONGER FOOL YOURSELF. OR ME.
BUT, YOU ARE ME.
WEIRD, HUH?

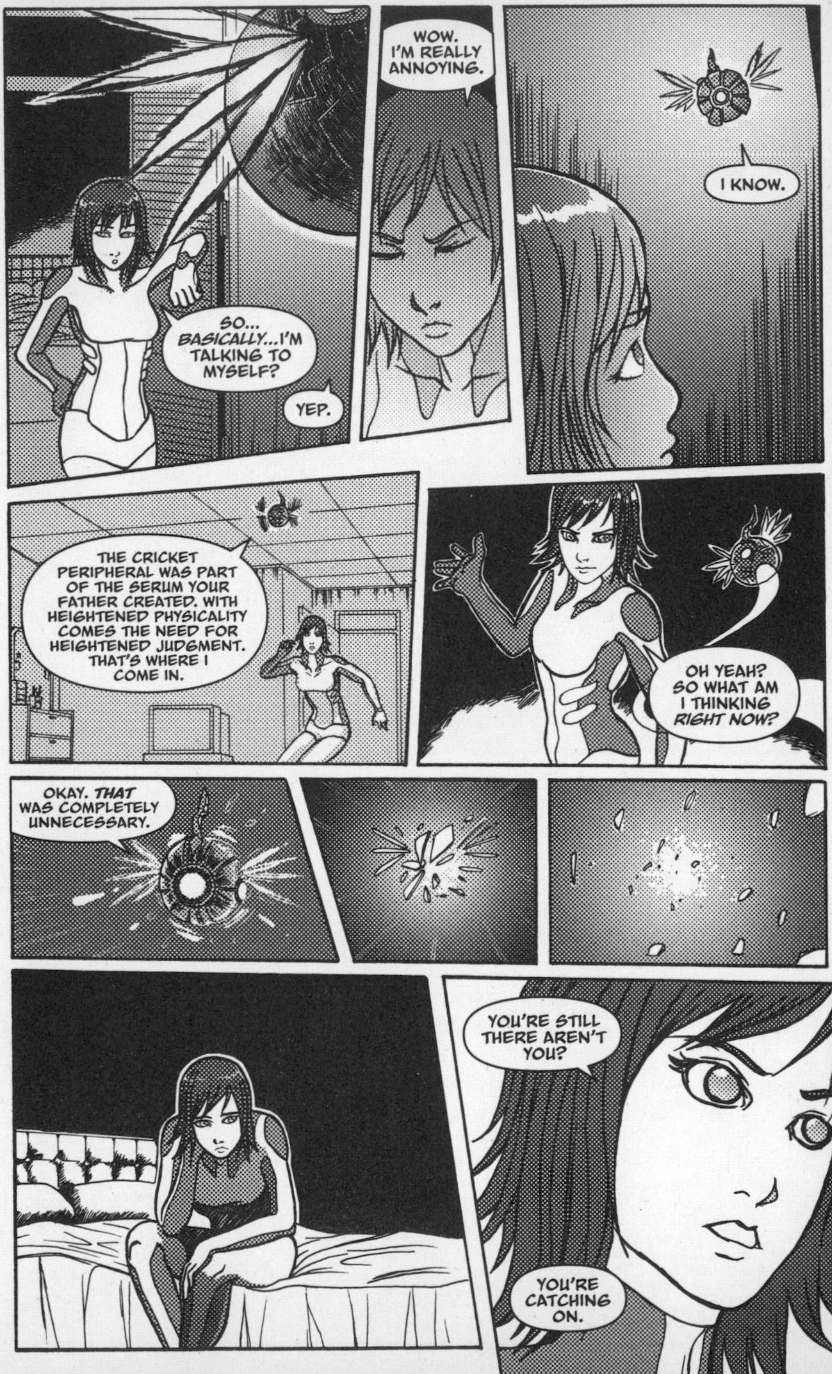
SO... BASICALLY...I'M TALKING TO MYSELF?
YEP.
WOW. I'M REALLY ANNOYING.
I KNOW.
THE CRICKET PERIPHERAL WAS PART OF THE SERUM YOUR FATHER CREATED. WITH HEIGHTENED PHYSICALITY COMES THE NEED FOR HEIGHTENED JUDGMENT. THAT'S WHERE I COME IN.
OH YEAH? SO WHAT AM I THINKING RIGHT NOW?
OKAY. THAT WAS COMPLETELY UNNECESSARY.
YOU'RE STILL THERE AREN'T YOU?
YOU'RE CATCHING ON.

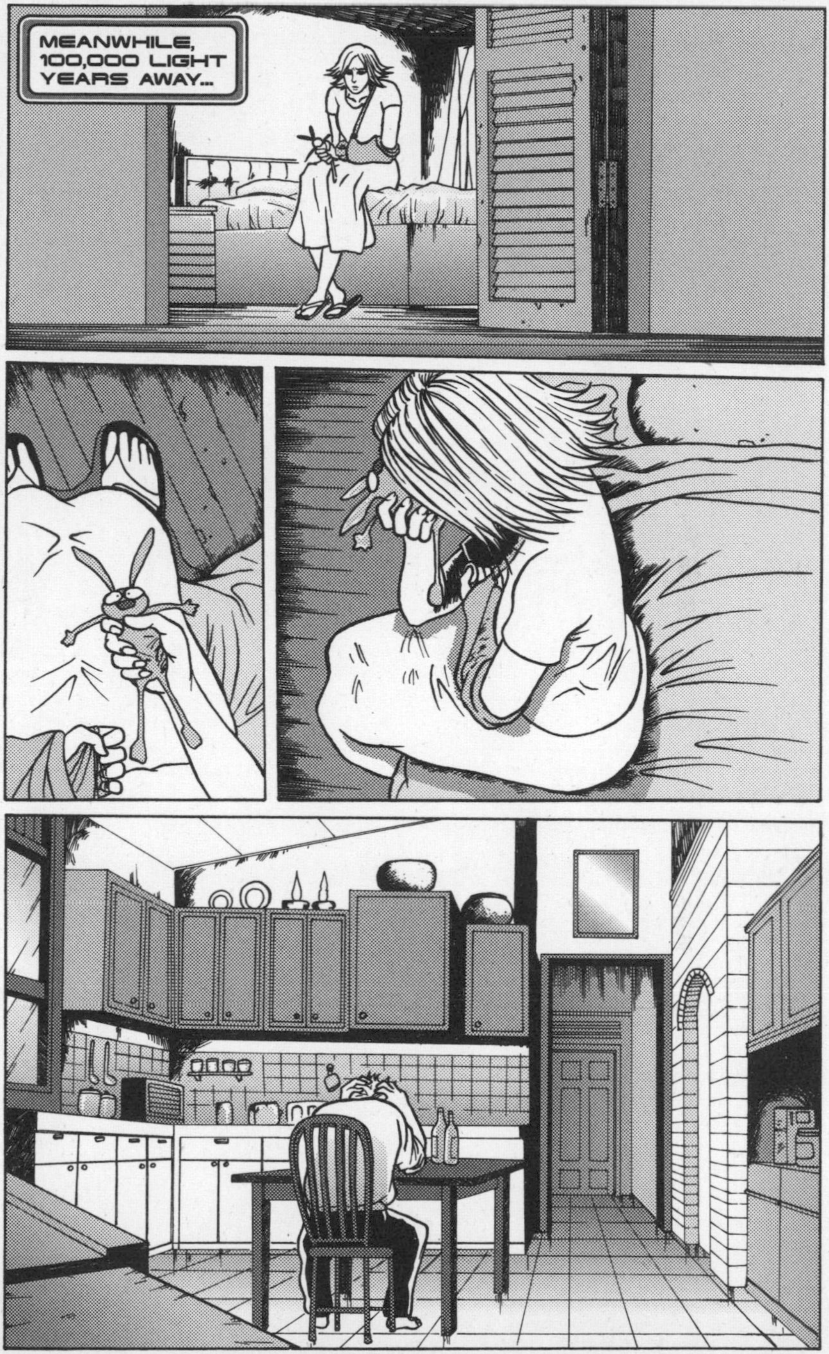
MEANWHILE, 100,000 LIGHT YEARS AWAY...

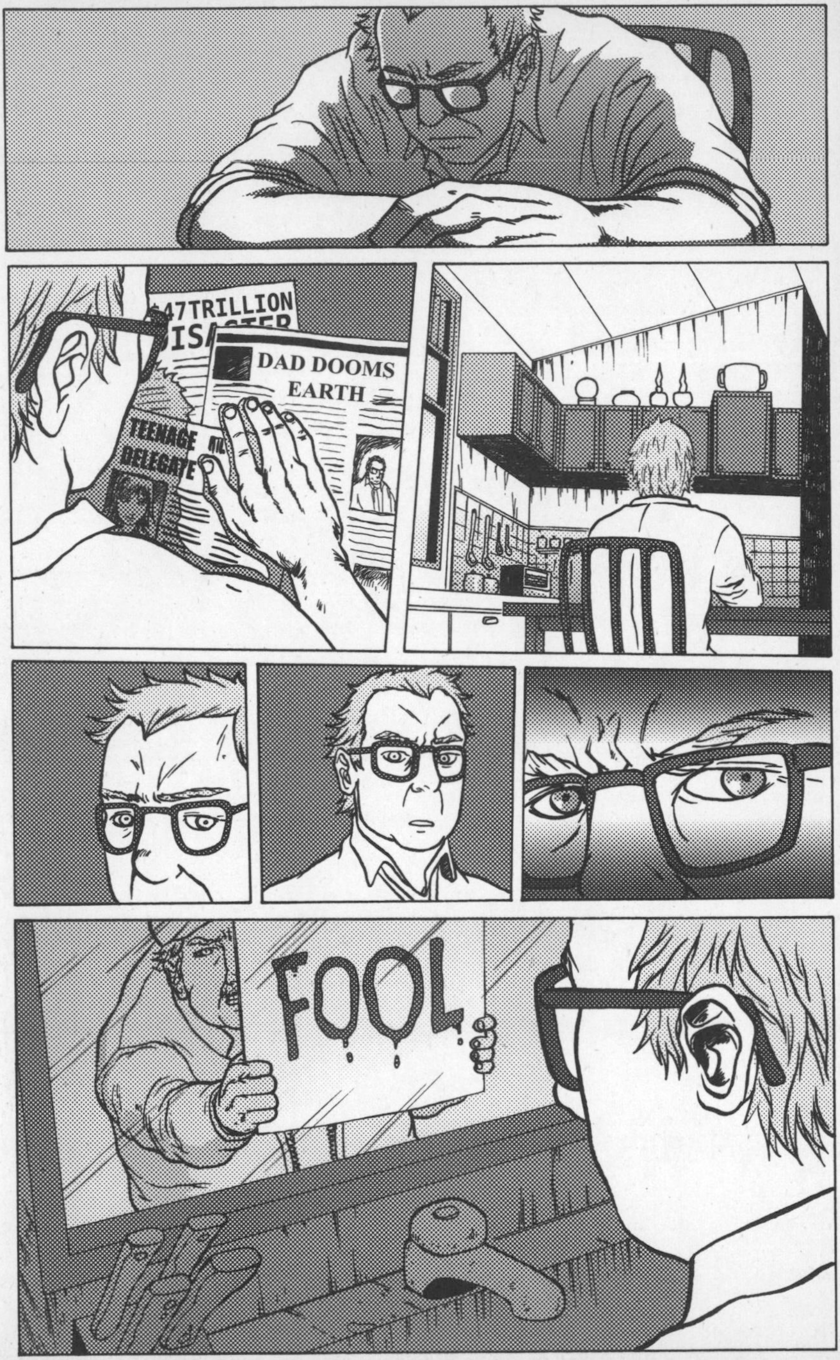

47TRILLION
DAD DOOMS EARTH
TEENAGE DELEGATE
FOOL

CHAPTER 03

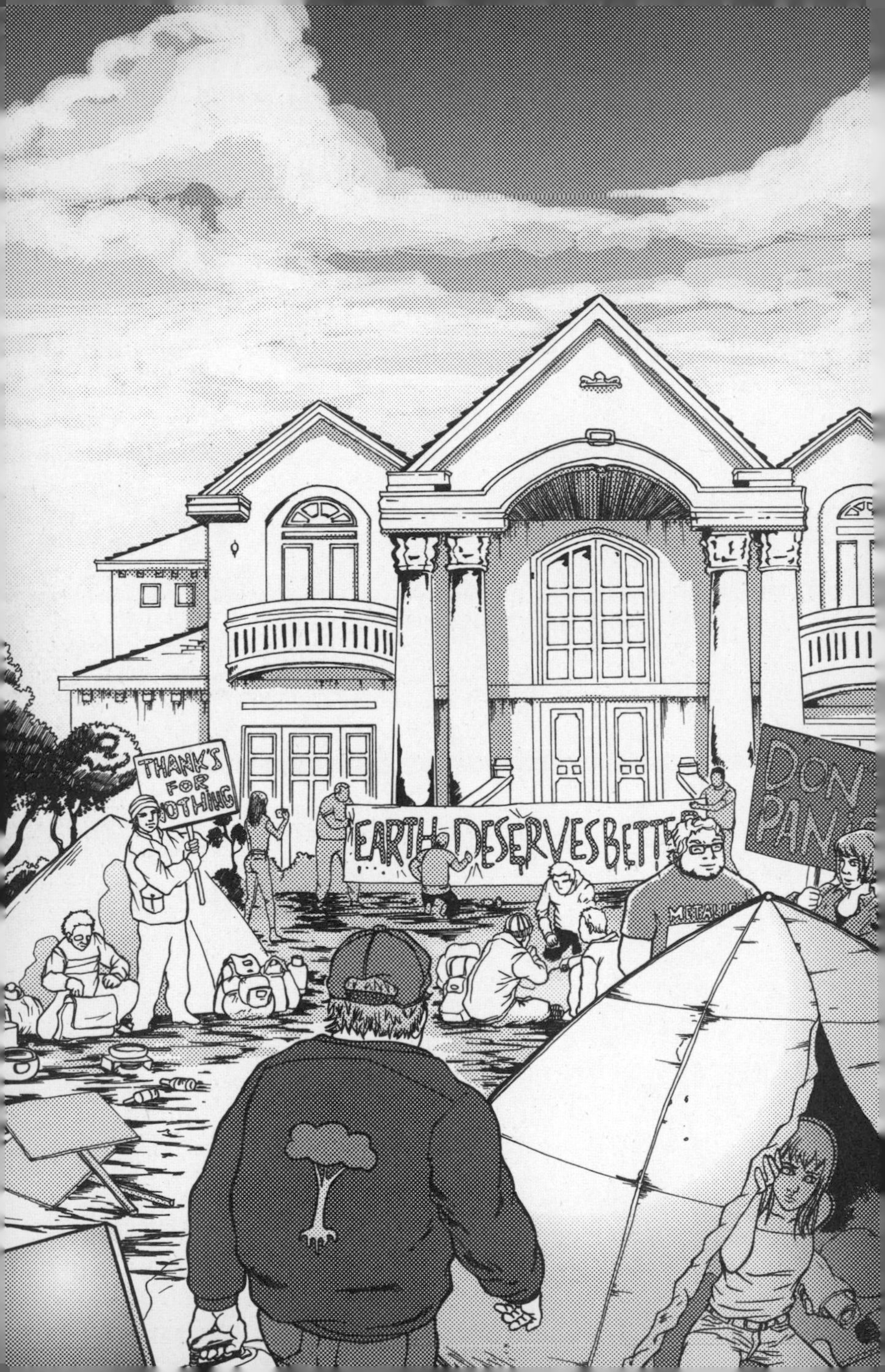
THANK'S FOR NOTHING
EARTH DESERVES BETTE
DON
PAN

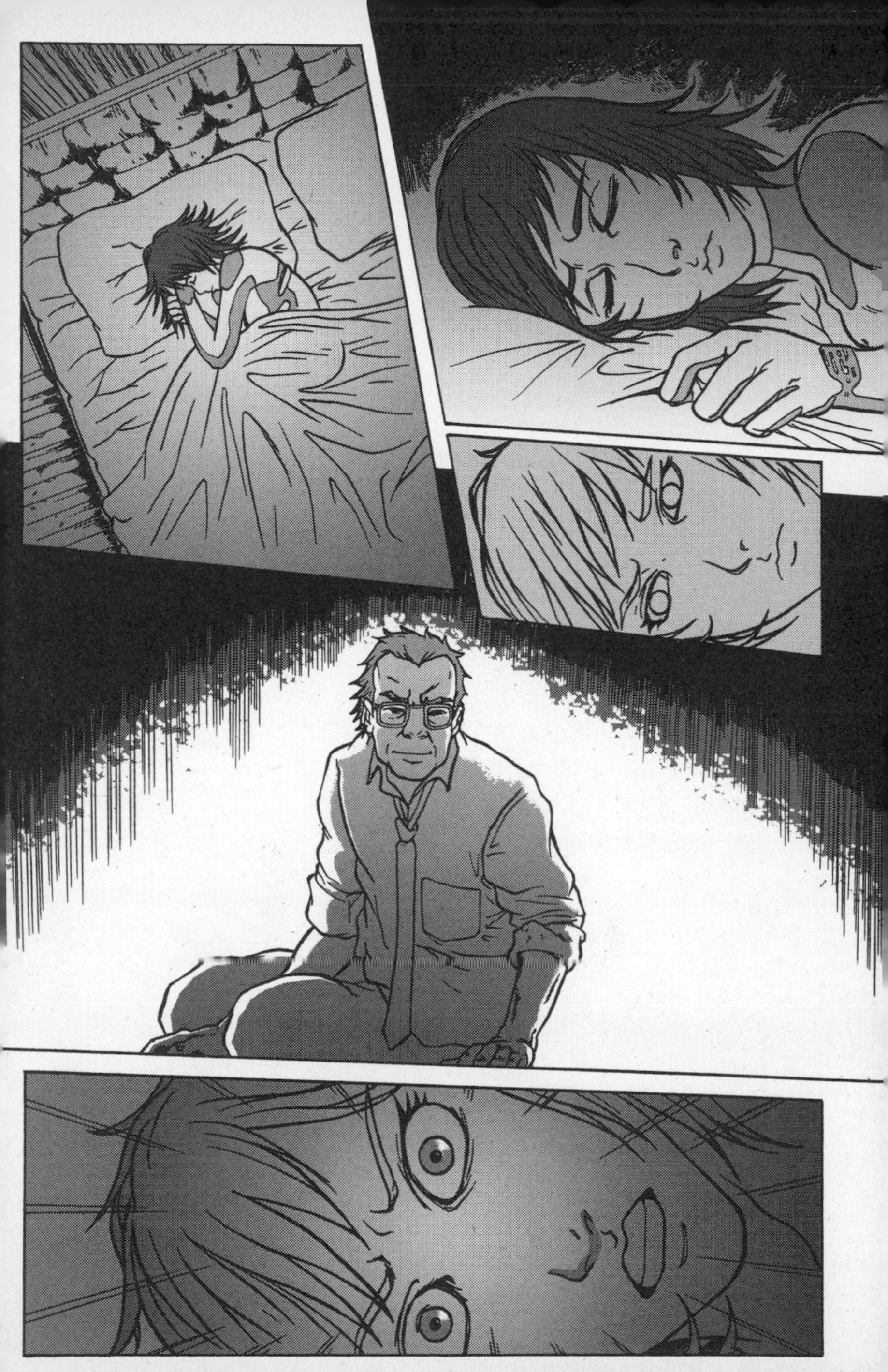

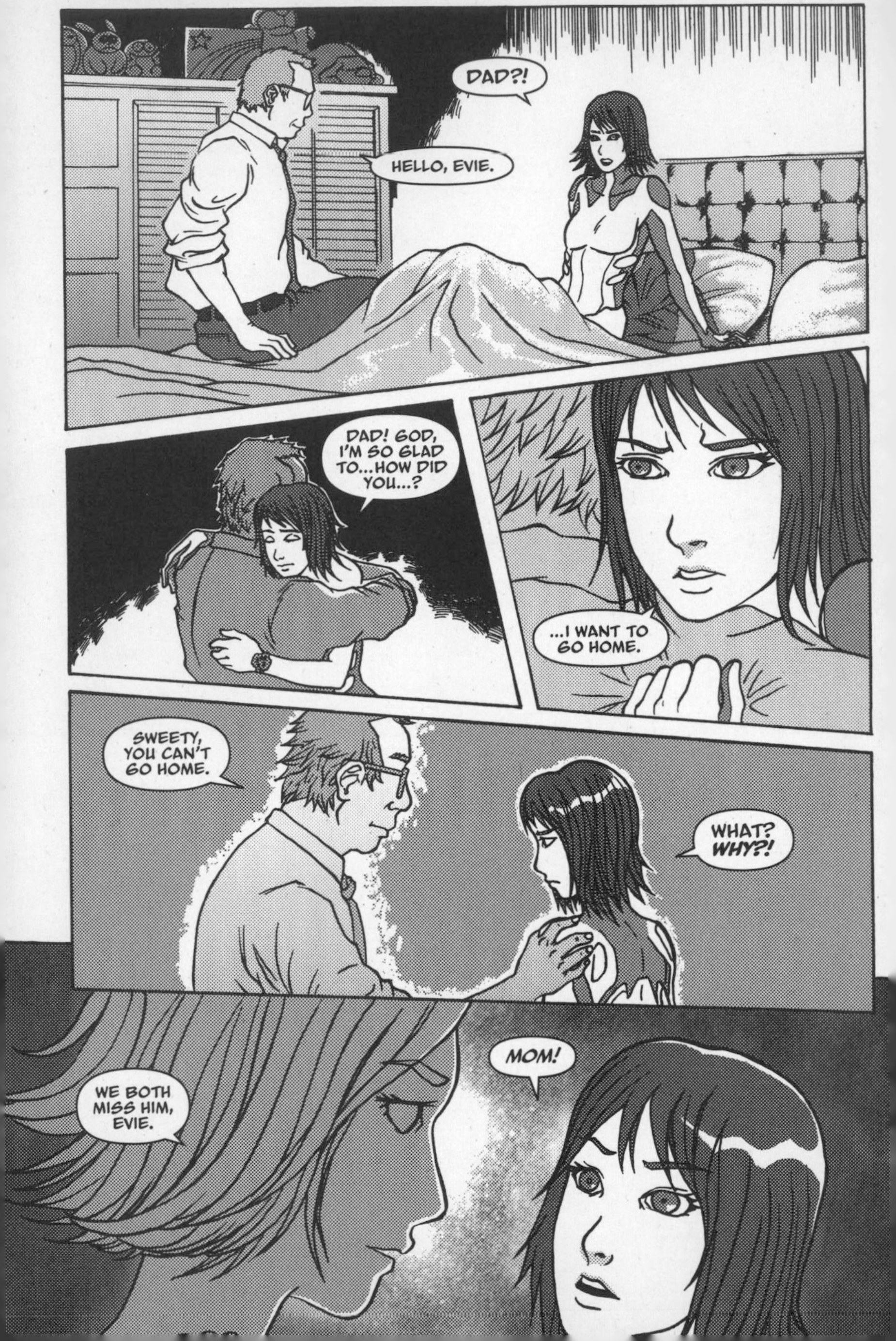
DAD?!
HELLO, EVIE.
DAD! GOD, I'M SO GLAD TO...HOW DID YOU...?
...I WANT TO GO HOME.
SWEETY, YOU CAN'T GO HOME.
WHAT? *WHY?!*
WE BOTH MISS HIM, EVIE.
MOM!

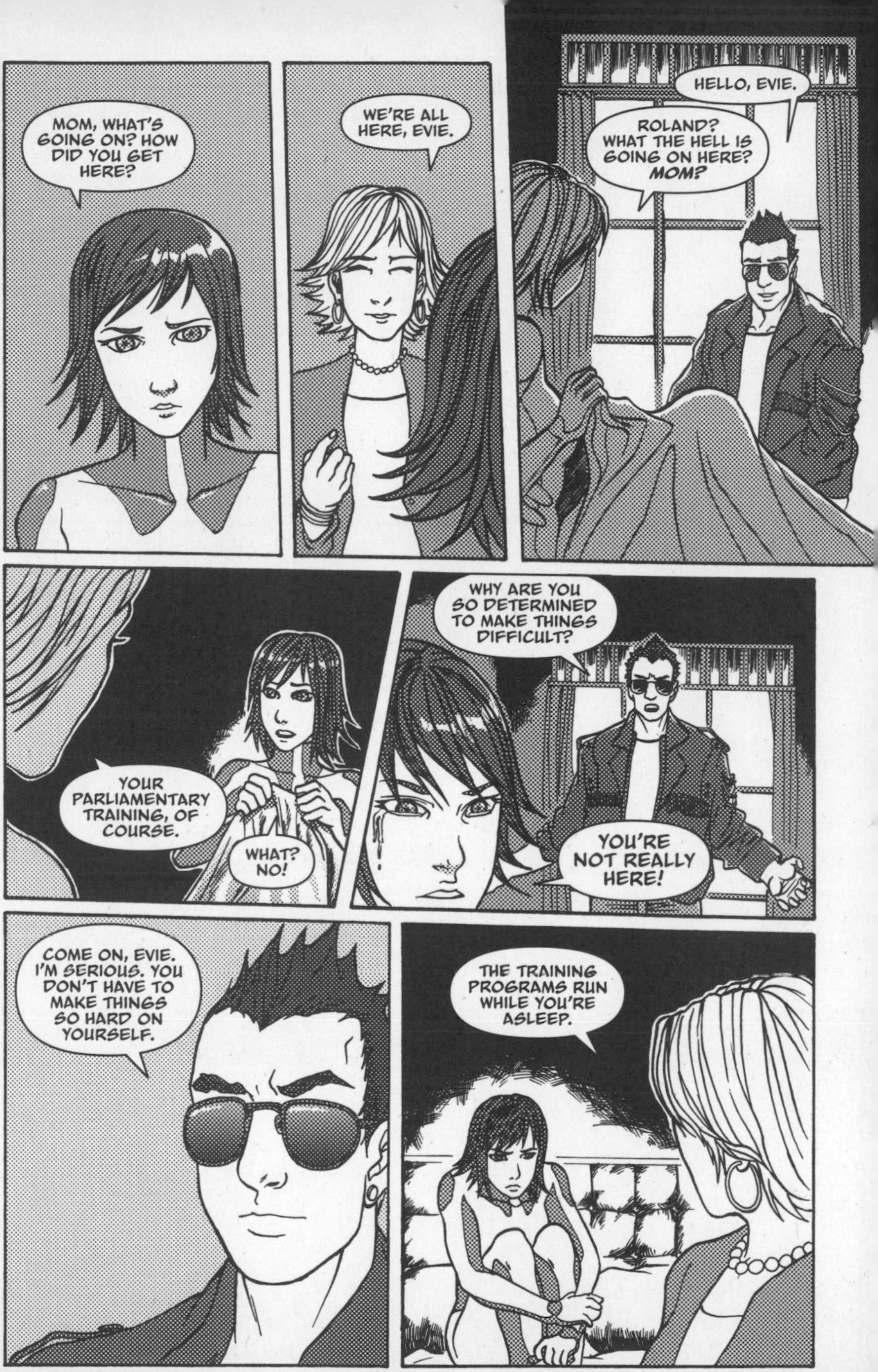
MOM, WHAT'S GOING ON? HOW DID YOU GET HERE?
WE'RE ALL HERE, EVIE.
HELLO, EVIE.
ROLAND? WHAT THE HELL IS GOING ON HERE? *MOM?*
YOUR PARLIAMENTARY TRAINING, OF COURSE.
WHAT? NO!
WHY ARE YOU SO DETERMINED TO MAKE THINGS DIFFICULT?
YOU'RE NOT REALLY HERE!
COME ON, EVIE. I'M SERIOUS. YOU DON'T HAVE TO MAKE THINGS SO HARD ON YOURSELF.
THE TRAINING PROGRAMS RUN WHILE YOU'RE ASLEEP.

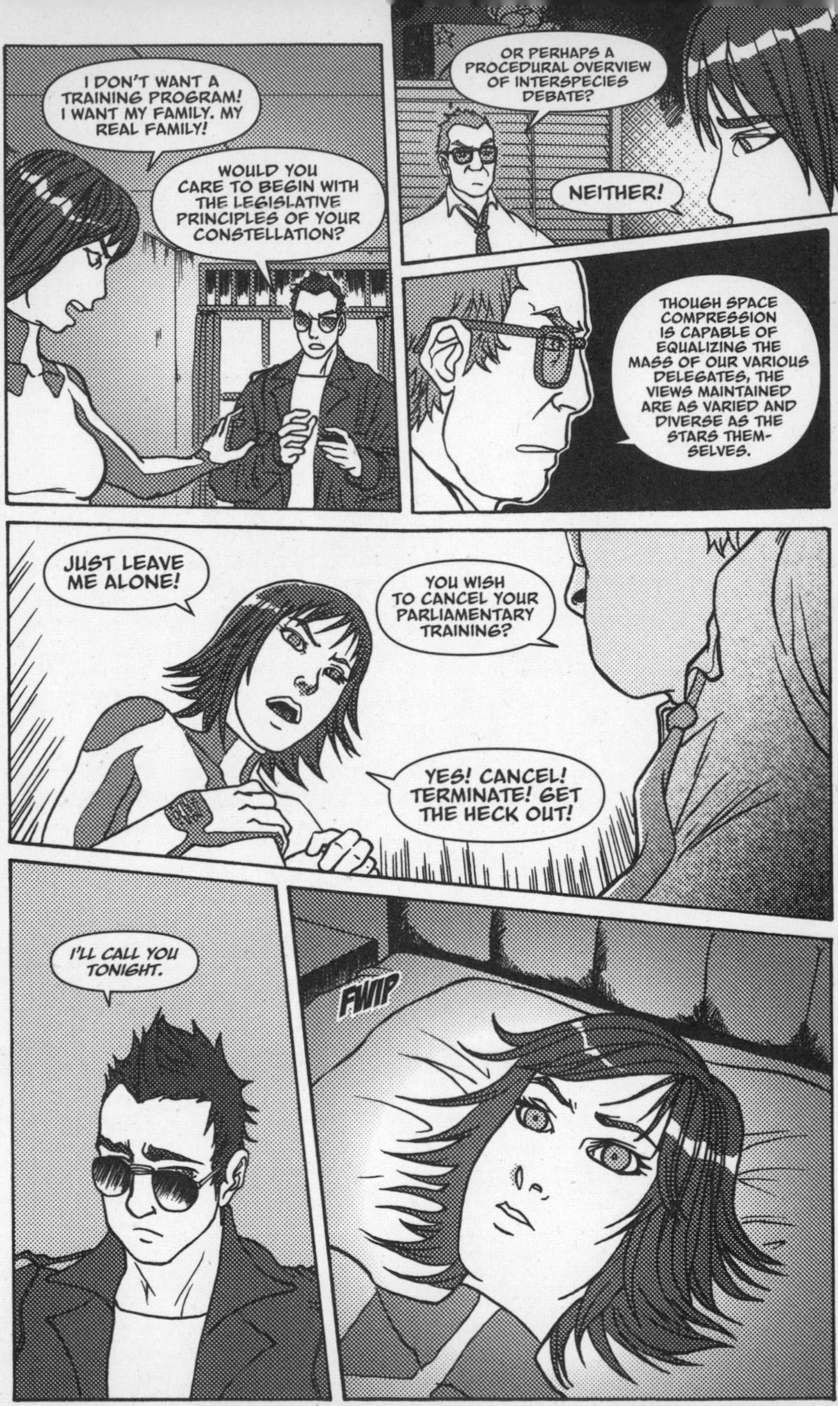
I DON'T WANT A TRAINING PROGRAM! I WANT MY FAMILY. MY REAL FAMILY!
WOULD YOU CARE TO BEGIN WITH THE LEGISLATIVE PRINCIPLES OF YOUR CONSTELLATION?
OR PERHAPS A PROCEDURAL OVERVIEW OF INTERSPECIES DEBATE?
NEITHER!
THOUGH SPACE COMPRESSION IS CAPABLE OF EQUALIZING THE MASS OF OUR VARIOUS DELEGATES, THE VIEWS MAINTAINED ARE AS VARIED AND DIVERSE AS THE STARS THEM-SELVES.
JUST LEAVE ME ALONE!
YOU WISH TO CANCEL YOUR PARLIAMENTARY TRAINING?
YES! CANCEL! TERMINATE! GET THE HECK OUT!
I'LL CALL YOU TONIGHT.
FWIP

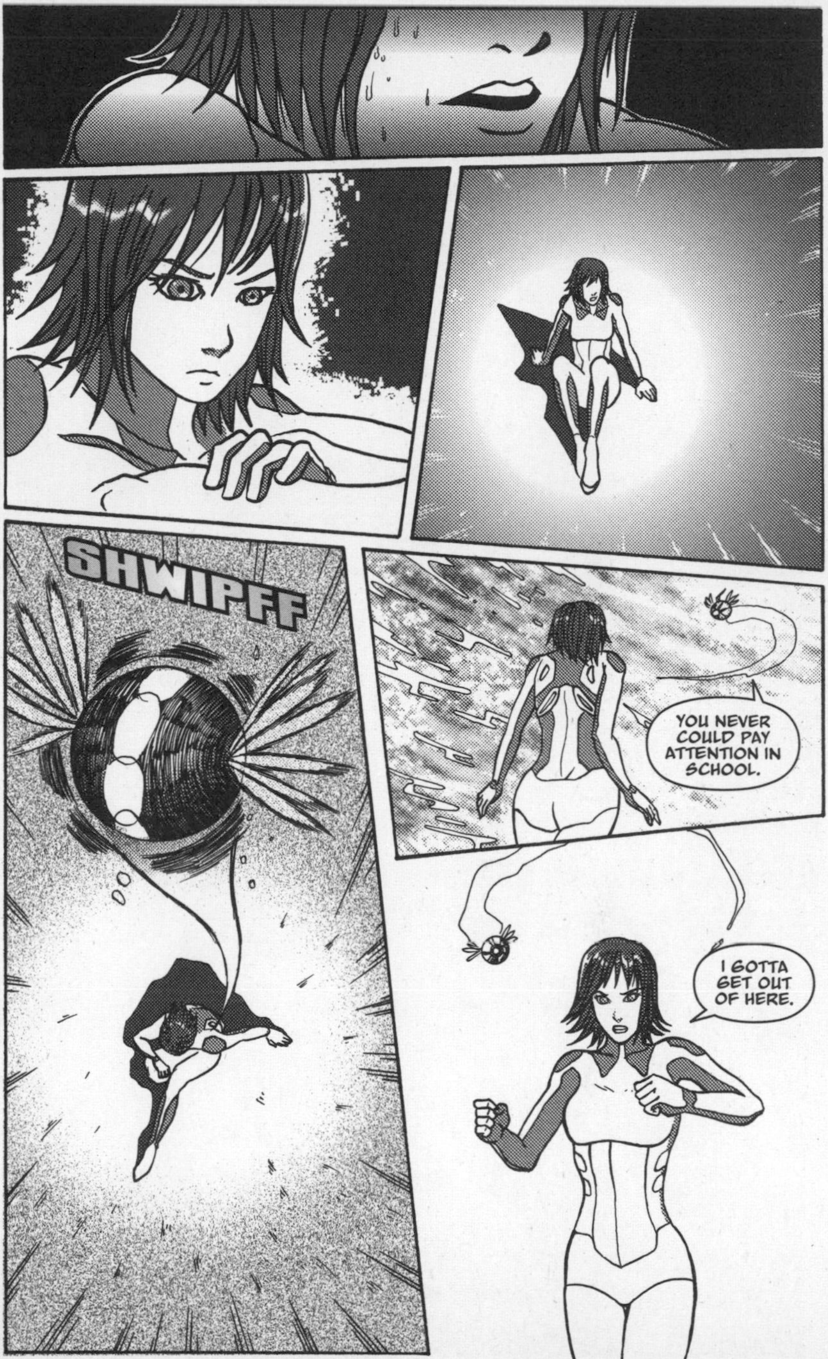
SHWIPFF
YOU NEVER COULD PAY ATTENTION IN SCHOOL.
I GOTTA GET OUT OF HERE.

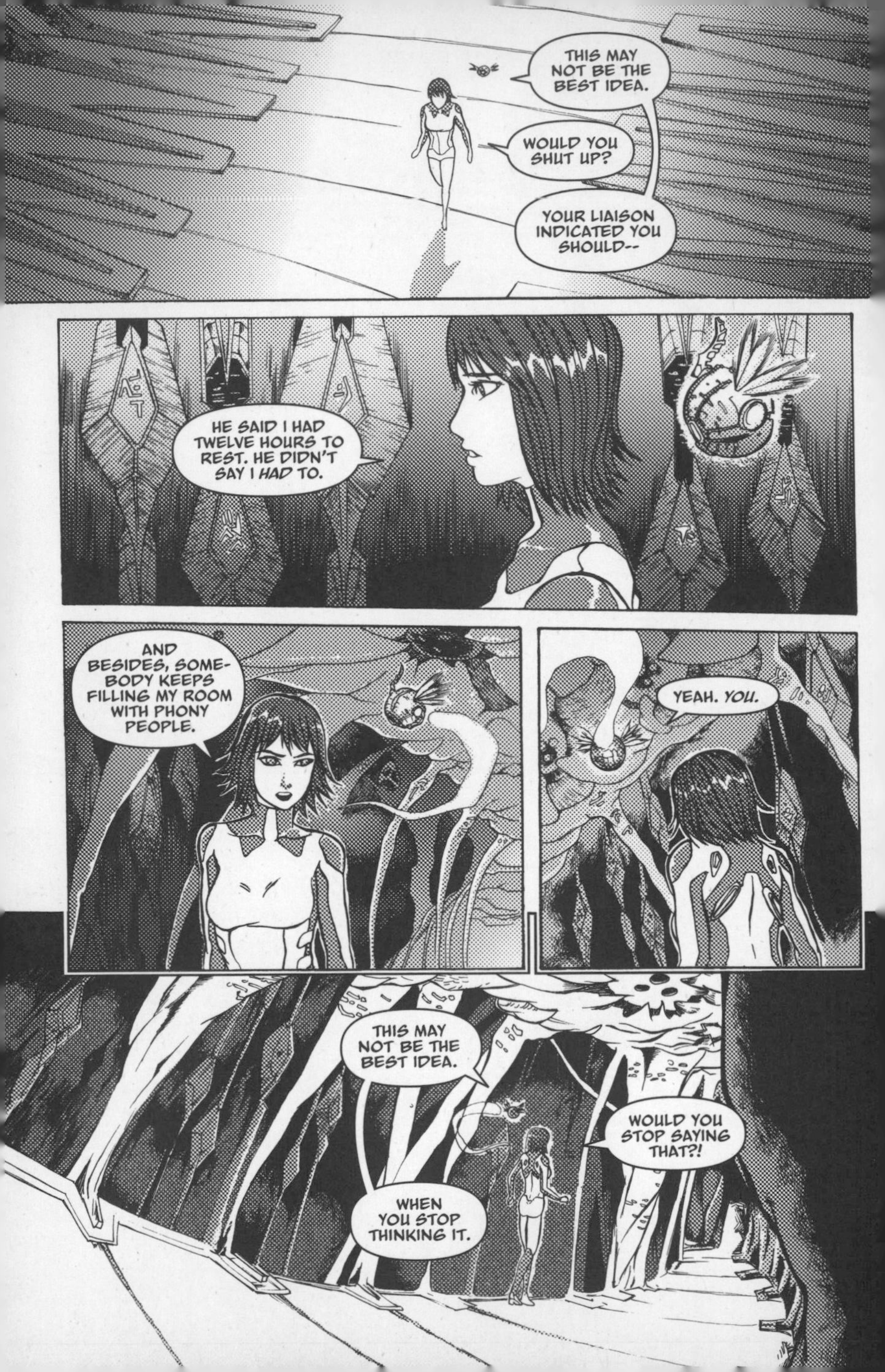
THIS MAY NOT BE THE BEST IDEA.
WOULD YOU SHUT UP?
YOUR LIAISON INDICATED YOU SHOULD--
HE SAID I HAD TWELVE HOURS TO REST. HE DIDN'T SAY I *HAD* TO.
AND BESIDES, SOME-BODY KEEPS FILLING MY ROOM WITH PHONY PEOPLE.
YEAH. *YOU.*
THIS MAY NOT BE THE BEST IDEA.
WOULD YOU STOP SAYING THAT?!
WHEN YOU STOP THINKING IT.

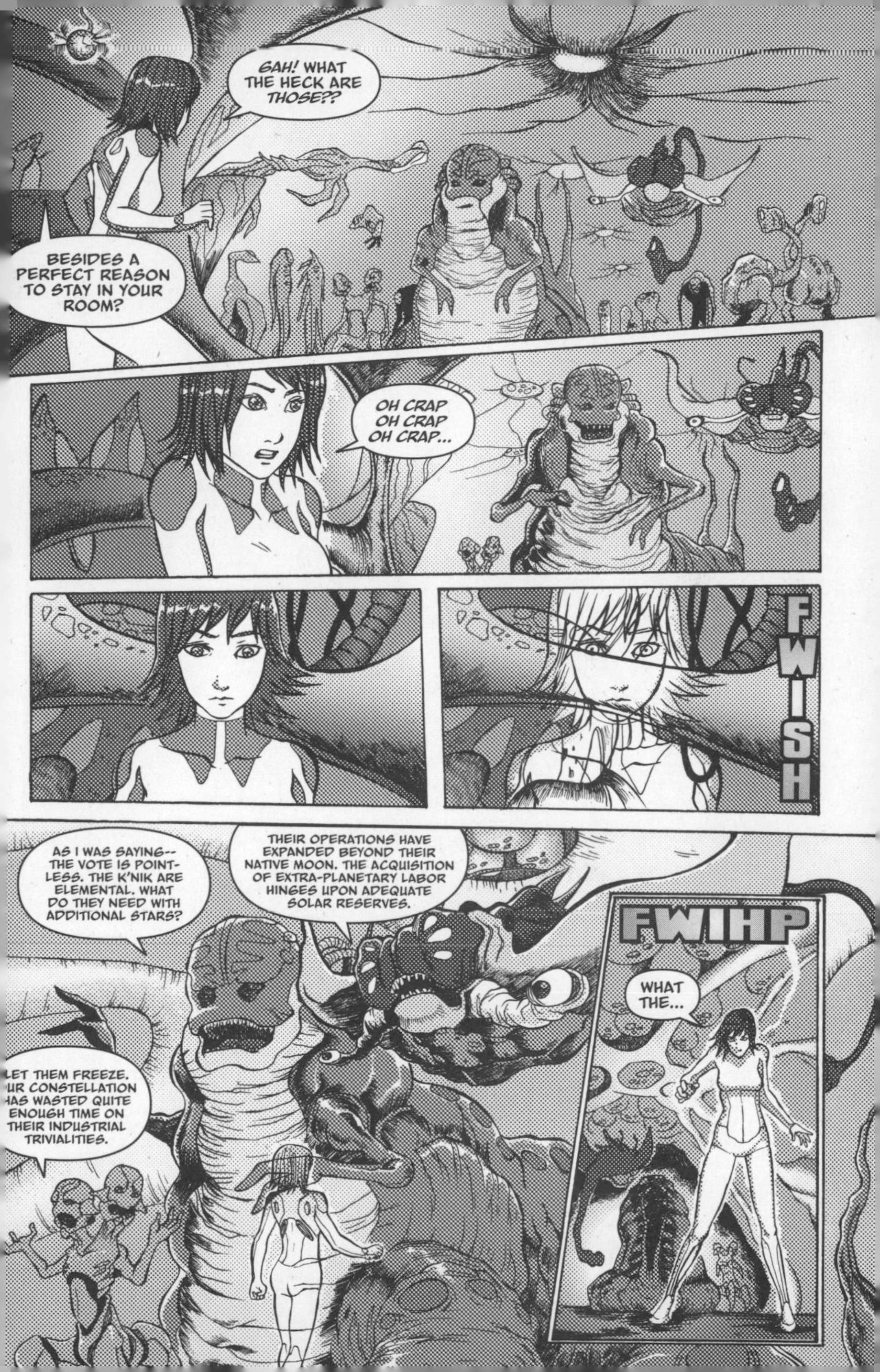
GAH! WHAT THE HECK ARE THOSE??
BESIDES A PERFECT REASON TO STAY IN YOUR ROOM?
OH CRAP OH CRAP OH CRAP...
FWISH
AS I WAS SAYING-- THE VOTE IS POINTLESS. THE K'NIK ARE ELEMENTAL. WHAT DO THEY NEED WITH ADDITIONAL STARS?
THEIR OPERATIONS HAVE EXPANDED BEYOND THEIR NATIVE MOON. THE ACQUISITION OF EXTRA-PLANETARY LABOR HINGES UPON ADEQUATE SOLAR RESERVES.
LET THEM FREEZE. UR CONSTELLATION HAS WASTED QUITE ENOUGH TIME ON THEIR INDUSTRIAL TRIVIALITIES.
FWIHP
WHAT THE...

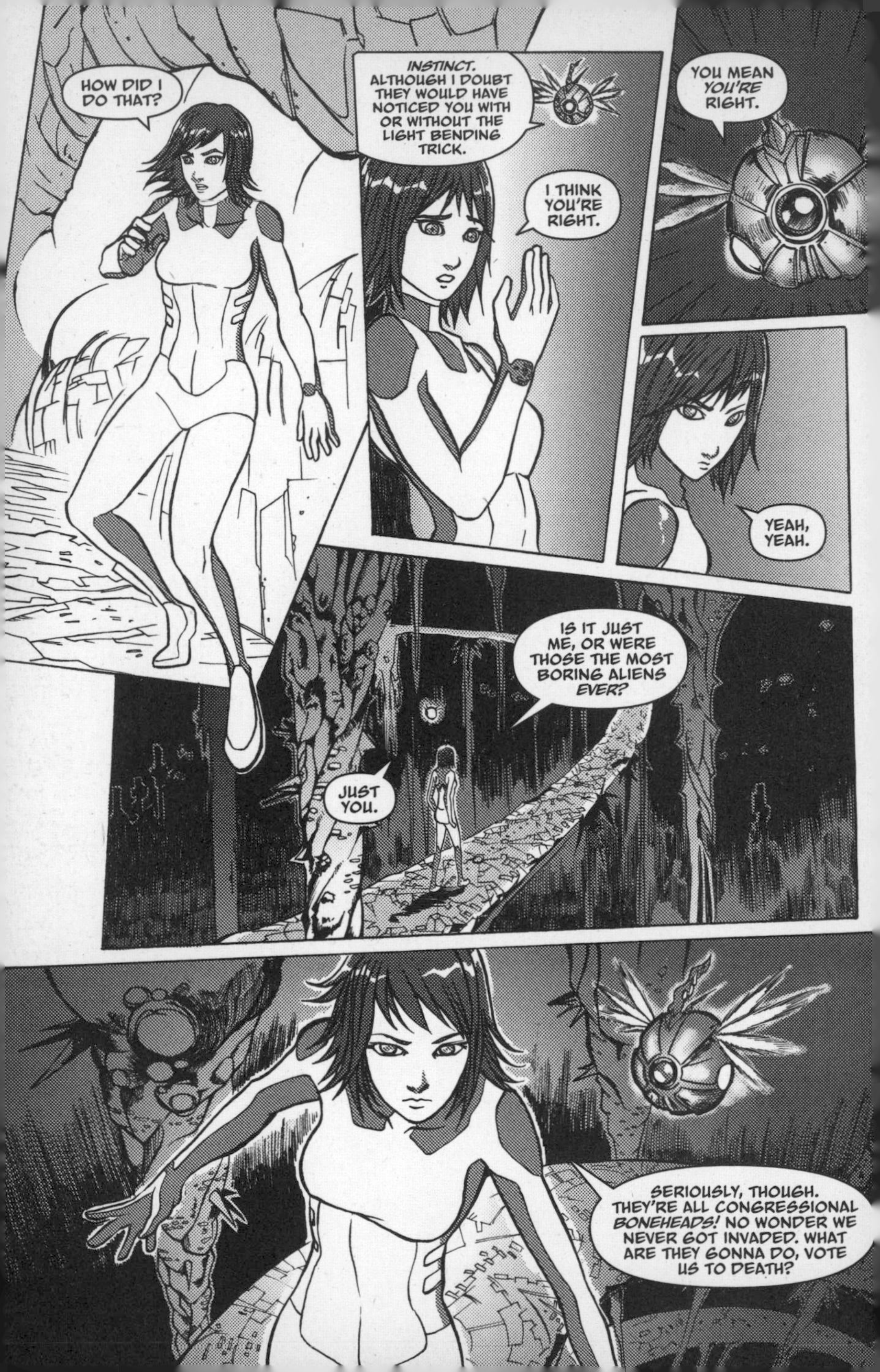
HOW DID I DO THAT?
INSTINCT. ALTHOUGH I DOUBT THEY WOULD HAVE NOTICED YOU WITH OR WITHOUT THE LIGHT BENDING TRICK.
I THINK YOU'RE RIGHT.
YOU MEAN *YOU'RE* RIGHT.
YEAH, YEAH.
IS IT JUST ME, OR WERE THOSE THE MOST BORING ALIENS *EVER?*
JUST YOU.
SERIOUSLY, THOUGH. THEY'RE ALL CONGRESSIONAL *BONEHEADS!* NO WONDER WE NEVER GOT INVADED. WHAT ARE THEY GONNA DO, VOTE US TO DEATH?

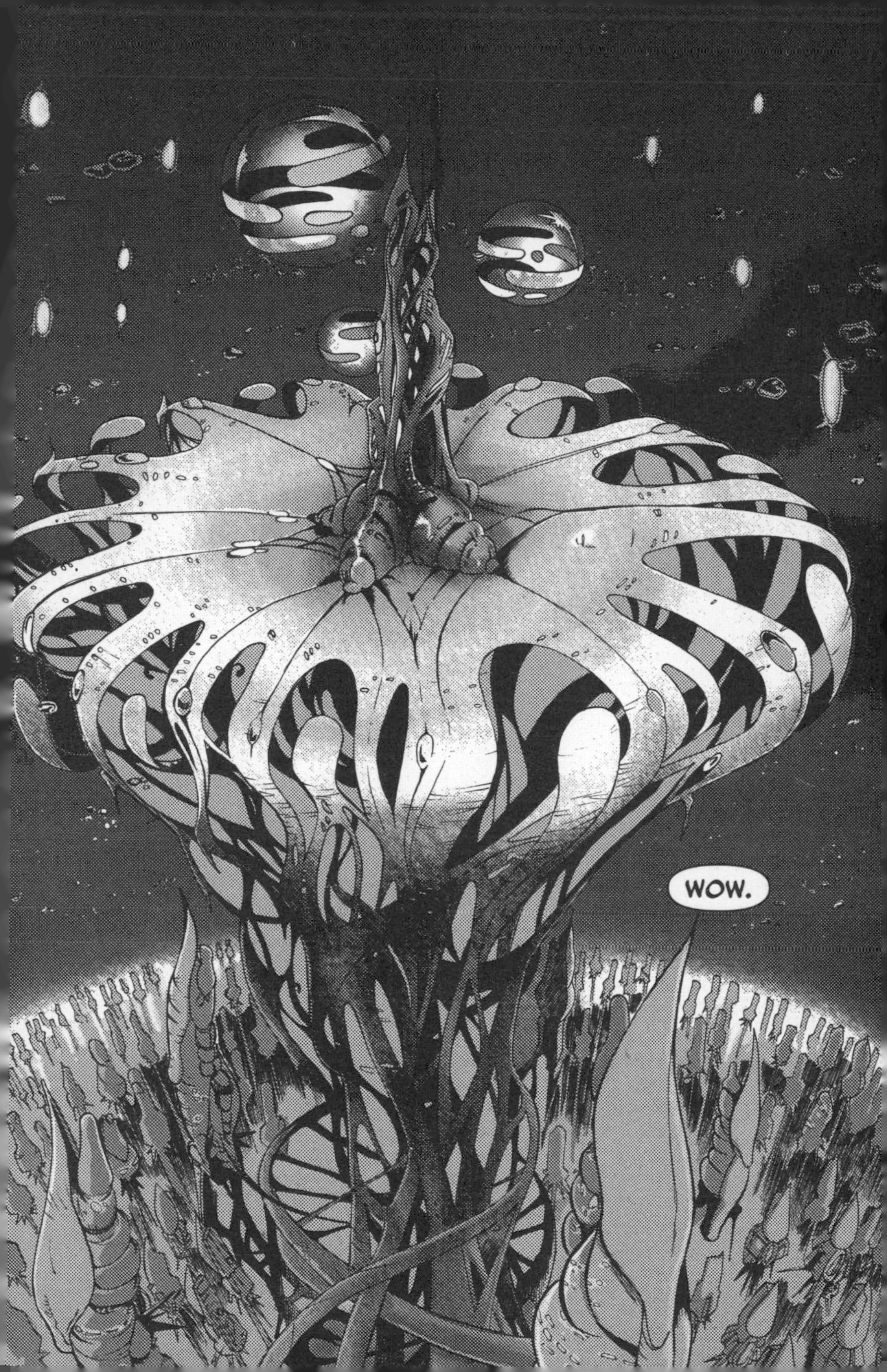
WOW.

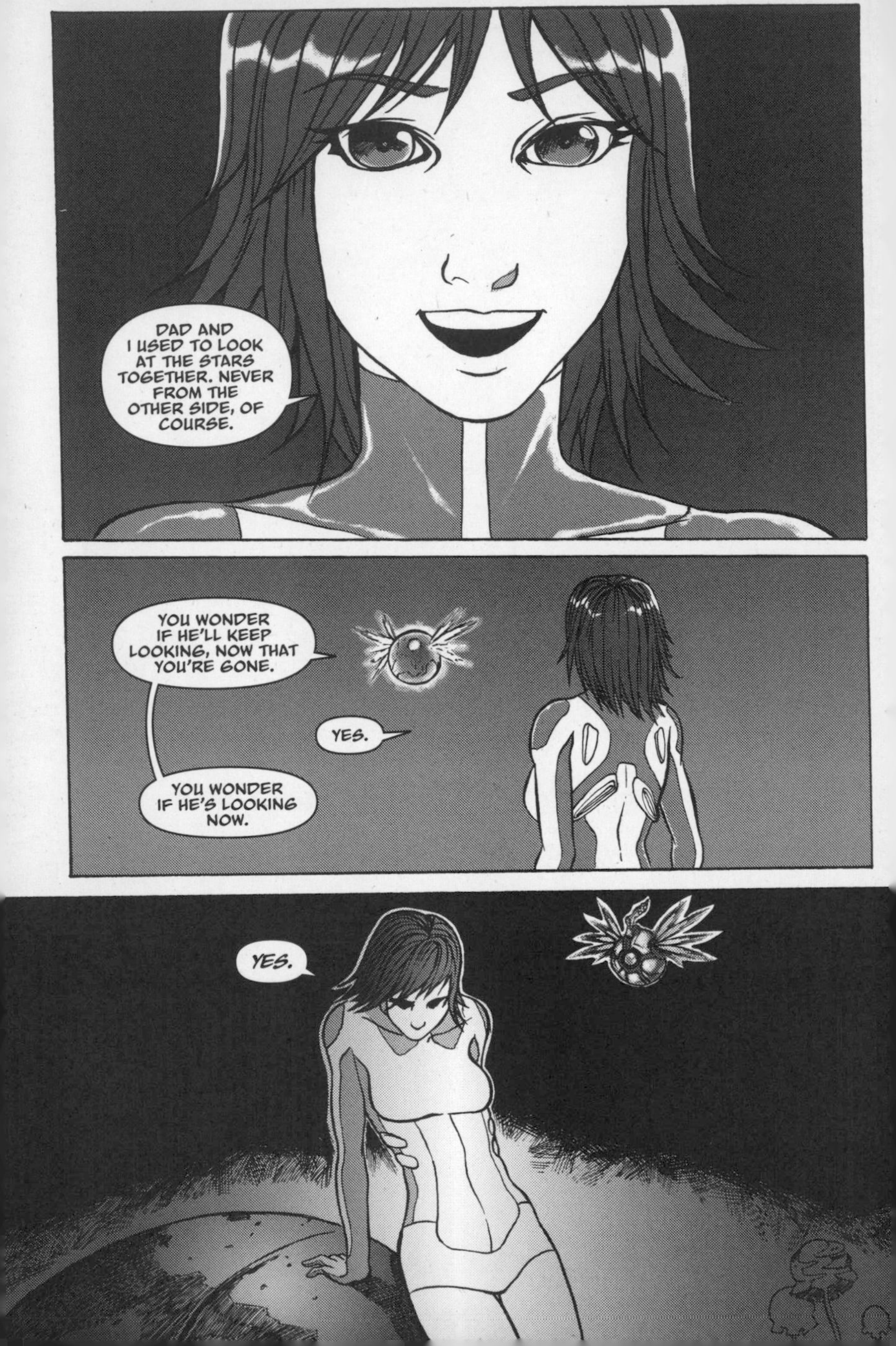
DAD AND I USED TO LOOK AT THE STARS TOGETHER. NEVER FROM THE OTHER SIDE, OF COURSE.
YOU WONDER IF HE'LL KEEP LOOKING, NOW THAT YOU'RE GONE.
YES.
YOU WONDER IF HE'S LOOKING NOW.
YES.

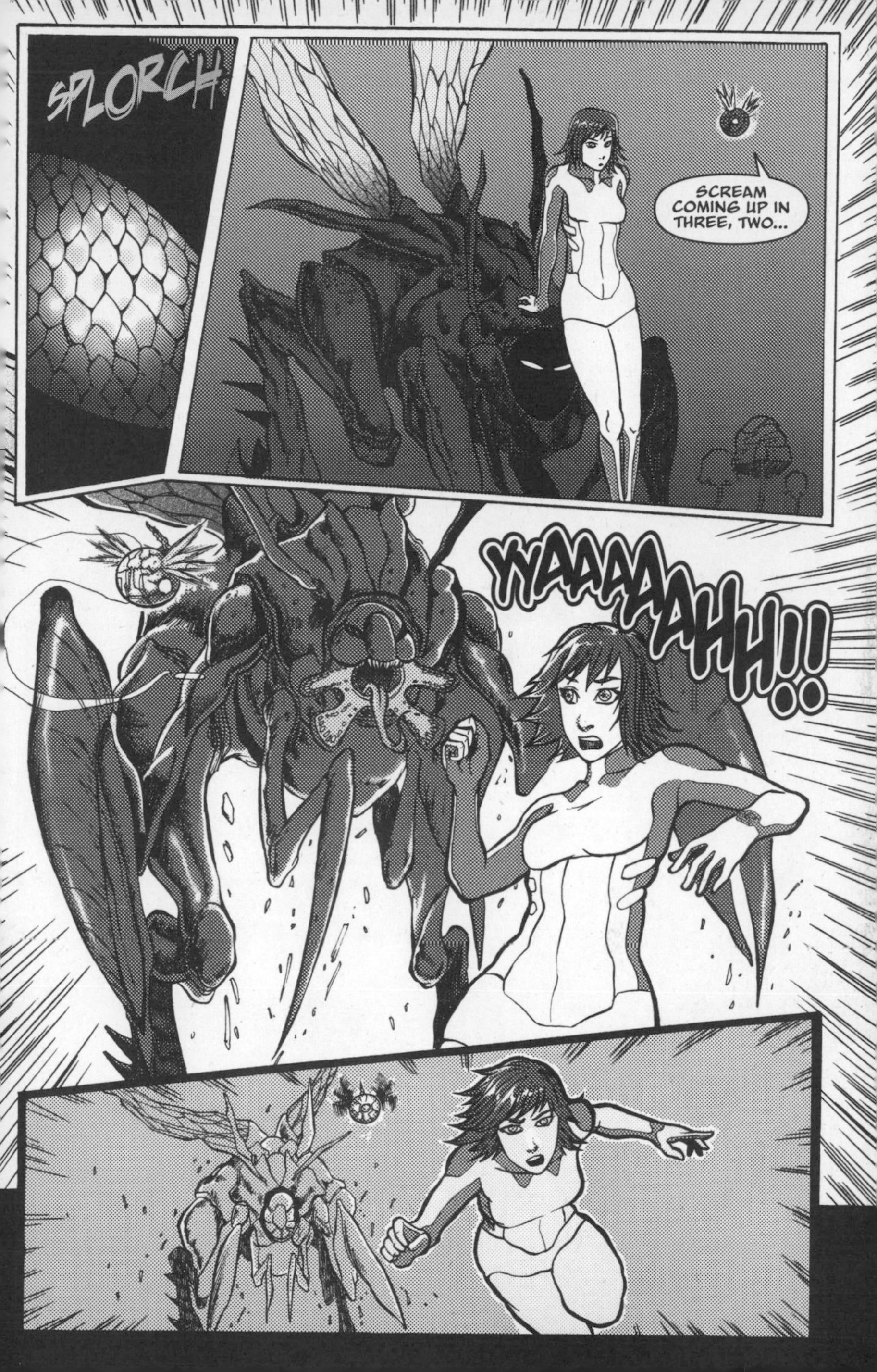
SPLORCH
SCREAM COMING UP IN THREE, TWO...
YAAAAAAHH!!

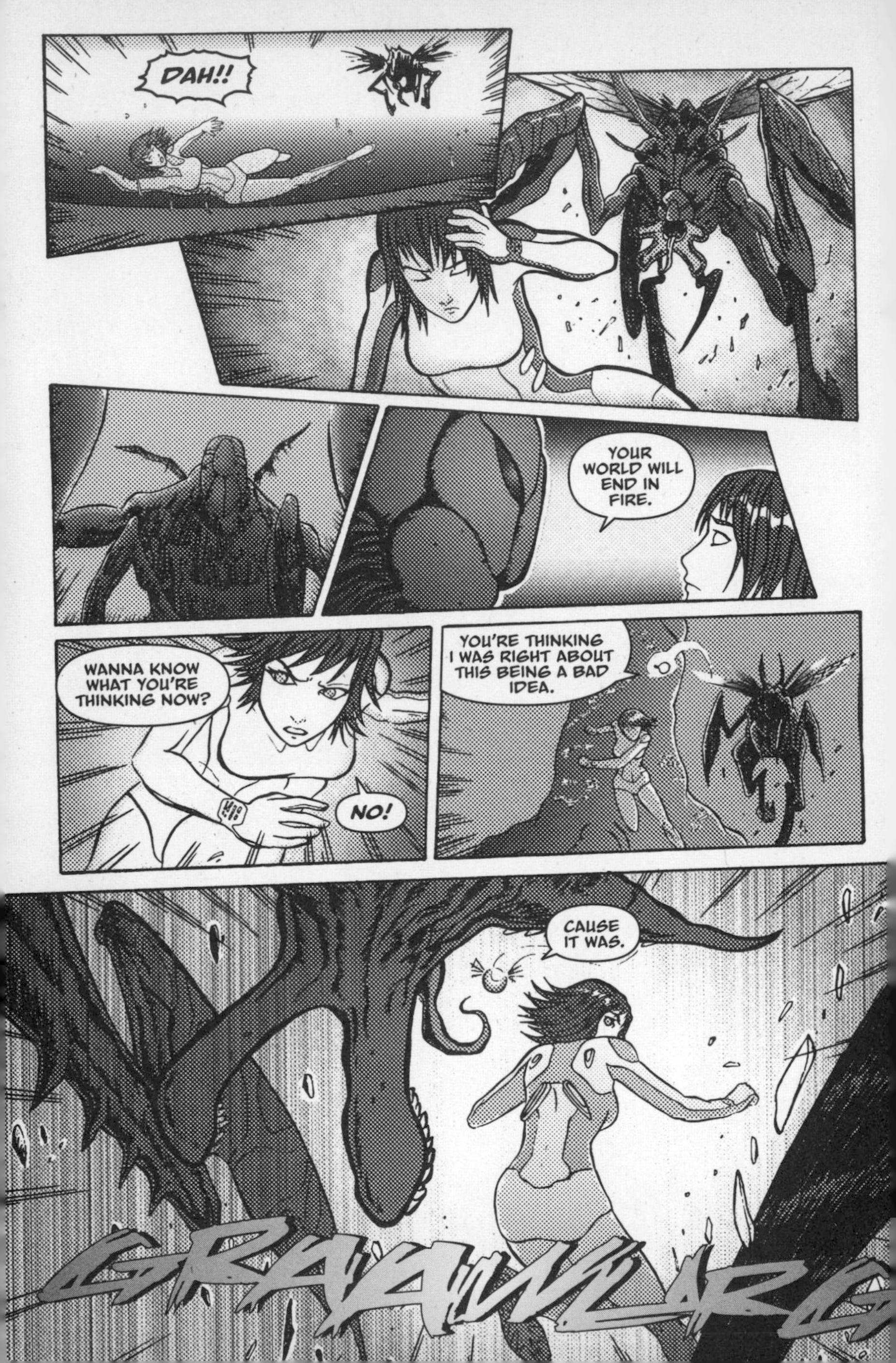
DAH!!
YOUR WORLD WILL END IN FIRE.
WANNA KNOW WHAT YOU'RE THINKING NOW?
NO!
YOU'RE THINKING I WAS RIGHT ABOUT THIS BEING A BAD IDEA.
CAUSE IT WAS.
GRAAWLARG

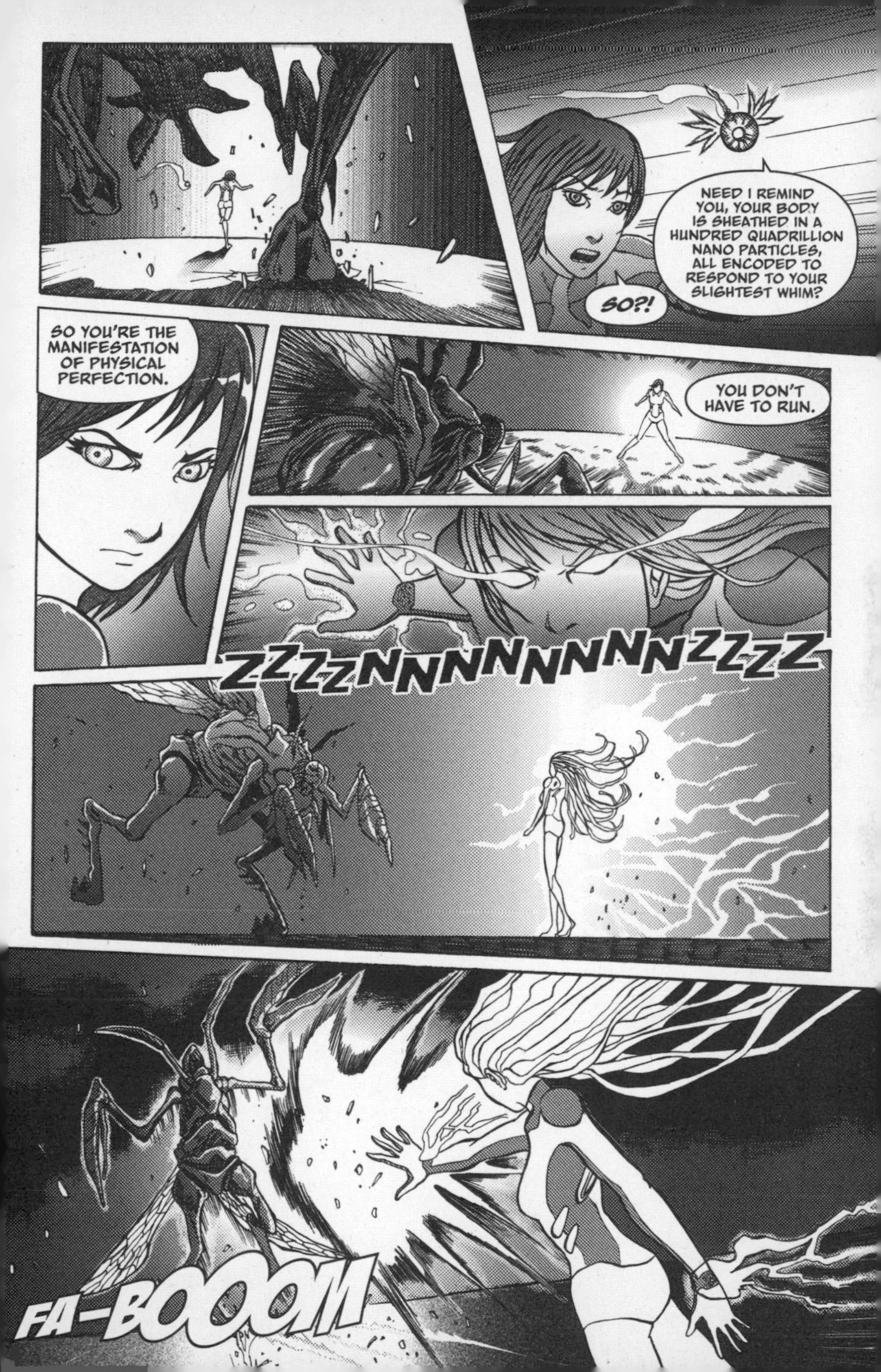
NEED I REMIND YOU, YOUR BODY IS SHEATHED IN A HUNDRED QUADRILLION NANO PARTICLES, ALL ENCODED TO RESPOND TO YOUR SLIGHTEST WHIM?
SO?!
SO YOU'RE THE MANIFESTATION OF PHYSICAL PERFECTION.
YOU DON'T HAVE TO RUN.
ZZZZNNNNNNNNZZZZ
FA-BOOOM

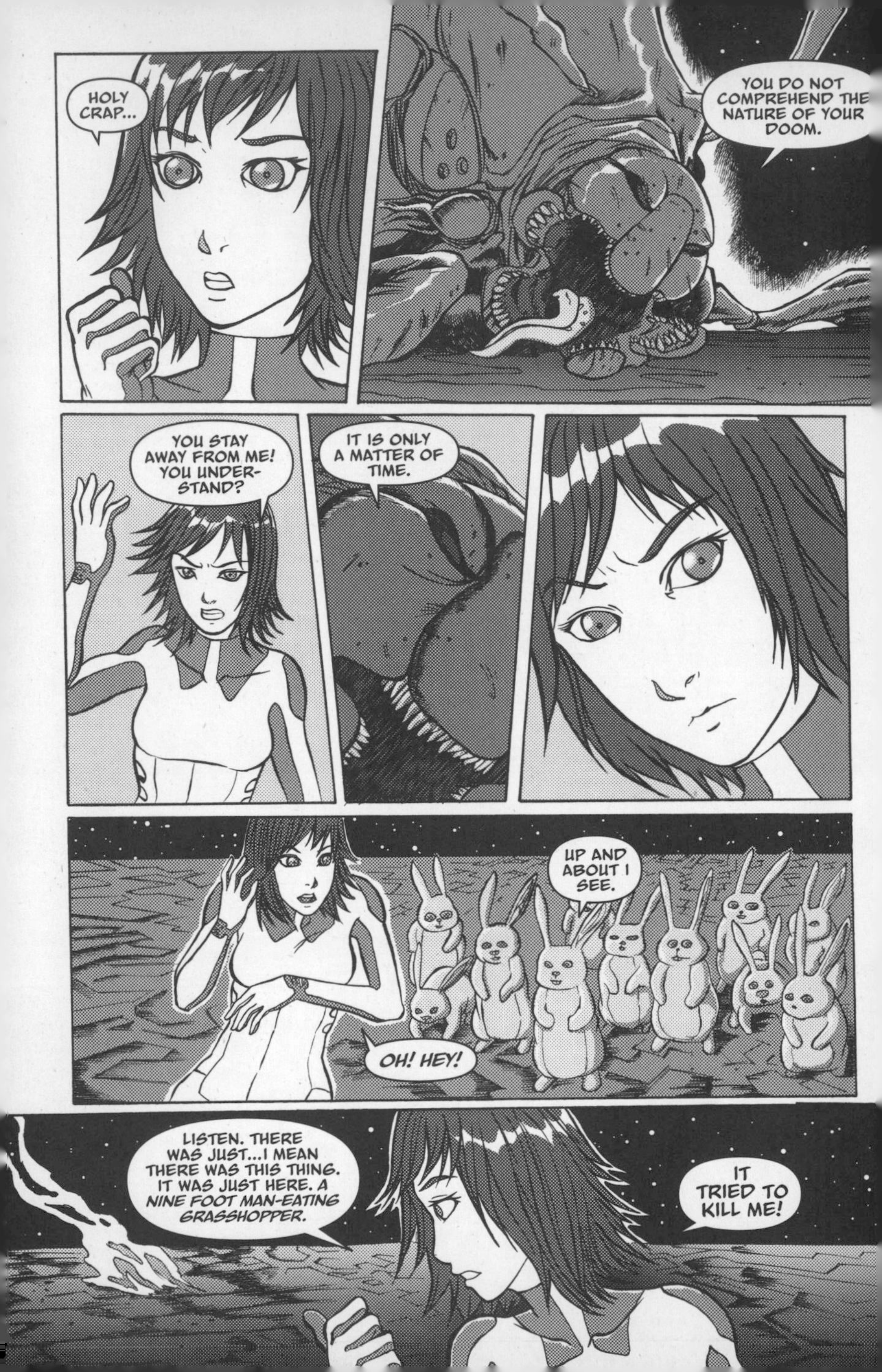
HOLY CRAP...
YOU DO NOT COMPREHEND THE NATURE OF YOUR DOOM.
YOU STAY AWAY FROM ME! YOU UNDER-STAND?
IT IS ONLY A MATTER OF TIME.
UP AND ABOUT I SEE.
OH! HEY!
LISTEN. THERE WAS JUST...I MEAN THERE WAS THIS THING. IT WAS JUST HERE. A NINE FOOT MAN-EATING GRASSHOPPER.
IT TRIED TO KILL ME!

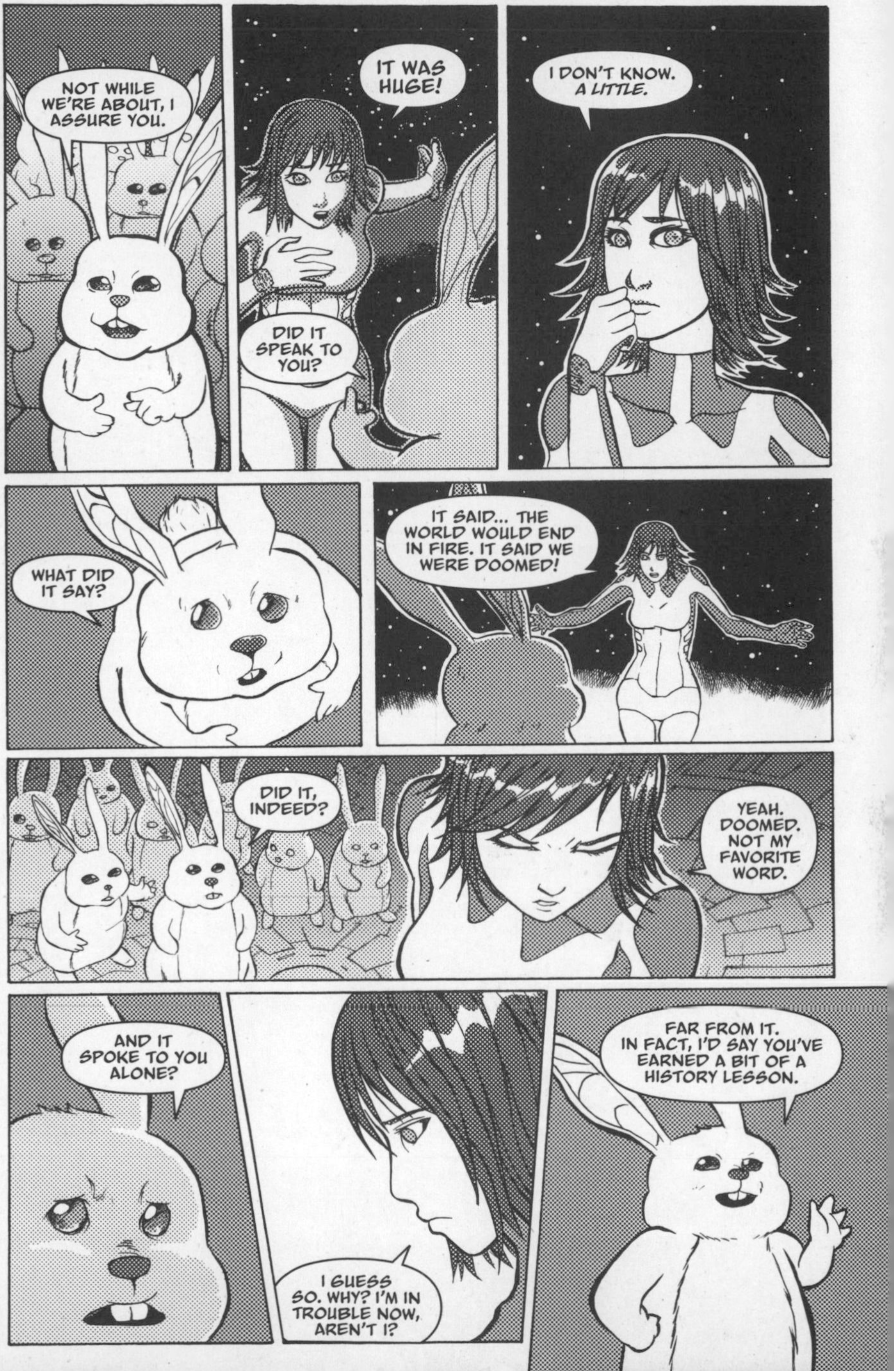
NOT WHILE WE'RE ABOUT, I ASSURE YOU.
IT WAS HUGE!
DID IT SPEAK TO YOU?
I DON'T KNOW. A *LITTLE.*
WHAT DID IT SAY?
IT SAID... THE WORLD WOULD END IN FIRE. IT SAID WE WERE DOOMED!
DID IT, INDEED?
YEAH. DOOMED. NOT MY FAVORITE WORD.
AND IT SPOKE TO YOU ALONE?
I GUESS SO. WHY? I'M IN TROUBLE NOW, AREN'T I?
FAR FROM IT. IN FACT, I'D SAY YOU'VE EARNED A BIT OF A HISTORY LESSON.

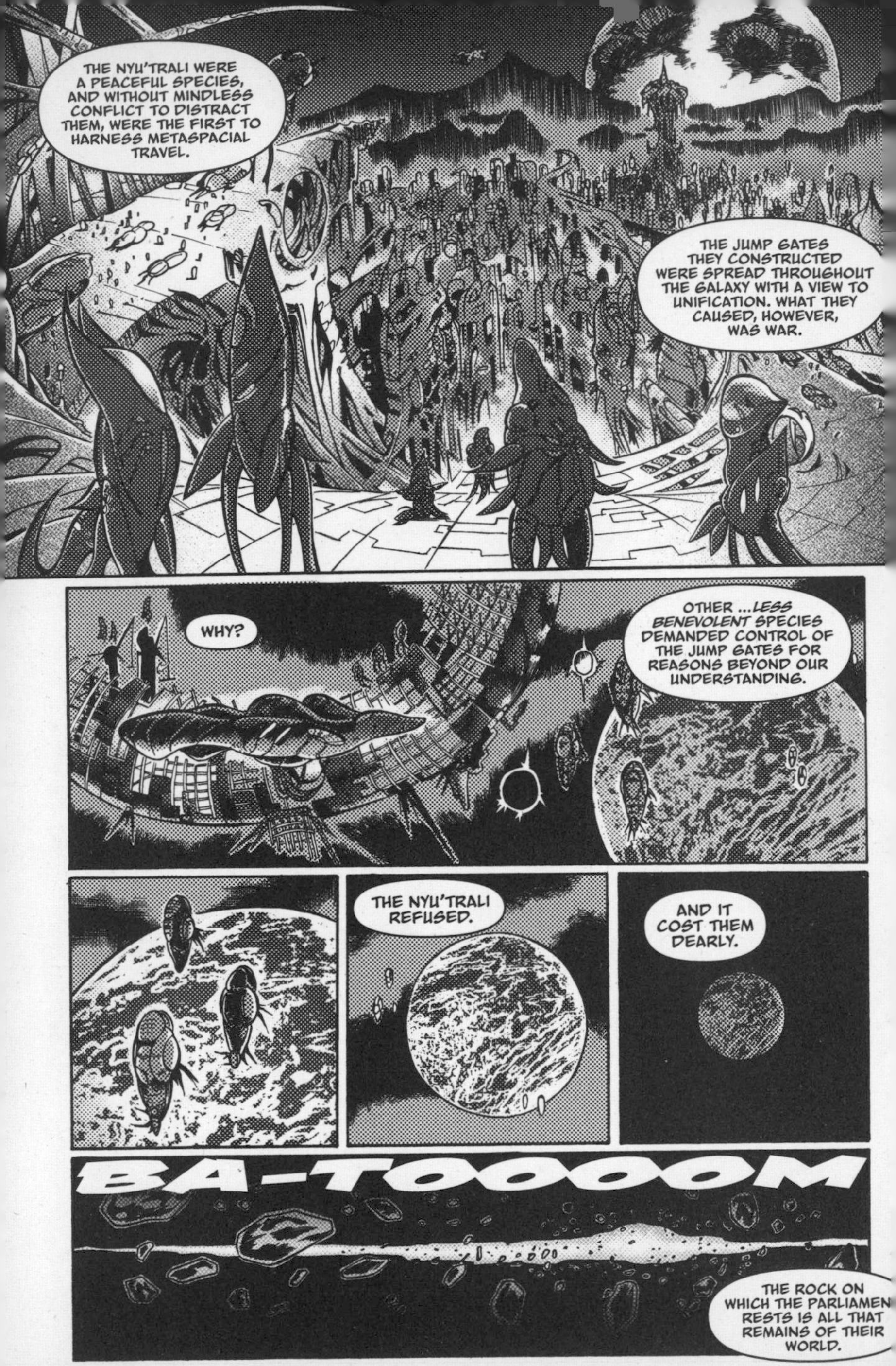
THE NYU'TRALI WERE A PEACEFUL SPECIES, AND WITHOUT MINDLESS CONFLICT TO DISTRACT THEM, WERE THE FIRST TO HARNESS METASPACIAL TRAVEL.
THE JUMP GATES THEY CONSTRUCTED WERE SPREAD THROUGHOUT THE GALAXY WITH A VIEW TO UNIFICATION. WHAT THEY CAUSED, HOWEVER, WAS WAR.
WHY?
OTHER ...LESS BENEVOLENT SPECIES DEMANDED CONTROL OF THE JUMP GATES FOR REASONS BEYOND OUR UNDERSTANDING.
THE NYU'TRALI REFUSED.
AND IT COST THEM DEARLY.
BA-TOOOOM
THE ROCK ON WHICH THE PARLIAMEN RESTS IS ALL THAT REMAINS OF THEIR WORLD.

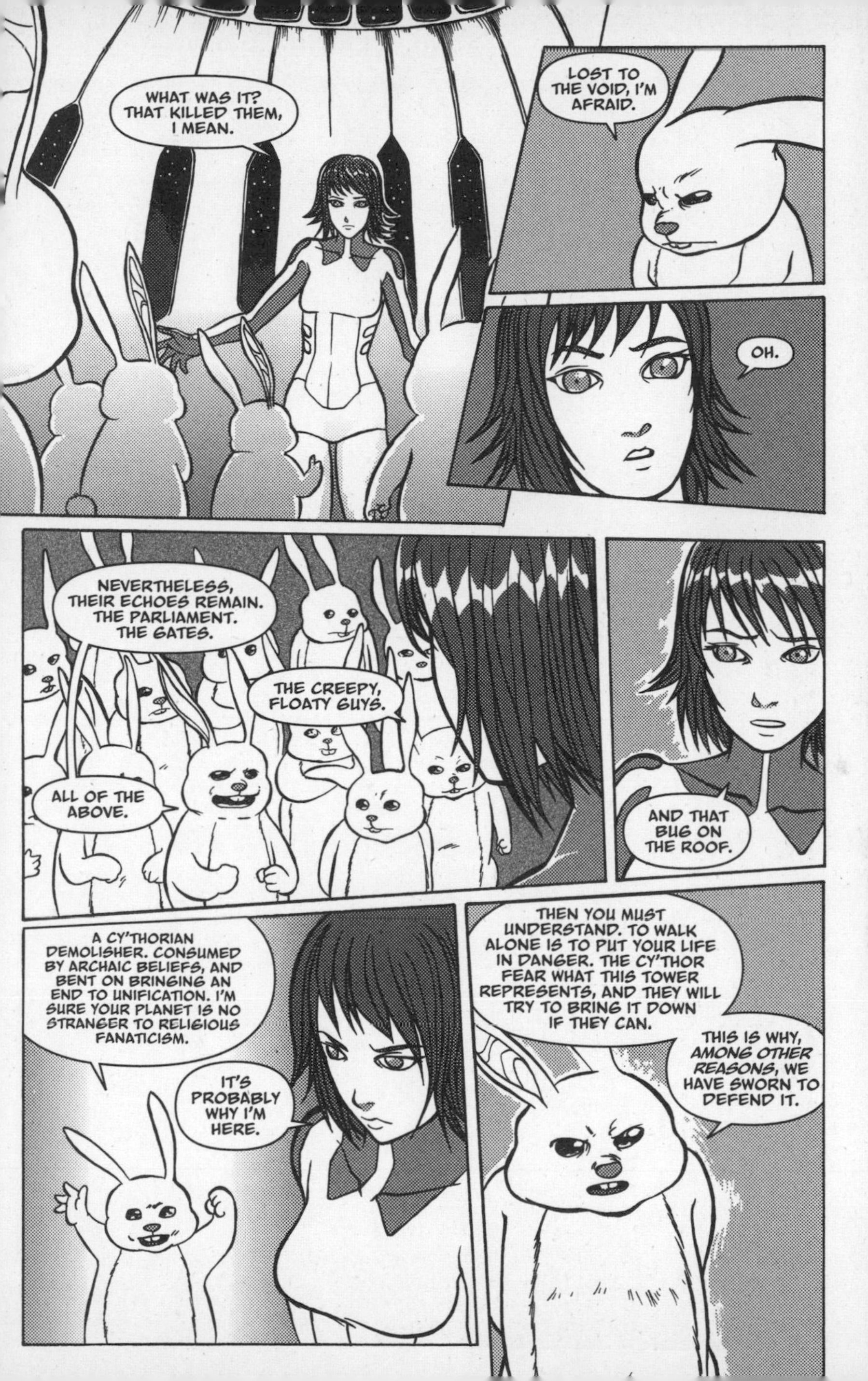
WHAT WAS IT? THAT KILLED THEM, I MEAN.
LOST TO THE VOID, I'M AFRAID.
OH.
NEVERTHELESS, THEIR ECHOES REMAIN. THE PARLIAMENT. THE GATES.
THE CREEPY, FLOATY GUYS.
ALL OF THE ABOVE.
AND THAT BUG ON THE ROOF.
A CY'THORIAN DEMOLISHER. CONSUMED BY ARCHAIC BELIEFS, AND BENT ON BRINGING AN END TO UNIFICATION. I'M SURE YOUR PLANET IS NO STRANGER TO RELIGIOUS FANATICISM.
IT'S PROBABLY WHY I'M HERE.
THEN YOU MUST UNDERSTAND. TO WALK ALONE IS TO PUT YOUR LIFE IN DANGER. THE CY'THOR FEAR WHAT THIS TOWER REPRESENTS, AND THEY WILL TRY TO BRING IT DOWN IF THEY CAN.
THIS IS WHY, *AMONG OTHER REASONS*, WE HAVE SWORN TO DEFEND IT.

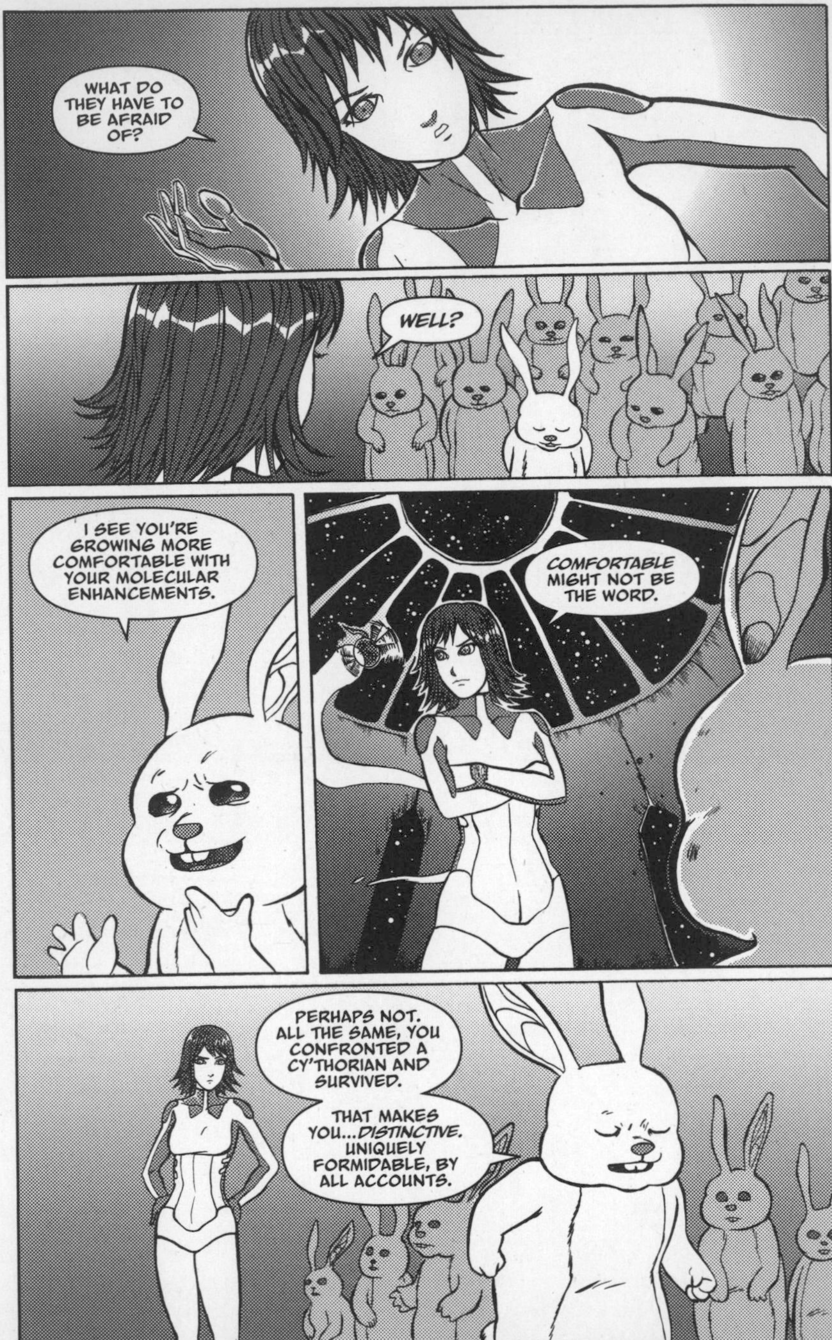
WHAT DO THEY HAVE TO BE AFRAID OF?
WELL?
I SEE YOU'RE GROWING MORE COMFORTABLE WITH YOUR MOLECULAR ENHANCEMENTS.
COMFORTABLE MIGHT NOT BE THE WORD.
PERHAPS NOT. ALL THE SAME, YOU CONFRONTED A CY'THORIAN AND SURVIVED.
THAT MAKES YOU...*DISTINCTIVE.* UNIQUELY FORMIDABLE, BY ALL ACCOUNTS.

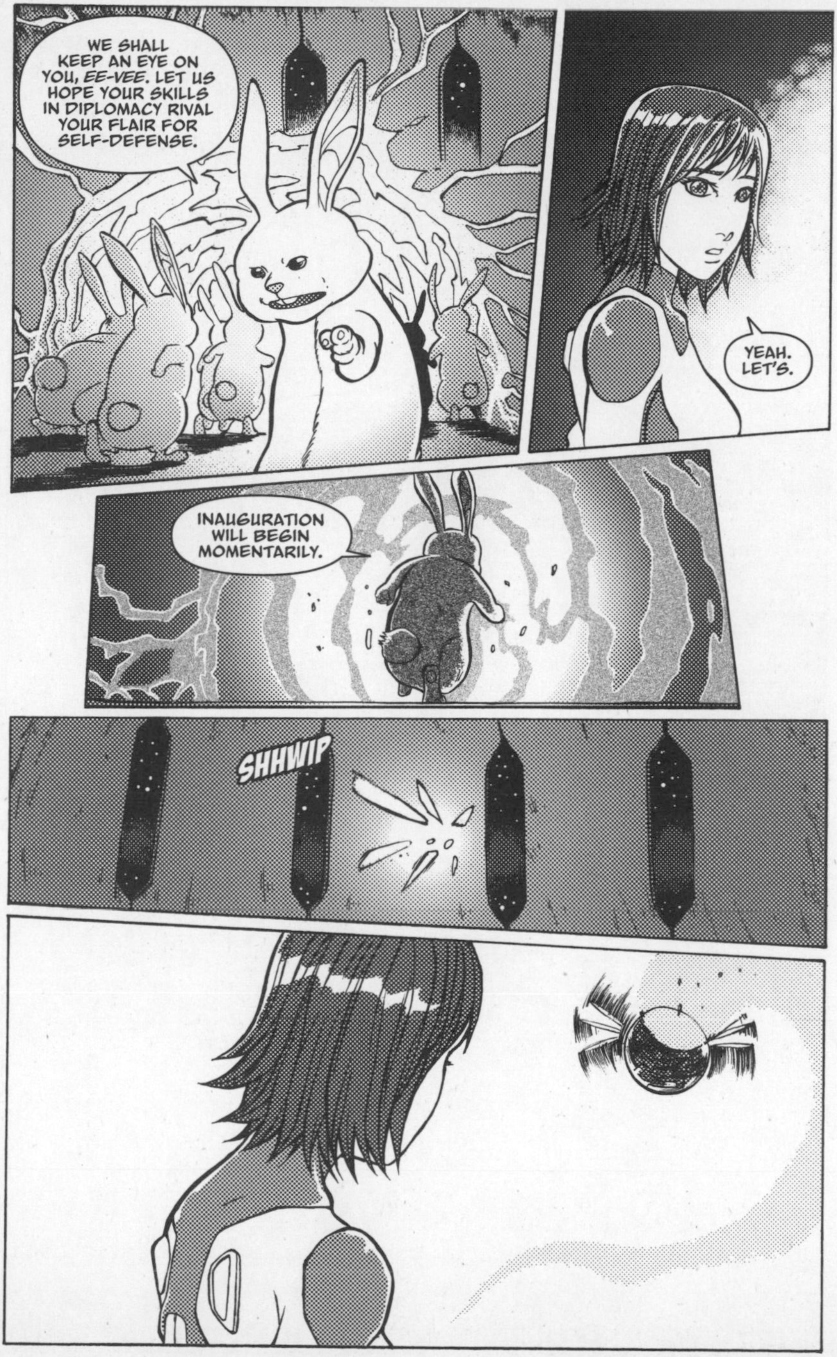
WE SHALL KEEP AN EYE ON YOU, *EE-VEE*. LET US HOPE YOUR SKILLS IN DIPLOMACY RIVAL YOUR FLAIR FOR SELF-DEFENSE.
YEAH. LET'S.
INAUGURATION WILL BEGIN MOMENTARILY.
SHHWIP

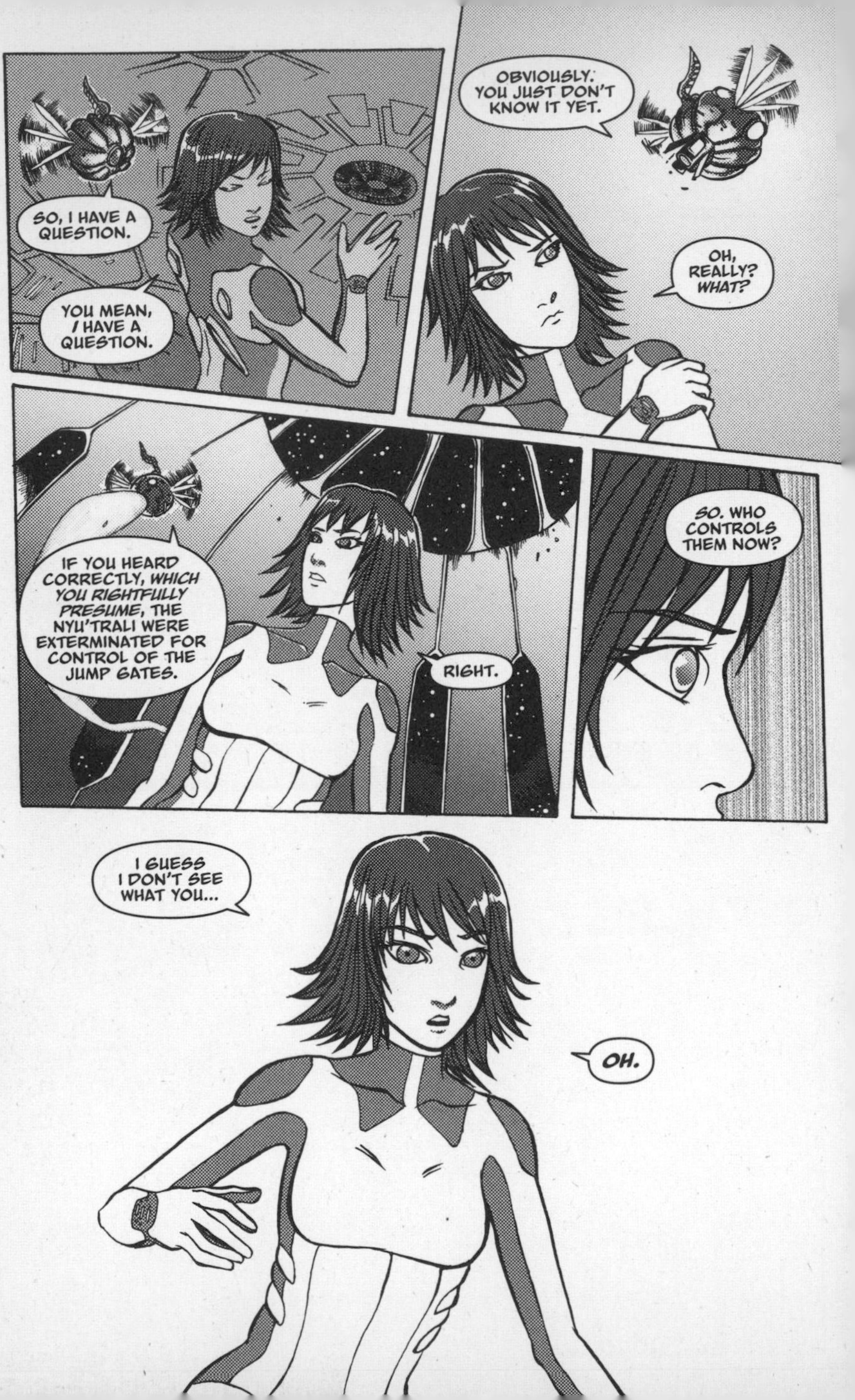
SO, I HAVE A QUESTION.
YOU MEAN, I HAVE A QUESTION.
OBVIOUSLY. YOU JUST DON'T KNOW IT YET.
OH, REALLY? WHAT?
IF YOU HEARD CORRECTLY, WHICH YOU RIGHTFULLY PRESUME, THE NYU'TRALI WERE EXTERMINATED FOR CONTROL OF THE JUMP GATES.
RIGHT.
SO. WHO CONTROLS THEM NOW?
I GUESS I DON'T SEE WHAT YOU...
OH.

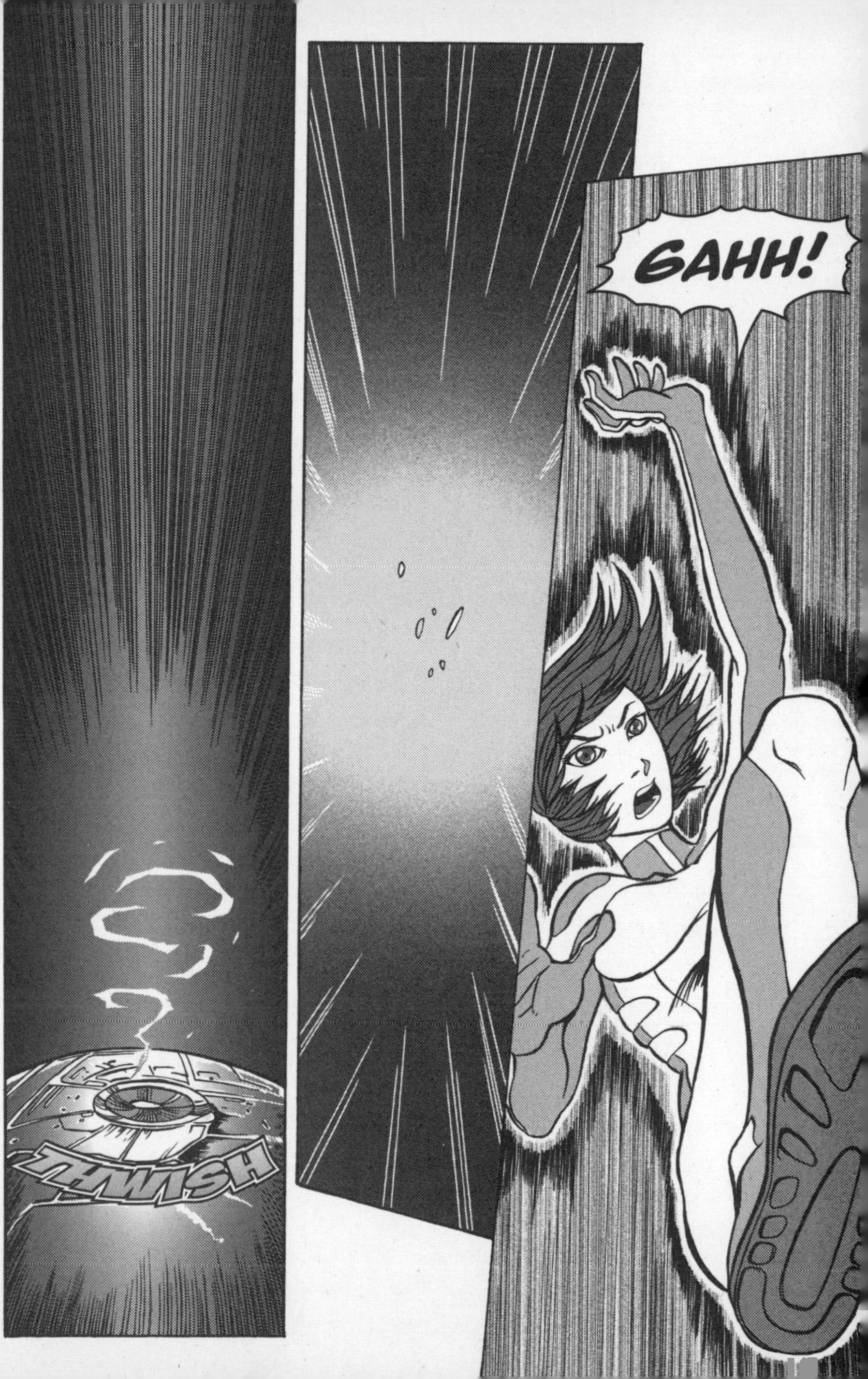
THWISH
GAHH!

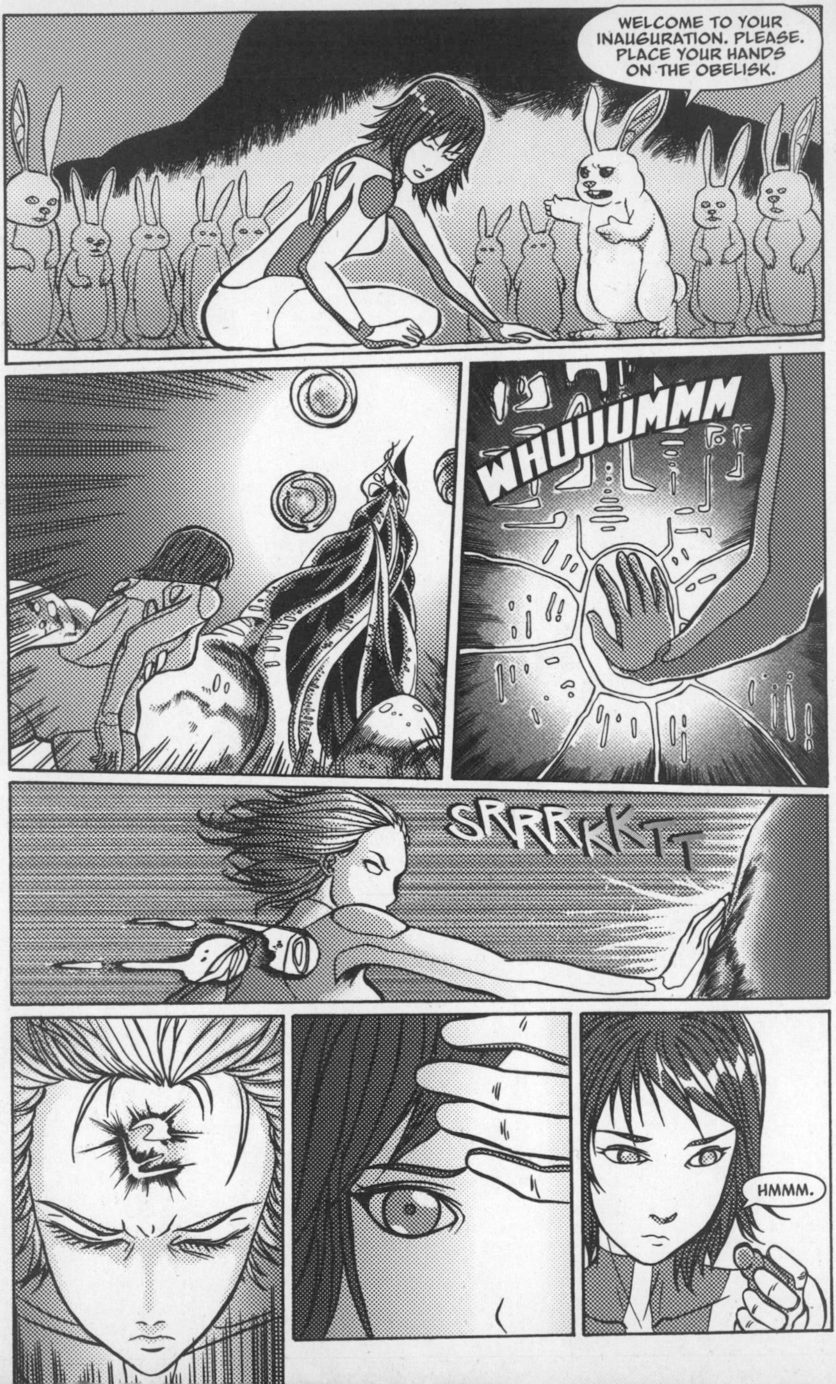
WELCOME TO YOUR INAUGURATION. PLEASE. PLACE YOUR HANDS ON THE OBELISK.
WHUUUMMM
SRRRKKTT
HMMM.

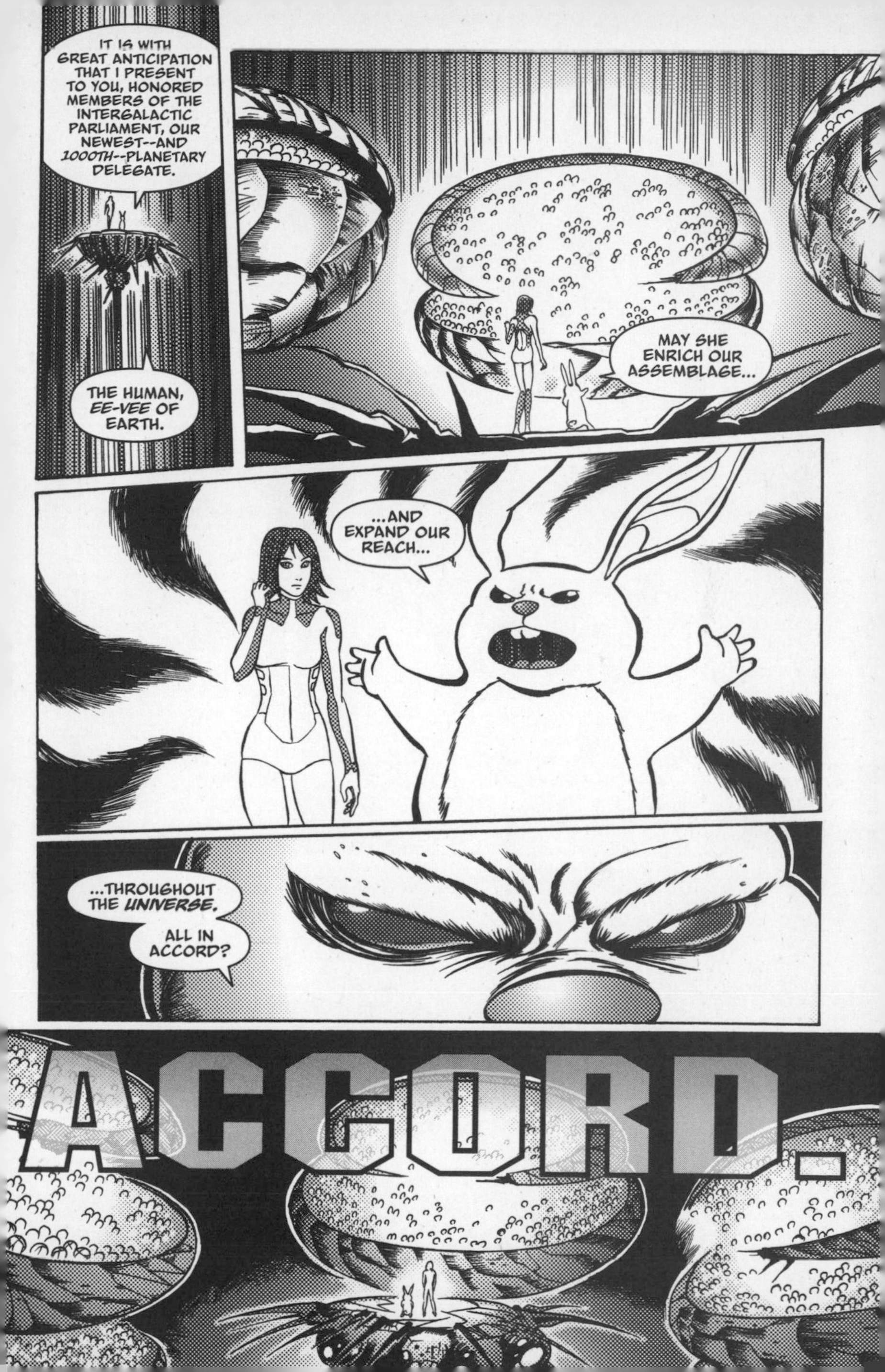
IT IS WITH GREAT ANTICIPATION THAT I PRESENT TO YOU, HONORED MEMBERS OF THE INTERGALACTIC PARLIAMENT, OUR NEWEST--AND 1000TH--PLANETARY DELEGATE.
THE HUMAN, EE-VEE OF EARTH.
MAY SHE ENRICH OUR ASSEMBLAGE...
...AND EXPAND OUR REACH...
...THROUGHOUT THE UNIVERSE.
ALL IN ACCORD?
ACCORD.

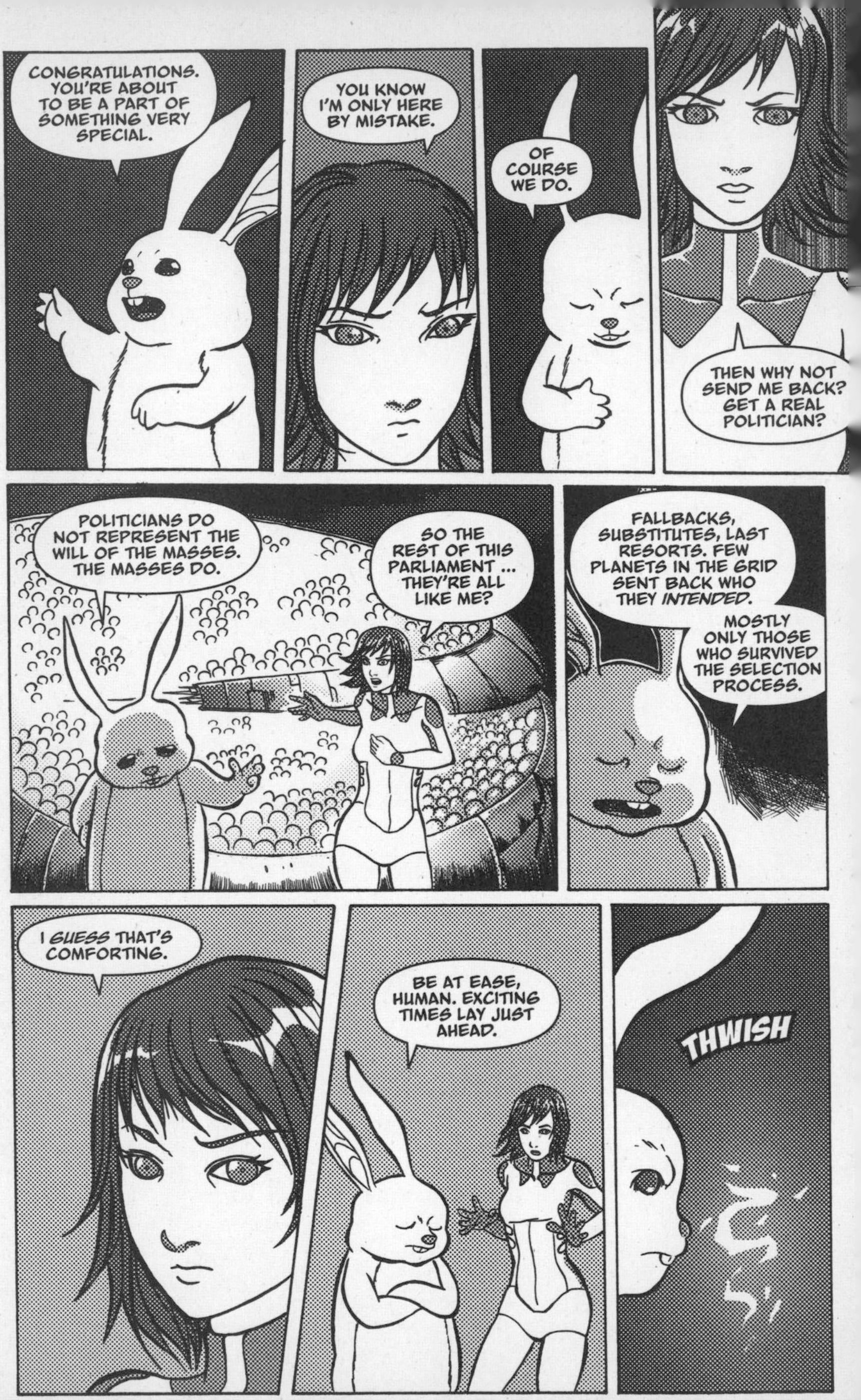
CONGRATULATIONS. YOU'RE ABOUT TO BE A PART OF SOMETHING VERY SPECIAL.
YOU KNOW I'M ONLY HERE BY MISTAKE.
OF COURSE WE DO.
THEN WHY NOT SEND ME BACK? GET A REAL POLITICIAN?
POLITICIANS DO NOT REPRESENT THE WILL OF THE MASSES. THE MASSES DO.
SO THE REST OF THIS PARLIAMENT ... THEY'RE ALL LIKE ME?
FALLBACKS, SUBSTITUTES, LAST RESORTS. FEW PLANETS IN THE GRID SENT BACK WHO THEY *INTENDED*.
MOSTLY ONLY THOSE WHO SURVIVED THE SELECTION PROCESS.
I GUESS THAT'S COMFORTING.
BE AT EASE, HUMAN. EXCITING TIMES LAY JUST AHEAD.
THWISH

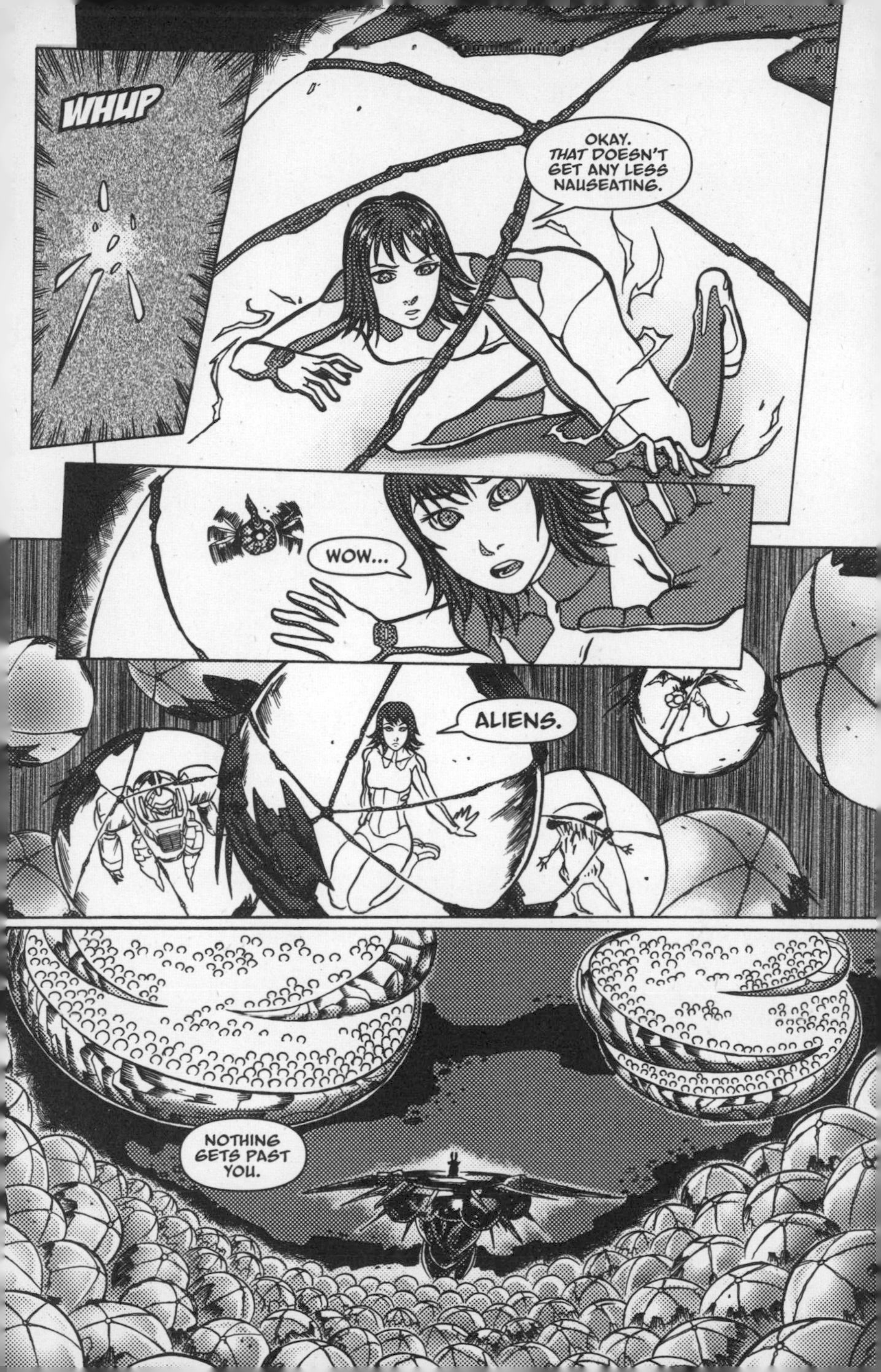
WHUP
OKAY. THAT DOESN'T GET ANY LESS NAUSEATING.
WOW...
ALIENS.
NOTHING GETS PAST YOU.

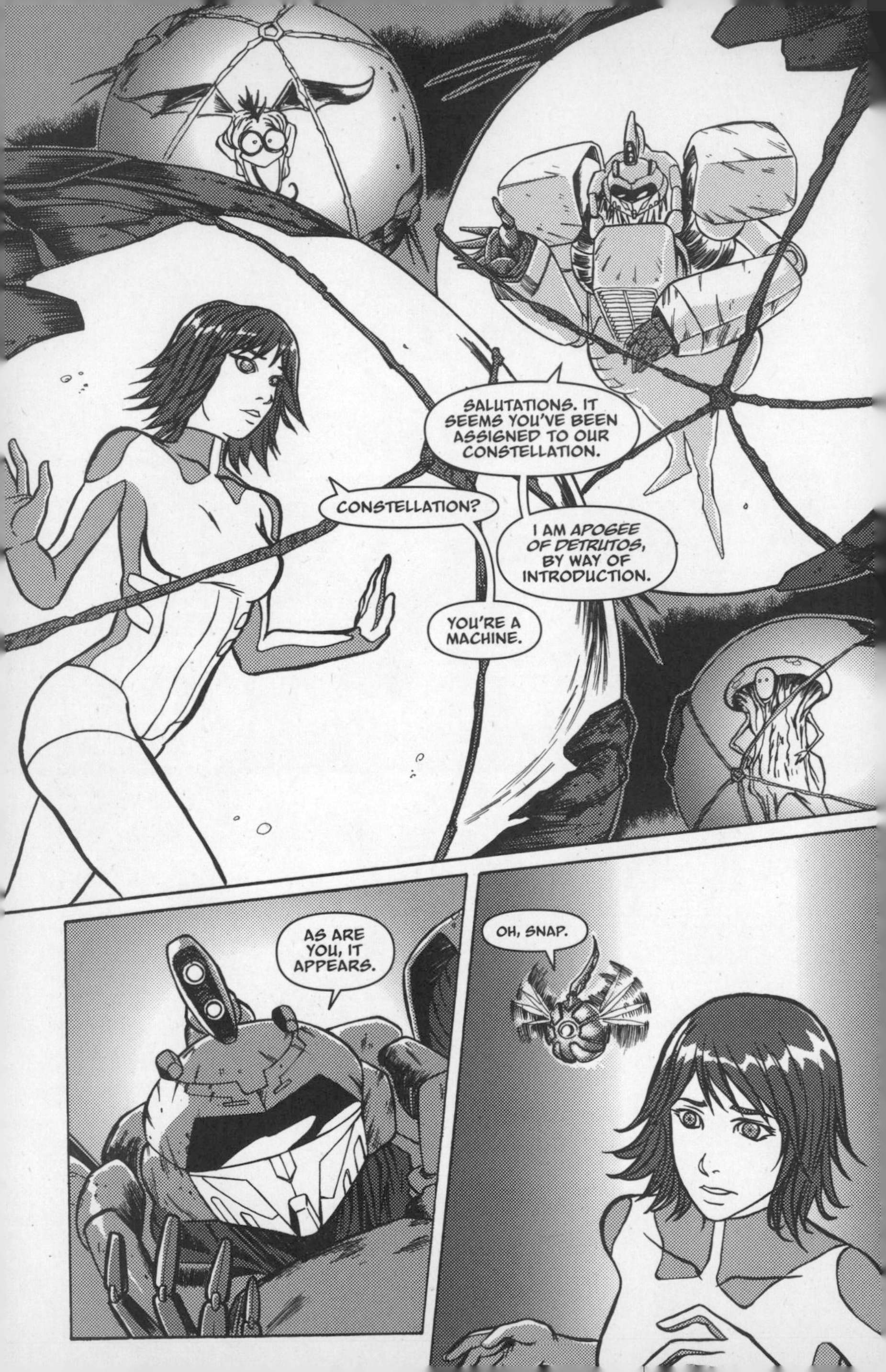
SALUTATIONS. IT SEEMS YOU'VE BEEN ASSIGNED TO OUR CONSTELLATION.
CONSTELLATION?
I AM APOGEE OF DETRUTOS, BY WAY OF INTRODUCTION.
YOU'RE A MACHINE.
AS ARE YOU, IT APPEARS.
OH, SNAP.

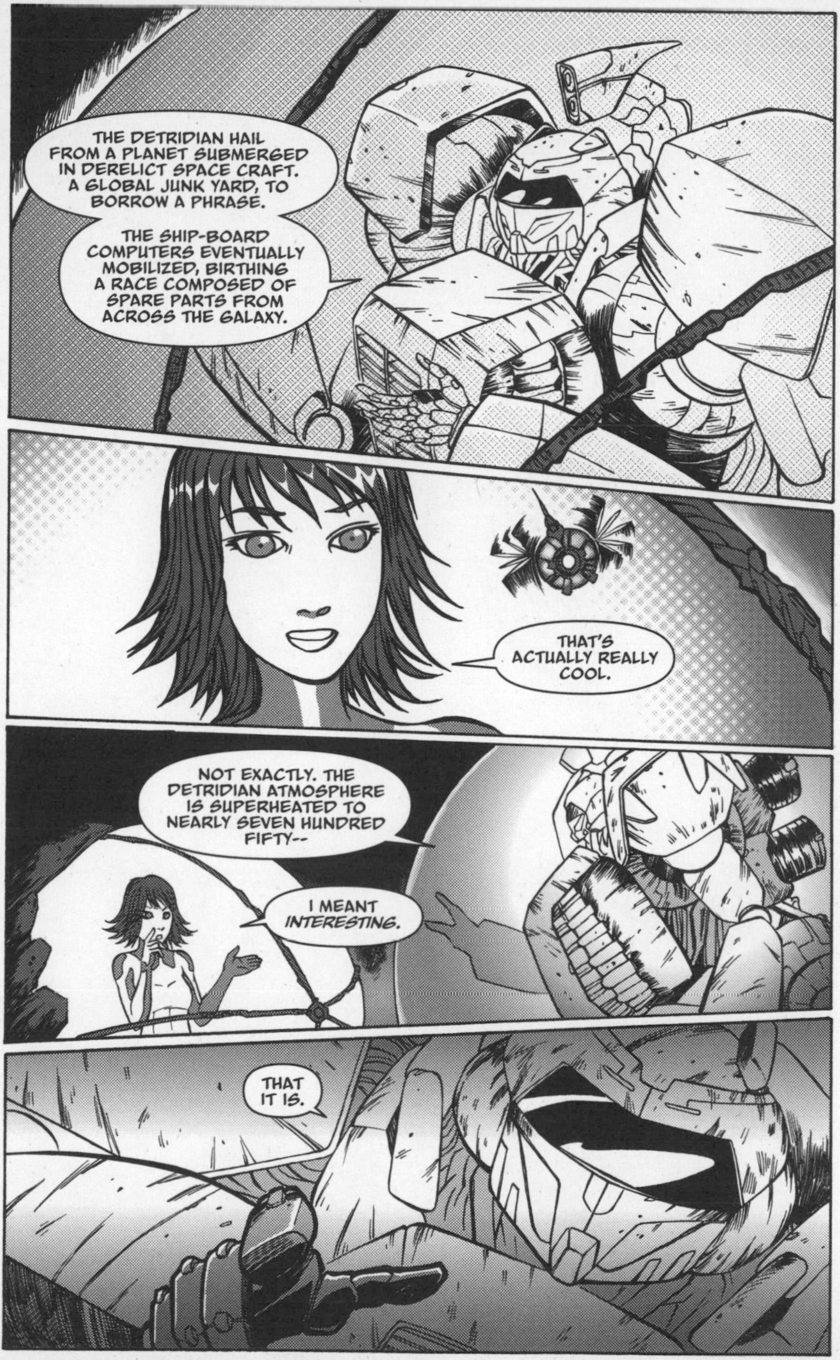
THE DETRIDIAN HAIL FROM A PLANET SUBMERGED IN DERELICT SPACE CRAFT. A GLOBAL JUNK YARD, TO BORROW A PHRASE.
THE SHIP-BOARD COMPUTERS EVENTUALLY MOBILIZED, BIRTHING A RACE COMPOSED OF SPARE PARTS FROM ACROSS THE GALAXY.
THAT'S ACTUALLY REALLY COOL.
NOT EXACTLY. THE DETRIDIAN ATMOSPHERE IS SUPERHEATED TO NEARLY SEVEN HUNDRED FIFTY--
I MEANT *INTERESTING*.
THAT IT IS.

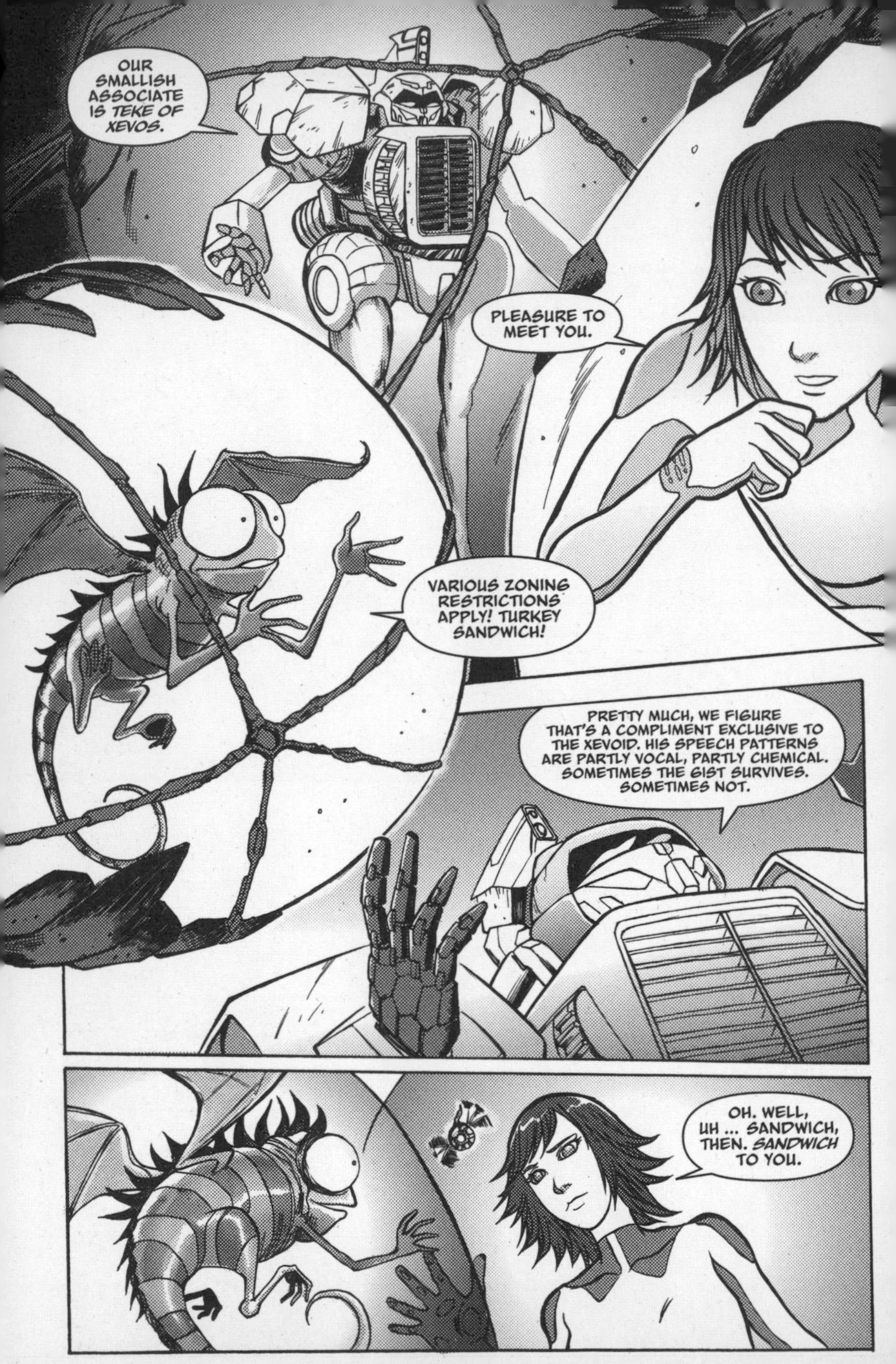
OUR SMALLISH ASSOCIATE IS TEKE OF XEVOS.
PLEASURE TO MEET YOU.
VARIOUS ZONING RESTRICTIONS APPLY! TURKEY SANDWICH!
PRETTY MUCH, WE FIGURE THAT'S A COMPLIMENT EXCLUSIVE TO THE XEVOID. HIS SPEECH PATTERNS ARE PARTLY VOCAL, PARTLY CHEMICAL. SOMETIMES THE GIST SURVIVES. SOMETIMES NOT.
OH. WELL, UH ... SANDWICH, THEN. SANDWICH TO YOU.

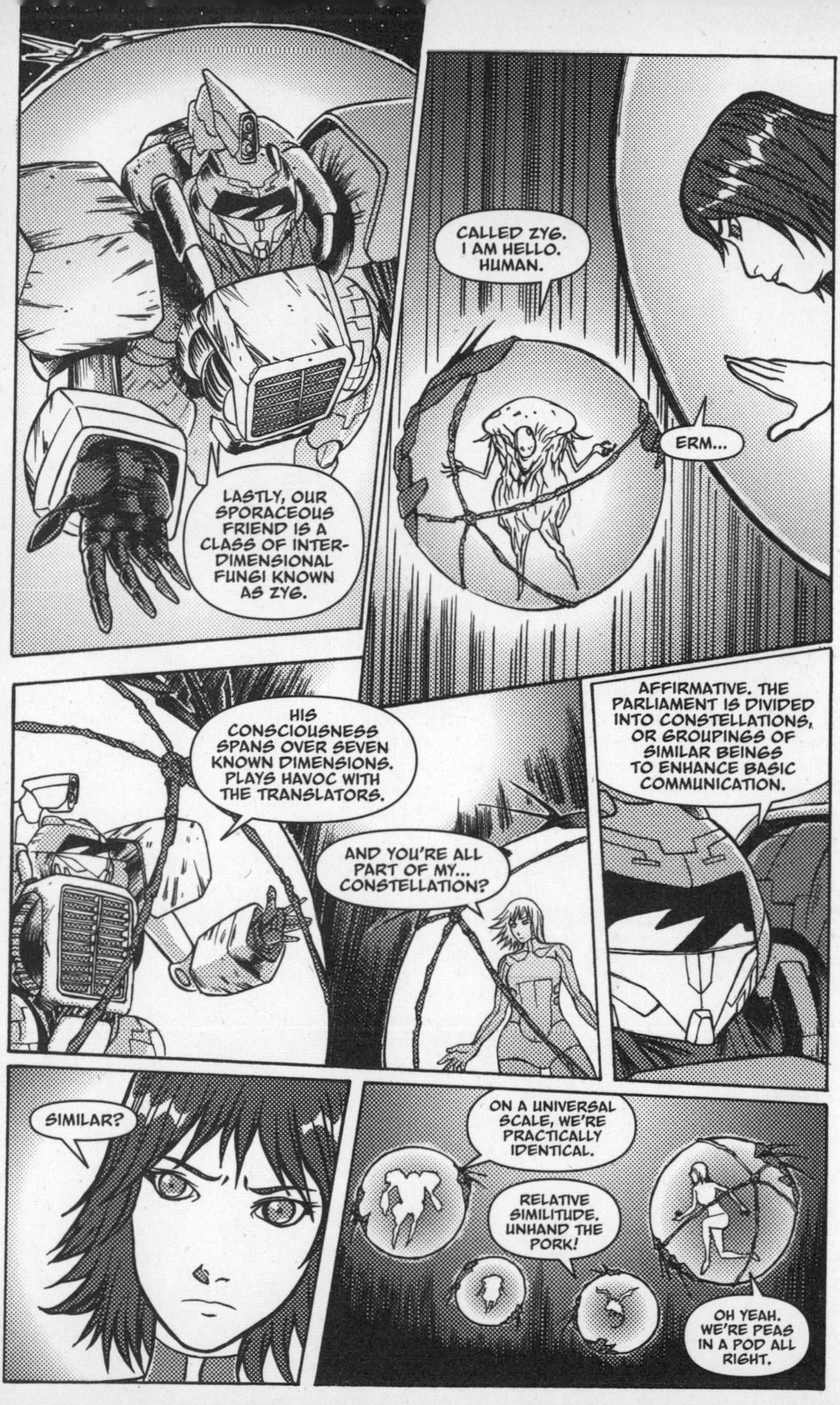
LASTLY, OUR SPORACEOUS FRIEND IS A CLASS OF INTER-DIMENSIONAL FUNGI KNOWN AS ZYG.
CALLED ZYG. I AM HELLO. HUMAN.
ERM...
HIS CONSCIOUSNESS SPANS OVER SEVEN KNOWN DIMENSIONS. PLAYS HAVOC WITH THE TRANSLATORS.
AND YOU'RE ALL PART OF MY... CONSTELLATION?
AFFIRMATIVE. THE PARLIAMENT IS DIVIDED INTO CONSTELLATIONS, OR GROUPINGS OF SIMILAR BEINGS TO ENHANCE BASIC COMMUNICATION.
SIMILAR?
ON A UNIVERSAL SCALE, WE'RE PRACTICALLY IDENTICAL.
RELATIVE SIMILITUDE. UNHAND THE PORK!
OH YEAH. WE'RE PEAS IN A POD ALL RIGHT.

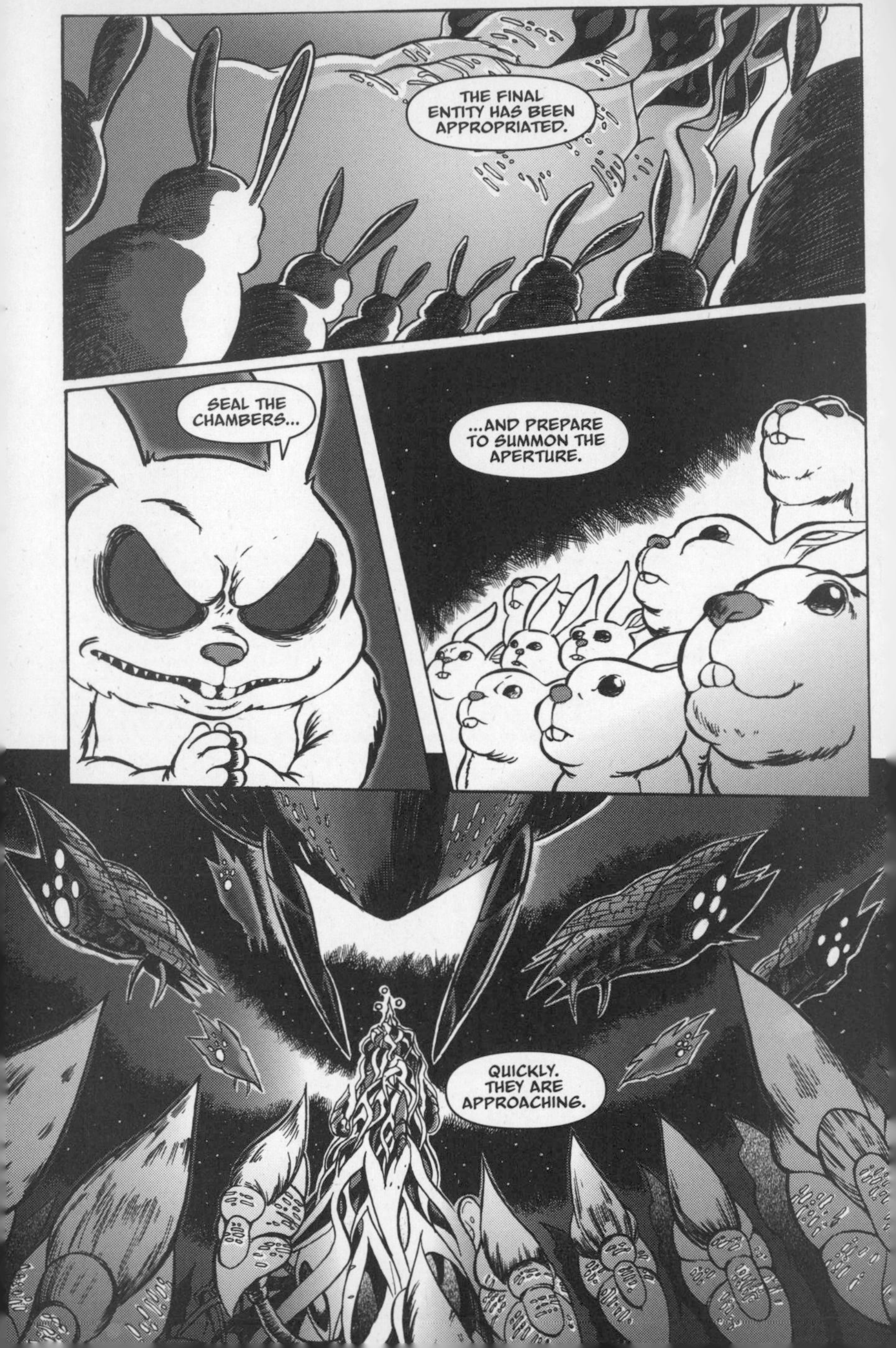
THE FINAL ENTITY HAS BEEN APPROPRIATED.
SEAL THE CHAMBERS...
...AND PREPARE TO SUMMON THE APERTURE.
QUICKLY. THEY ARE APPROACHING.

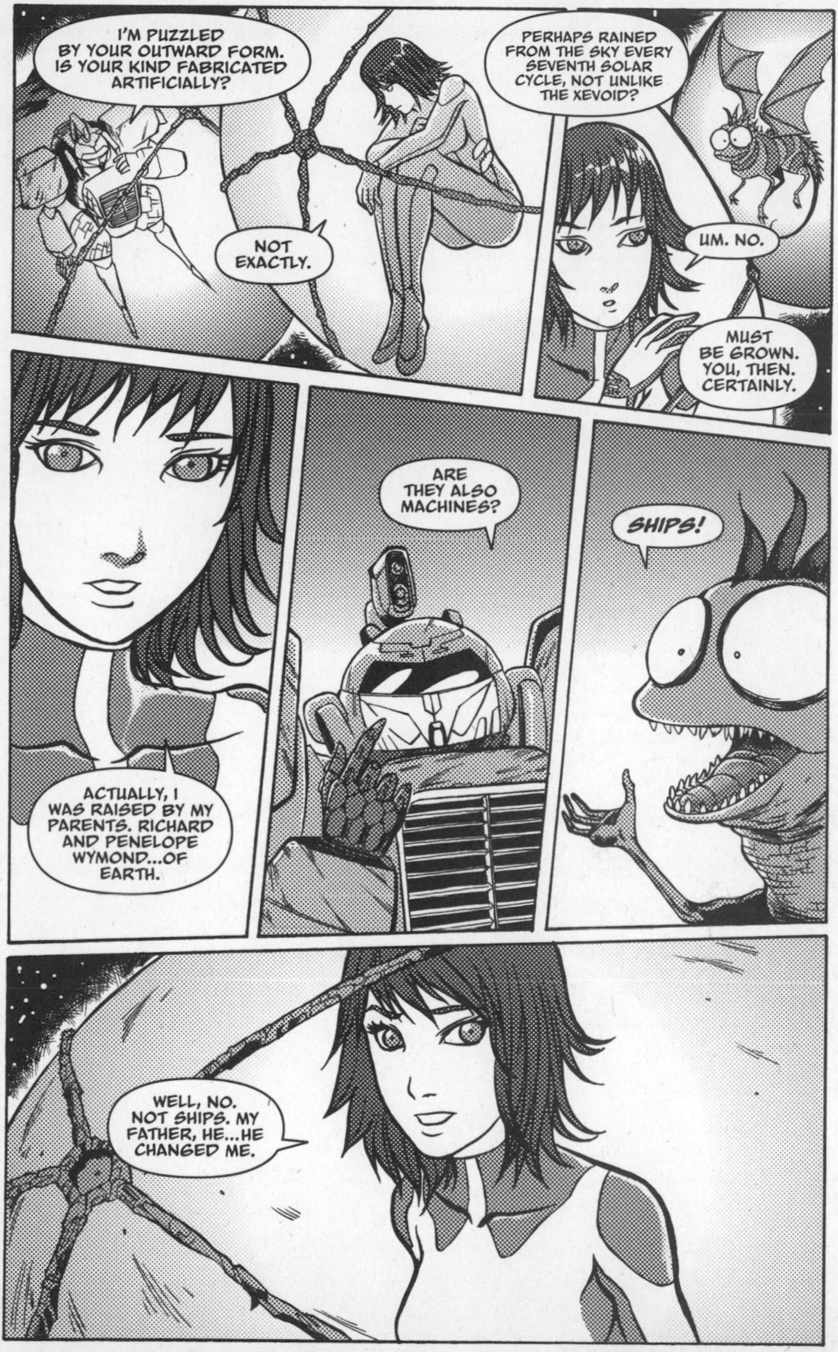
I'M PUZZLED BY YOUR OUTWARD FORM. IS YOUR KIND FABRICATED ARTIFICIALLY?
NOT EXACTLY.
PERHAPS RAINED FROM THE SKY EVERY SEVENTH SOLAR CYCLE, NOT UNLIKE THE XEVOID?
UM. NO.
MUST BE GROWN. YOU, THEN. CERTAINLY.
ACTUALLY, I WAS RAISED BY MY PARENTS. RICHARD AND PENELOPE WYMOND...OF EARTH.
ARE THEY ALSO MACHINES?
SHIPS!
WELL, NO. NOT SHIPS. MY FATHER, HE...HE CHANGED ME.

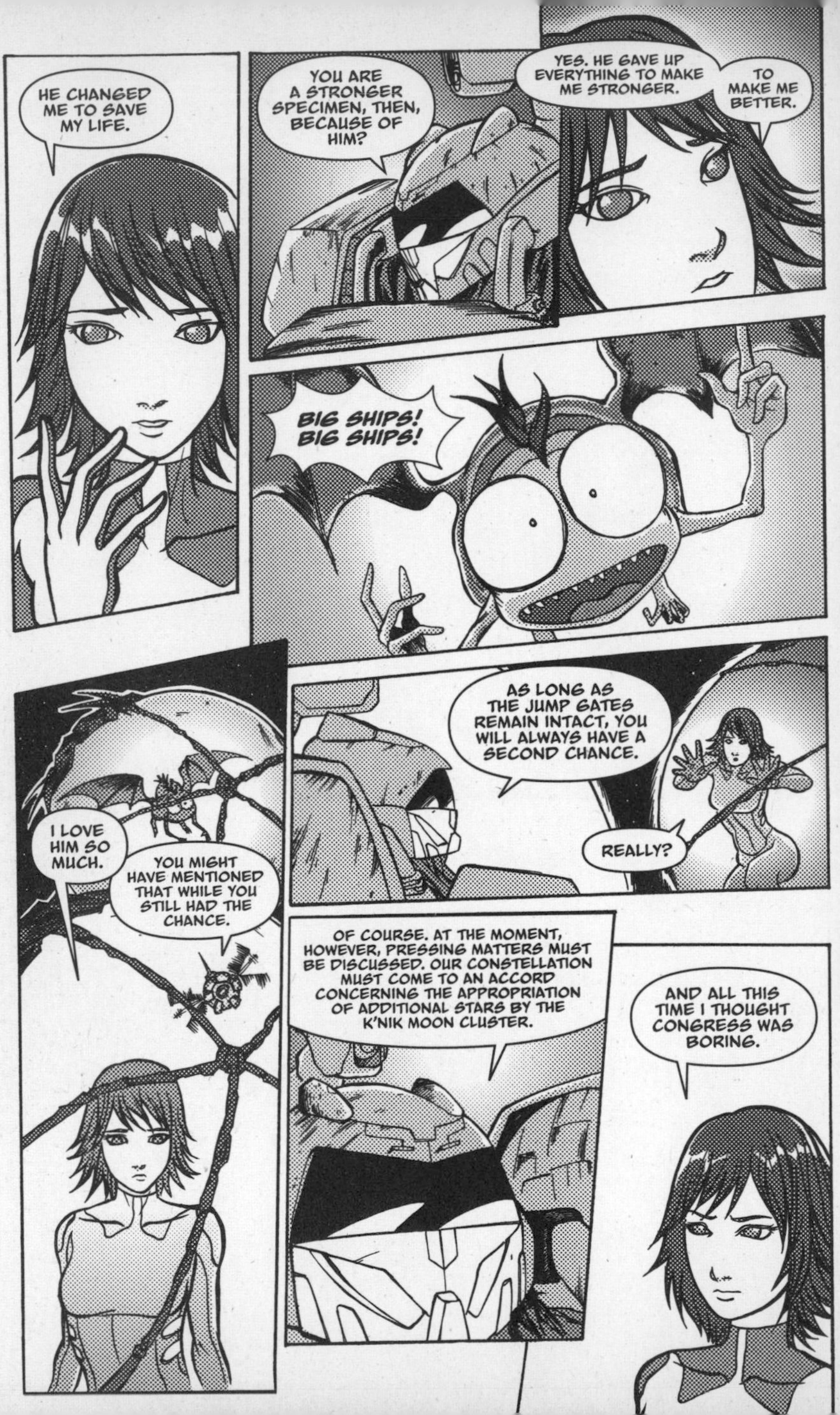
HE CHANGED ME TO SAVE MY LIFE.
YOU ARE A STRONGER SPECIMEN, THEN, BECAUSE OF HIM?
YES. HE GAVE UP EVERYTHING TO MAKE ME STRONGER.
TO MAKE ME BETTER.
BIG SHIPS! BIG SHIPS!
I LOVE HIM SO MUCH.
YOU MIGHT HAVE MENTIONED THAT WHILE YOU STILL HAD THE CHANCE.
AS LONG AS THE JUMP GATES REMAIN INTACT, YOU WILL ALWAYS HAVE A SECOND CHANCE.
REALLY?
OF COURSE. AT THE MOMENT, HOWEVER, PRESSING MATTERS MUST BE DISCUSSED. OUR CONSTELLATION MUST COME TO AN ACCORD CONCERNING THE APPROPRIATION OF ADDITIONAL STARS BY THE K'NIK MOON CLUSTER.
AND ALL THIS TIME I THOUGHT CONGRESS WAS BORING.

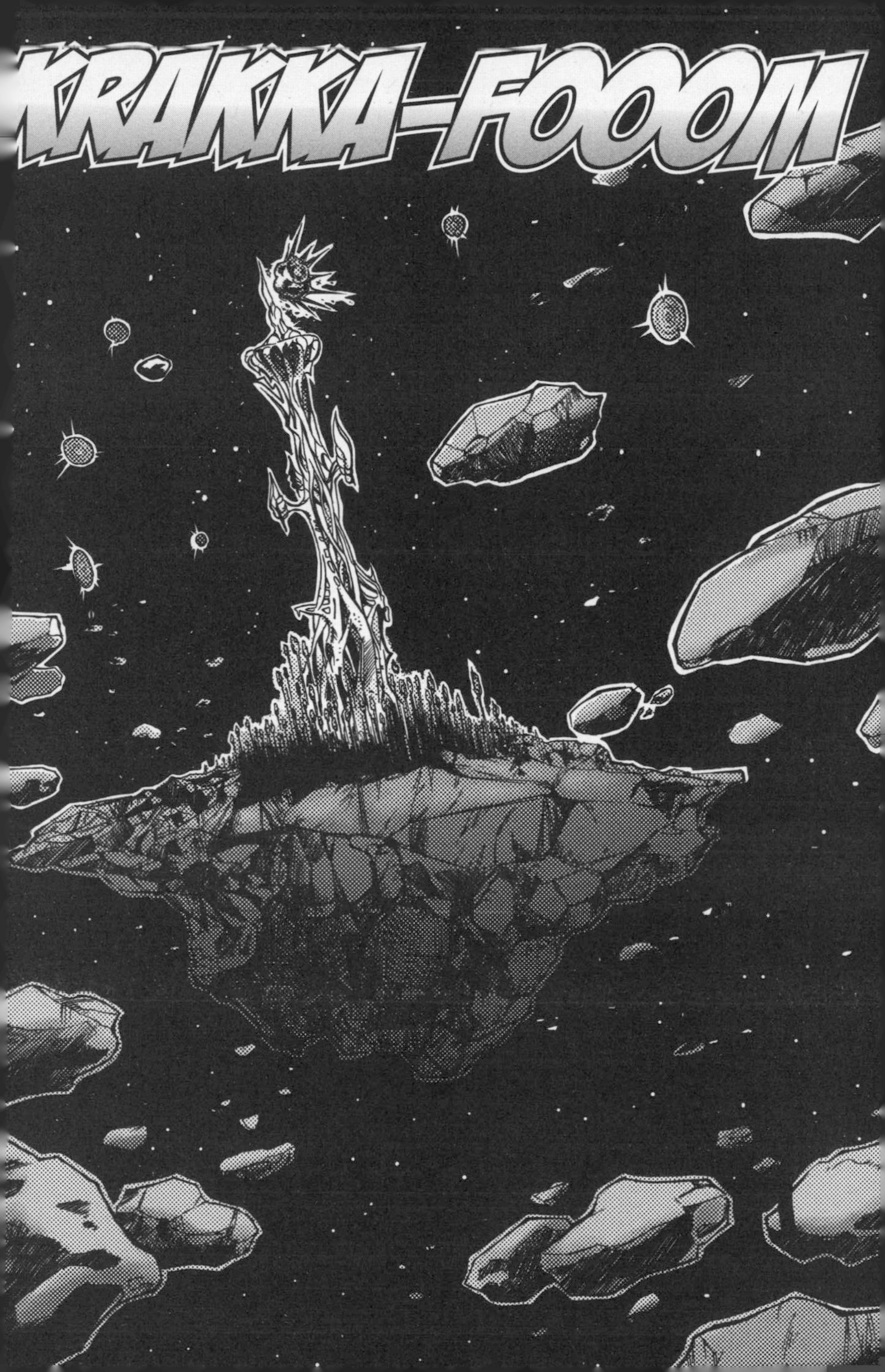
KRAKKA-FOOOM

CHAPTER 04

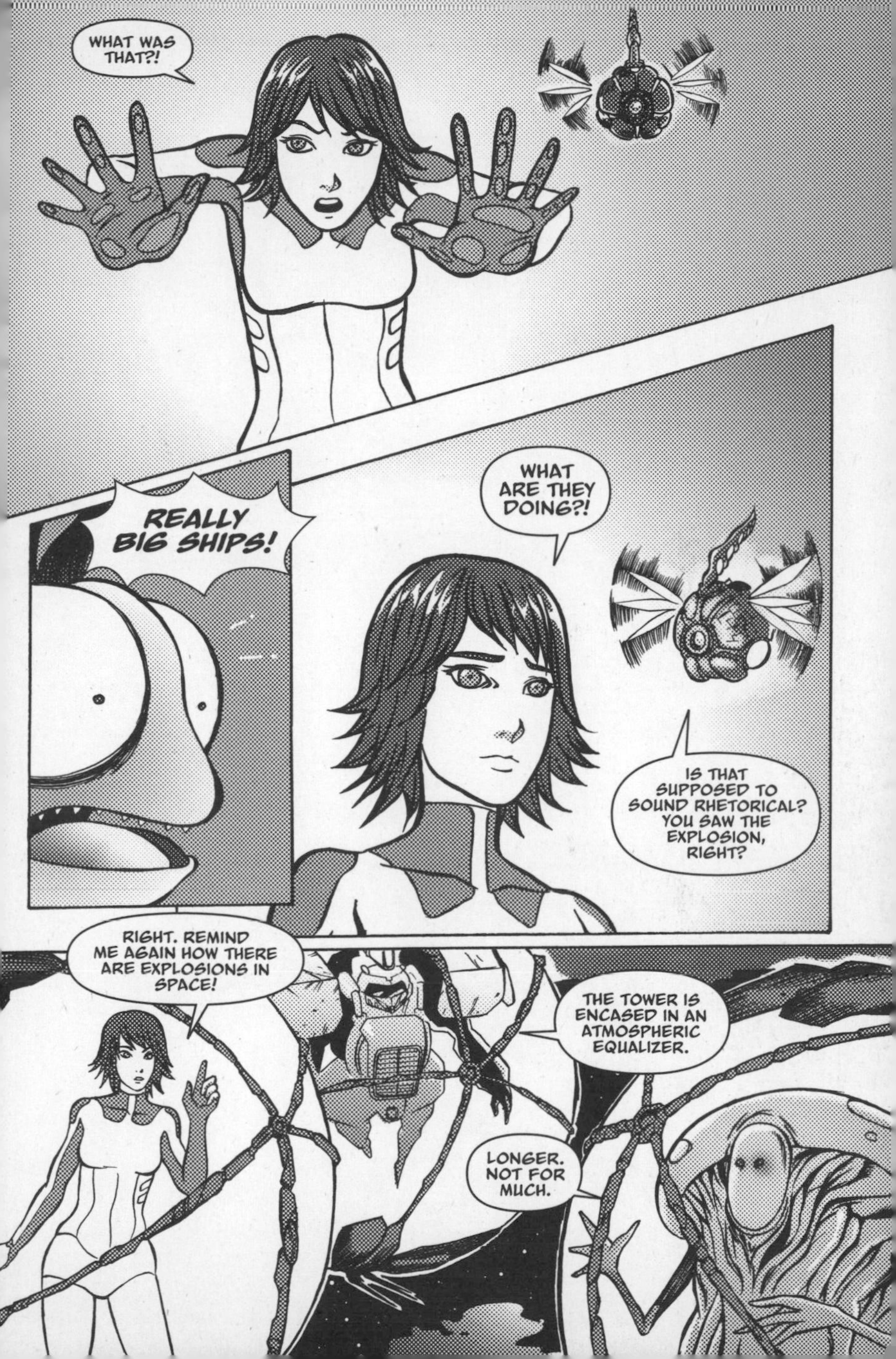

WHAT WAS THAT?!
REALLY BIG SHIPS!
WHAT ARE THEY DOING?!
IS THAT SUPPOSED TO SOUND RHETORICAL? YOU SAW THE EXPLOSION, RIGHT?
RIGHT. REMIND ME AGAIN HOW THERE ARE EXPLOSIONS IN SPACE!
THE TOWER IS ENCASED IN AN ATMOSPHERIC EQUALIZER.
LONGER. NOT FOR MUCH.

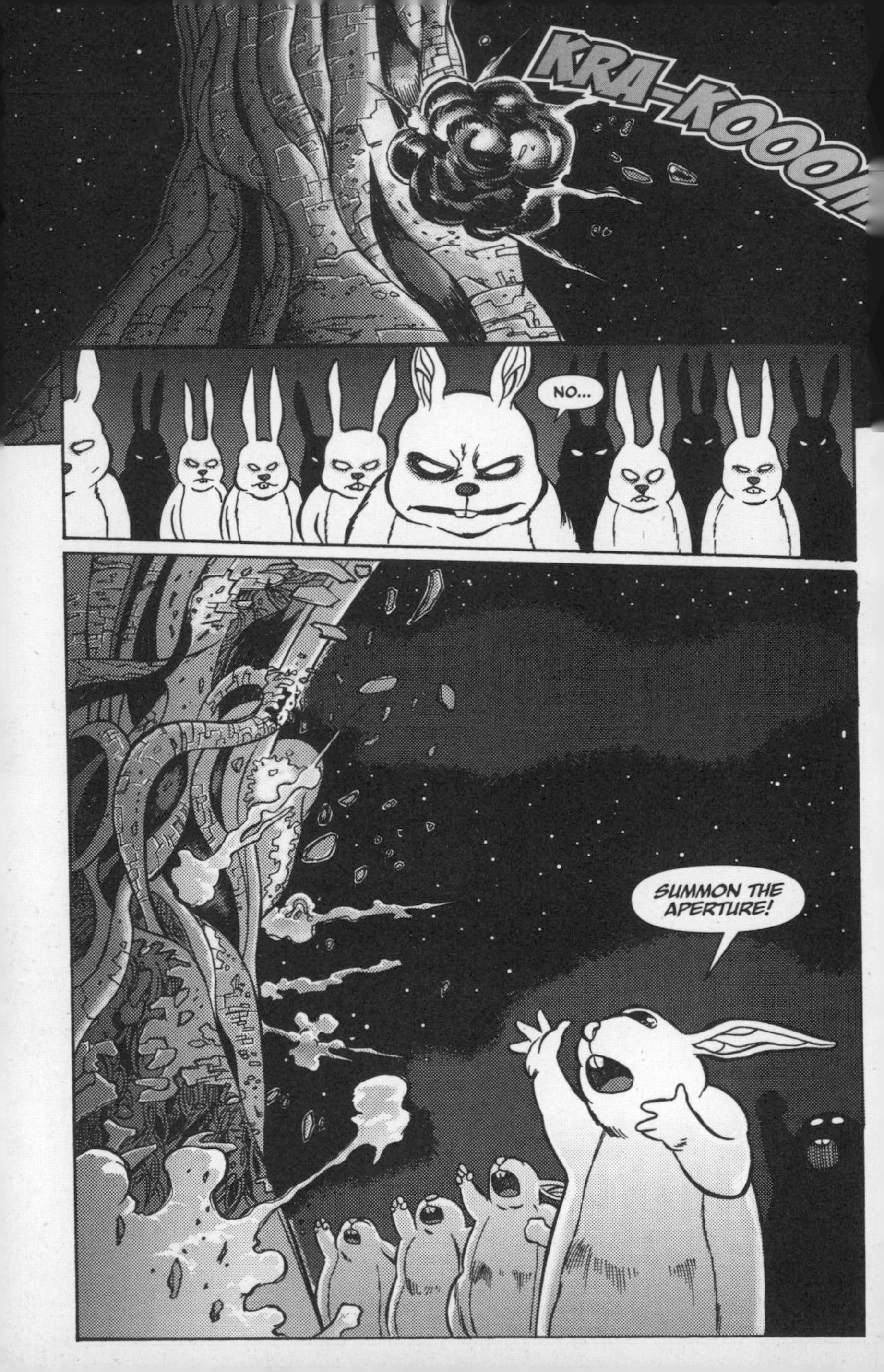
KRA-KOOOM!!
NO...
SUMMON THE APERTURE!

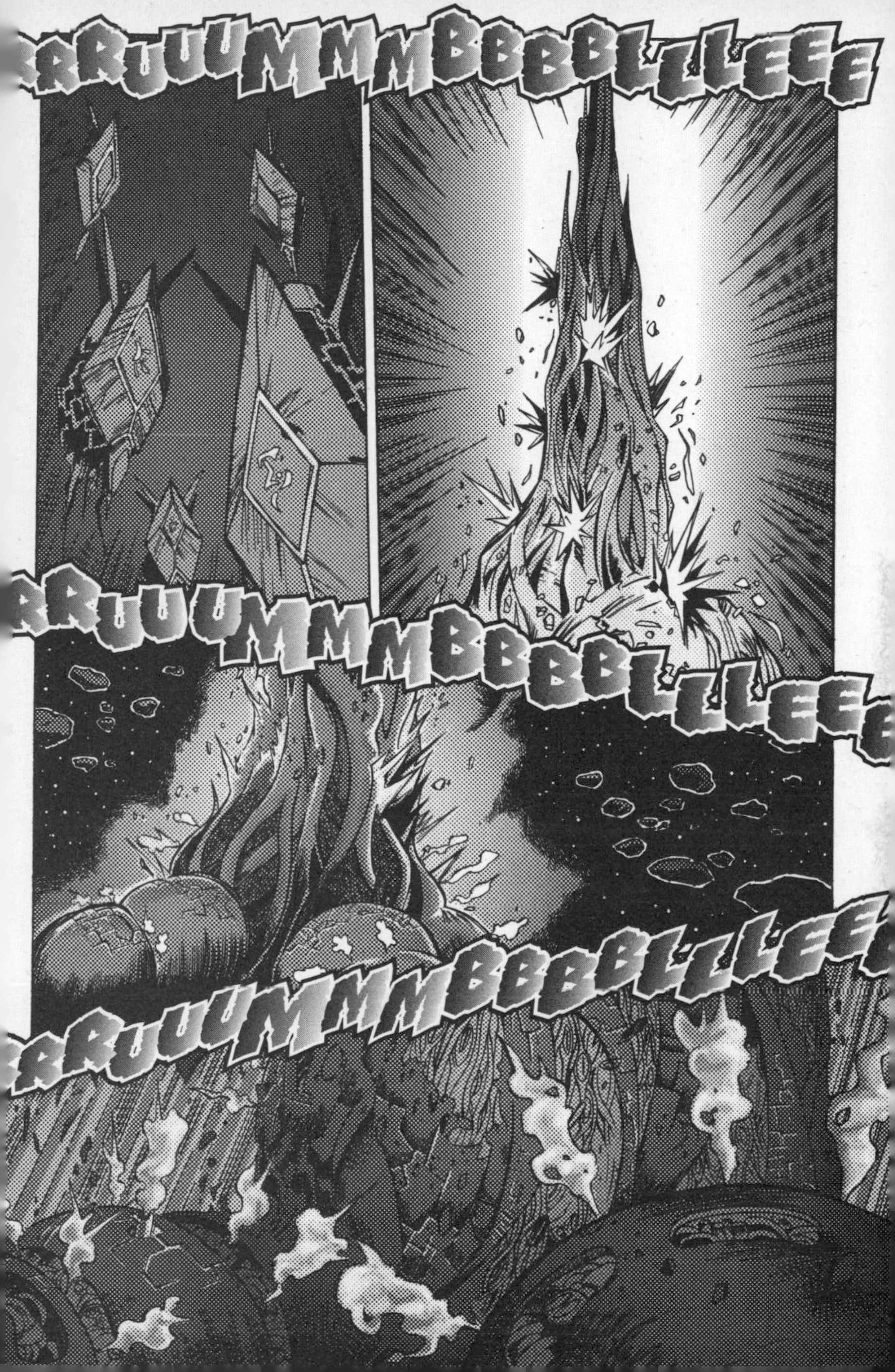
RRUUUMMMBBBBLLLEEE
RRUUUMMMBBBBLLLEEE
RRUUUMMMBBBBLLLEE

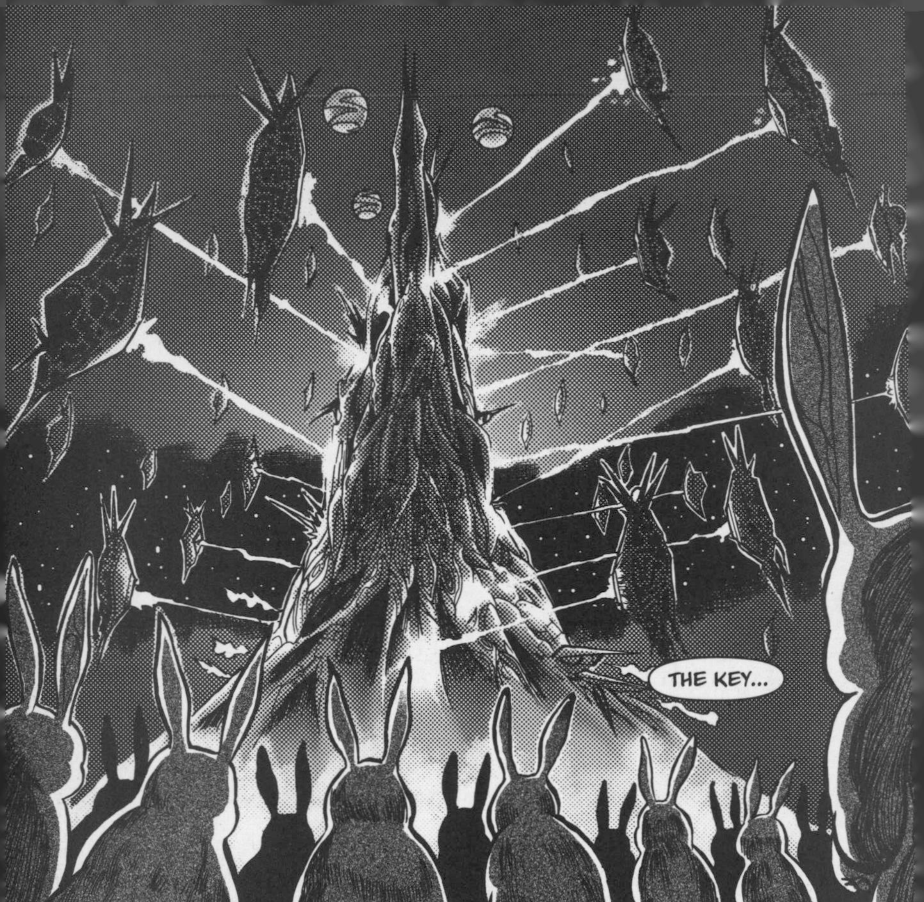
THE KEY...
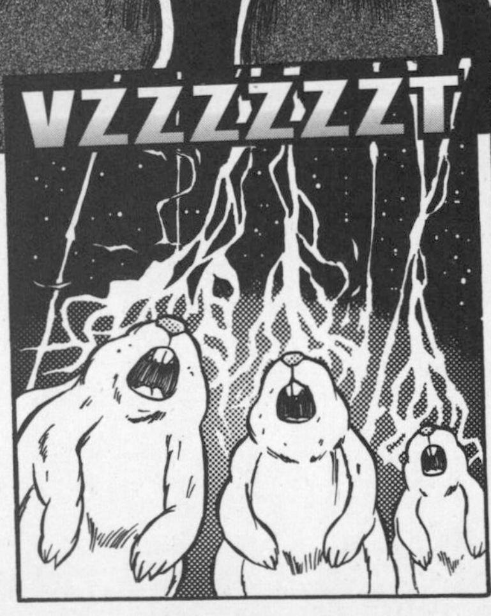
VZZZZZZZT
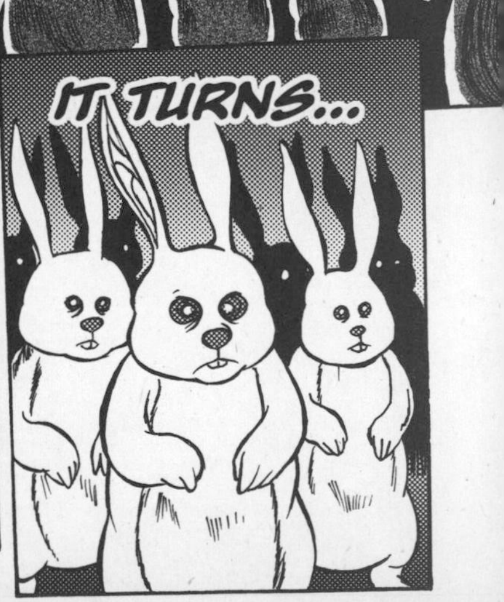
IT TURNS...

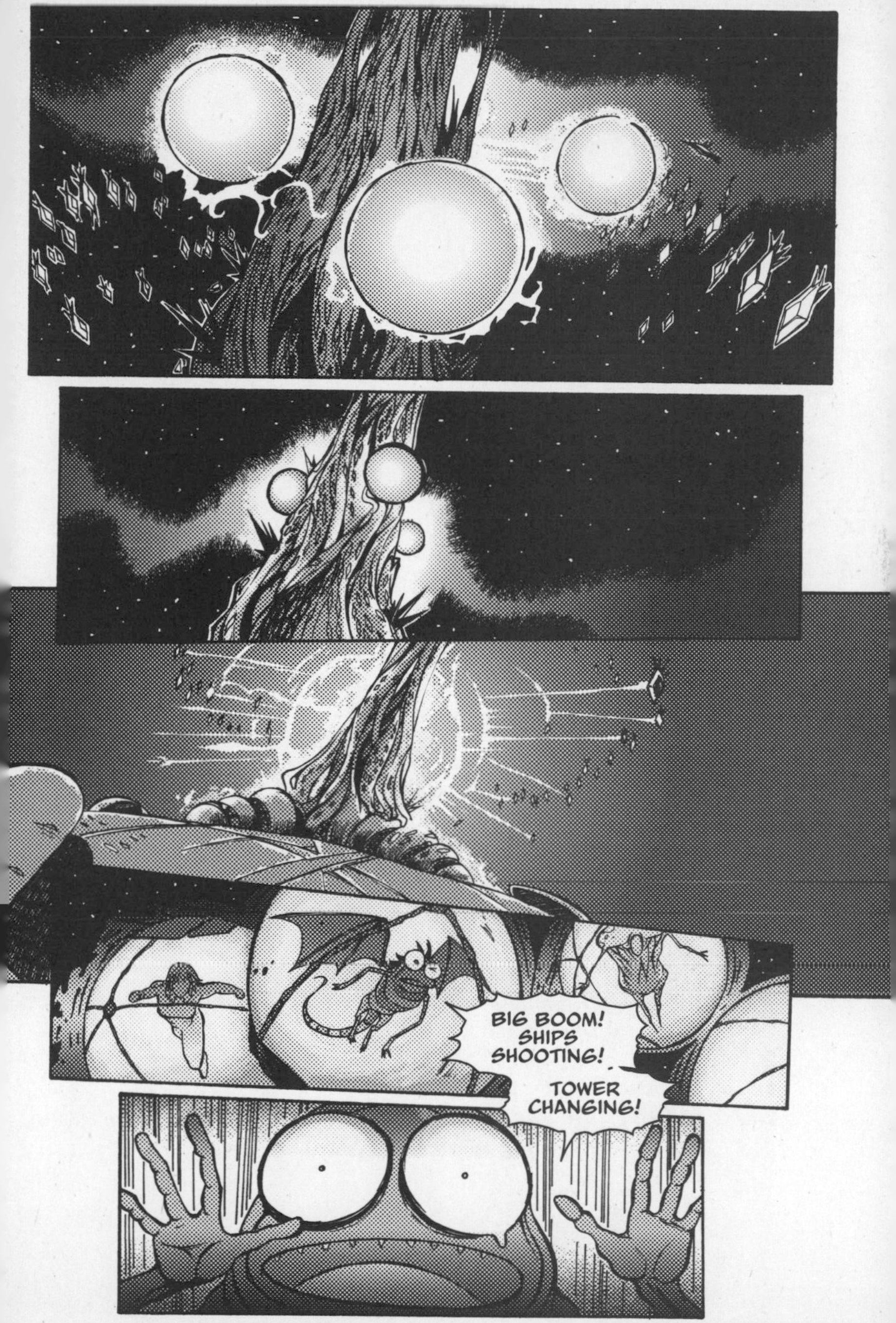
BIG BOOM! SHIPS SHOOTING!
TOWER CHANGING!

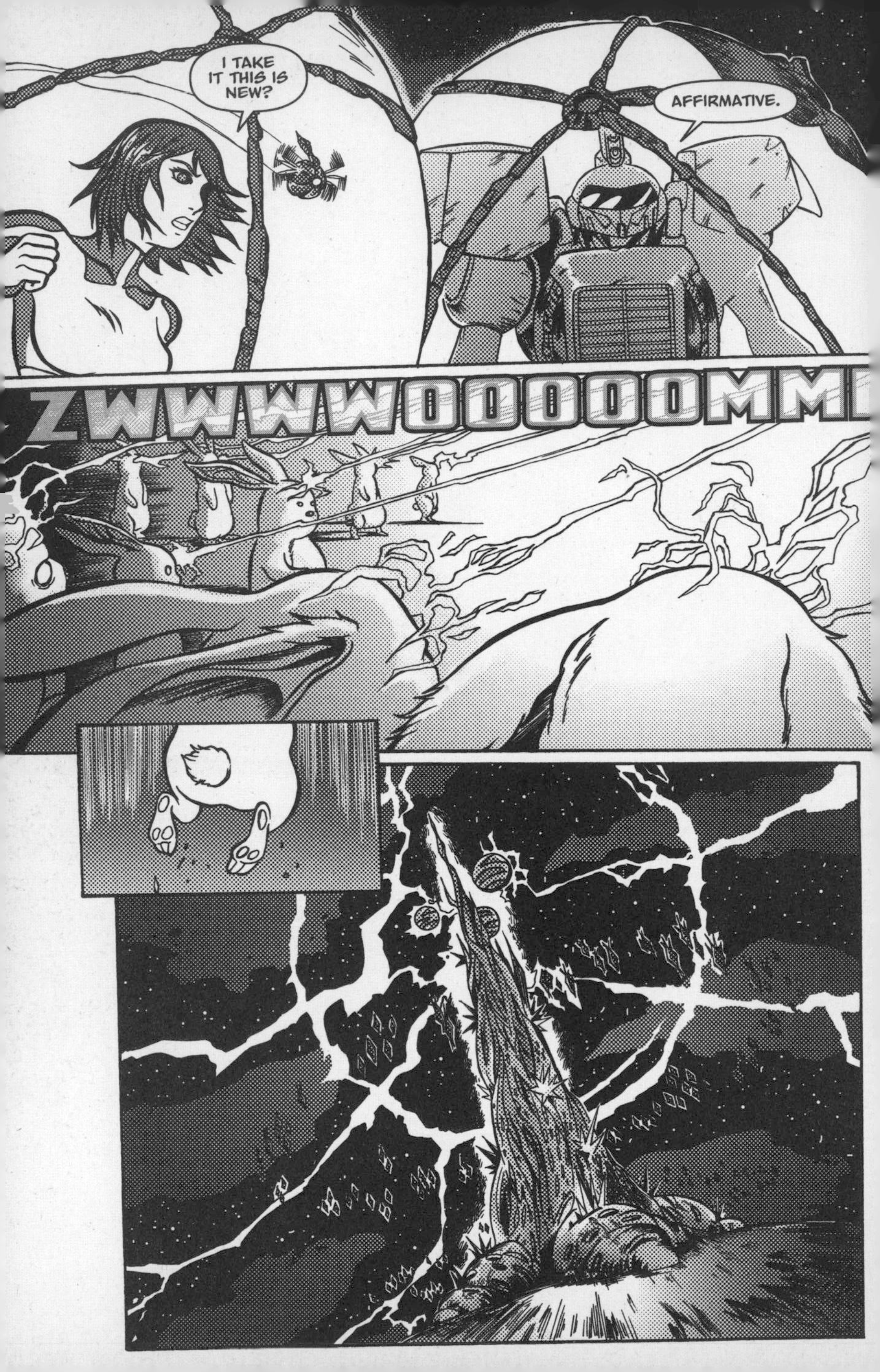
I TAKE IT THIS IS NEW?
AFFIRMATIVE.
ZWWWWOOOOOOMMM

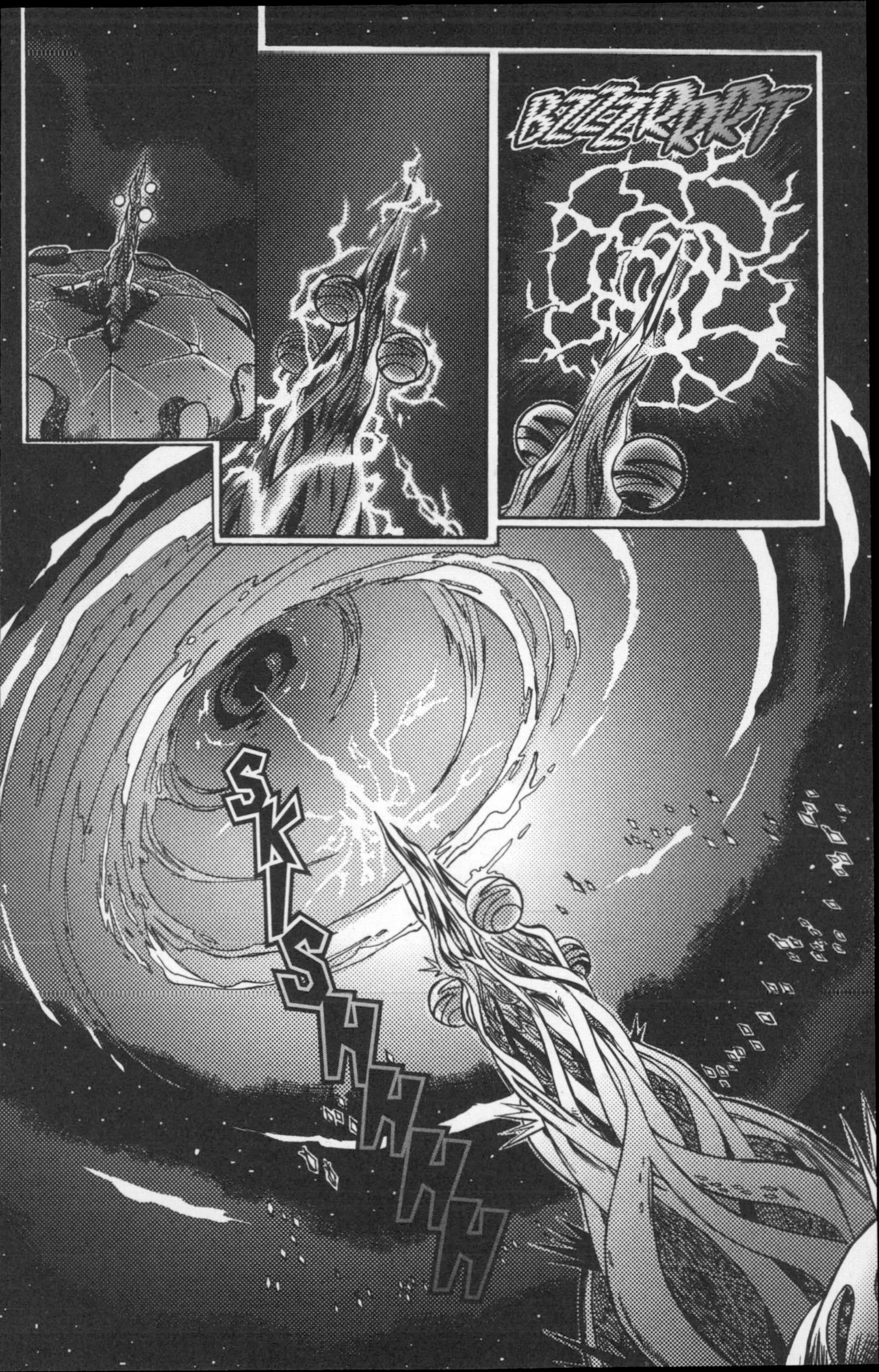
BZZZRRRT
SKISHHHHH

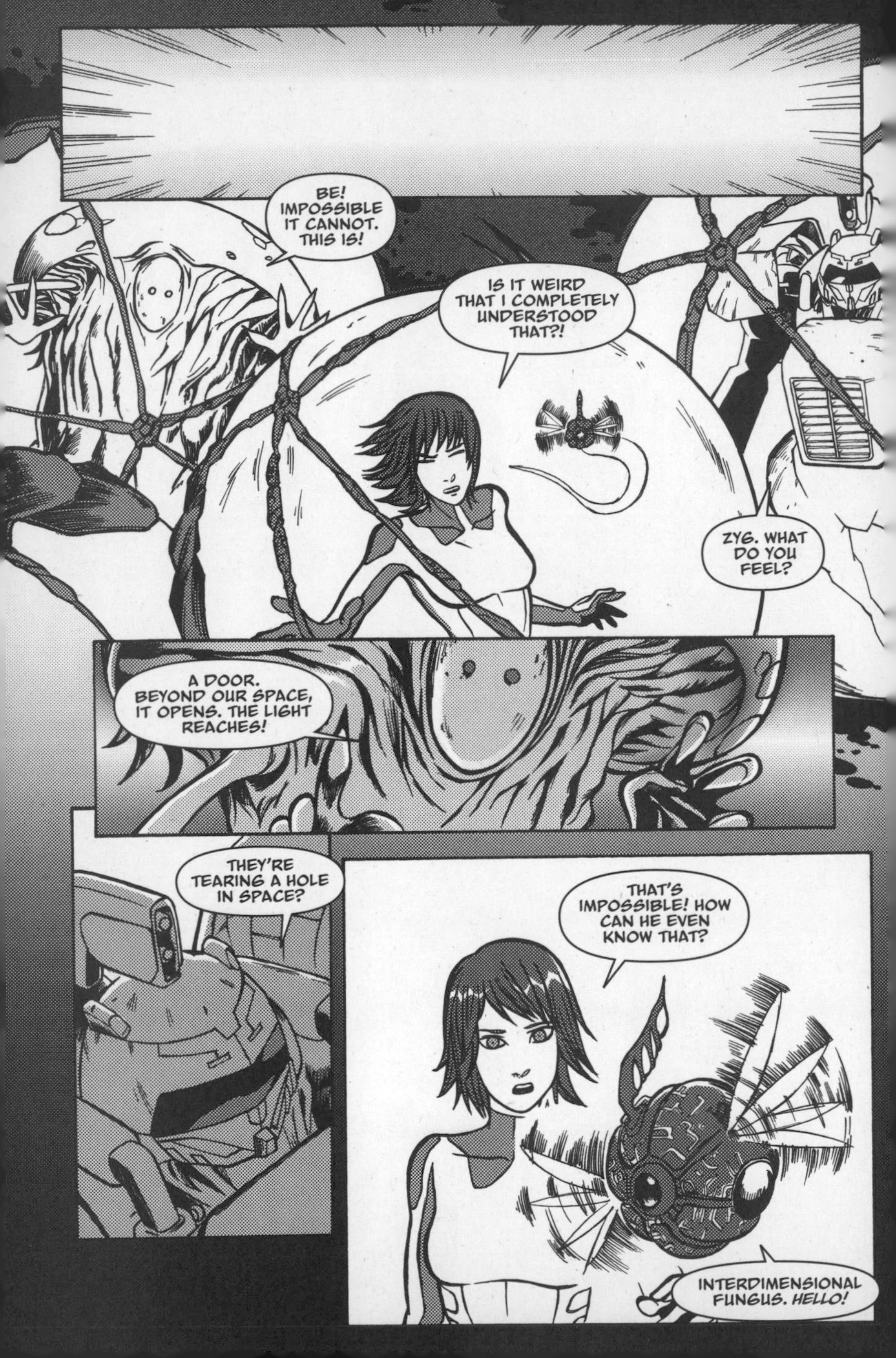
BE! IMPOSSIBLE IT CANNOT. THIS IS!
IS IT WEIRD THAT I COMPLETELY UNDERSTOOD THAT?!
ZYG. WHAT DO YOU FEEL?
A DOOR. BEYOND OUR SPACE, IT OPENS. THE LIGHT REACHES!
THEY'RE TEARING A HOLE IN SPACE?
THAT'S IMPOSSIBLE! HOW CAN HE EVEN KNOW THAT?
INTERDIMENSIONAL FUNGUS. *HELLO!*

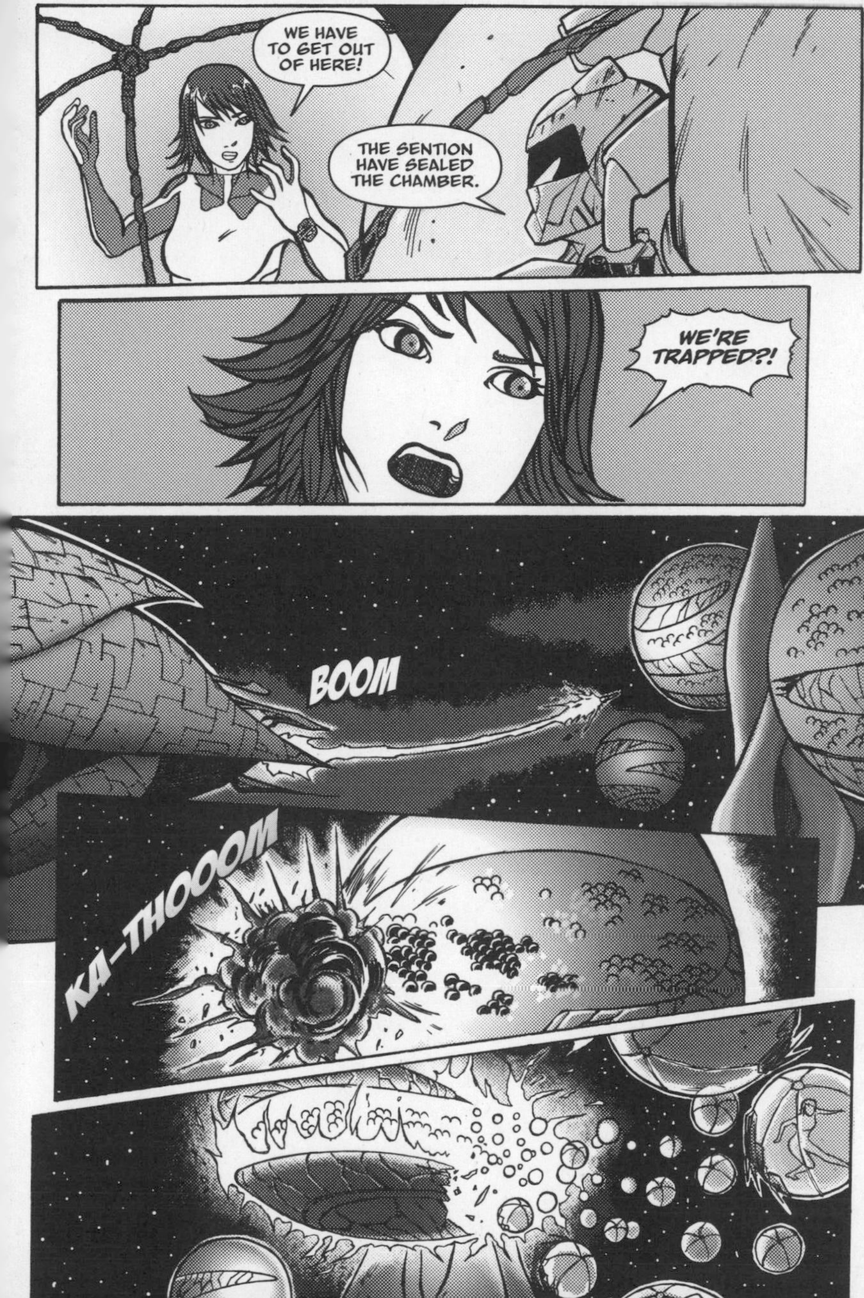
WE HAVE TO GET OUT OF HERE!
THE SENTION HAVE SEALED THE CHAMBER.
WE'RE TRAPPED?!
BOOM
KA-THOOOM

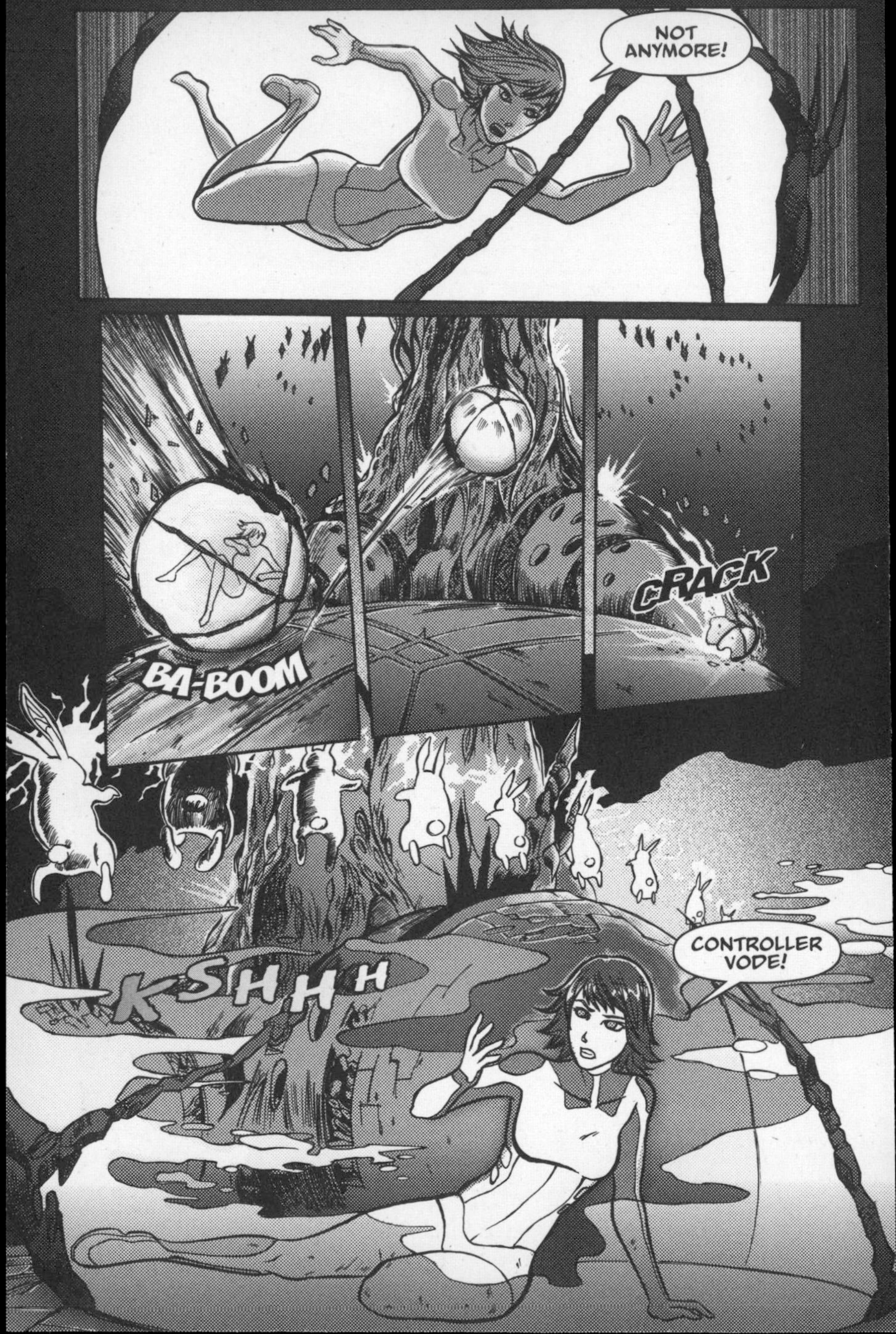
NOT ANYMORE!
BA-BOOM
CRACK
KSHHHH
CONTROLLER VODE!

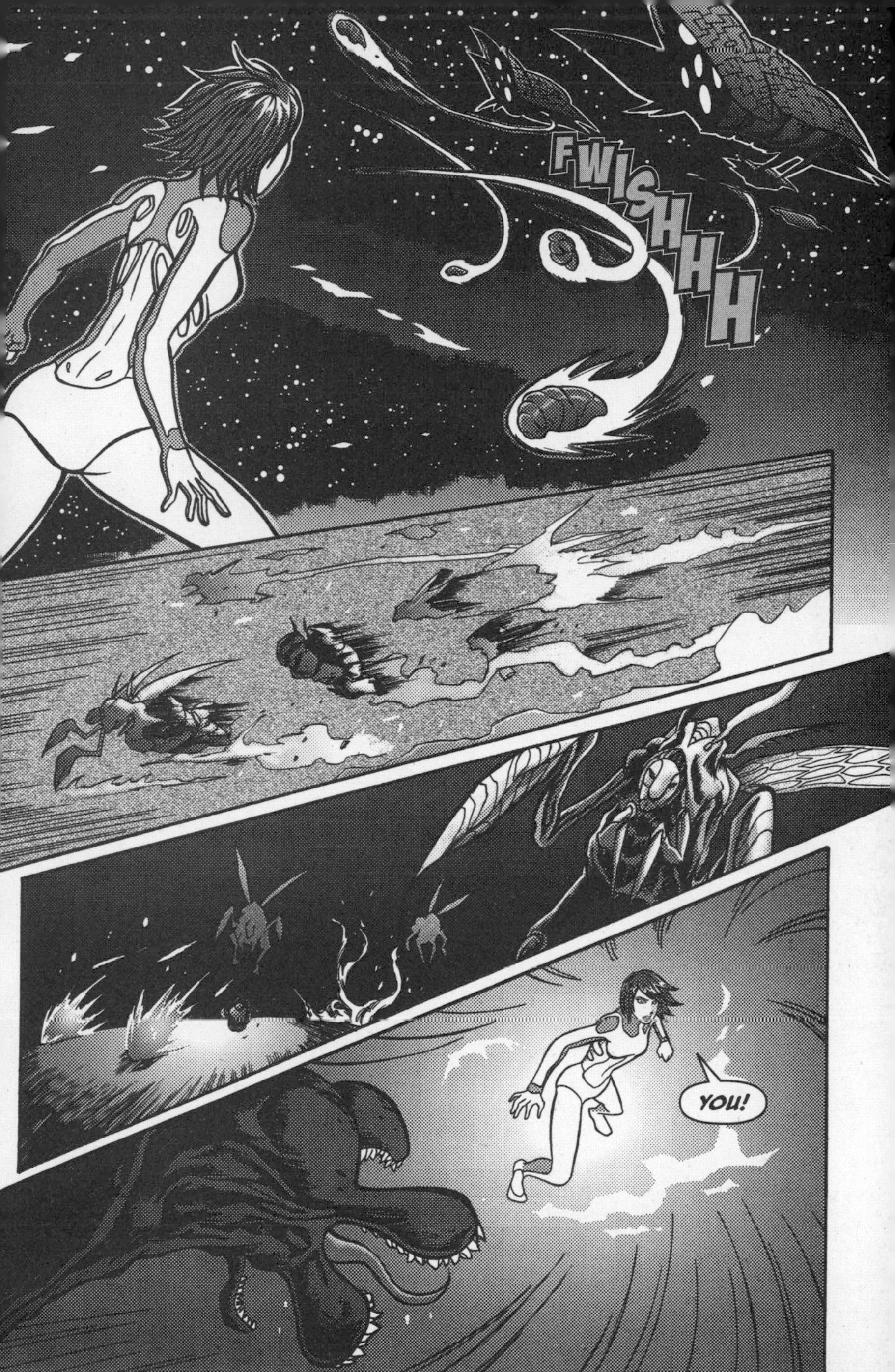
FWISHHHH
YOU!

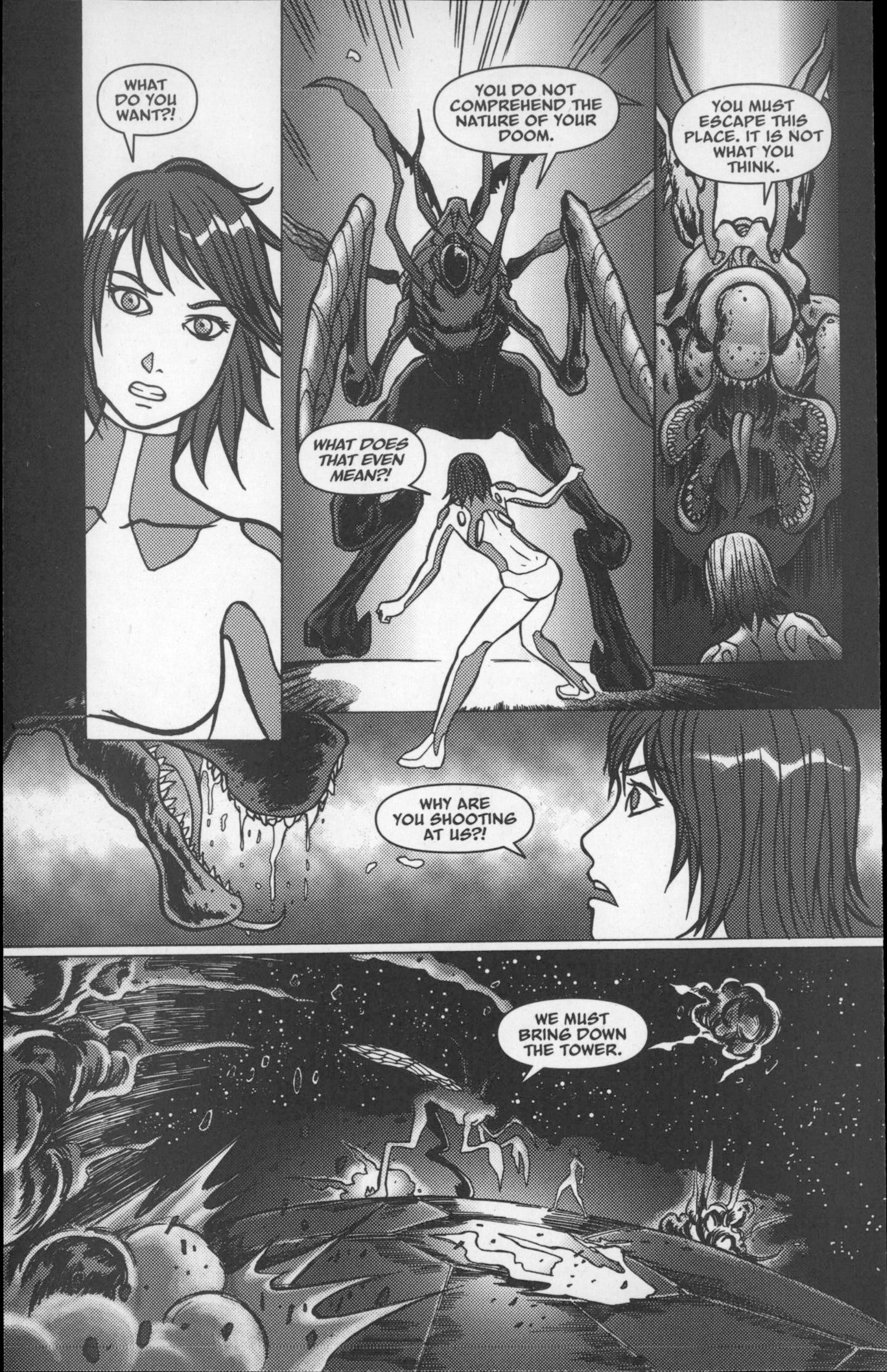
WHAT DO YOU WANT?!
YOU DO NOT COMPREHEND THE NATURE OF YOUR DOOM.
WHAT DOES THAT EVEN MEAN?!
YOU MUST ESCAPE THIS PLACE. IT IS NOT WHAT YOU THINK.
WHY ARE YOU SHOOTING AT US?!
WE MUST BRING DOWN THE TOWER.

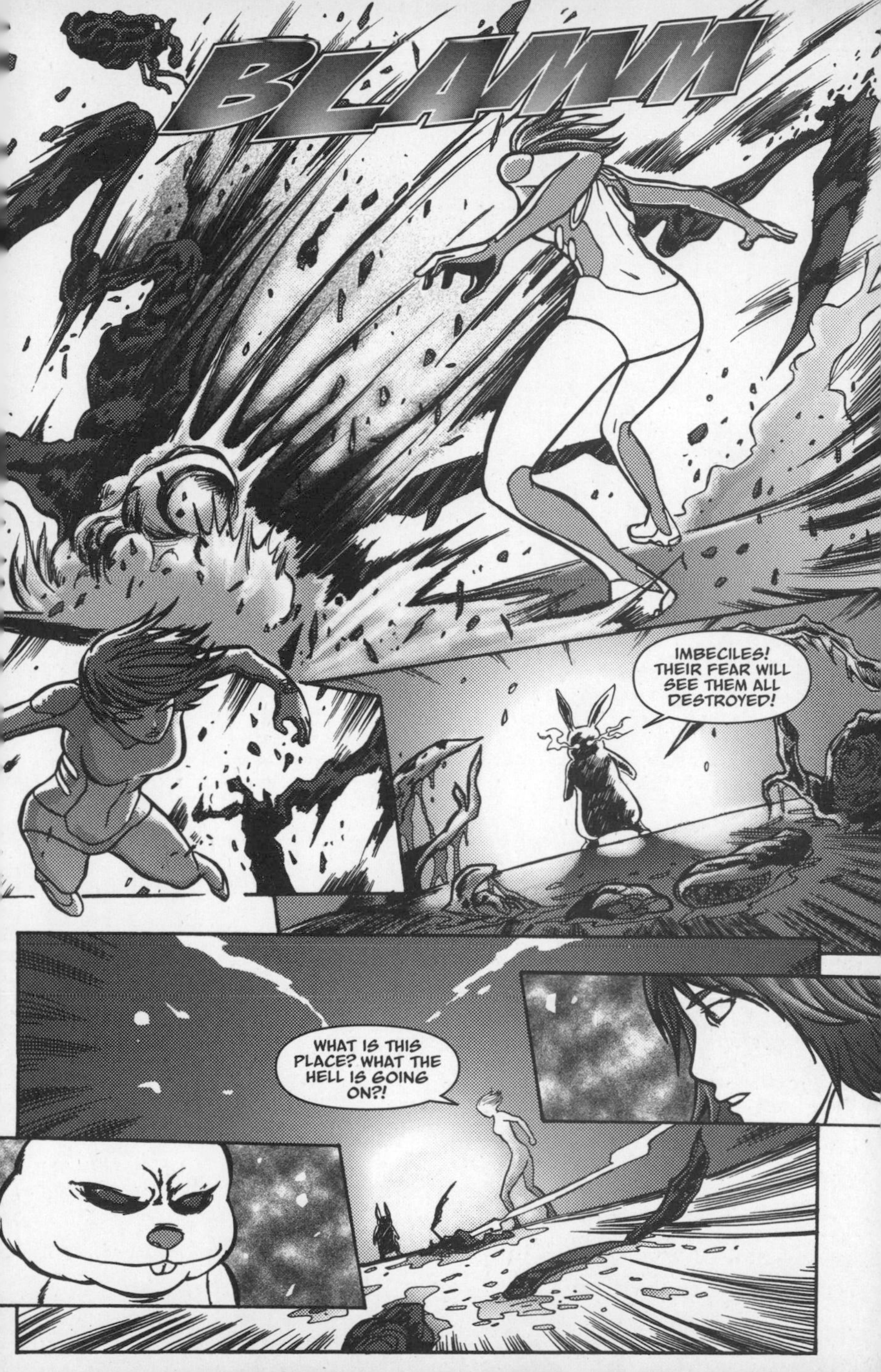
BLAMM
IMBECILES! THEIR FEAR WILL SEE THEM ALL DESTROYED!
WHAT IS THIS PLACE? WHAT THE HELL IS GOING ON?!

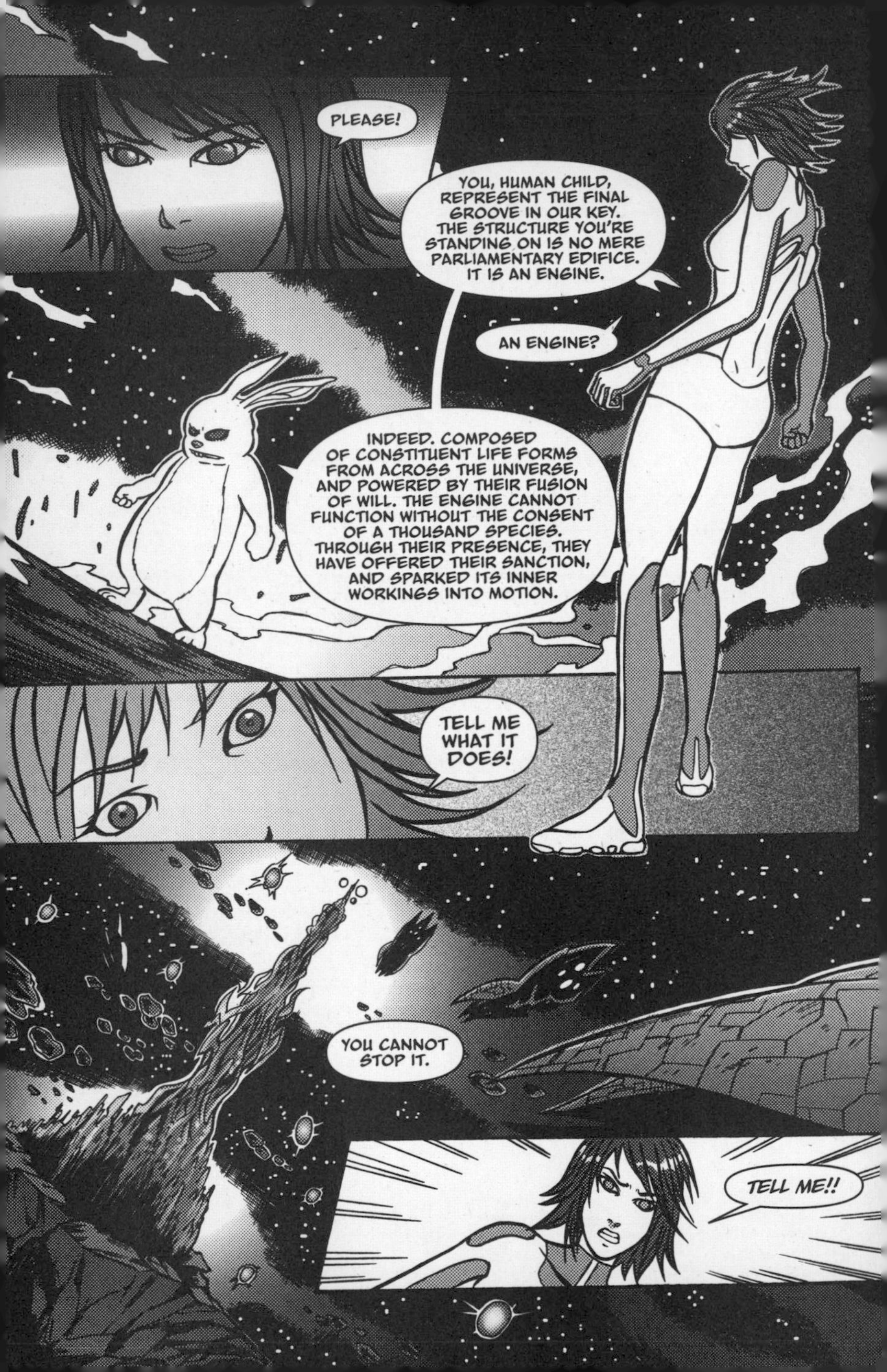
PLEASE!
YOU, HUMAN CHILD, REPRESENT THE FINAL GROOVE IN OUR KEY. THE STRUCTURE YOU'RE STANDING ON IS NO MERE PARLIAMENTARY EDIFICE. IT IS AN ENGINE.
AN ENGINE?
INDEED. COMPOSED OF CONSTITUENT LIFE FORMS FROM ACROSS THE UNIVERSE, AND POWERED BY THEIR FUSION OF WILL. THE ENGINE CANNOT FUNCTION WITHOUT THE CONSENT OF A THOUSAND SPECIES. THROUGH THEIR PRESENCE, THEY HAVE OFFERED THEIR SANCTION, AND SPARKED ITS INNER WORKINGS INTO MOTION.
TELL ME WHAT IT DOES!
YOU CANNOT STOP IT.
TELL ME!!

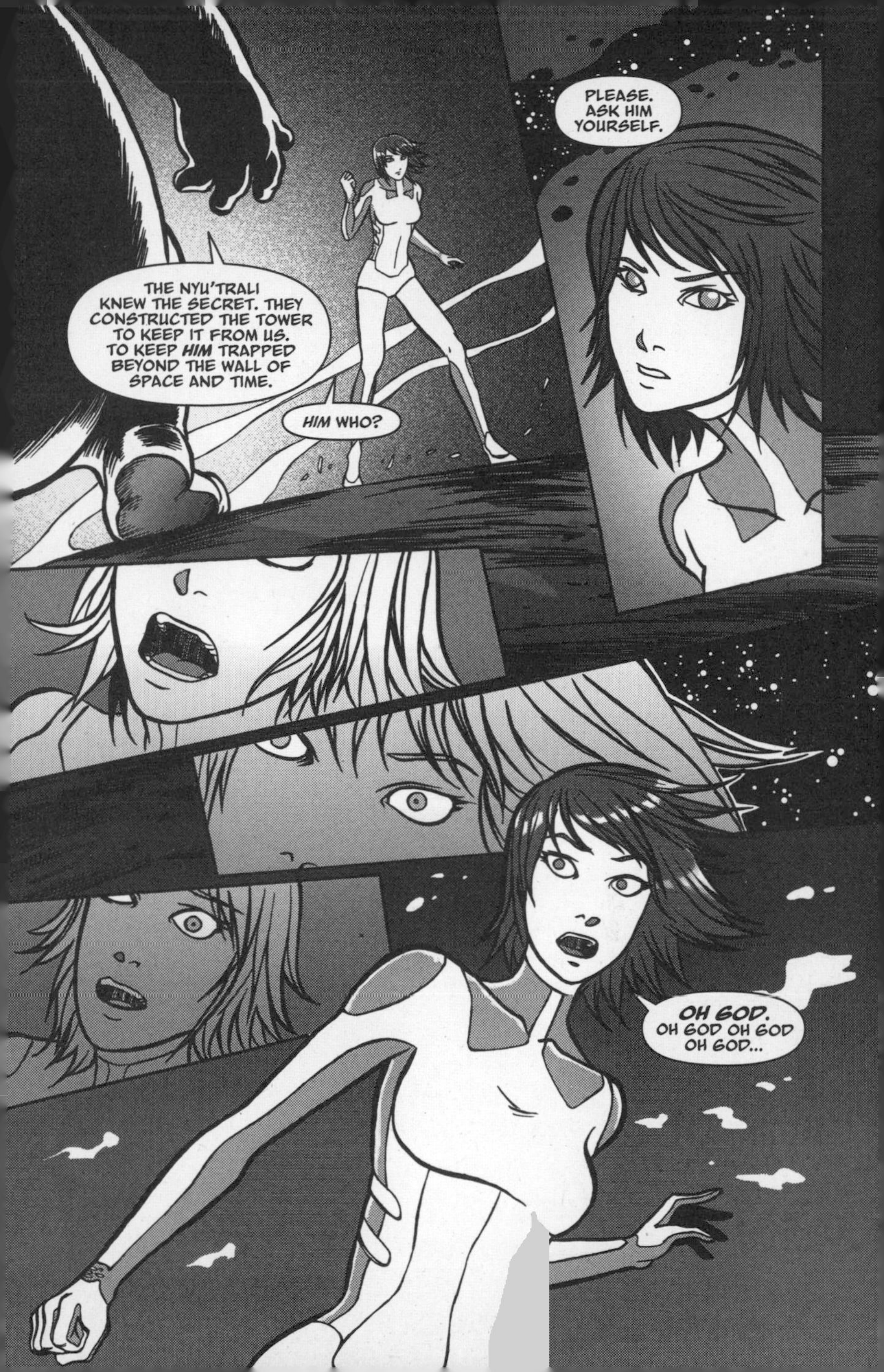
THE NYU'TRALI KNEW THE SECRET. THEY CONSTRUCTED THE TOWER TO KEEP IT FROM US. TO KEEP HIM TRAPPED BEYOND THE WALL OF SPACE AND TIME.
HIM WHO?
PLEASE. ASK HIM YOURSELF.
OH GOD. OH GOD OH GOD OH GOD...

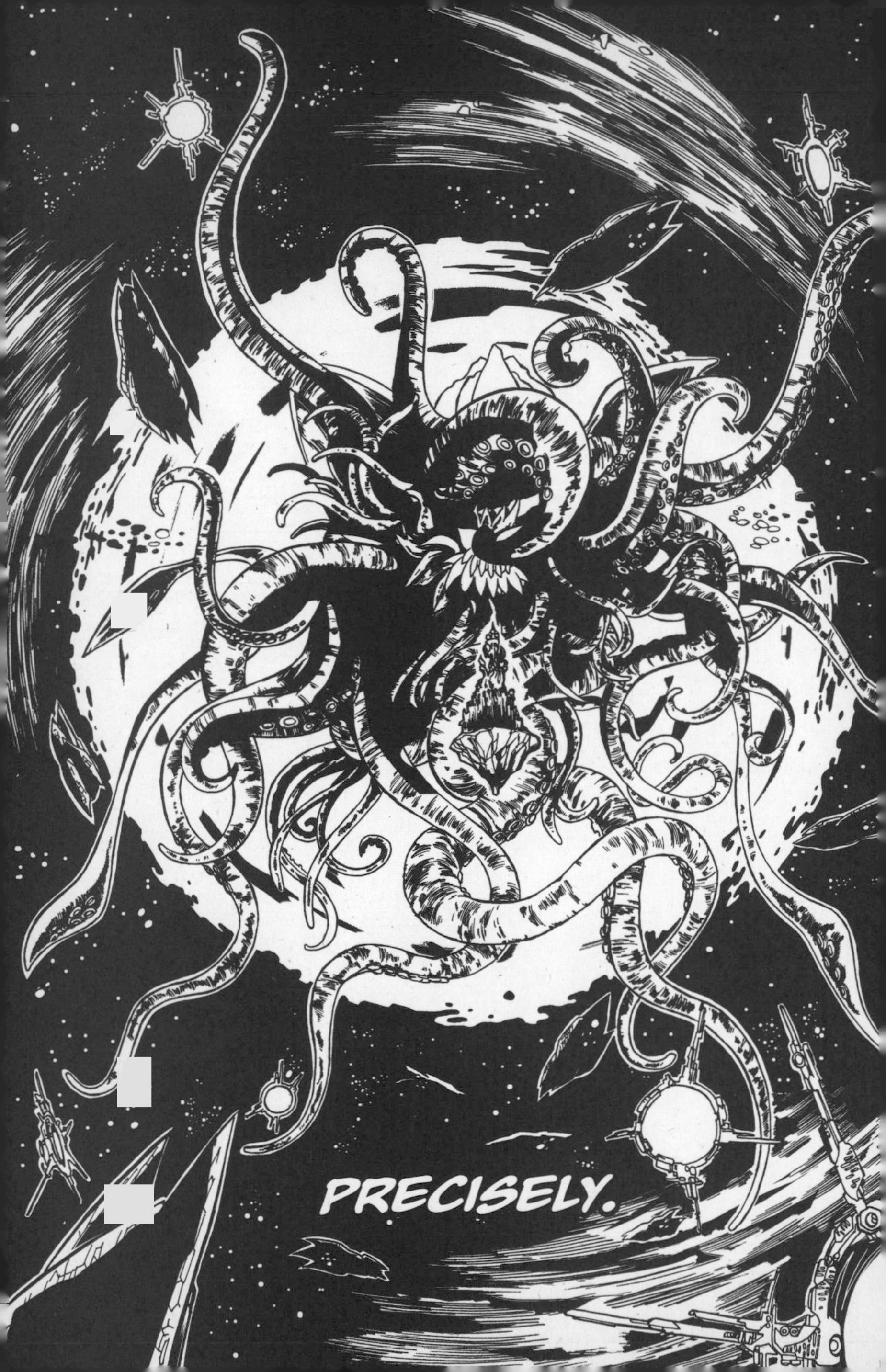
PRECISELY.

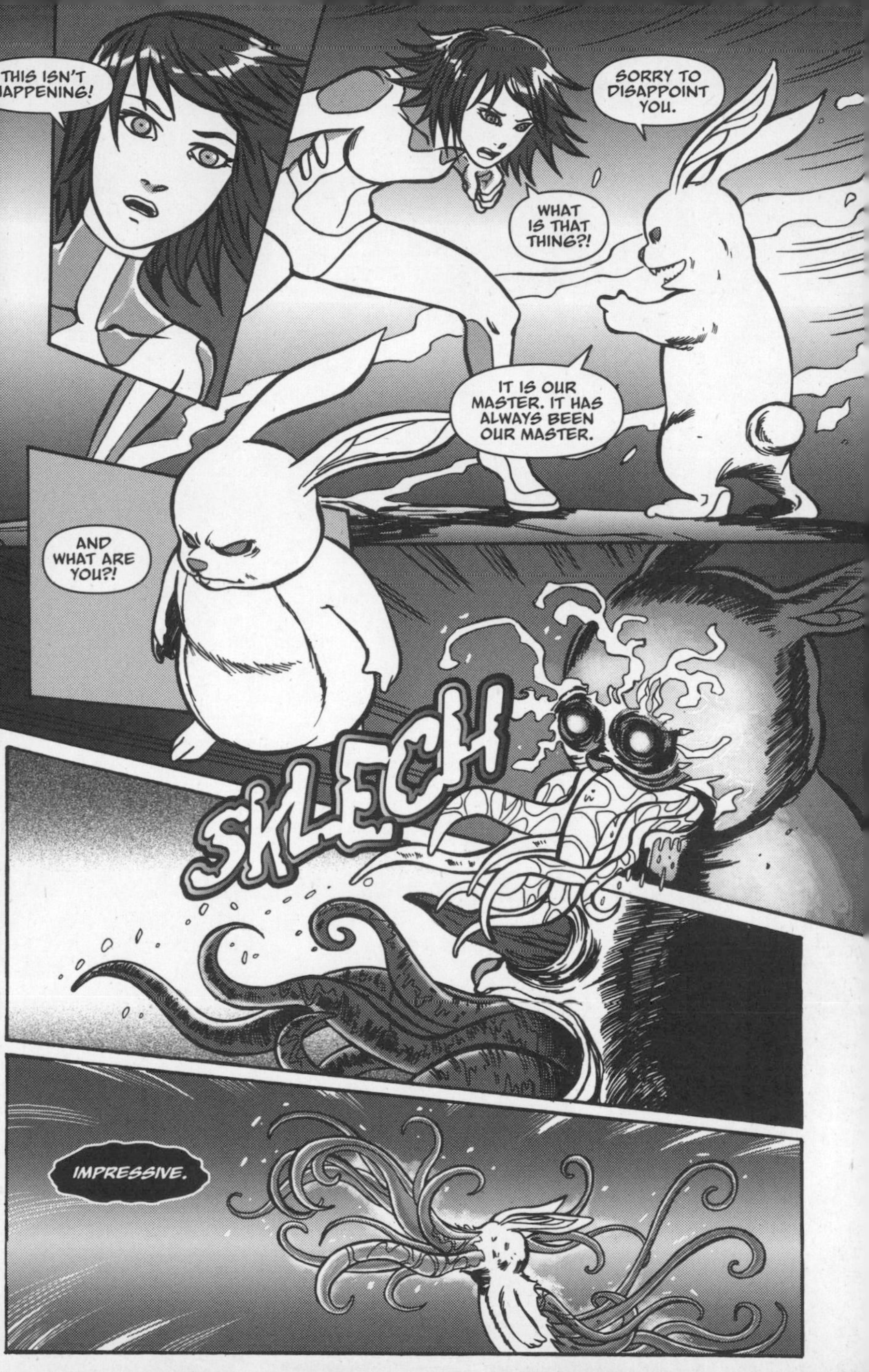
THIS ISN'T HAPPENING!
SORRY TO DISAPPOINT YOU.
WHAT IS THAT THING?!
IT IS OUR MASTER. IT HAS ALWAYS BEEN OUR MASTER.
AND WHAT ARE YOU?!
SKLECH
IMPRESSIVE.

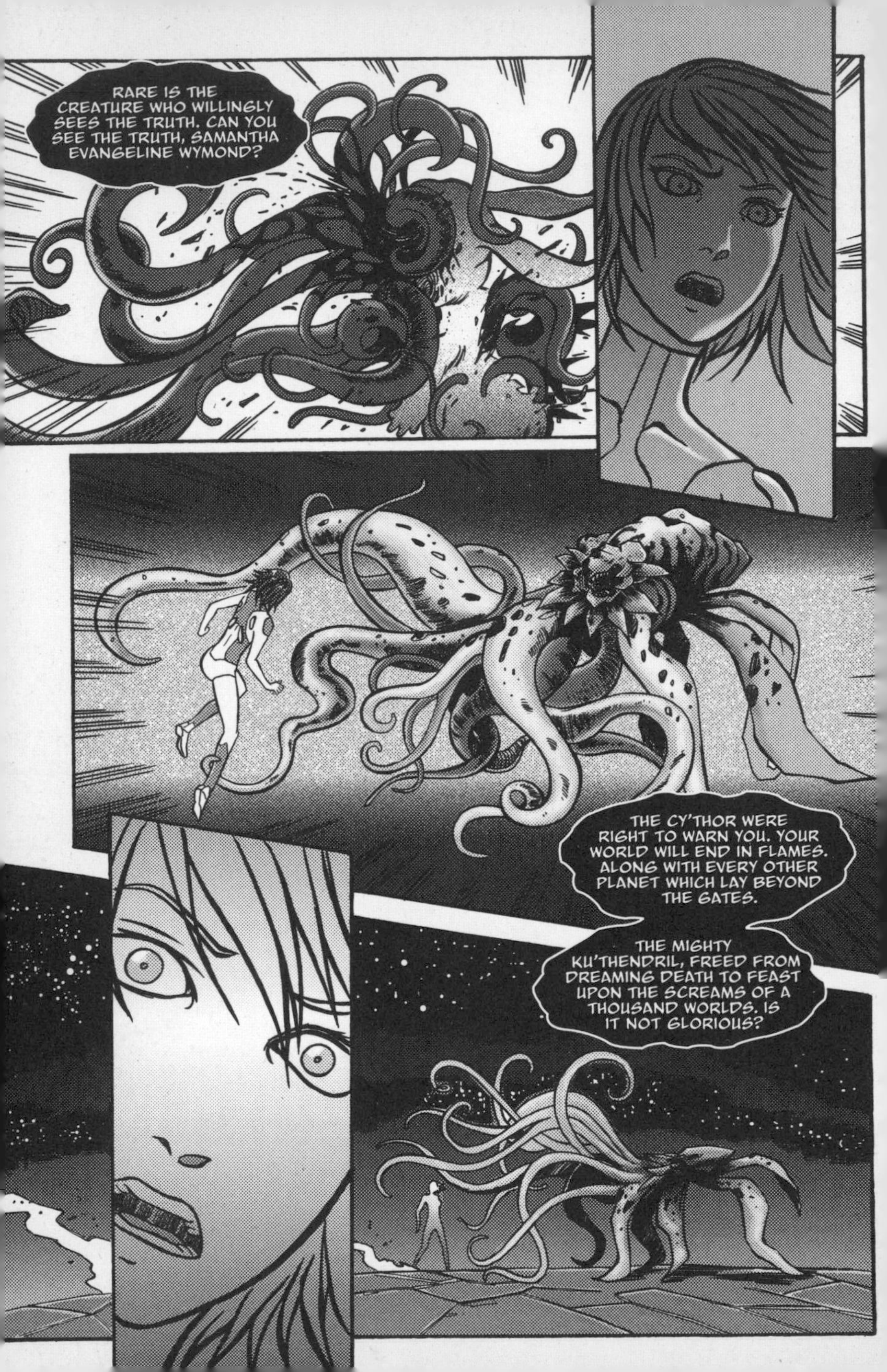
RARE IS THE CREATURE WHO WILLINGLY SEES THE TRUTH. CAN YOU SEE THE TRUTH, SAMANTHA EVANGELINE WYMOND?
THE CY'THOR WERE RIGHT TO WARN YOU. YOUR WORLD WILL END IN FLAMES. ALONG WITH EVERY OTHER PLANET WHICH LAY BEYOND THE GATES.
THE MIGHTY KU'THENDRIL, FREED FROM DREAMING DEATH TO FEAST UPON THE SCREAMS OF A THOUSAND WORLDS. IS IT NOT GLORIOUS?

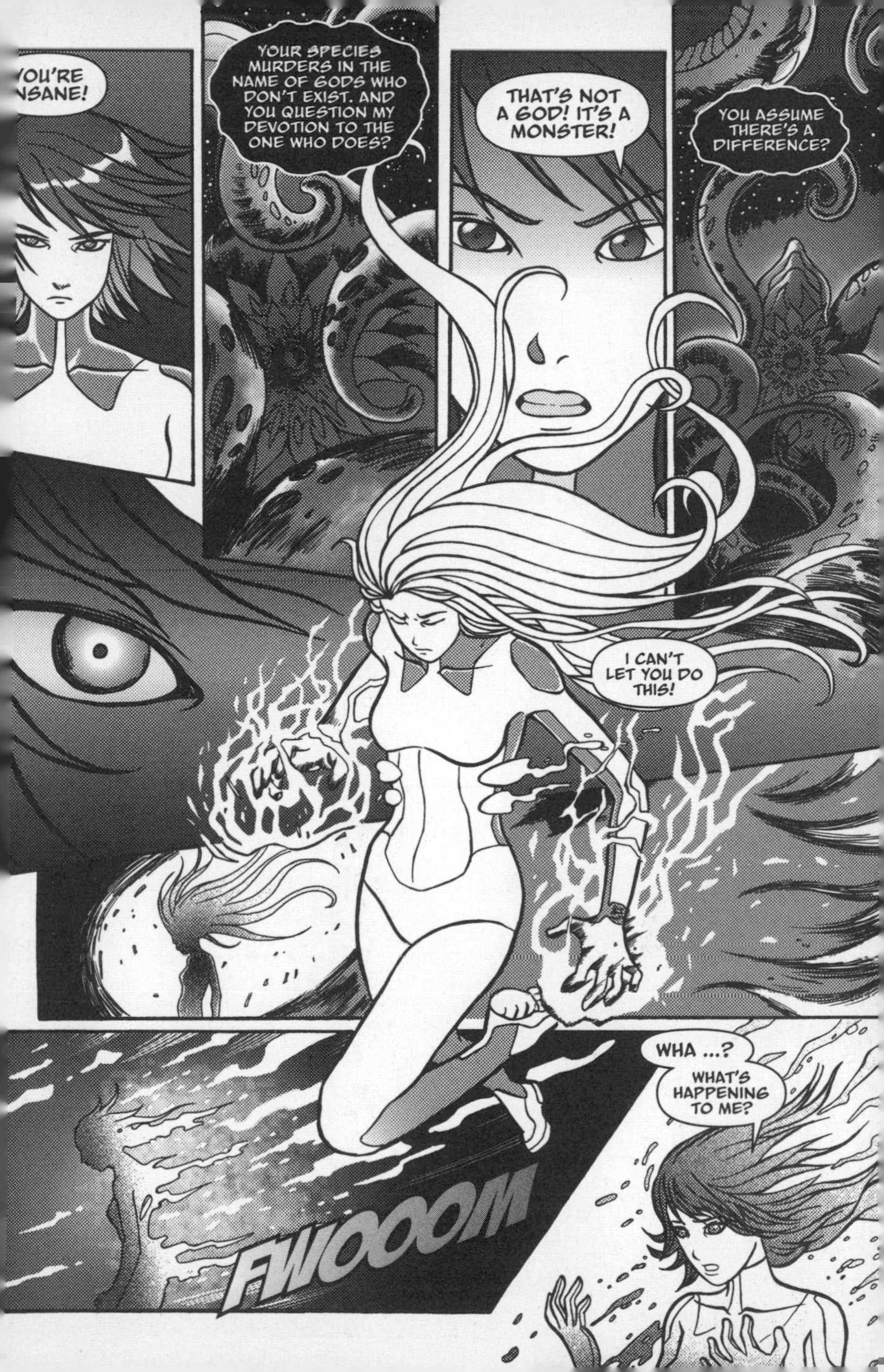
YOU'RE INSANE!
YOUR SPECIES MURDERS IN THE NAME OF GODS WHO DON'T EXIST. AND YOU QUESTION MY DEVOTION TO THE ONE WHO DOES?
THAT'S NOT A GOD! IT'S A MONSTER!
YOU ASSUME THERE'S A DIFFERENCE?
I CAN'T LET YOU DO THIS!
FWOOOM
WHA ...?
WHAT'S HAPPENING TO ME?

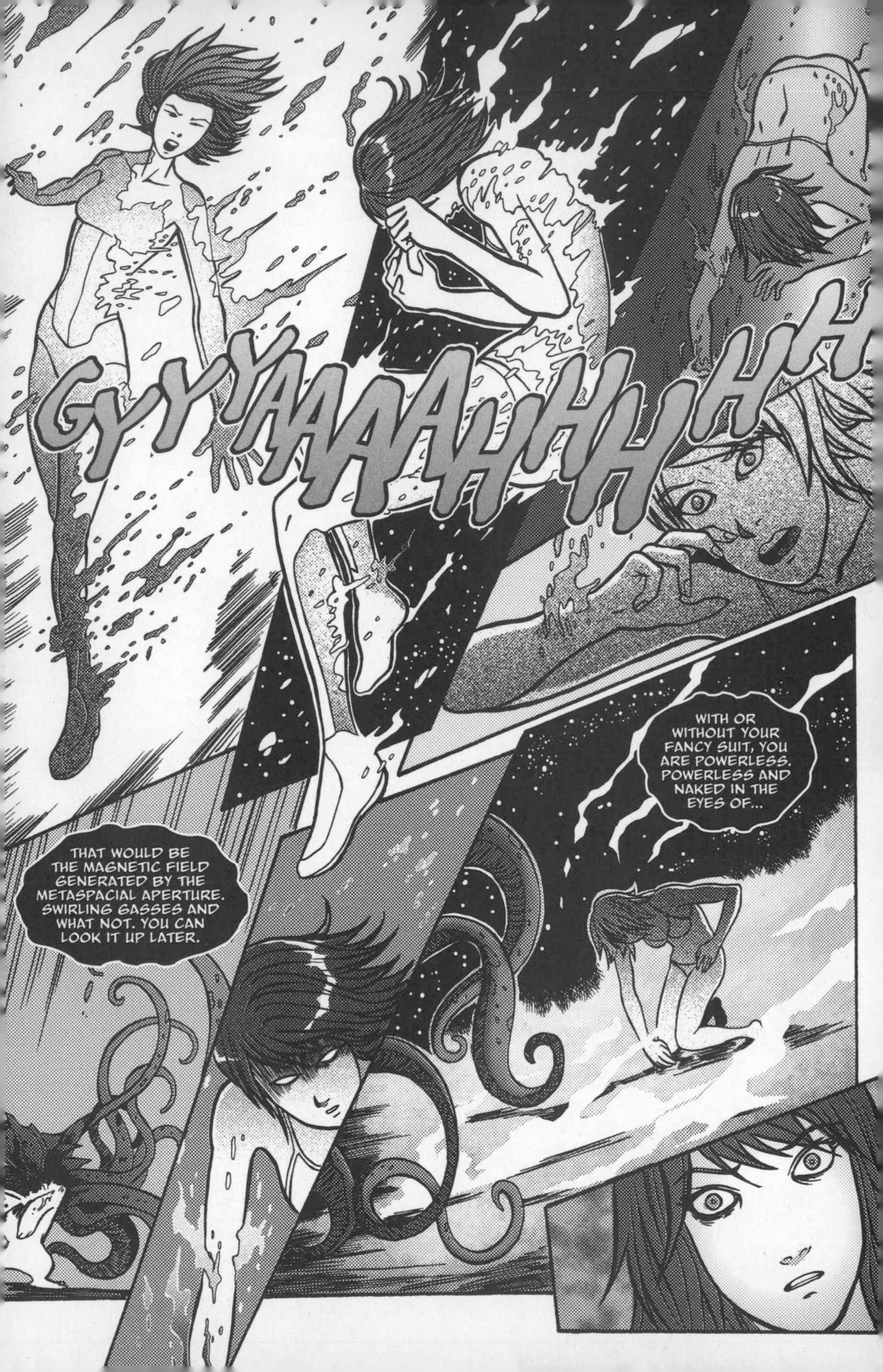
GYYYAAAAAHHHHHH
THAT WOULD BE THE MAGNETIC FIELD GENERATED BY THE METASPACIAL APERTURE. SWIRLING GASSES AND WHAT NOT. YOU CAN LOOK IT UP LATER.
WITH OR WITHOUT YOUR FANCY SUIT, YOU ARE POWERLESS. POWERLESS AND NAKED IN THE EYES OF...

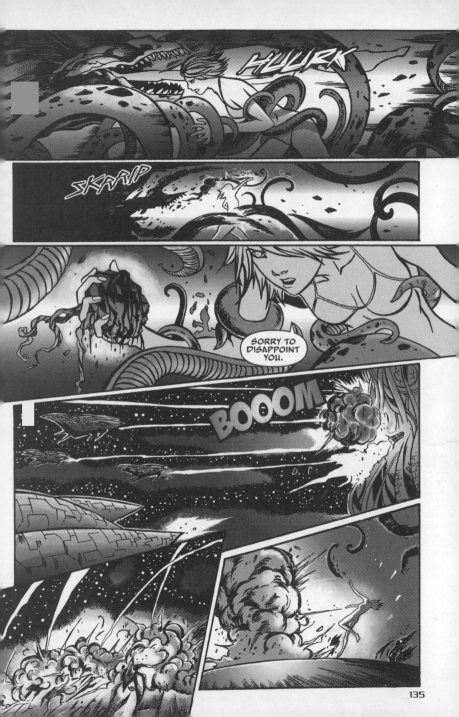

SORRY TO DISAPPOINT YOU.

135

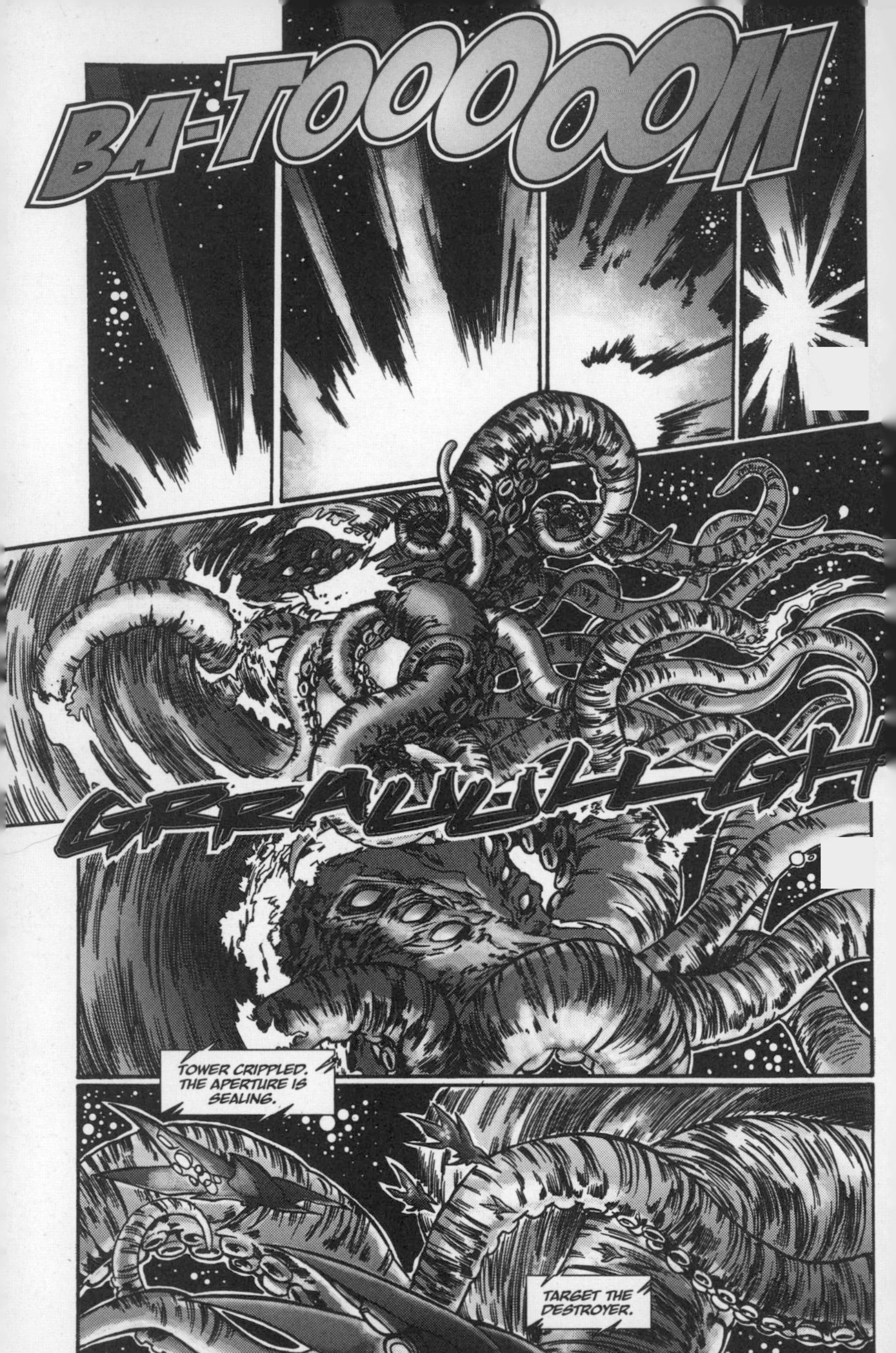
BA-TOOOOOM
GRRALLLLGH
TOWER CRIPPLED. THE APERTURE IS SEALING.
TARGET THE DESTROYER.

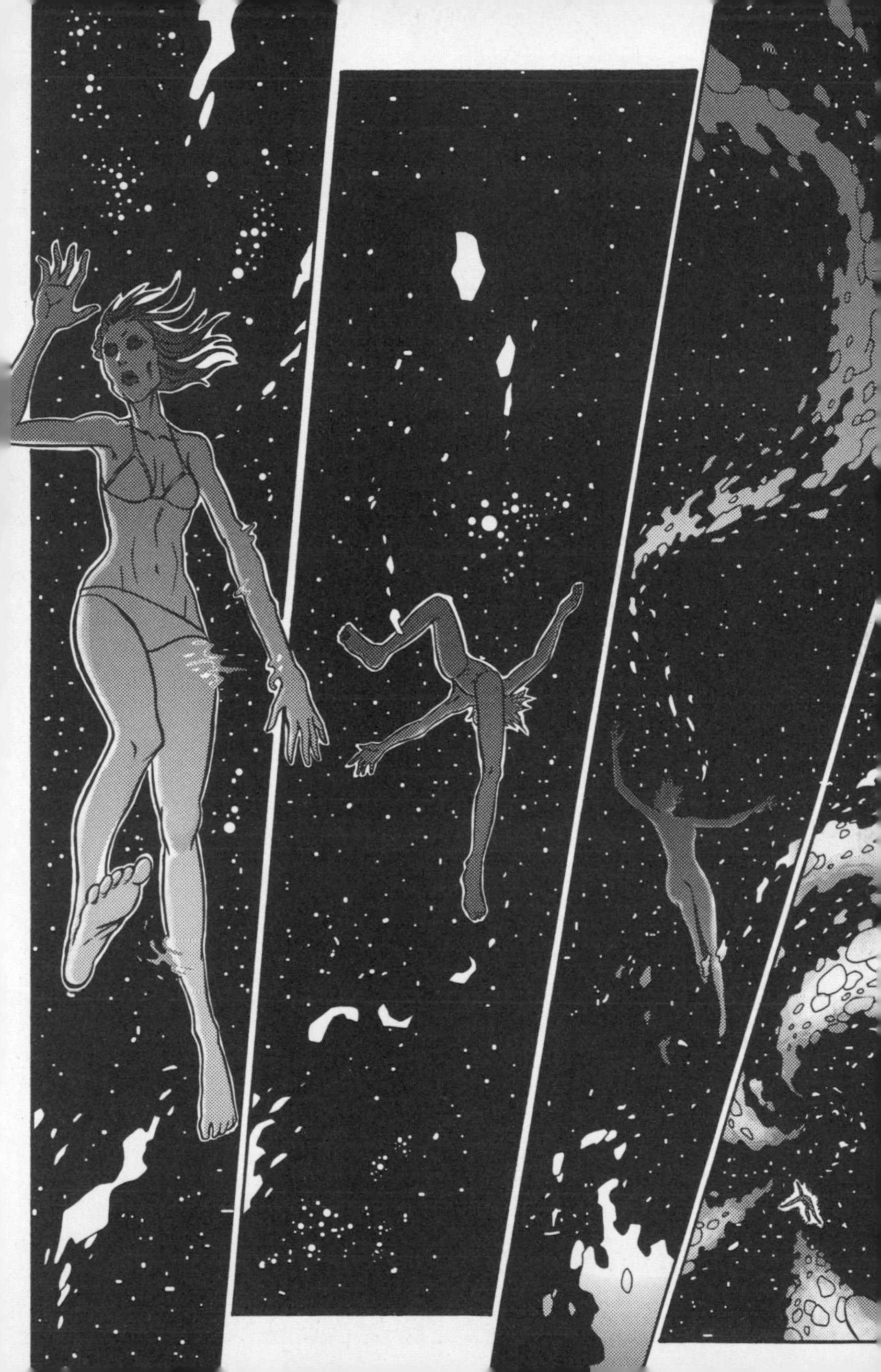

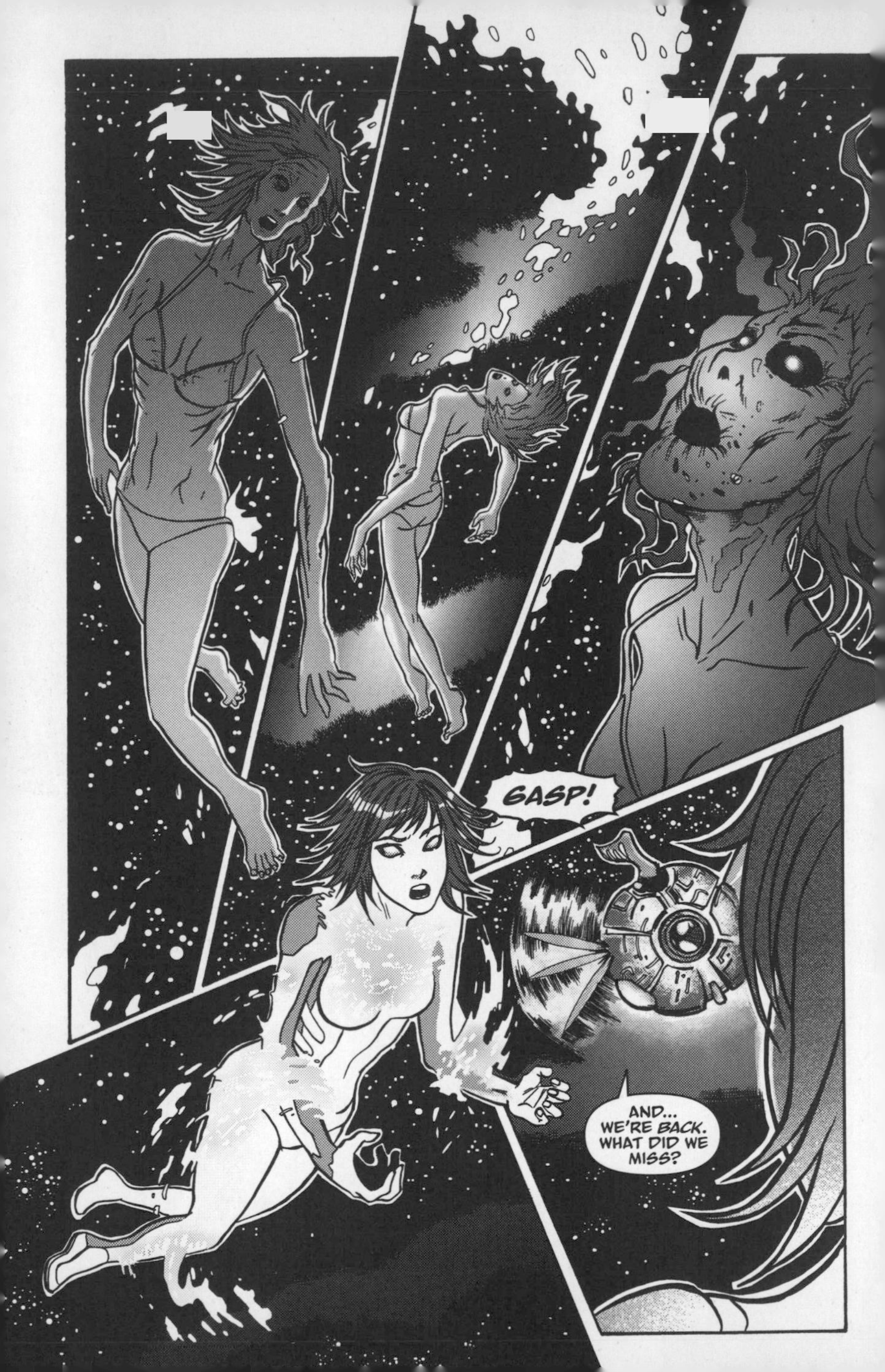
GASP!
AND... WE'RE BACK. WHAT DID WE MISS?

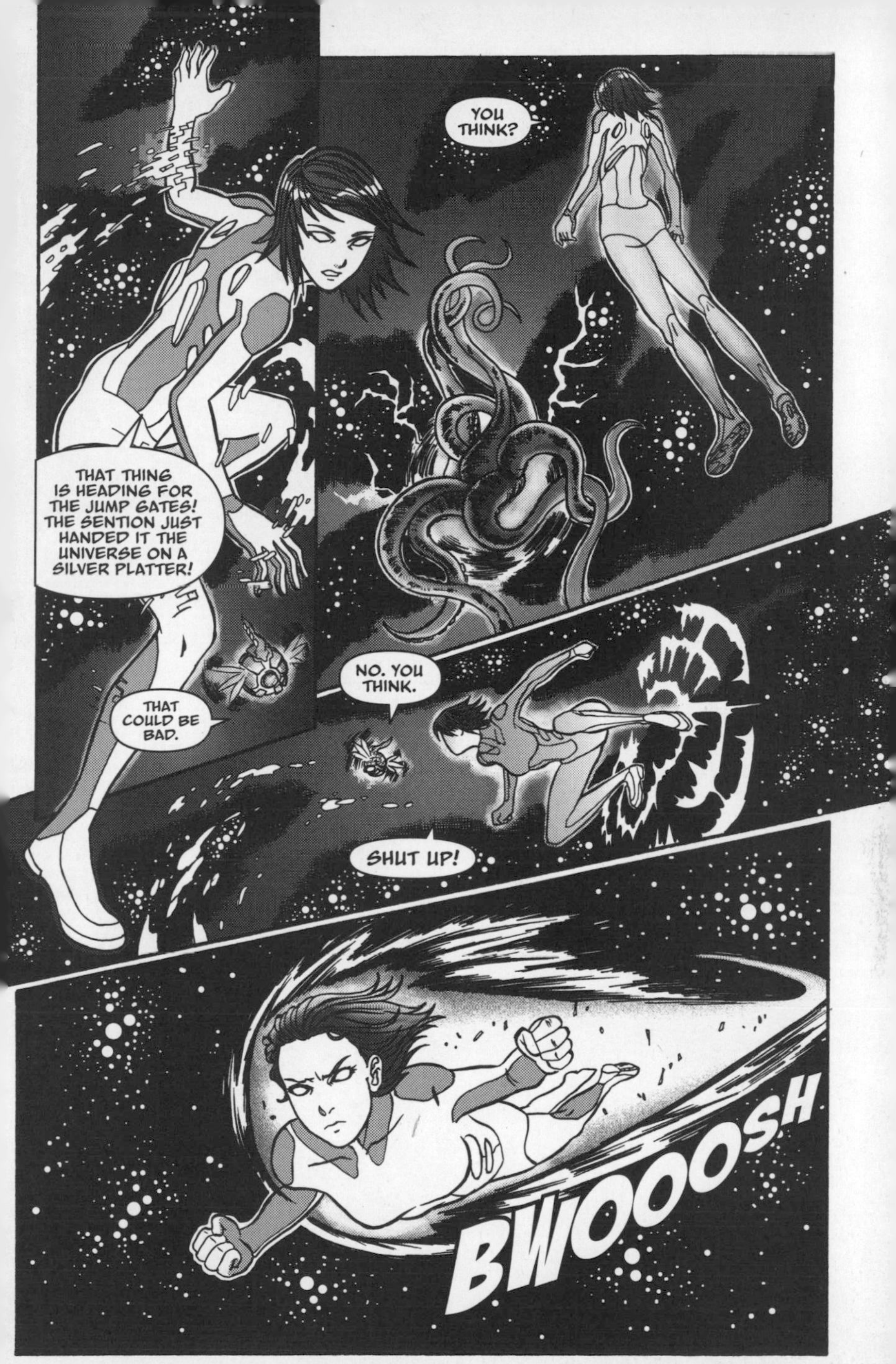

THAT THING IS HEADING FOR THE JUMP GATES! THE SENTION JUST HANDED IT THE UNIVERSE ON A SILVER PLATTER!
YOU THINK?
THAT COULD BE BAD.
NO. YOU THINK.
SHUT UP!
BWOOOOSH

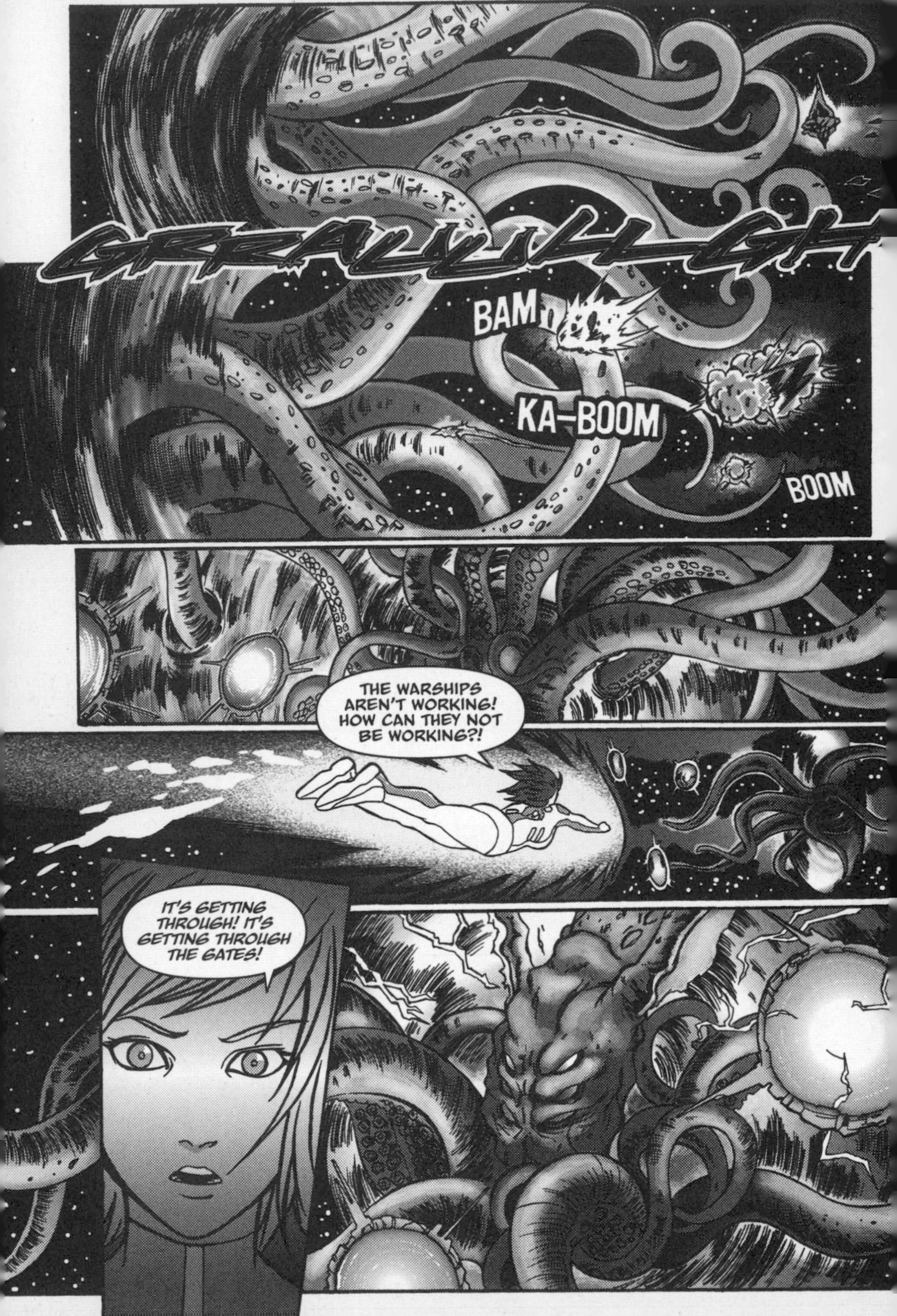
GRRAUUUGH
BAM
KA-BOOM
BOOM
THE WARSHIPS AREN'T WORKING! HOW CAN THEY NOT BE WORKING?!
IT'S GETTING THROUGH! IT'S GETTING THROUGH THE GATES!

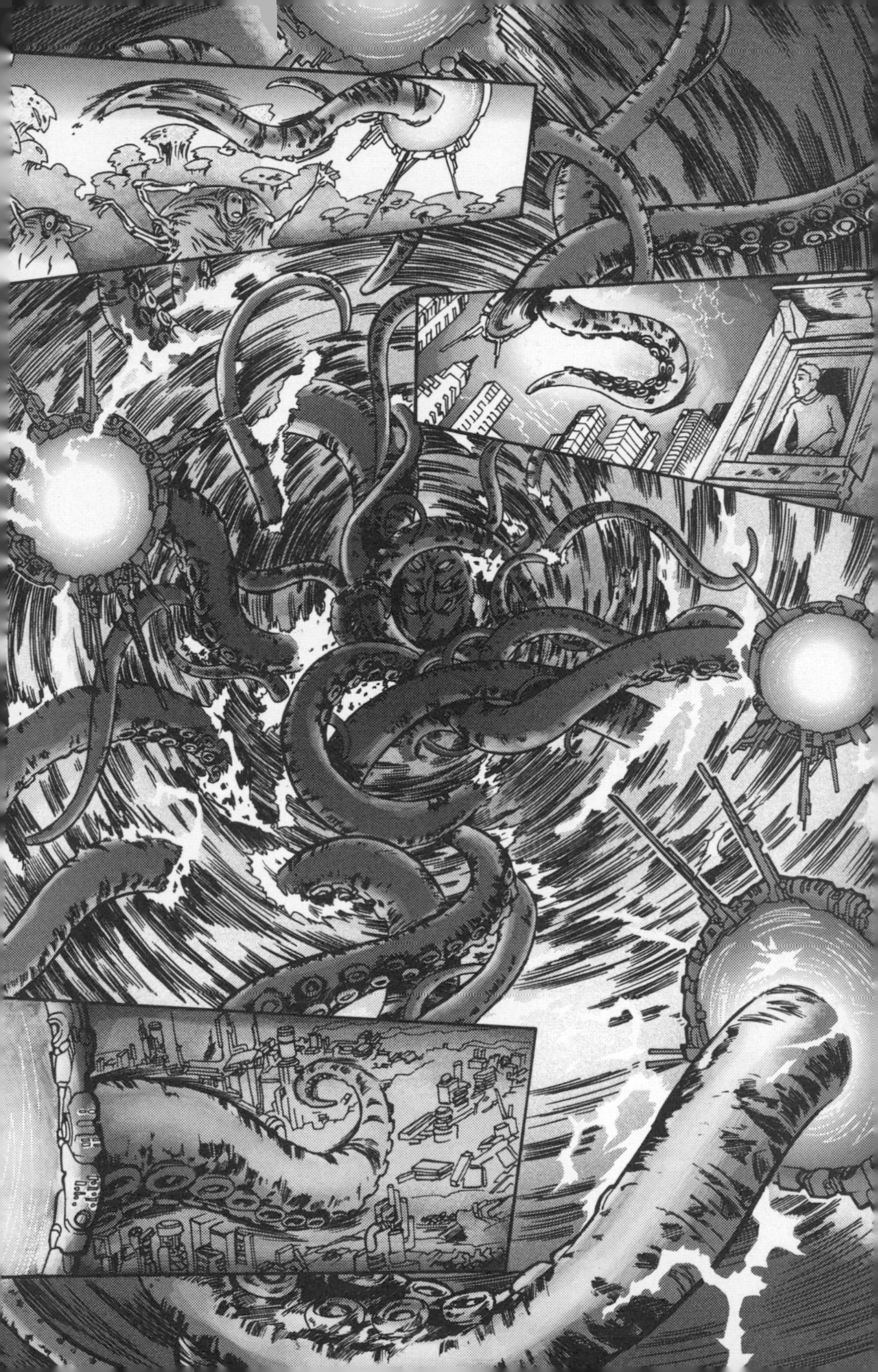

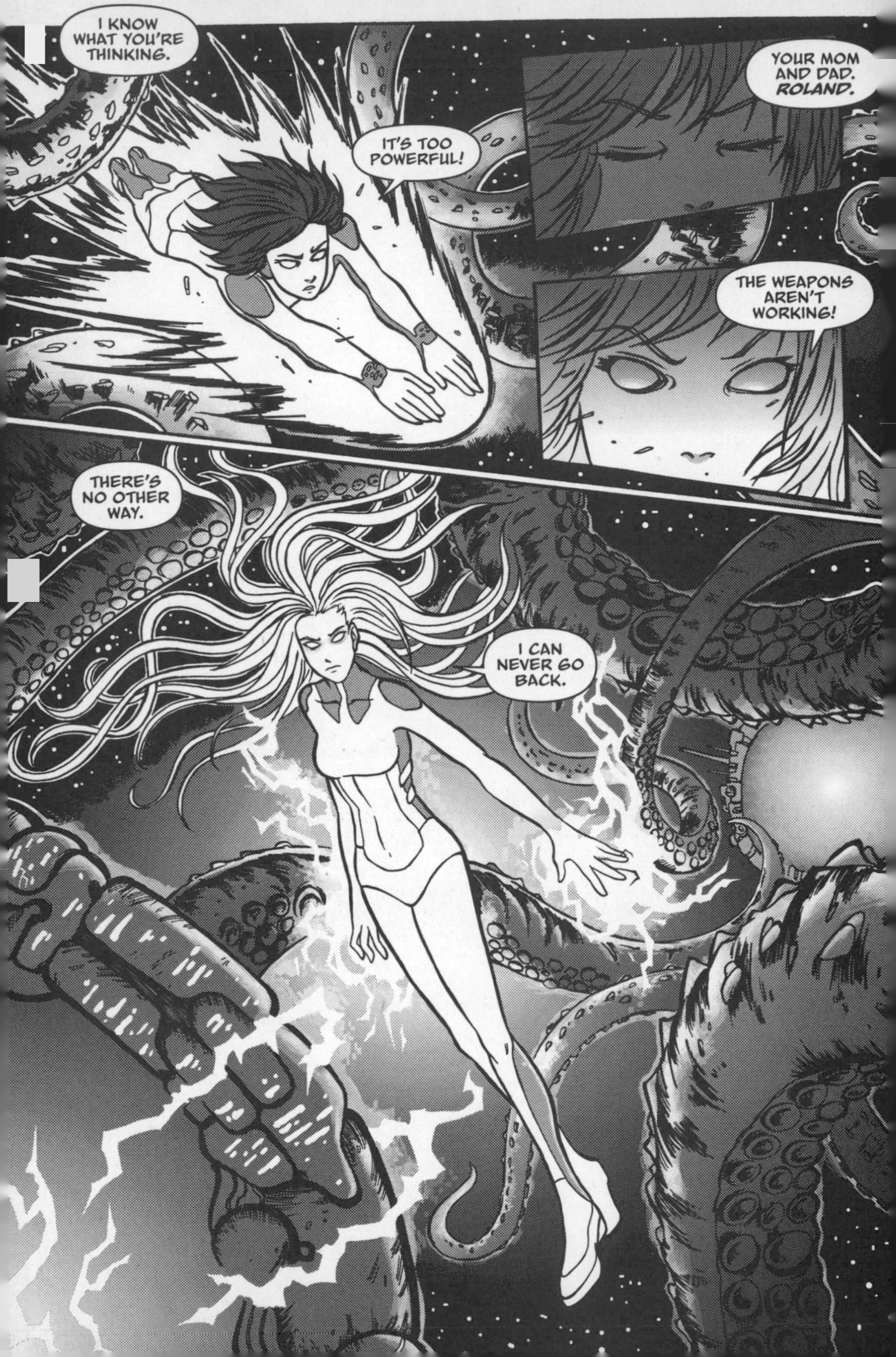
I KNOW WHAT YOU'RE THINKING.
IT'S TOO POWERFUL!
YOUR MOM AND DAD. *ROLAND.*
THE WEAPONS AREN'T WORKING!
THERE'S NO OTHER WAY.
I CAN NEVER GO BACK.

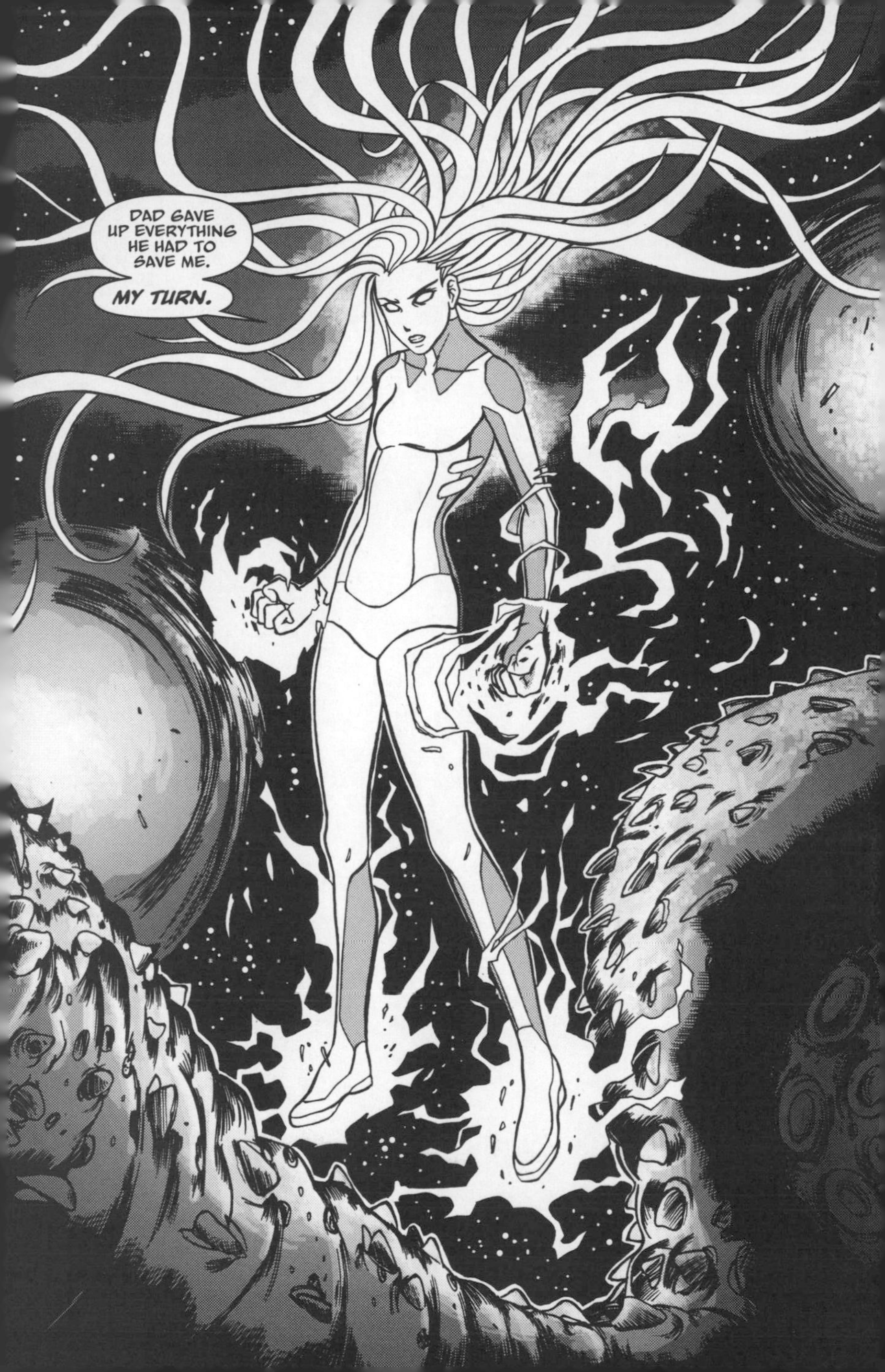
DAD GAVE UP EVERYTHING HE HAD TO SAVE ME.
MY TURN.

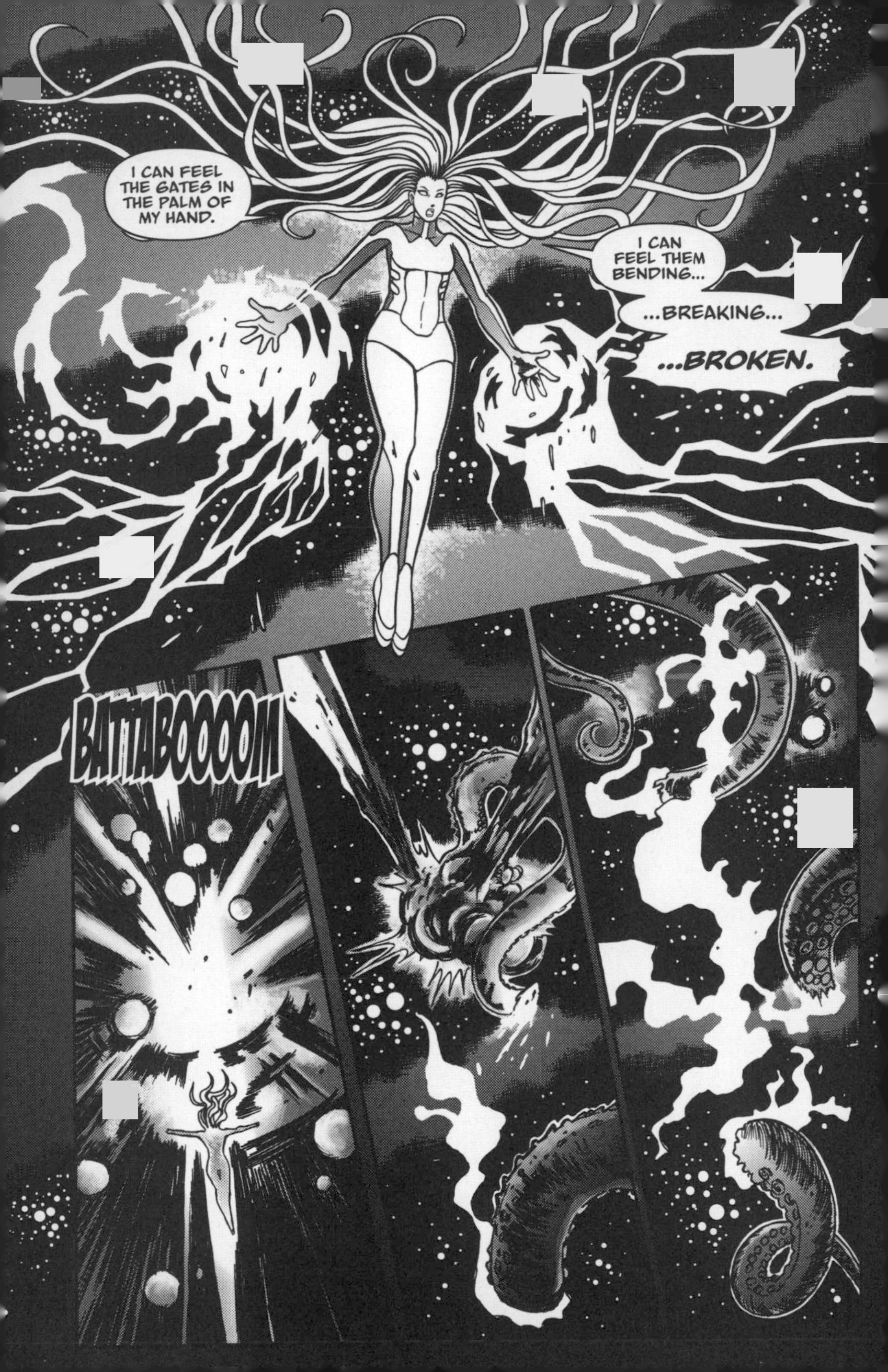
I CAN FEEL THE GATES IN THE PALM OF MY HAND.
I CAN FEEL THEM BENDING...
...BREAKING...
...BROKEN.
BATTABOOOOM

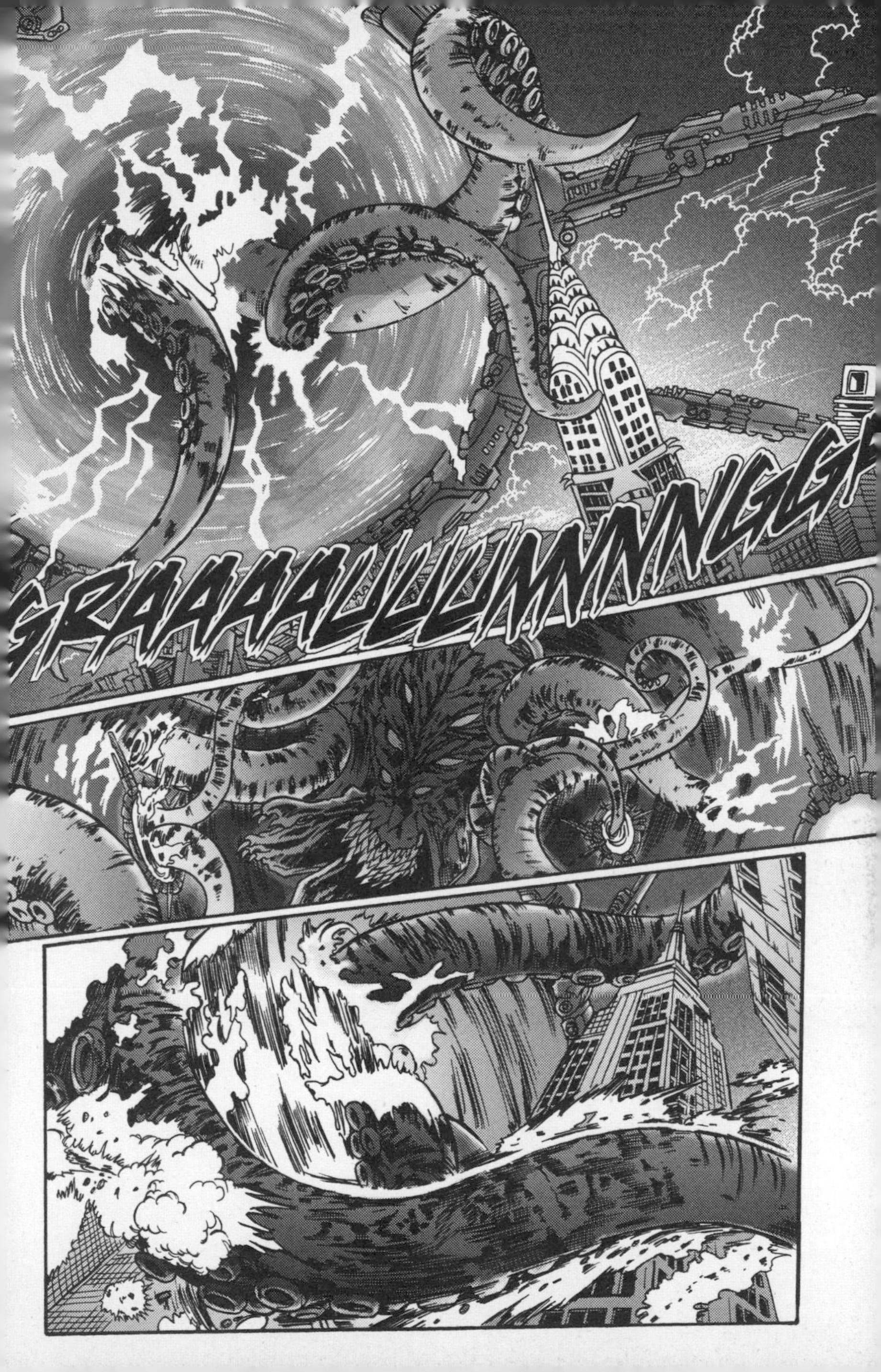
GRAAAUUUMMMNNGG

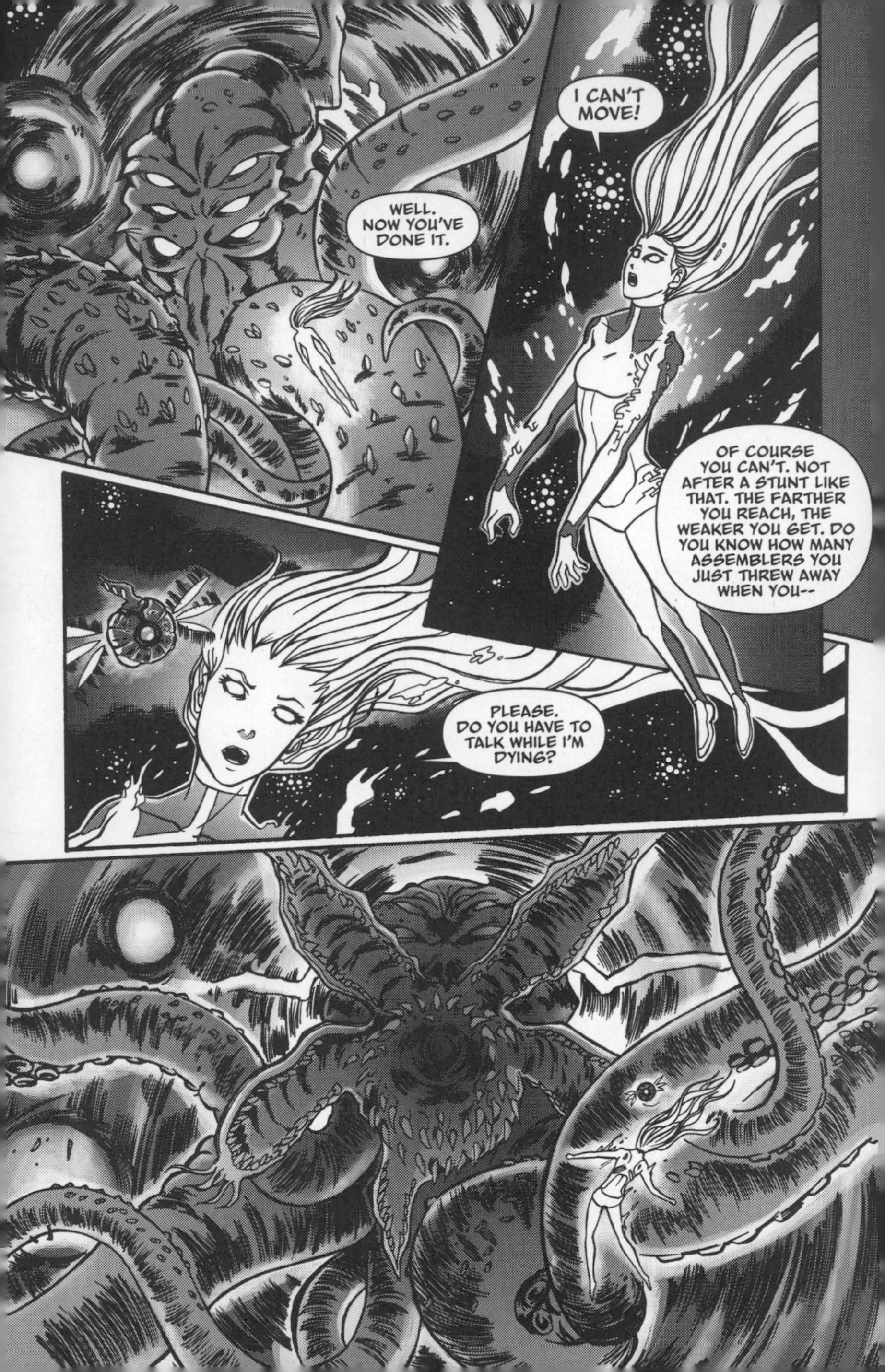
WELL. NOW YOU'VE DONE IT.
I CAN'T MOVE!
OF COURSE YOU CAN'T. NOT AFTER A STUNT LIKE THAT. THE FARTHER YOU REACH, THE WEAKER YOU GET. DO YOU KNOW HOW MANY ASSEMBLERS YOU JUST THREW AWAY WHEN YOU--
PLEASE. DO YOU HAVE TO TALK WHILE I'M DYING?

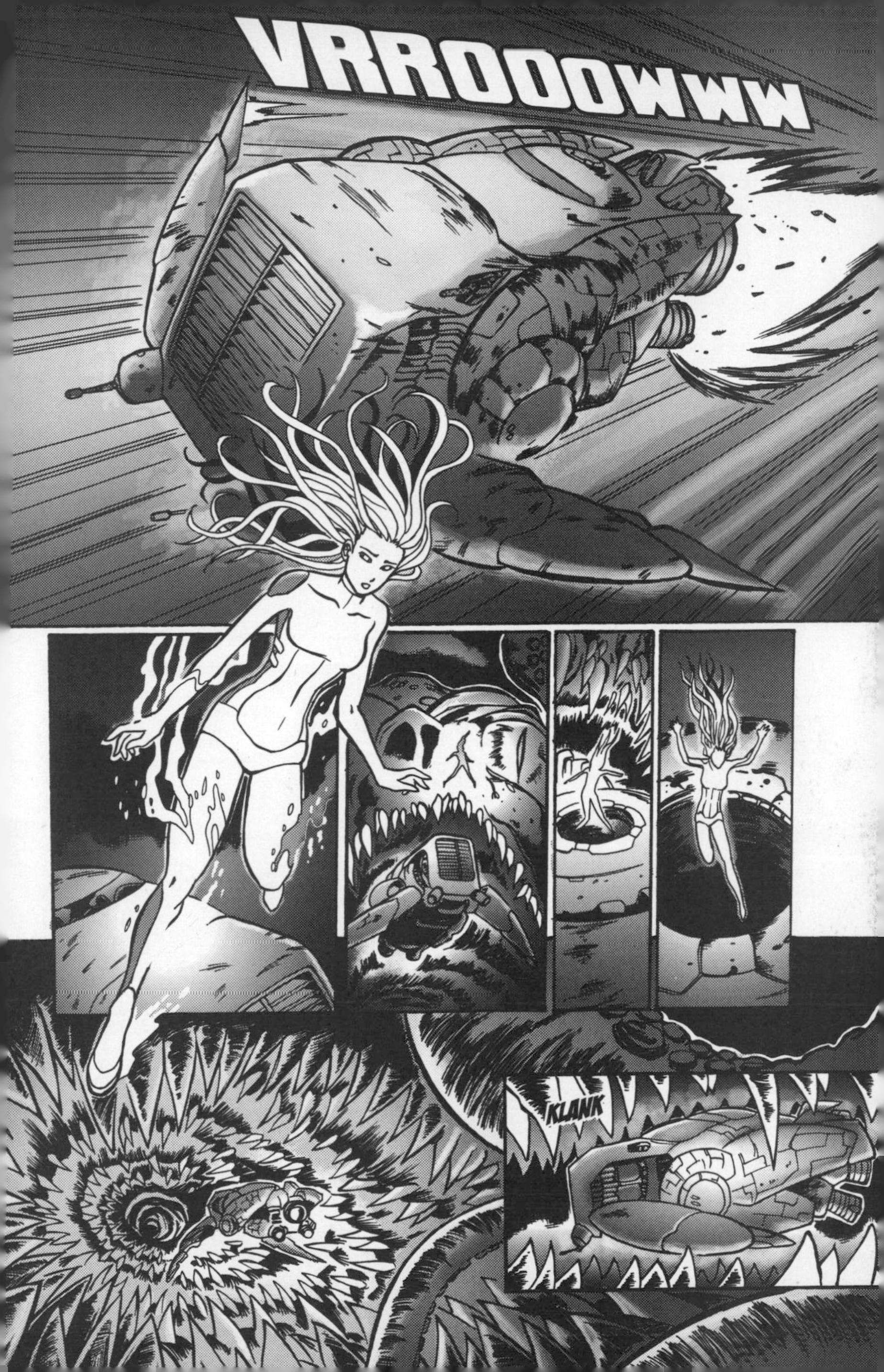
VRROOOOWWW
KLANK

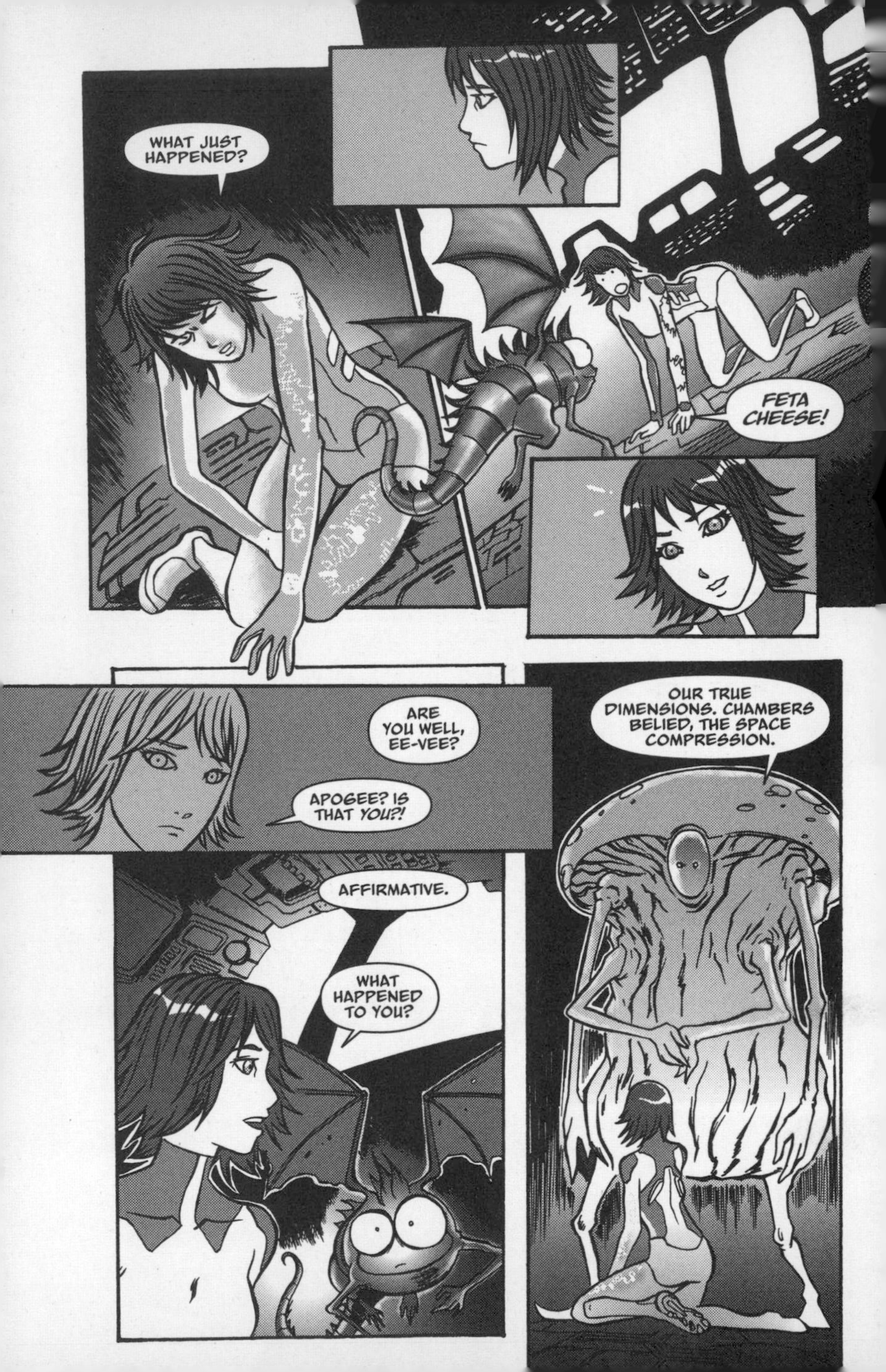
WHAT JUST HAPPENED?
FETA CHEESE!
ARE YOU WELL, EE-VEE?
APOGEE? IS THAT *YOU*?!
AFFIRMATIVE.
WHAT HAPPENED TO YOU?
OUR TRUE DIMENSIONS. CHAMBERS BELIED, THE SPACE COMPRESSION.

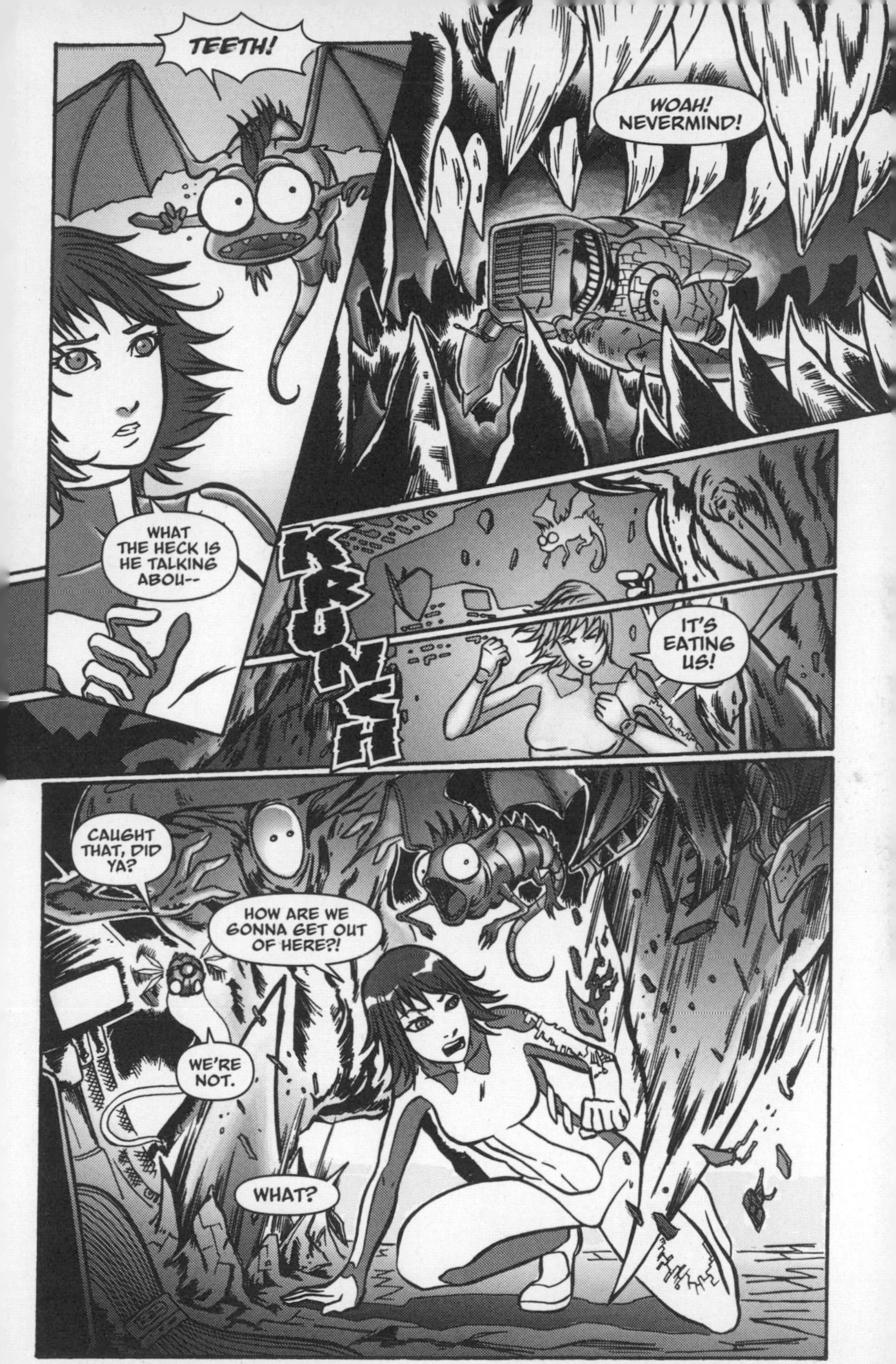
TEETH!
WOAH! NEVERMIND!
WHAT THE HECK IS HE TALKING ABOU--
KRUNCH
IT'S EATING US!
CAUGHT THAT, DID YA?
HOW ARE WE GONNA GET OUT OF HERE?!
WE'RE NOT.
WHAT?

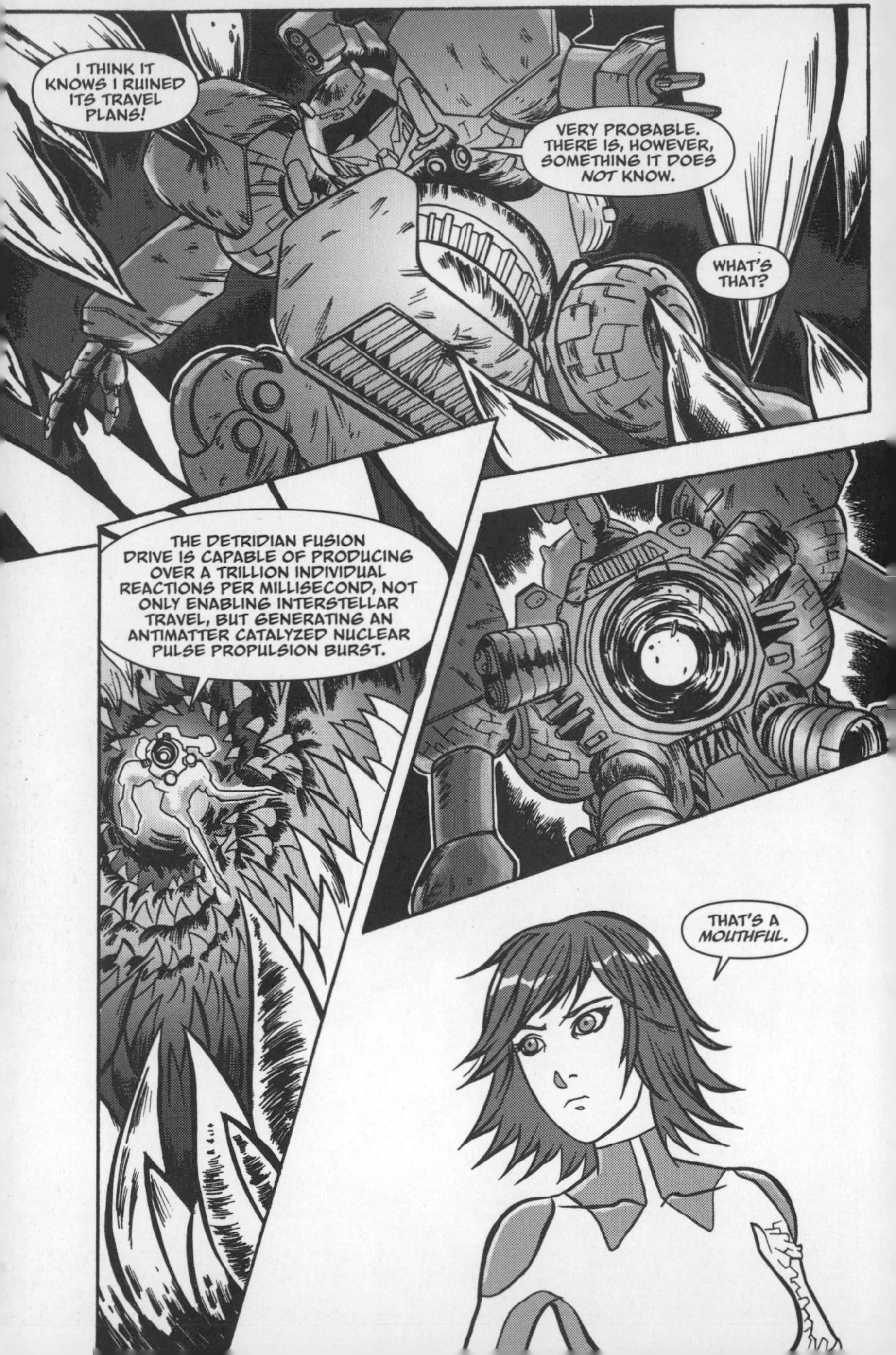
I THINK IT KNOWS I RUINED ITS TRAVEL PLANS!
VERY PROBABLE. THERE IS, HOWEVER, SOMETHING IT DOES *NOT* KNOW.
WHAT'S THAT?
THE DETRIDIAN FUSION DRIVE IS CAPABLE OF PRODUCING OVER A TRILLION INDIVIDUAL REACTIONS PER MILLISECOND, NOT ONLY ENABLING INTERSTELLAR TRAVEL, BUT GENERATING AN ANTIMATTER CATALYZED NUCLEAR PULSE PROPULSION BURST.
THAT'S A *MOUTHFUL.*

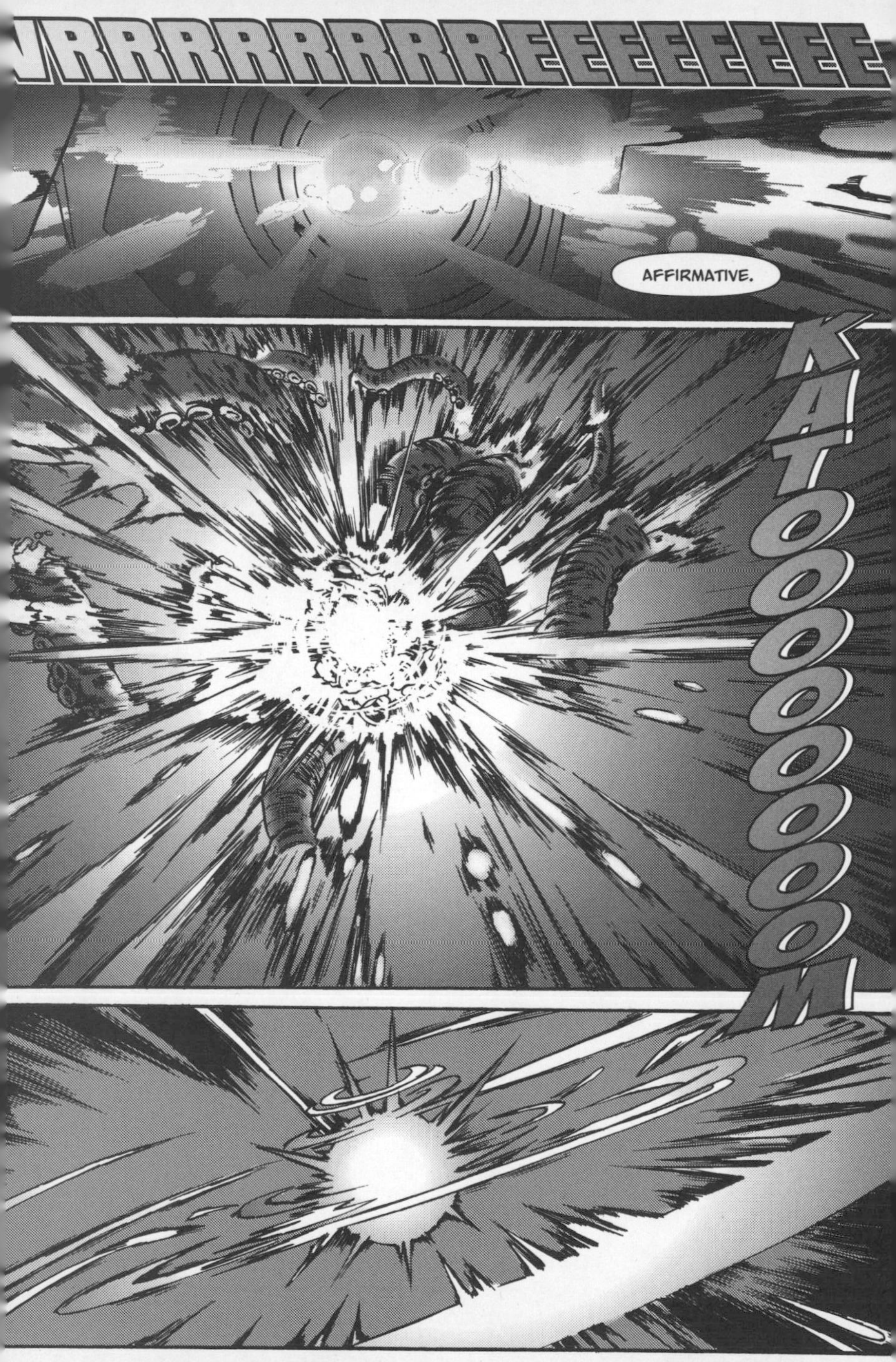
VRRRRRRRRRREEEEEEEEEE
AFFIRMATIVE.
KATOOOOOOOOM

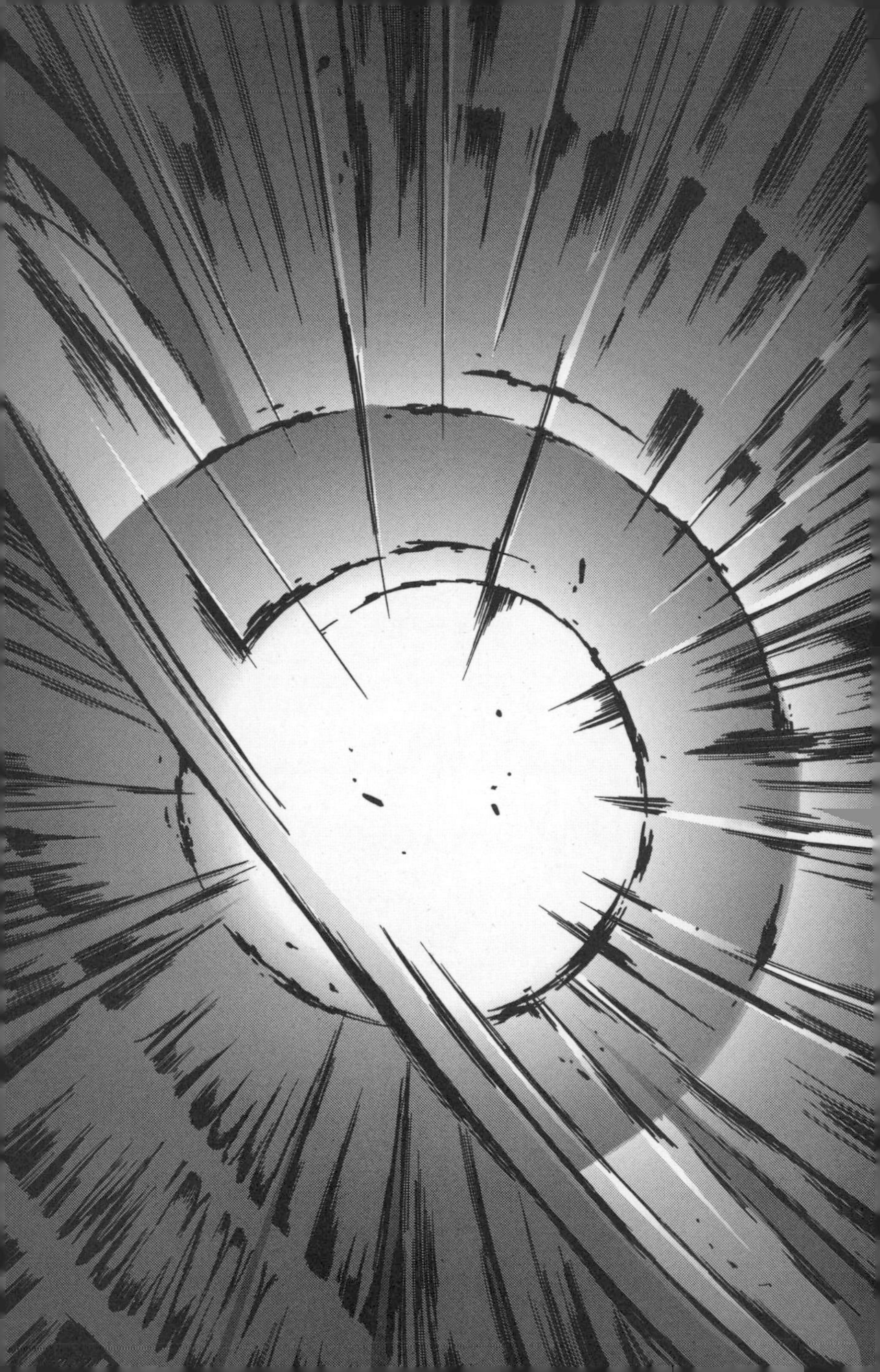

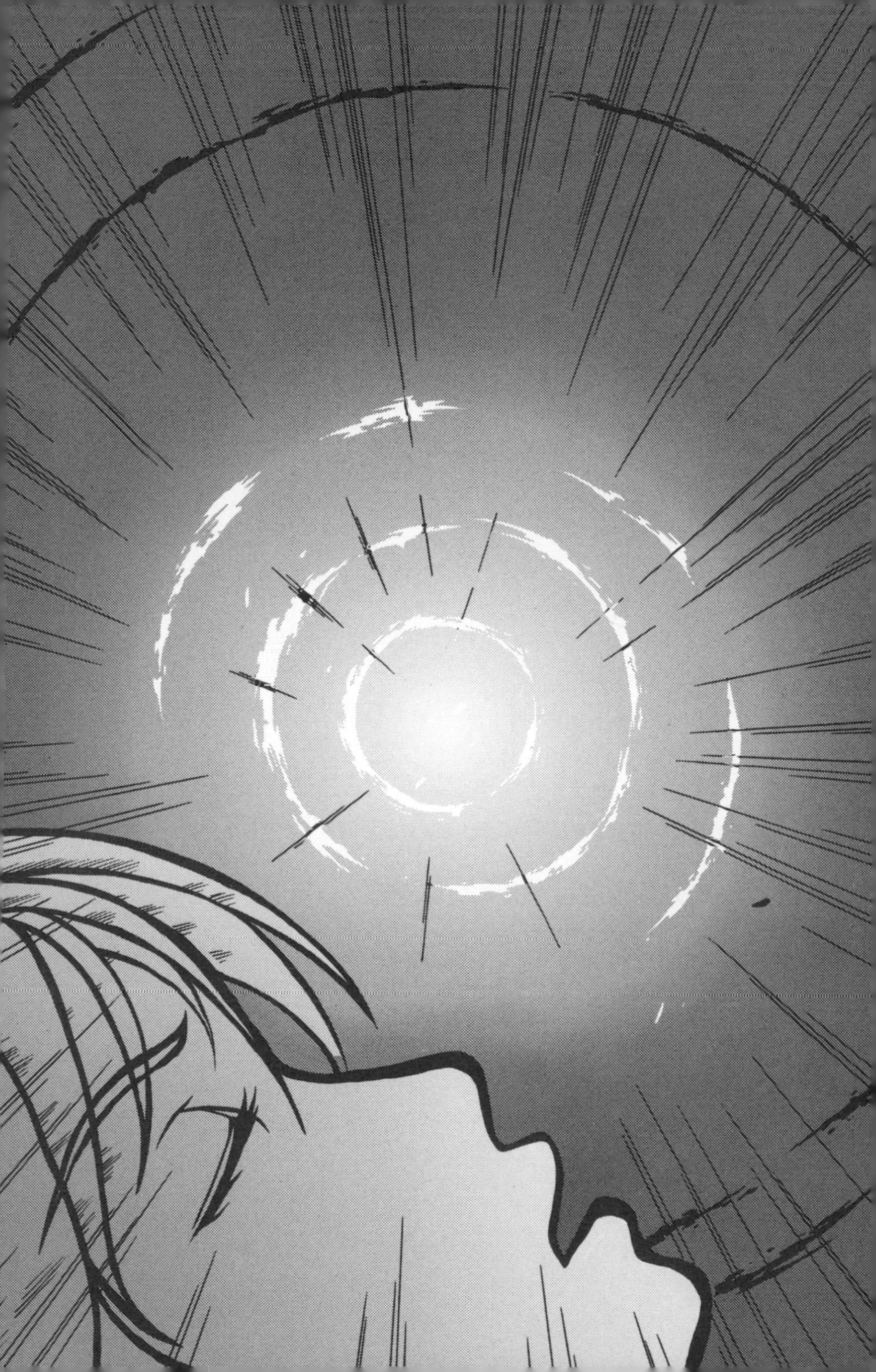

EPILOGUE

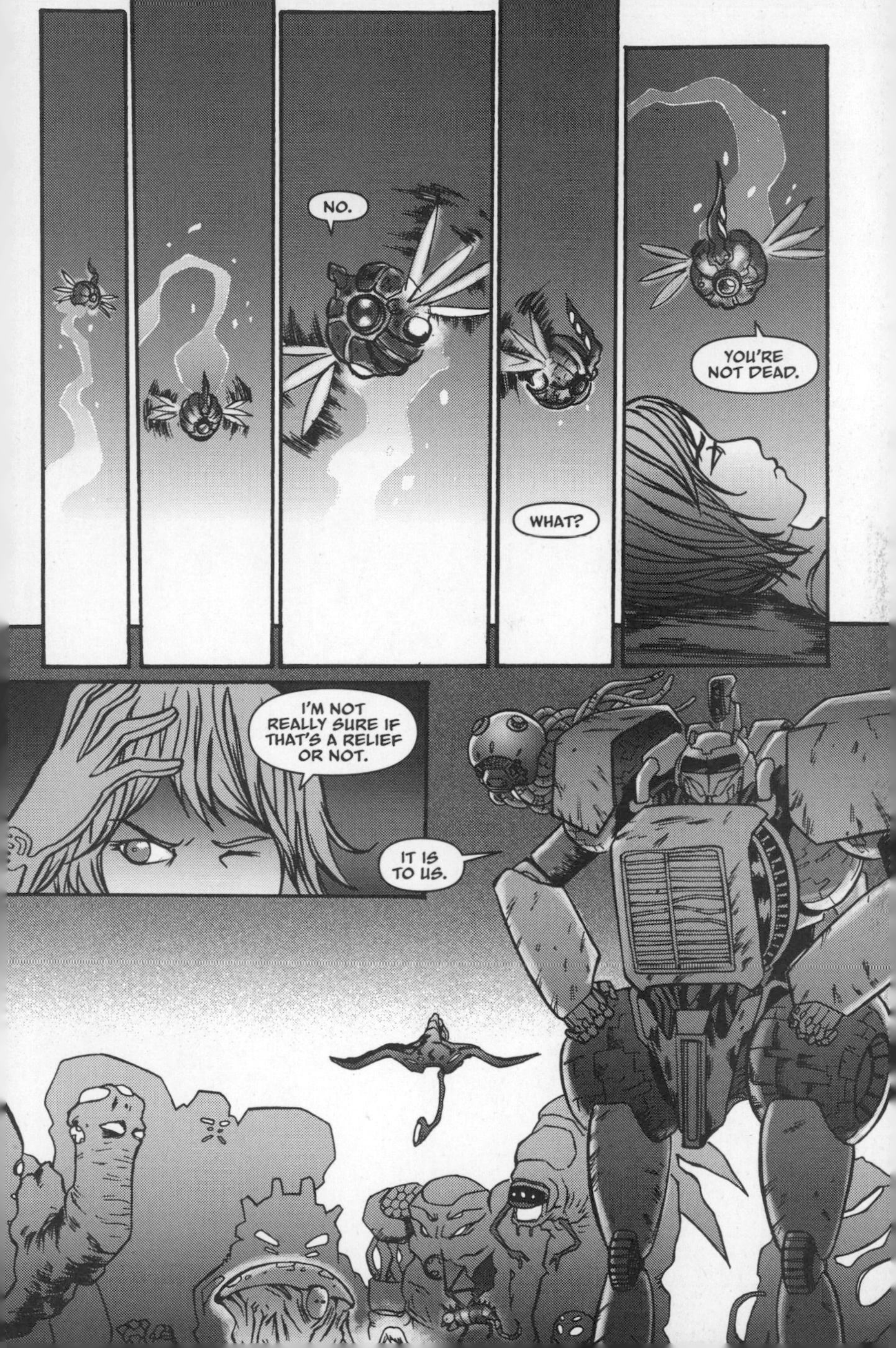
NO.
WHAT?
YOU'RE NOT DEAD.
I'M NOT REALLY SURE IF THAT'S A RELIEF OR NOT.
IT IS TO US.

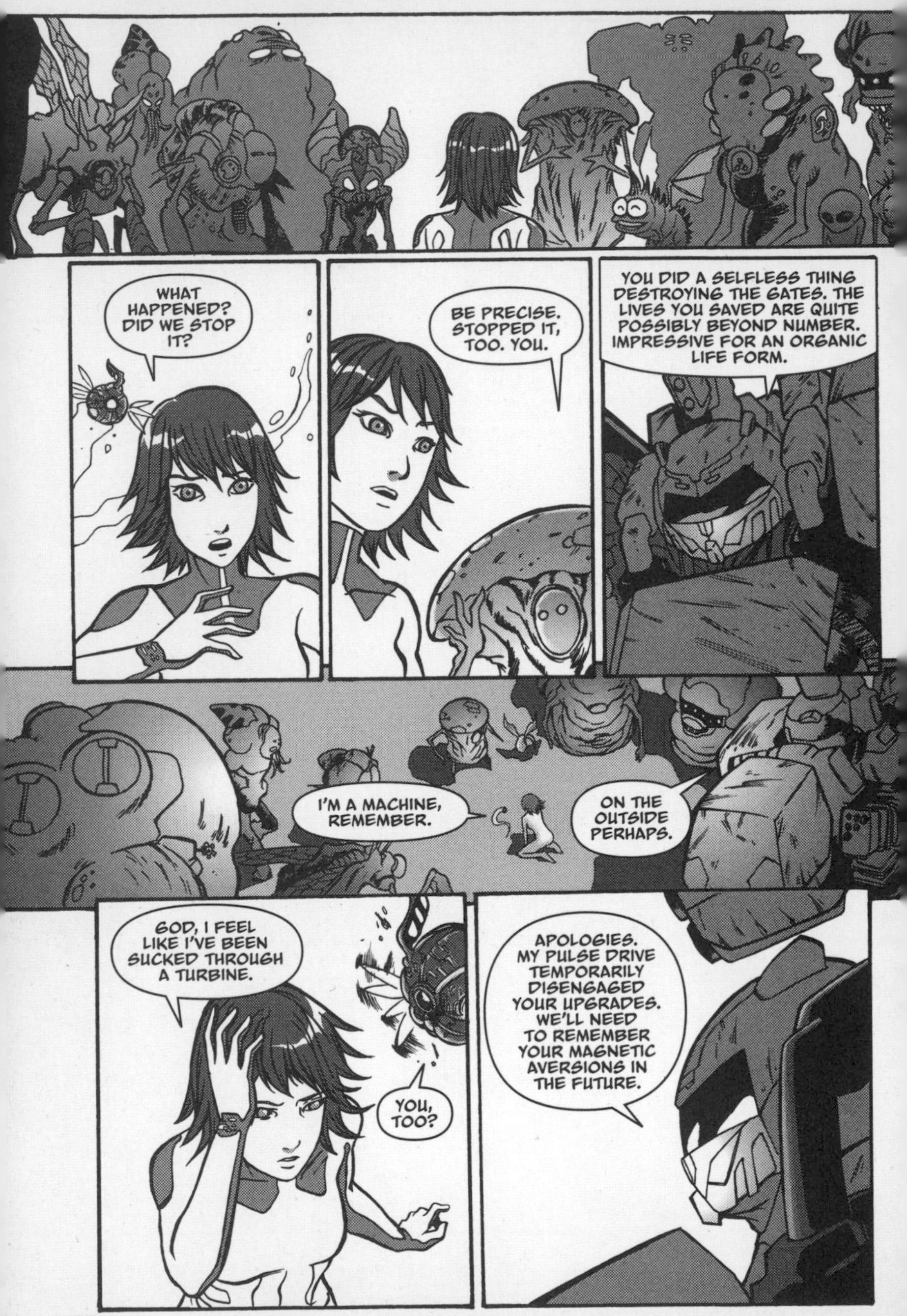
WHAT HAPPENED? DID WE STOP IT?
BE PRECISE. STOPPED IT, TOO. YOU.
YOU DID A SELFLESS THING DESTROYING THE GATES. THE LIVES YOU SAVED ARE QUITE POSSIBLY BEYOND NUMBER. IMPRESSIVE FOR AN ORGANIC LIFE FORM.
I'M A MACHINE, REMEMBER.
ON THE OUTSIDE PERHAPS.
GOD, I FEEL LIKE I'VE BEEN SUCKED THROUGH A TURBINE.
YOU, TOO?
APOLOGIES. MY PULSE DRIVE TEMPORARILY DISENGAGED YOUR UPGRADES. WE'LL NEED TO REMEMBER YOUR MAGNETIC AVERSIONS IN THE FUTURE.

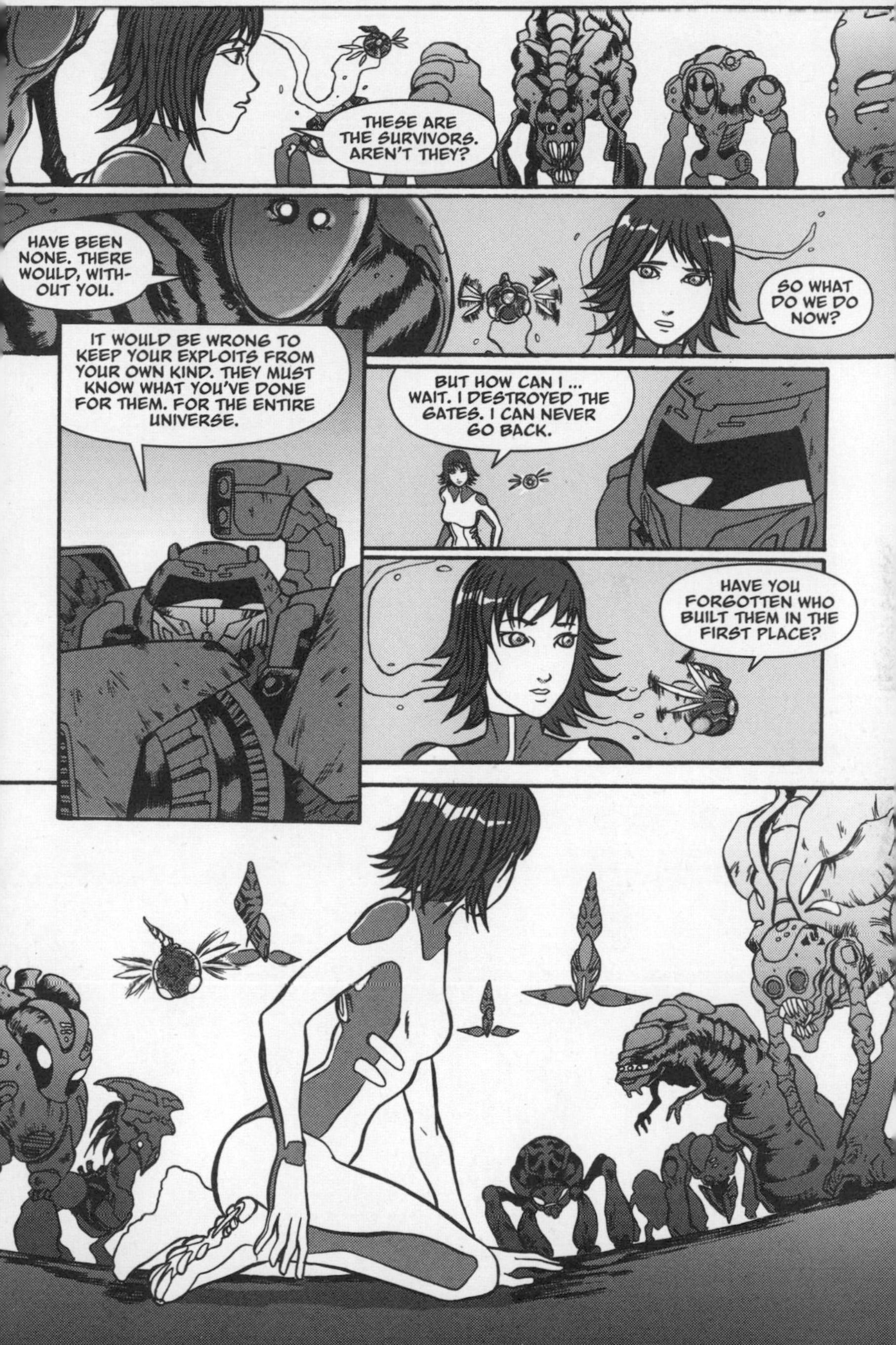
THESE ARE THE SURVIVORS. AREN'T THEY?
HAVE BEEN NONE. THERE WOULD, WITHOUT YOU.
SO WHAT DO WE DO NOW?
IT WOULD BE WRONG TO KEEP YOUR EXPLOITS FROM YOUR OWN KIND. THEY MUST KNOW WHAT YOU'VE DONE FOR THEM. FOR THE ENTIRE UNIVERSE.
BUT HOW CAN I ... WAIT. I DESTROYED THE GATES. I CAN NEVER GO BACK.
HAVE YOU FORGOTTEN WHO BUILT THEM IN THE FIRST PLACE?

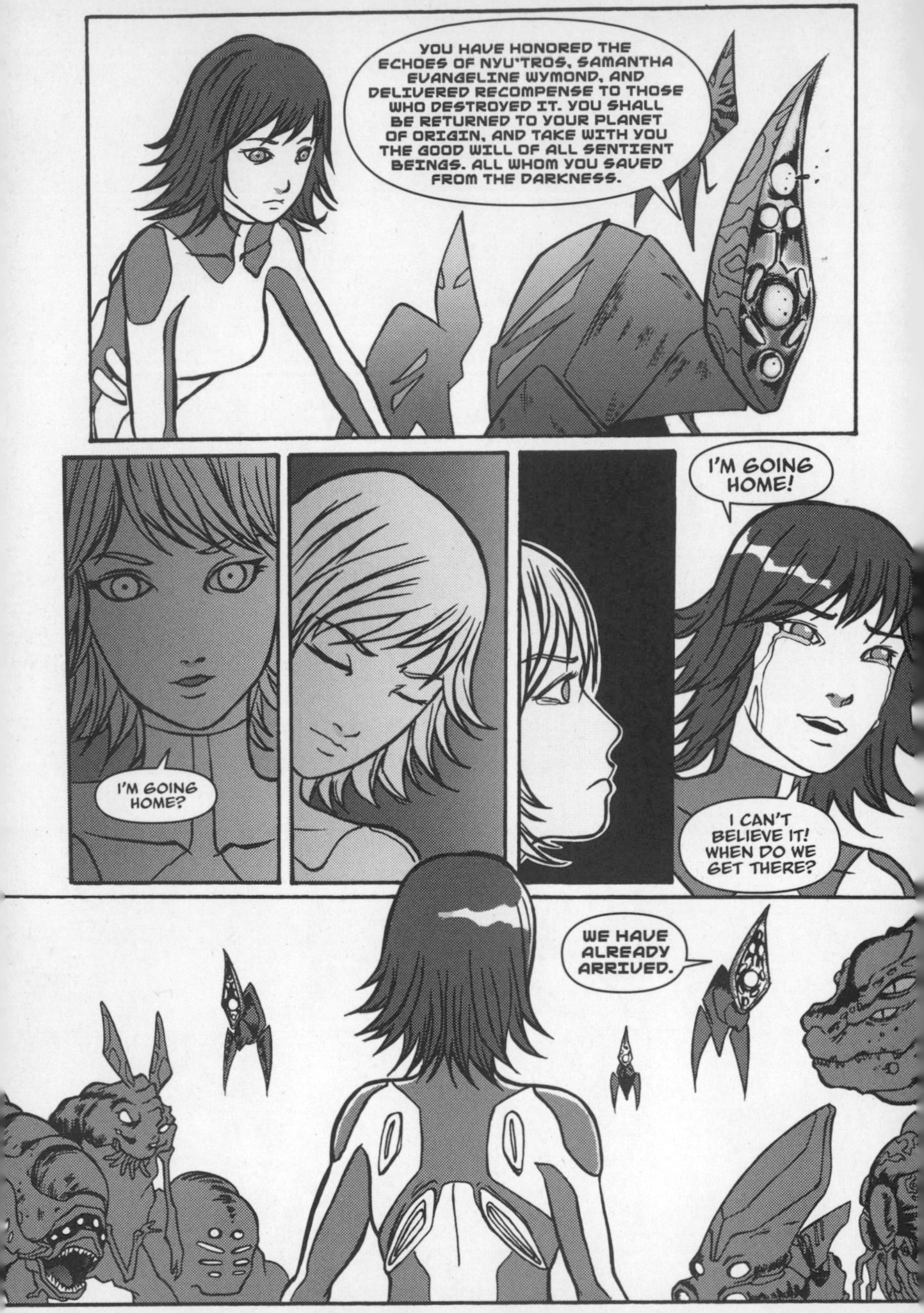
YOU HAVE HONORED THE ECHOES OF NYU'TROS, SAMANTHA EVANGELINE WYMOND, AND DELIVERED RECOMPENSE TO THOSE WHO DESTROYED IT. YOU SHALL BE RETURNED TO YOUR PLANET OF ORIGIN, AND TAKE WITH YOU THE GOOD WILL OF ALL SENTIENT BEINGS. ALL WHOM YOU SAVED FROM THE DARKNESS.
I'M GOING HOME?
I'M GOING HOME!
I CAN'T BELIEVE IT! WHEN DO WE GET THERE?
WE HAVE ALREADY ARRIVED.

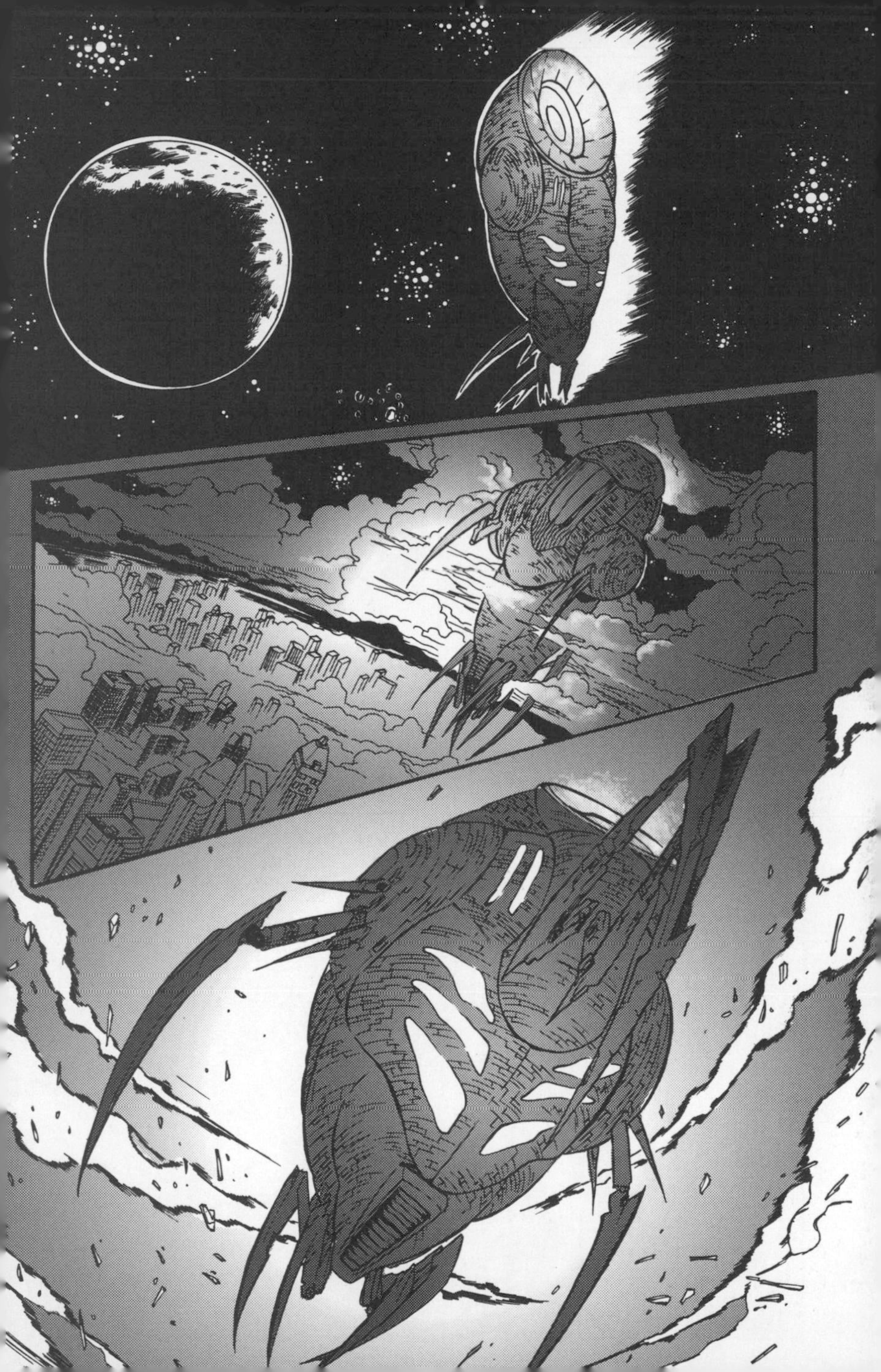

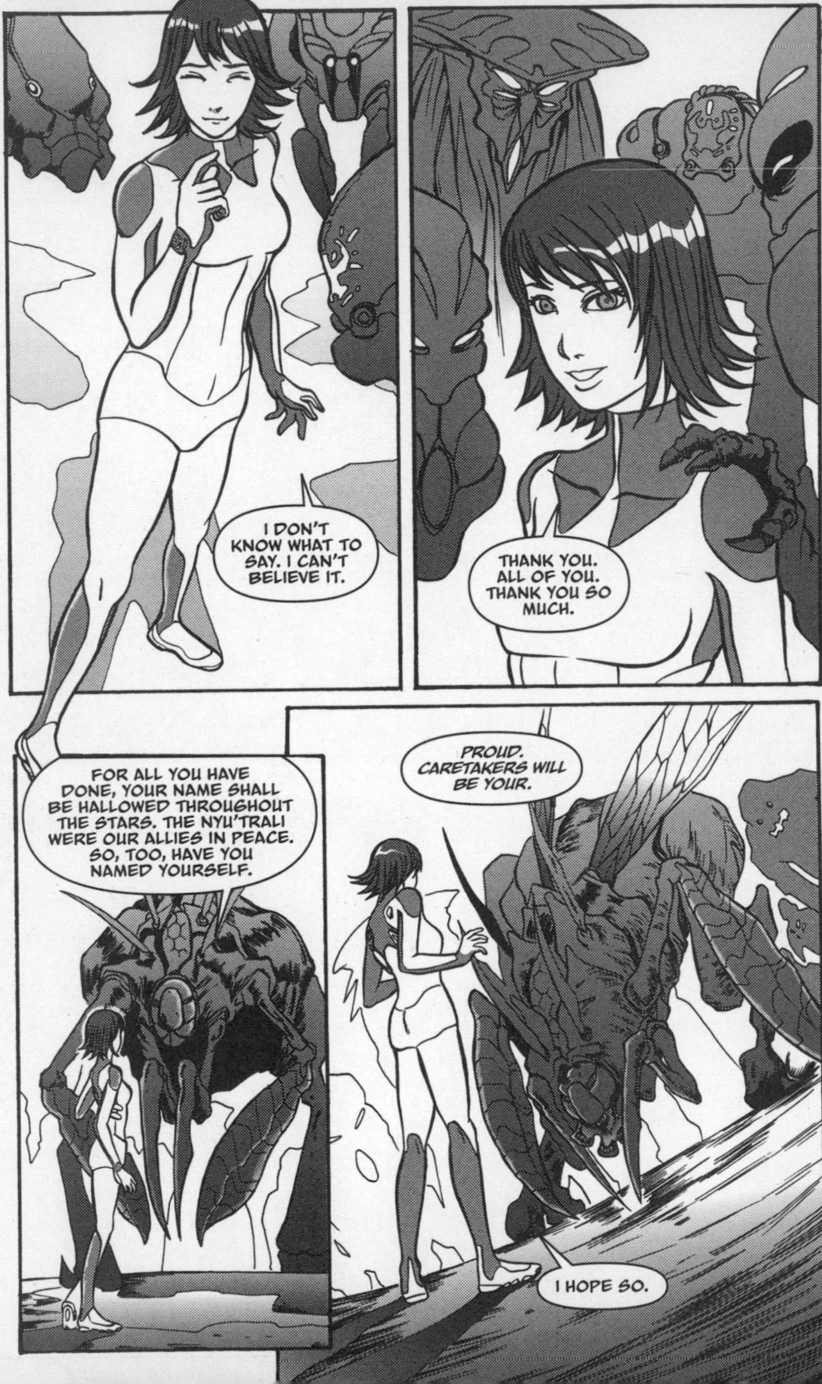
I DON'T KNOW WHAT TO SAY. I CAN'T BELIEVE IT.
THANK YOU. ALL OF YOU. THANK YOU SO MUCH.
FOR ALL YOU HAVE DONE, YOUR NAME SHALL BE HALLOWED THROUGHOUT THE STARS. THE NYU'TRALI WERE OUR ALLIES IN PEACE. SO, TOO, HAVE YOU NAMED YOURSELF.
PROUD. CARETAKERS WILL BE YOUR.
I HOPE SO.

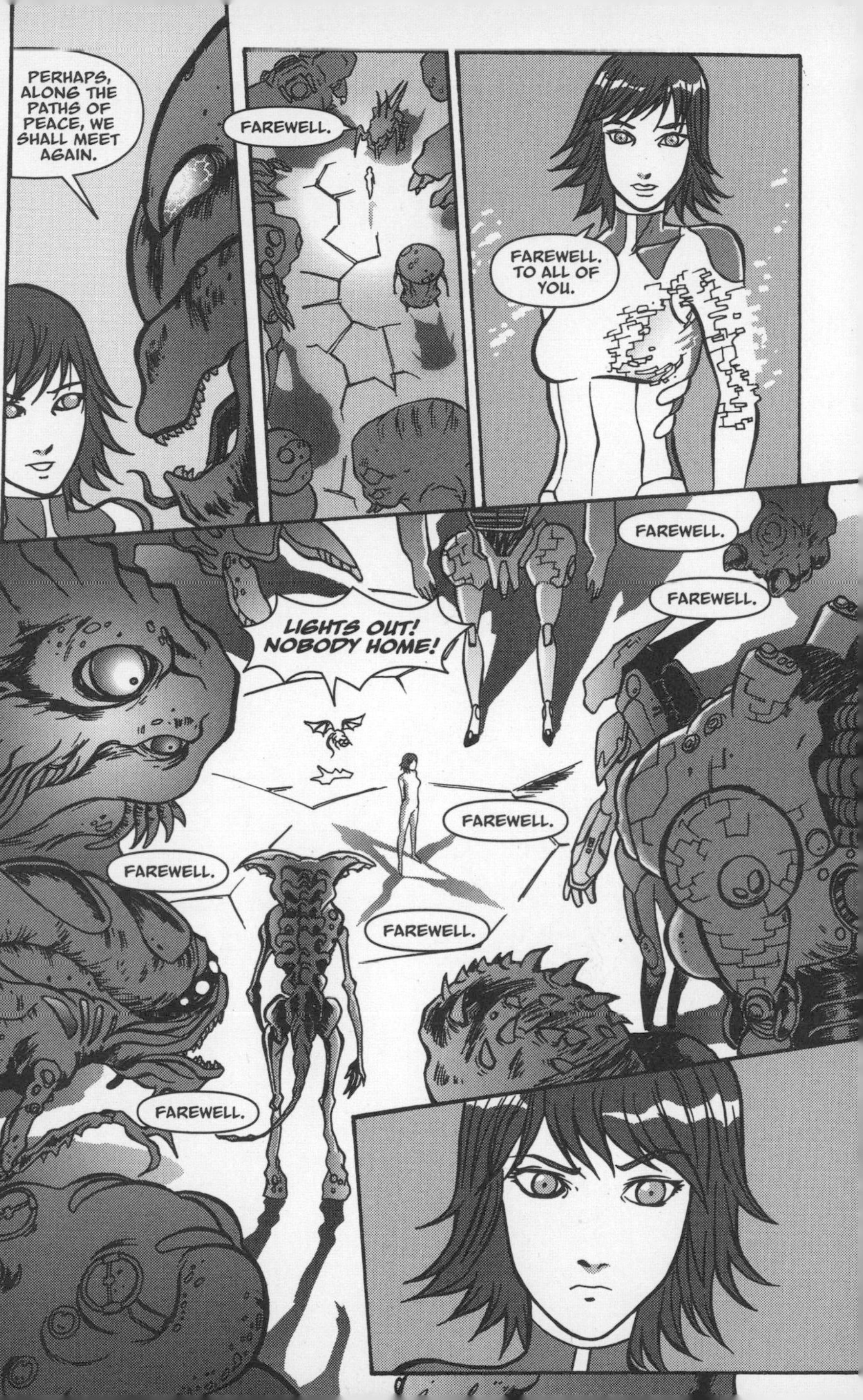
PERHAPS, ALONG THE PATHS OF PEACE, WE SHALL MEET AGAIN.
FAREWELL.
FAREWELL. TO ALL OF YOU.
FAREWELL.
LIGHTS OUT! NOBODY HOME!
FAREWELL.
FAREWELL.
FAREWELL.
FAREWELL.
FAREWELL.

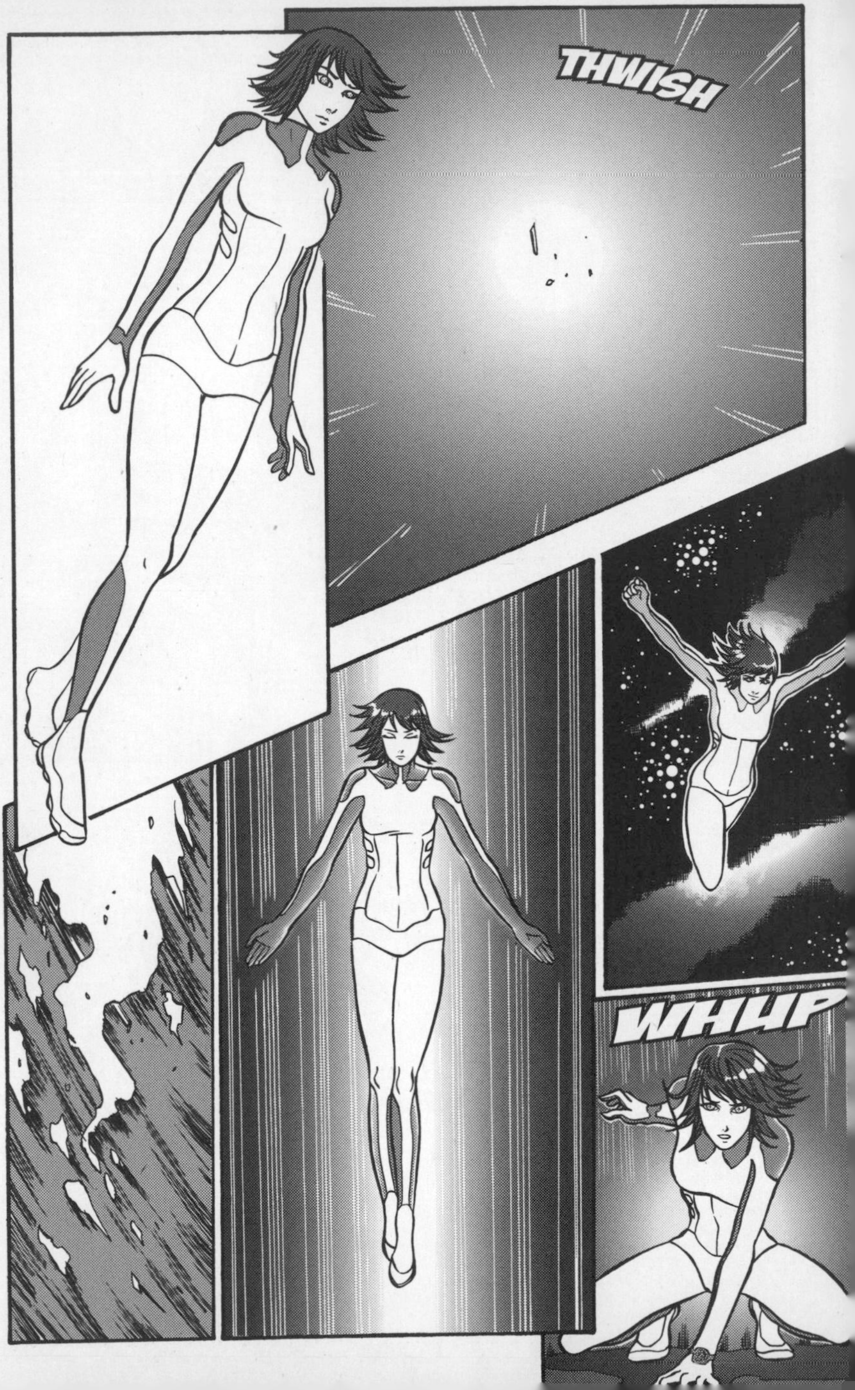
THWISH
WHUP

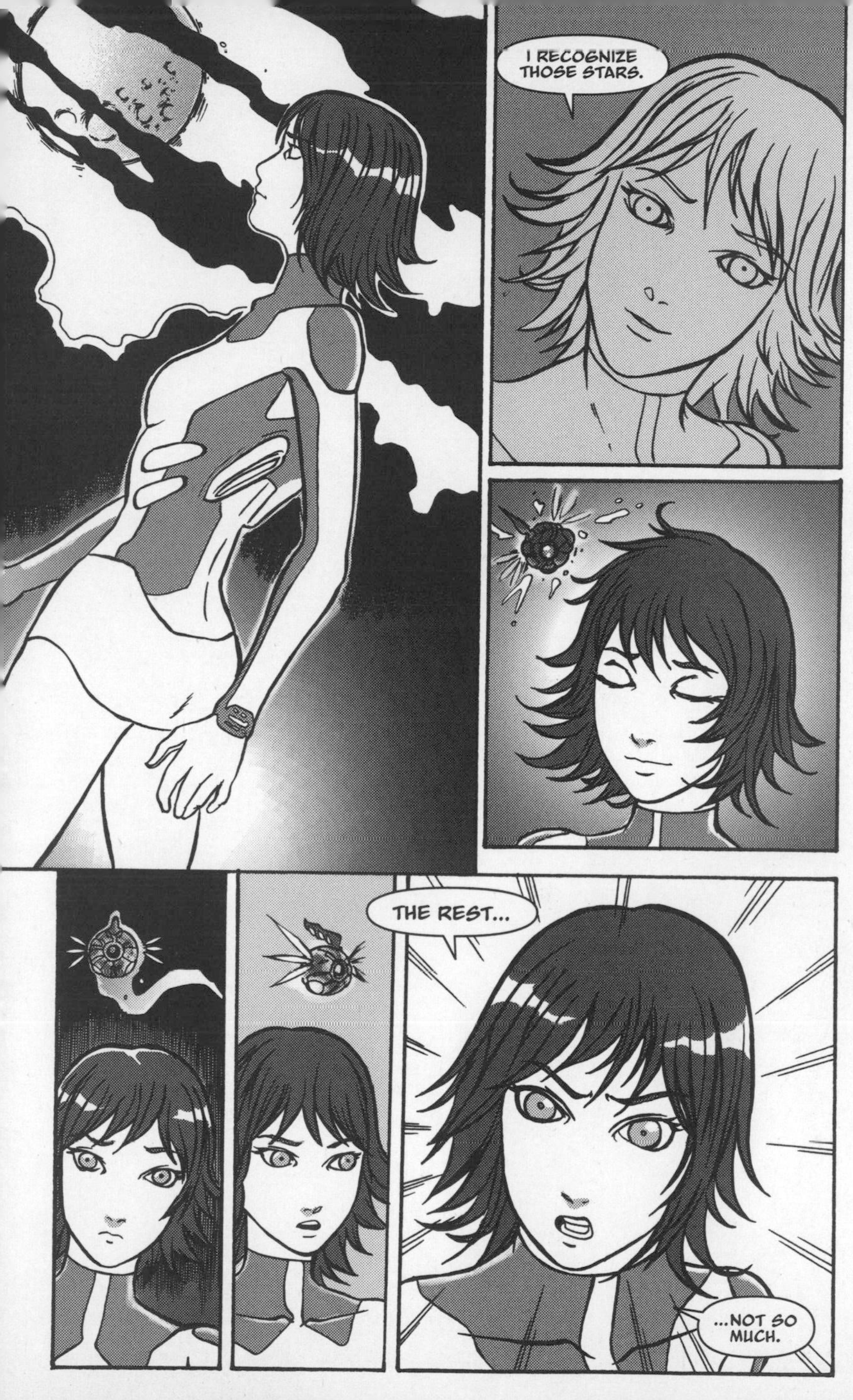
I RECOGNIZE THOSE STARS.
THE REST...
...NOT SO MUCH.

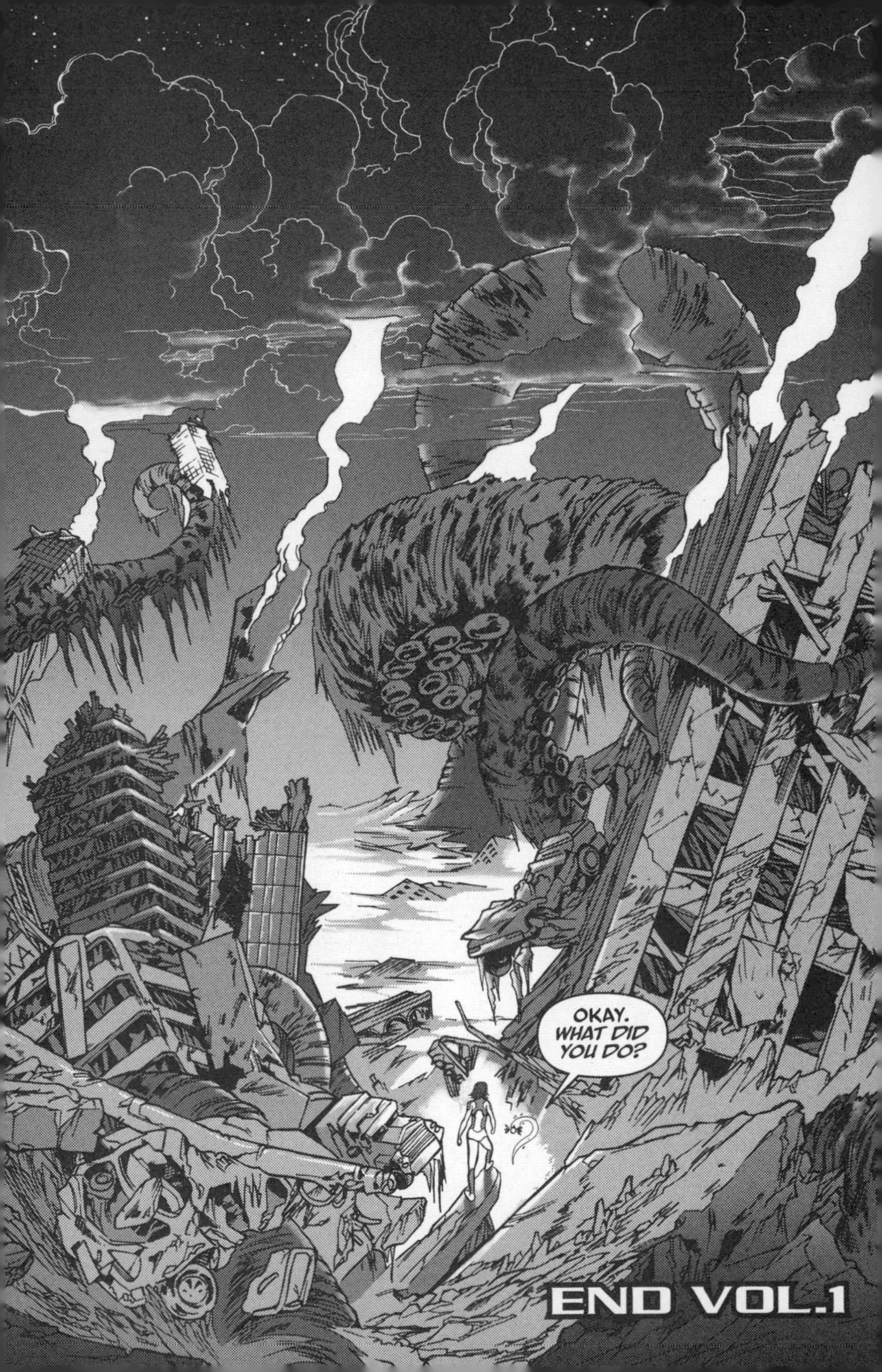
OKAY. WHAT DID YOU DO?
END VOL.1

IN THE NEXT VOLUME OF

WITH EARTH AND A MULTITUDE OF OTHER
PLANETS IN RUIN, AND KU'THENDRIL'S EVIL
CONTINUING TO SPREAD, EVIE MUST RETURN TO
A RE-FORMED INTERGALACTIC CONGRESS AND
WORK TO REBUILD THESE SHATTERED WORLDS.
IN THE EXCITING NEXT CHAPTER, SHE WILL
FACE BOTH THE PERILS OF CONGRESS, WHERE
ENEMIES OFTEN POSE AS ALLIES, AS WELL AS
A NEW BREED OF EVIL FROM THE FARTHEST
REACHES OF THE GALAXY...

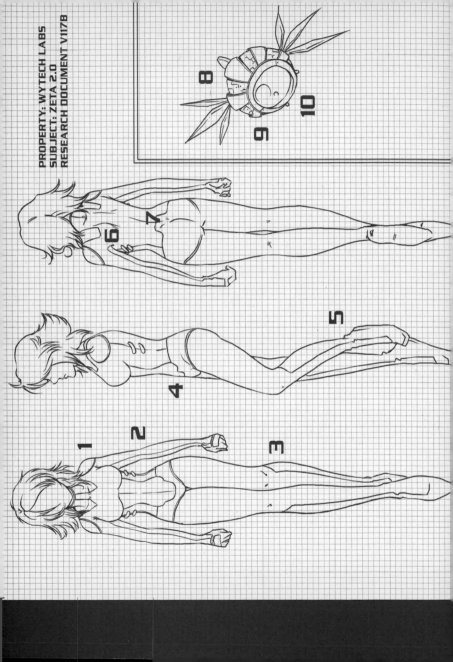

PROPERTY: WYTECH LABS
SUBJECT: ZETA 2.0
RESEARCH DOCUMENT V117B

ABSTRACT: SUBJECT'S EXODERMUS AND VITAL SYSTEMS NOW MERGED WITH ZETA COMPLEX. HYBRID ENTITY CAPABLE OF PROJECTING, CONTROLLING NANITE CLOUDS. HYPOTHETICAL RESULTS: VARIABLE OPACITY, DENSITY, WEIGHT, REACH.

1. GLENOHUMERAL FACILITATOR

A HYPERFLEXIBLE ENHANCEMENT TO BOTH THE GLENOID AND ARTICULAR CARTILAGE, ENABLING NOT ONLY INCREASED REACH, ROTATION AND RECOIL, BUT INCALCULABLE SOCKET DURABILITY.

2. BICIPITAL STRUT

A SKELETAL BRACE AND MUSCULAR ENHANCEMENT, DESIGNED TO BOTH PROTECT AND EMPOWER THE ARM. THE STRUT IS CALCULATED TO ENHANCE APPLIED STRENGTH BY WELL OVER 720%.

3. GASTROCNEMIAL ACTUATOR

A TARGETED KINETIC EXPANSION, INTENDED TO BOTH REDUCE LOCOMOTIVE STRESS AND AUGMENT FORCEFUL EXTENSION. EARLY TRIALS SUGGESTED A SIGNIFICANT INCREASE IN POTENTIAL SPEED, HEIGHT AND DISTANCE.

4. ABDOMINAL BUFFER

A DUAL-PURPOSE SHIELD, DESIGNED TO WITHSTAND ELECTRICAL, BALLISTIC AND/ OR BLUNT FORCE TRAUMA AT POINT-BLANK RANGE, THEREBY SAFEGUARDING VITAL INTERNAL SYSTEMS. CONVERSELY, THE SHIELD PROVIDES AMPLE FLEXIBILITY, ALLOWING FOR INCREASED FREEDOM OF MOVEMENT, AND ADDED ABDOMINAL STRENGTH.

5. ACHILLES STABILIZER

SIMILAR IN DESIGN TO THE GASTROCNEMIAL ACTUATOR, BUT HONED SPECIFICALLY FOR INCREASED FORWARD PROPULSION; NOT UNLIKE A LATTICE OF PNEUMATIC MUSCULATURE.

6. CIRCULATORY ACCELERATORS

A FULLY-INTEGRATED CARDIOLOGICAL STIMULANT, ENABLING FASTER, MORE EFFICIENT BLOOD-FLOW TO TARGETED MUSCLE SYSTEMS DURING STRESS, FLIGHT OR OTHER HIGH-ENDURANCE ACTIVITIES.

7. SEGMENTED SPINAL BUOY

A VARIABLE-STATE NANITE BRACE, CAPABLE OF SOFTENING THE SPINAL COLUMN FOR HYPER-ELASTICITY, OR SOLIDIFYING TO INSULATE AGAINST TRAUMA, VIOLENT GRAVITATIONAL SHIFT, LIFE-THREATENING IMPACT AND THE LIKE.

8. NAVIGATIONAL FLAGELLUM (*CRICKET PERIPHERAL)

A CROSS-PURPOSE WING AND RUDDER ARRAY, HINGED UPON A WEB OF MOLECULAR MOTORS AND ALLOWING THE CRICKET PROJECTION TO MANEUVER UNHINDERED THROUGH 3-DIMENSIONAL SPACE.

9. VARIABLE-STATE CASING (*CRICKET PERIPHERAL)

AN EXTENSION OF THE HOST'S NANITE-BASED EXODERMUS, THE CRICKET'S SHELL IS CAPABLE OF VARYING IN SOLIDITY, TRANSPARENCY, AND SIZE.

10. SUB-NEURAL TRANSDUCER (*CRICKET PERIPHERAL)

A FULLY ADAPTABLE AI CORE, DESIGNED TO BOTH FILTER AND INTERPRET ITS HOST'S SYNAPTIC ACTIVITY, DISTILLING OVER A BILLION NEUROLOGICAL PROCESSES PER SECOND, AND DELIVERING THEM IN AUDIBLE FORMAT.

DRAMATIS PERSONÆ

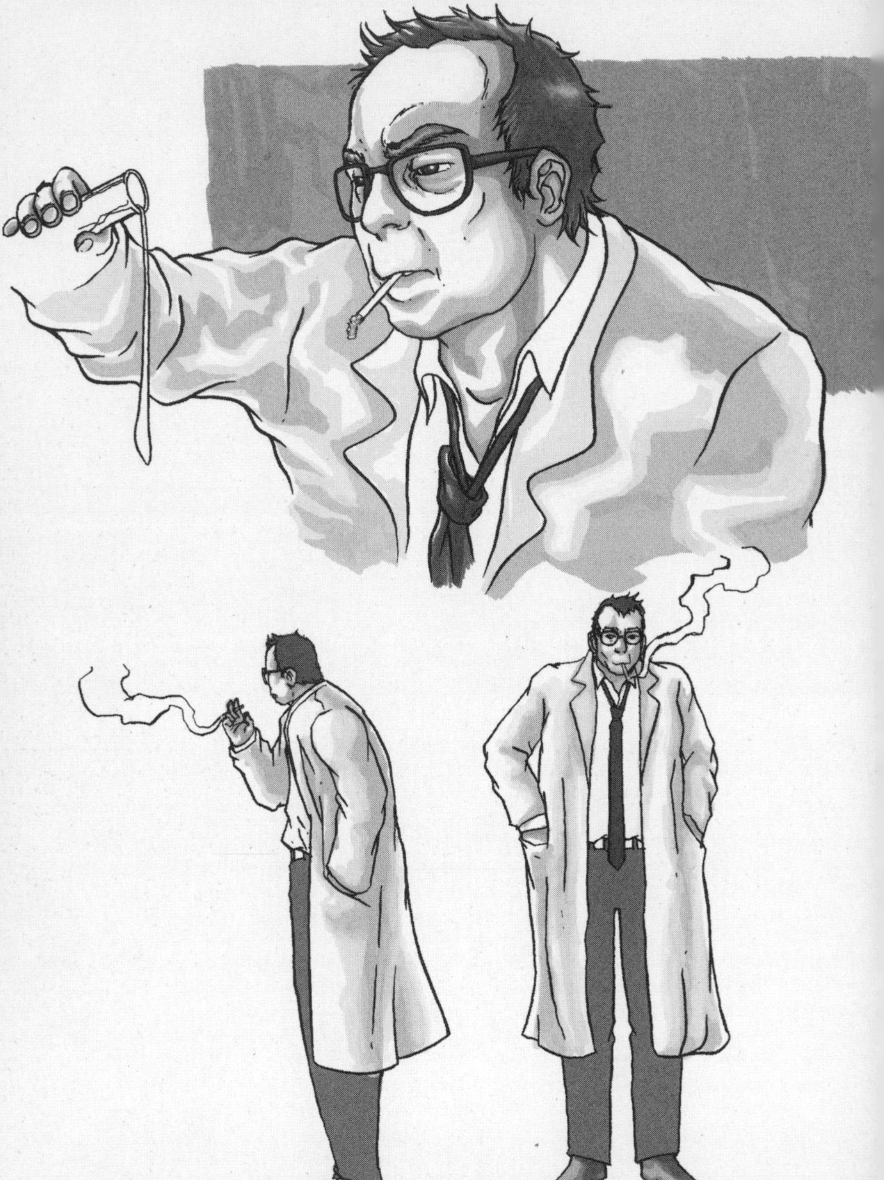

RICHARD LYNDON WYMOND

AGE: 53 YEARS
CLASSIFICATION: HUMAN
STATUS: ACTIVE
PARLIAMENTARY RECORD SECTION 0002.9
MARK XL-RLW.A

LAUDED AS THE EARTH'S LEADING NANOBIOLOGIST, RICHARD WYMOND ROSE FROM HUMBLE BEGINNINGS TO INTERNATIONAL SCIENTIFIC ACCLAIM.

GRADUATING WITH HONORS FROM THE MASSACHUSETTS INSTITUTE OF TECHNOLOGY AT CAMBRIDGE, RICHARD QUICKLY SECURED A STRING OF GENEROUS GRANTS, POURING ALL HIS RESOURCES INTO THE RESEARCH AND DEVELOPMENT OF FORMERLY THEORETICAL NANO COMPONENTS. HIS COMPANY, WYTECH LABS, PIONEERED A MODEST ARRAY OF NANITE BASED PRODUCTIVITY PACKAGES. WITH AN INITIAL FOCUS ON INDUSTRIAL APPLICATIONS, WYTECH SOON FOUND SUCCESS WITH MEDICALLY TARGETED PRODUCTS.

THE SIGMA SERUM, ABLE TO DELIVER MEDICINES AT THE CELLULAR LEVEL, PREDATED THE NOBEL-PRIZE-WINNING UPSILON SERUM; A SINGLE DOSE OF WHICH BOTH TARGETED AND ELIMINATED CANCEROUS CELLS FROM THE BODY.

THOUGH HIS SUCCESS WAS WELL-DESERVED, IT CAME AT THE PRICE OF HIS FAMILY. UNABLE TO BALANCE HIS HECTIC CORPORATE SCHEDULE, RICHARD FOUND HIMSELF AT THE OFFICE MORE AND MORE, AND AT HIS HOME LESS AND LESS. THE ARRIVAL OF THE EMISSARIES WOULD ONLY PROVE TO FURTHER DELAY HIS RETIREMENT, AND HASTEN THE DEVELOPMENT OF THE GOVERNMENT-FUNDED **ZETTA** SERUM, THE EFFECTS OF WHICH ARE NOW WELL-DOCUMENTED THE WORLD OVER.

DRAMATIS PERSONÆ

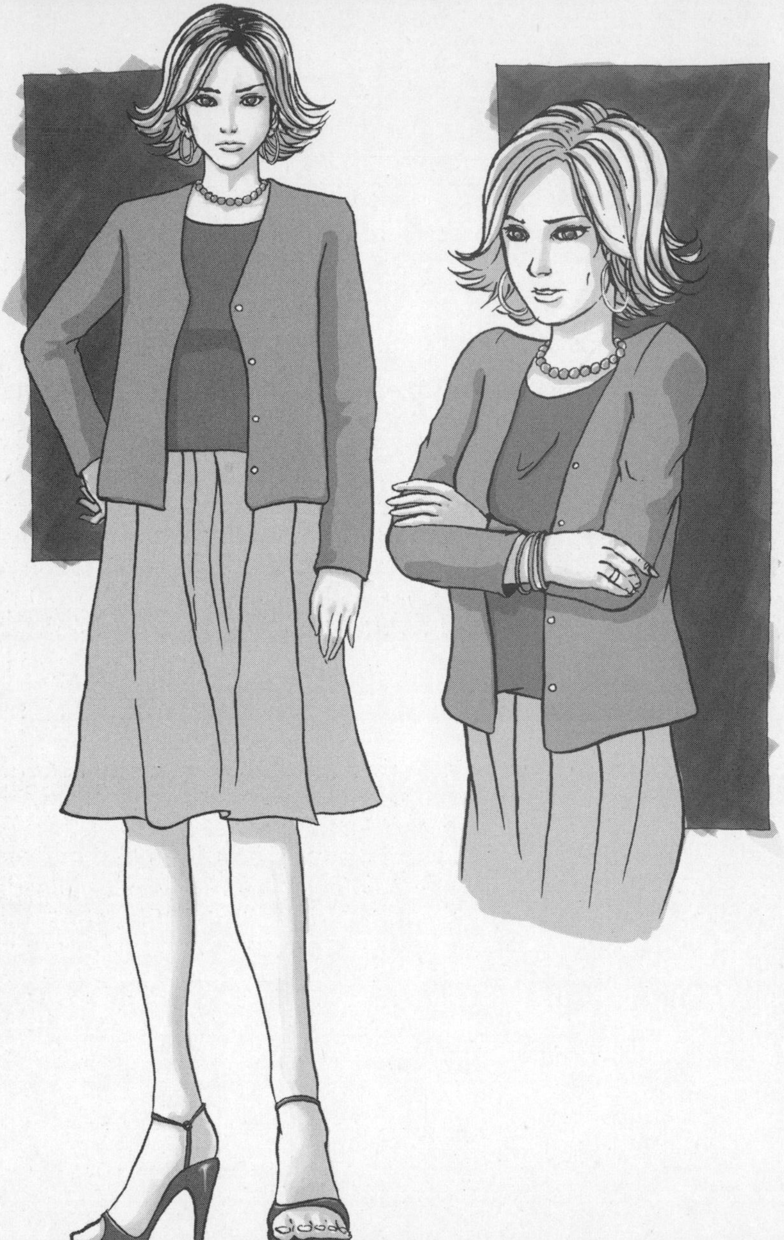

PENELOPE LYNN WYMOND
AGE: 44 YEARS
CLASSIFICATION: HUMAN
STATUS: ACTIVE
PARLIAMENTARY RECORD SECTION O118.3
MARK XL-PLW.D

AN AVID FOLLOWER OF RICHARD WYMOND'S GROUNDBREAKING WORK, PENELOPE'S LONGTIME FASCINATION LED TO AN ENTRY LEVEL POSITION AT WYTECH LABS, WHICH IN TURN LED TO MARRIAGE SHORTLY THEREAFTER.

THE DEATH OF HER PARENTS, BOTH AT THE HANDS OF CANCER, NOT ONLY PROMPTED HER INTENSE INTEREST IN THE SUBJECT OF NANO MEDICINES, BUT HER HUSBAND'S RESEARCH AND DEVELOPMENT OF THE UPSILON SERUM.

ELECTING TO STAY HOME FOLLOWING THE BIRTH OF THEIR DAUGHTER, PENELOPE CONTENTED HERSELF TO KEEP PACE WITH WYTECH LABS BY PROXY, WATCHING AS HER HUSBAND DISAPPEARED FARTHER AND FARTHER INTO THE OBSCURITY OF HIS BLEEDING-EDGE RESEARCH.

DRAMATIS PERSONÆ

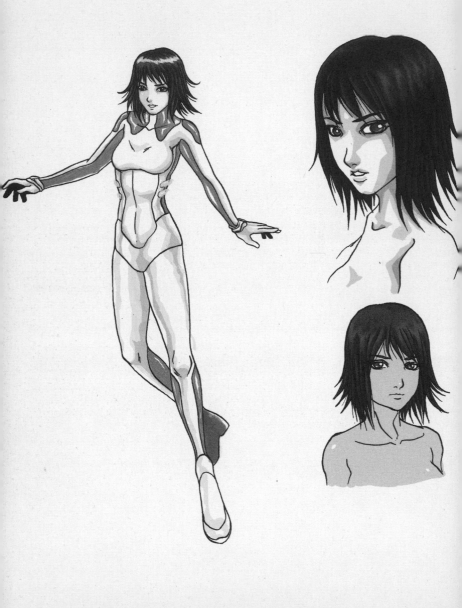

SAMANTHA EVANGELINE WYMOND
AGE: 17 YEARS
CLASSIFICATION: HUMAN
STATUS: ACTIVE
PARLIAMENTARY RECORD SECTION 1121.2 MARK
XL-SEW.Q

UNABLE TO CONNECT MEANINGFULLY WITH HER MOTHER, AND
CONFUSED BY THE PERSISTENT ABSENCE OF HER FATHER, SAMANTHA
EVANGELINE WYMOND SKEWED GRADUALLY OFF COURSE. DESPITE AN
UNCANNY KNACK FOR ALMOST EVERY SUBJECT, EVIE (AS SHE'S CALLED
BY FRIENDS AND FAMILY) CHOOSES TO RAIL AGAINST HER TEACHERS
(BOTH HUMAN AND NON-HUMAN), HER BITTERNESS MATERIALIZING
AS COLD SARCASM AND SELF-DESTRUCTIVE BEHAVIOR.

SEEKING OUT THE PERSISTENT DIN OF HER EARPHONES, EVIE
STUBBORNLY IGNORES HER OWN TALENTS IN FAVOR OF MOUNTING
BITTERNESS, TURNING AWAY THE FEW WHO CARE ENOUGH TO REACH
OUT. AFTER ALL, NOBODY SHE LOVED EVER LOVED HER BACK. NOT FOR
LONG, ANYWAY.

FOR EVIE, THE ARRIVAL OF THE *EMISSARIES* WAS NOT A WELCOME ONE.
IN ADDITION TO AROUSING CHAOS THROUGHOUT THE WORLD, THEIR
PRESENCE PULLED HER FATHER EVEN FARTHER AWAY THAN BEFORE.
LITTLE DID SHE KNOW THEY WOULD BOTH BE REUNITED IN THE SHADOW
OF EARTH'S STRANGE, NEW VISITORS – IF ONLY FOR A SHORT AMOUNT
OF TIME.

DRAMATIS PERSONÆ

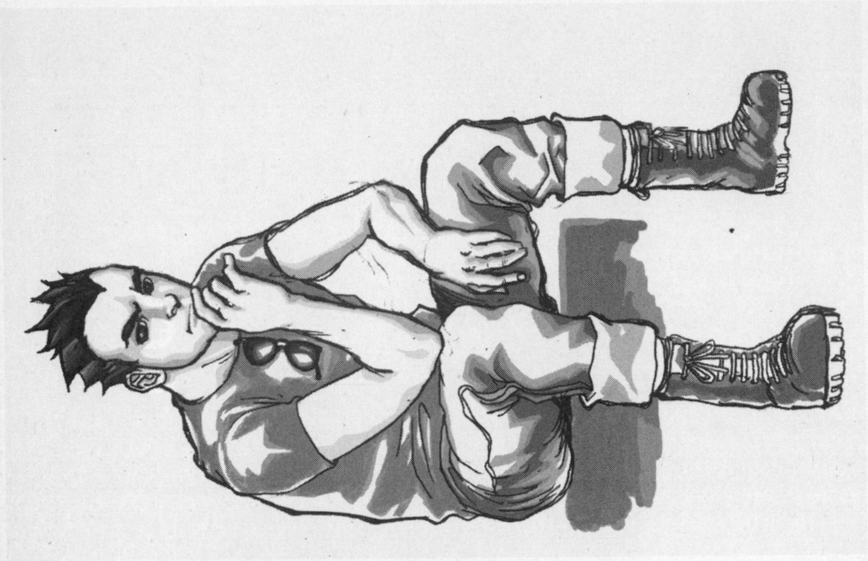

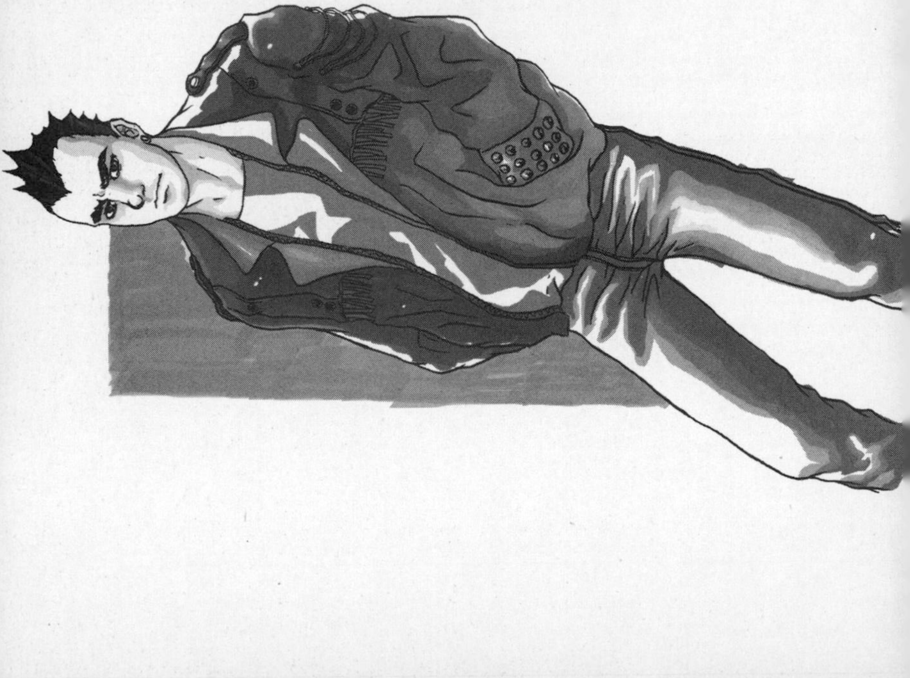

ROLAND JOSEPH WATSON
AGE: 18 YEARS
CLASSIFICATION: HUMAN
STATUS: ACTIVE
PARLIAMENTARY RECORD SECTION 7610.0
MARK XL-RJW.I

BOTH FRUSTRATED BY AND ATTRACTED TO HIS CLASSMATE EVIE, ROLAND WATSON OFFERS SOUND ADVICE DISGUISED BY SUBTLE FLIRTATION. HIS CALM AND COOL EXTERIOR BELIES HIS UPBRINGING AS THE SON OF A MILITARY OFFICER, NOT TO MENTION A LIFETIME OF CHAOS AND CONSTANT CROSS-COUNTRY MOVES.

AN A STUDENT HIMSELF, ROLAND'S TRUE PASSION IS HIS MUSIC. TEACHING GUITAR LESSONS IN HIS SPARE TIME, ROLAND SPENDS EVERY EXTRA DOLLAR ON AMPS AND EQUIPMENT WITH THE ASPIRATION OF ONE DAY STARTING HIS OWN BAND AND – JUST MAYBE – PLAYING THE SONG HE WROTE FOR EVIE THEIR FIRST YEAR OF HIGH SCHOOL.

WHEREAS SHE USES MUSIC TO ESCAPE THE WORLD, ROLAND USES MUSIC TO UNDERSTAND IT. TO SEE THROUGH IT. WITHOUT THE CALMING FILTER HIS ART CREATES, ROLAND ISN'T SURE HE COULD HANDLE THE STRESSES OF DAY-TO-DAY LIFE. LET ALONE THE ARRIVAL OF THE EMISSARIES.

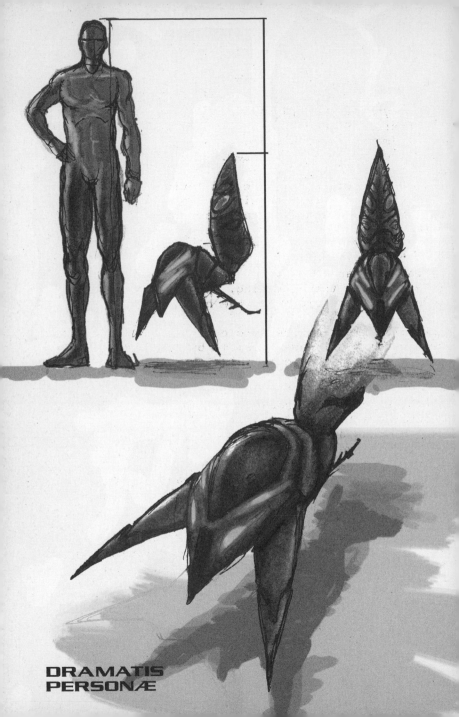

DRAMATIS PERSONÆ

THE EMISSARIES
AGE: INDETERMINATE
CLASSIFICATION: ARTIFICIAL
STATUS: ACTIVE
PARLIAMENTARY RECORD SECTION 0000.9
MARK XZ-NTE.Q

CONSTRUCTED COUNTLESS EONS AGO BY THE PEACEFUL NYU'TRALI, THESE ARTIFICIAL RECRUITMENT DRONES TIRELESSLY SCOUR THE UNIVERSE, WANDERING SILENTLY FROM ONE GALAXY TO THE NEXT IN SEARCH OF SENTIENT LIFE. WITHOUT THE NEED FOR FOOD OR SLEEP, AND DESIGNED TO PERSIST INDEFINITELY, THE EMISSARIES SERVE AS THE PERFECT COSMIC EXPLORERS.

ONCE UNCOVERED, A NEW AND SUFFICIENTLY ADVANCED CIVILIZATION IS INVITED TO JOIN THE INTERGALACTIC PARLIAMENT, AND IS GIVEN 5 YEARS (OR LOCAL EQUIVALENT) TO SELECT A WORTHY REPRESENTATIVE.

IN ADDITION TO THE DESIGN AND CONSTRUCTION OF GEOSYNCHRONOUS JUMP GATES FOR EACH CONSTITUENT PLANET, THE EMISSARIES ARE TASKED WITH ESCORTING EACH NEW DELEGATE TO THE PARLIAMENT ITSELF, SITUATED ATOP THE FREE-FLOATING REMNANTS OF PLANET NYU'TROS.

DRAMATIS PERSONÆ

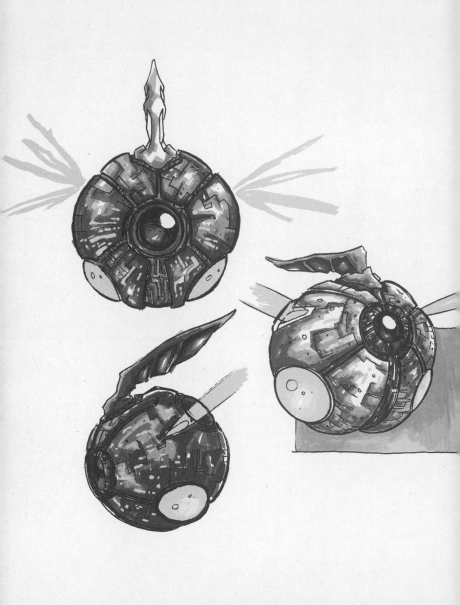

CRICKET

AGE: VARIABLE / HOST SPECIFIC
CLASSIFICATION: ARTIFICIAL
STATUS: ACTIVE
PARLIAMENTARY RECORD SECTION 1121.2
MARK XZ-SEW.Q2

NICKNAMED SO AS TO AVOID TERMINALLY LONG TECHNICAL SEMINARS, THE COGNITIVE REACTION AND INTUITIVE CONCEPTUAL KNOWLEDGE EXPERT WAS PROGRAMMED BY WYTECH LABS IN CONJUNCTION WITH THE ZETTA SERUM, AND PRESET TO INSTALL ITSELF WITHIN THE AUGMENTED CONSCIOUSNESS OF ITS RECIPIENT.

PROJECTED INTO VISIBLE SPACE ON A THREE-DIMENSIONAL GRID OF NANO PARTICLES, CRICKET'S CODE IS EXECUTED AT LIGHTNING SPEED BY A MENTALLY-INTEGRATED LATTICE OF MOLECULAR COMPUTERS. IN SHORT, CRICKET *KNOWS WHAT YOU KNOW BEFORE YOU KNOW IT, EVEN IF YOU DON'T THINK YOU KNOW IT.* WHEREAS A CONSCIENCE IS ONE'S GUIDE, CRICKET IS THEIR SPOTLIGHT — OFTEN GIVING VOICE TO THOUGHTS OR MOTIVATIONS LAYING HIDDEN BENEATH THE SURFACE.

THE LONG-TERM EFFECTS OF CRICKET INSTALLATION ARE CURRENTLY UNDOCUMENTED, THOUGH IT IS CONJECTURED THAT HUMAN MENTAL CAPACITY COULD QUADRUPLE GIVEN THE GRADUAL LOSS OF SELF-DECEPTION, AND HEIGHTENED LEVEL OF FOCUS INHERENT IN THE UNIT.

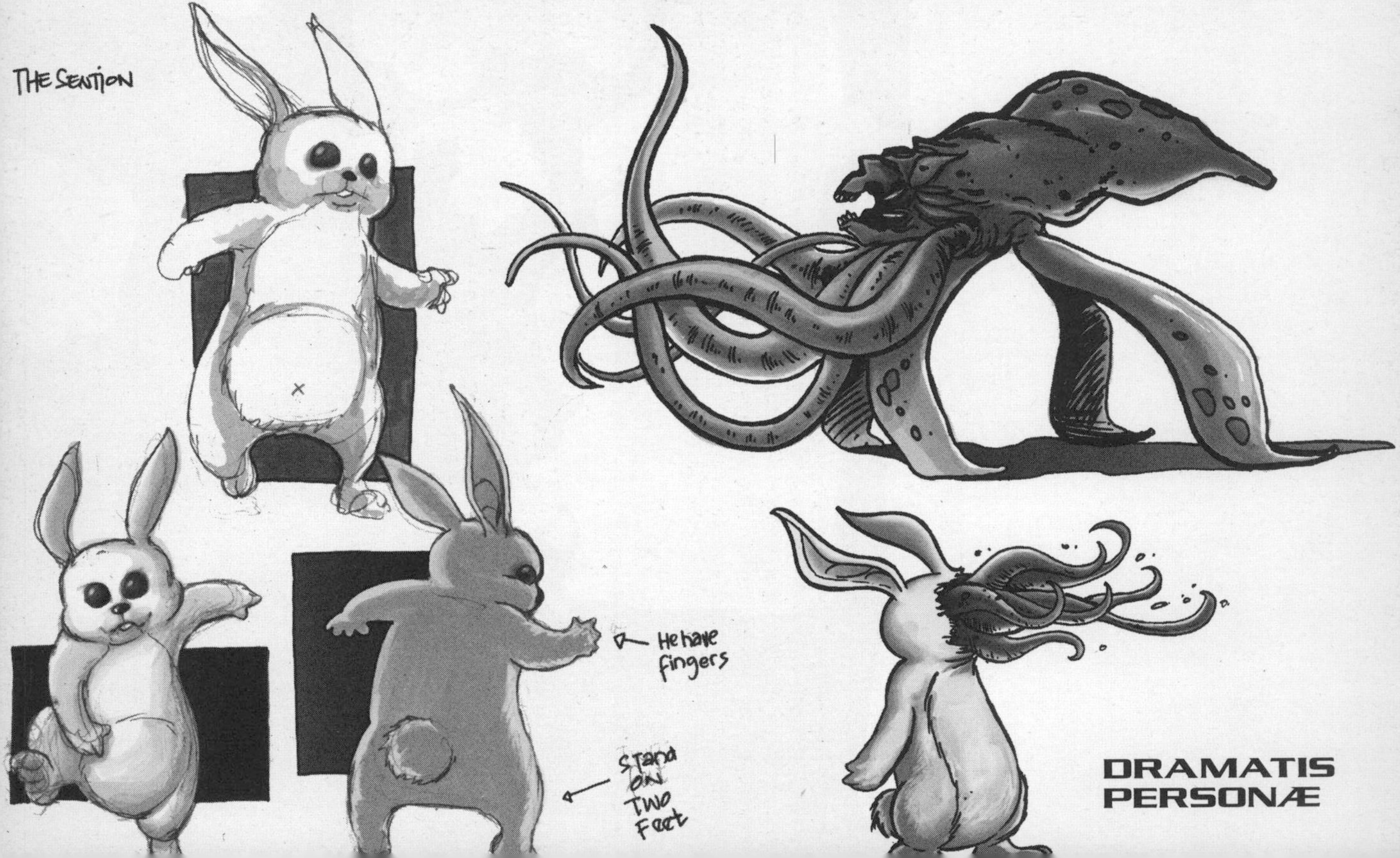
THE SENTION
He have fingers
Stand on two feet

DRAMATIS PERSONÆ

CONTROLLER VODE
AGE: INDETERMINATE
CLASSIFICATION: SENTION
STATUS: ACTIVE
PARLIAMENTARY RECORD SECTION 03417.1
MARK XX-STN.Q

AS THE NEBULOUS CUSTODIAN OF THE INTERGALACTIC PARLIAMENT,
CONTROLLER VODE RELIES ON HIS SENTION HERITAGE TO CLOTHE
HIM IN A FAVORABLE GUISE. HAVING EVOLVED OVER COUNTLESS
MILLENNIA FROM BEINGS NOT UNLIKE CHAMELEONS, THE SENTION ARE
CHRONICLED AS HAVING DEVELOPED THE MOST SUCCESSFUL FORM OF
CAMOUFLAGE KNOWN THROUGHOUT THE UNIVERSE.

AS OPPOSED TO DRAWING THEIR DISGUISE FROM ENVIRONMENTAL
SHAPES AND PATTERNS, THE SENTION ARE ABLE TO PLUMB THE
PSYCHE OF BOTH FRIEND AND FOE FOR APPROPRIATE (AND OFTEN
BENEVOLENT) CAMOUFLAGE. LIKEWISE, THE TRUE FORM OF THE
SENTION – AND CONTROLLER VODE HIMSELF - IS A THING LONG
FORGOTTEN AMONGST THE STARS.

TOGETHER WITH HIS ASSOCIATES, VODE CHANNELS HIS TALENTS TO
EASE THE MINDS OF NEW RECRUITS, ACTING AS LIAISON, TOUR GUIDE
AND DISCIPLINARIAN. AS THE PARLIAMENT PLAYS HOME TO NEARLY
1000 ALIEN LIFE FORMS, AND THEREFORE 1000 DIVERGENT POLITICAL
VIEWS, VODE MAKES IT HIS JOB TO KEEP BELLIGERENCE AT BAY, AND
THE PARLIAMENT SAFELY INTACT.

DRAMATIS PERSONÆ

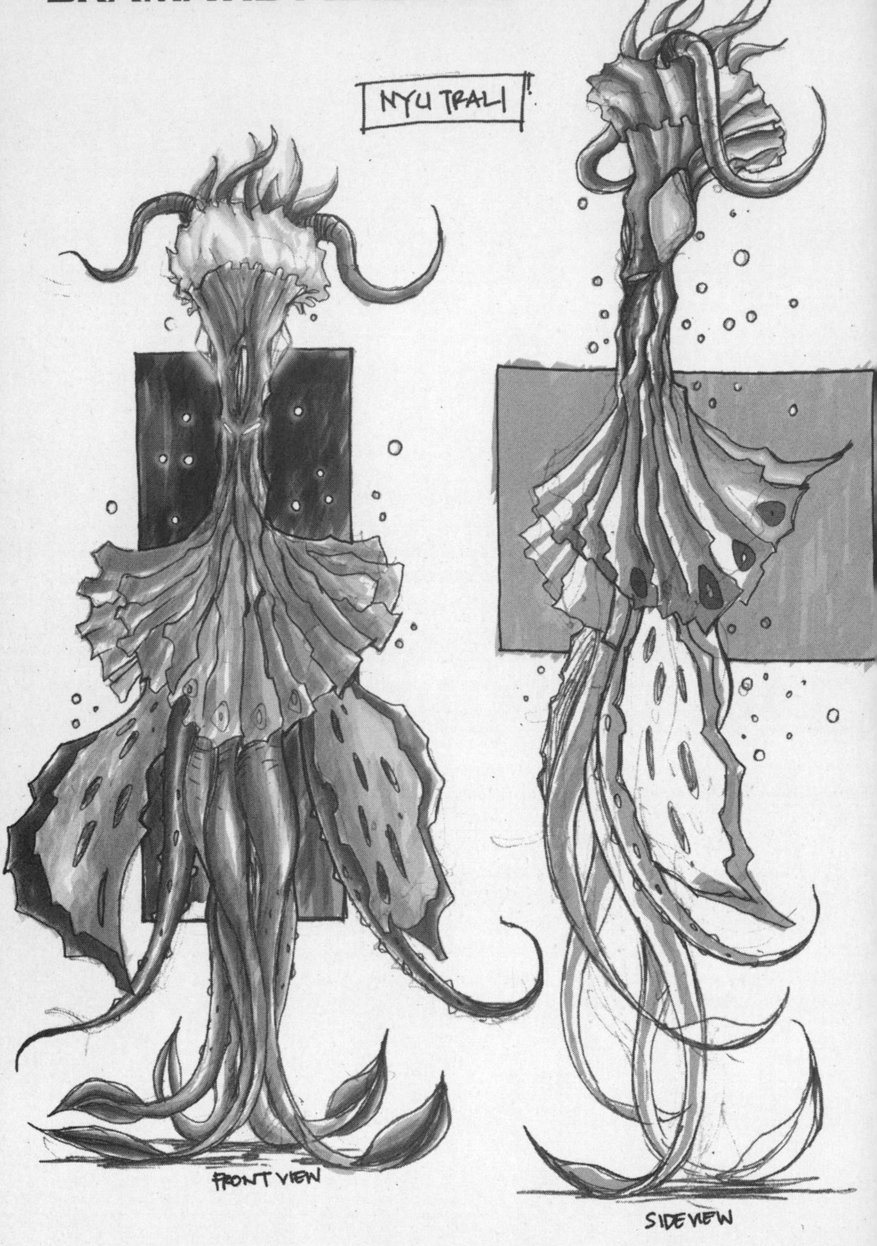
NYU TRALI
FRONT VIEW
SIDE VIEW

THE NYU'TRALI
STATUS: EXTINCT
PARLIAMENTARY RECORD SECTION 0000.3
MARK XP-NTI.A

THE NYU'TRALI WERE A PEACEFUL SPECIES, PERHAPS THE FIRST AND ONLY TRULY PEACE-LOVING ORGANISMS TO EVER EXIST THROUGHOUT THE KNOWN UNIVERSE.

BRILLIANT AND WISE, YET PLANT-LIKE IN NATURE, THE NYU'TRALI FORGED THEIR HOMES, TECHNOLOGIES AND EVEN THEIR CAPITAL CITIES ENTIRELY OF SOPHISTICATED PHOTOSYNTHETIC MATERIALS, EFFECTIVELY ENABLING THEIR ENTIRE CIVILIZATION TO HEAL ITSELF BY STARLIGHT. FOR THIS REASON, AND OTHERS, IT IS CONJECTURED THAT WAR WAS ABANDONED AT A VERY EARLY STAGE, AND LIKELY VIEWED AS A BOTHERSOME AND WHOLLY POINTLESS WASTE OF TIME. ANY EXTERNAL FORCES, LARGE OR SMALL, THOUGHT TO INVOKE AGGRESSION OR BRUTALITY WERE JUDICIOUSLY ABOLISHED – IF NOT ELIMINATED ALTOGETHER.

WITHOUT MINDLESS CONFLICT TO DISTRACT THEM, THE NYU'TRALI WERE ALSO THE FIRST TO HARNESS METASPACIAL – AND ALLEGEDLY PAN-DIMENSIONAL - TRAVEL, PERFECTING THE DESIGN AND DISTRIBUTION OF GEOSYNCHRONOUS JUMP GATES THROUGHOUT THEIR GALAXY. IN FACT, IT IS THE SPACE-BENDING TECHNOLOGIES PIONEERED BY THE NYU'TRALI WHICH STILL FACILITATE THE VAST MAJORITY OF INTERSTELLAR TRAVEL.

IT IS UNKNOWN PRECISELY WHEN THEY WERE ATTACKED, OR FROM WHENCE THEIR EXECUTIONERS ORIGINATED. IT IS BELIEVED, HOWEVER, THAT THEIR ENEMIES HID AMONGST THEM FOR SOME TIME; WATCHING, WAITING AND STRIKING WITH DEADLY PRECISION. THE ENTIRE PLANET NYU'TROS WAS SUMMARILY DESTROYED, SURVIVED ONLY BY THE SPIRE OF THEIR INTERGALACTIC PARLIAMENT, AND A SCATTERED FLEET OF EMISSARY SCOUTS.

DRAMATIS PERSONÆ

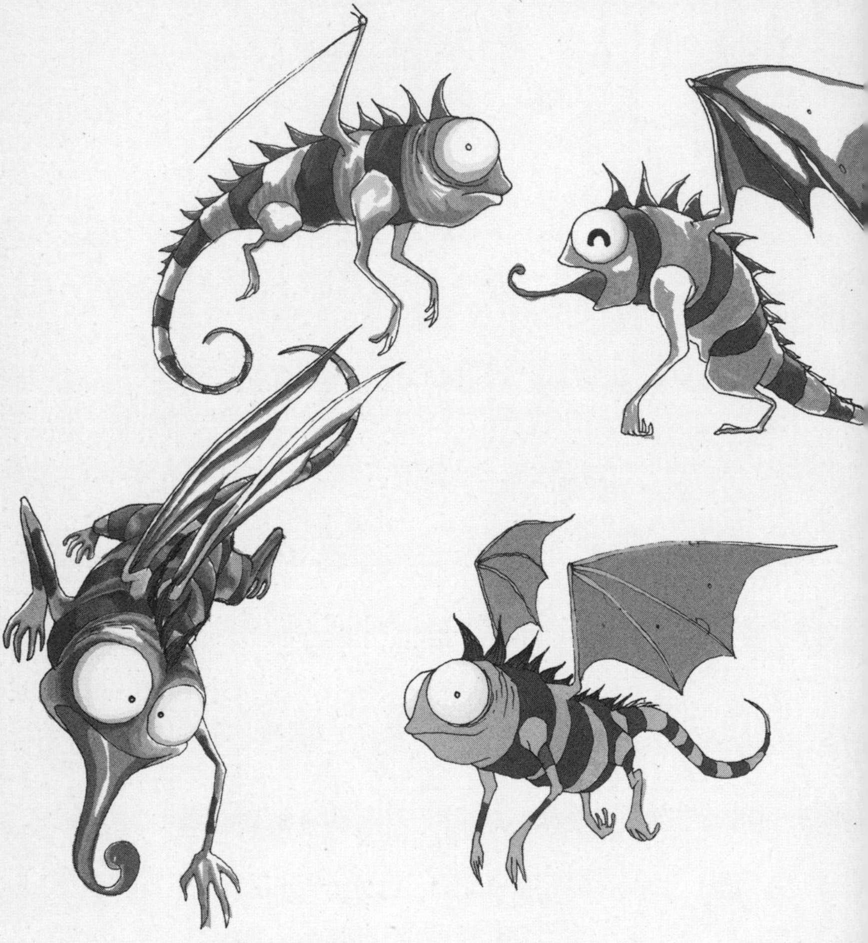

TEKE
AGE: INDETERMINATE
CLASSIFICATION: XEVOID
STATUS: ACTIVE
PARLIAMENTARY RECORD SECTION 1979.0
MARK XD-TKE.H

HAILING FROM THE PLANET XEVOS, AND ACCUSTOMED TO THE BLUEISH
GLOW OF NOT ONE, BUT THREE DISTANT SUNS, TEKE MAKES FOR MUCH
MORE THAN A CHALLENGING CONVERSATIONALIST.

SMALLISH AND PSEUDO-REPTILIAN, TEKE IS ABLE TO HOVER ON
A PAIR OF THIN, MEMBRANOUS WINGS. DEEMED TOO DIMINUTIVE
FOR MILITARY SERVICE, AND ENTIRELY TOO ABSENT-MINDED FOR
SCIENTIFIC PURSUITS, TEKE WAS SELECTED AS XEVOS' SOLE POLITICAL
REPRESENTATIVE.

THOUGH HIS HYPERACTIVE NATURE AND CHEMICALLY-AUGMENTED
SPEECH PATTERNS MAKE HIM TRICKY TO UNDERSTAND, ONE LATENT
ABILITY PROVES CONSISTENTLY INVALUABLE. DEVELOPED AS AN
EVOLUTIONARY DEFENSE AGAINST THE LARGER, MORE DANGEROUS
RESIDENTS OF XEVOS, XEVOID HATCHLINGS ARE CAPABLE OF SEEING
AT LEAST 10, IF NOT 20, SECONDS INTO THE FUTURE. NOT ONLY DOES
THIS MAKE THE XEVOID ALMOST IMPOSSIBLE TO CATCH, BUT DOUBLY
IMPOSSIBLE TO KILL, DESPITE VARIOUS PREDATORS' EVENTUAL
DEVELOPMENT OF TARGETED TEMPORAL DISTORTION.

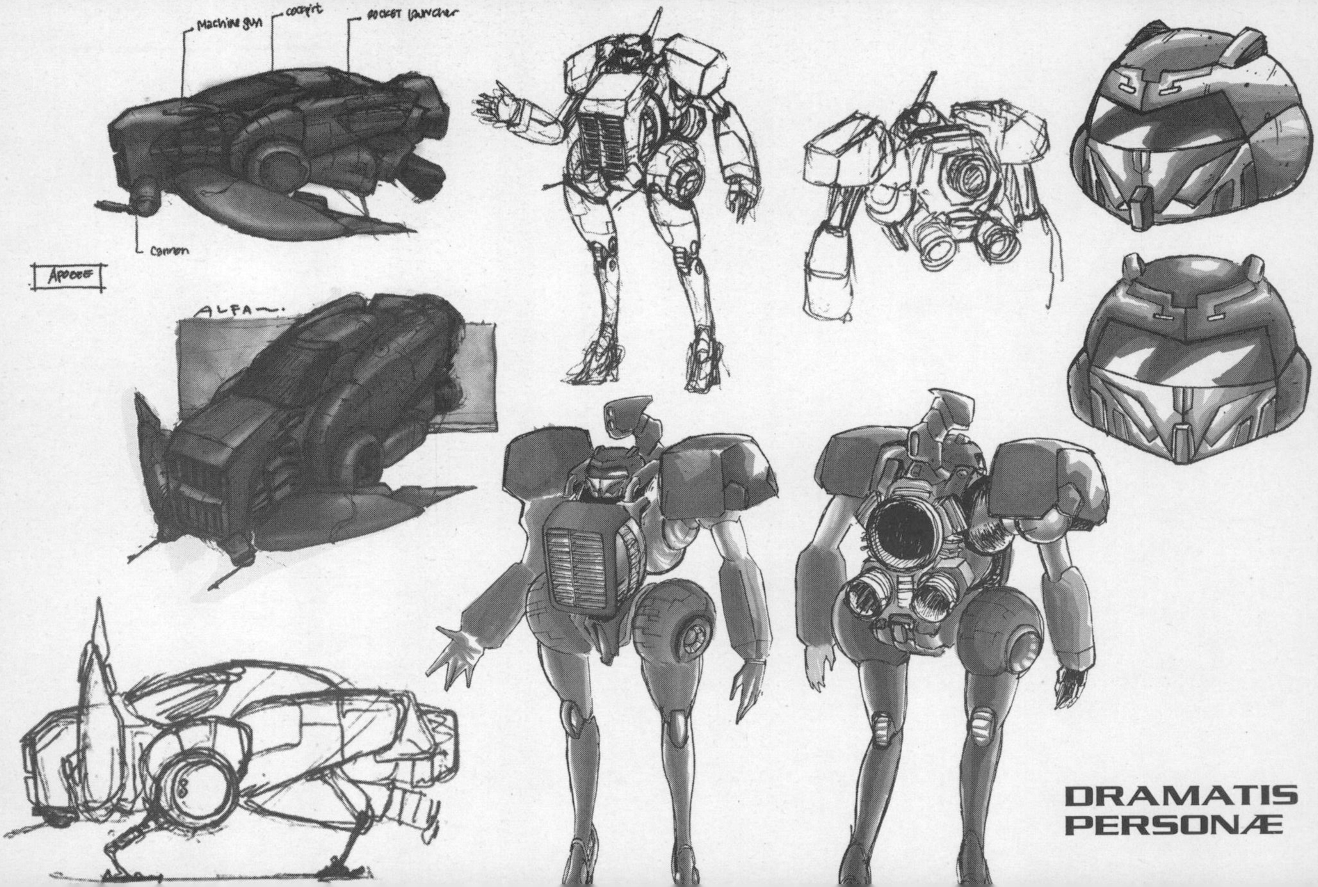
Machine gun
cockpit
Rocket launcher
Cannon
ALFA

DRAMATIS PERSONÆ

APOGEE
AGE: INDETERMINATE
CLASSIFICATION: DETRIDIAN
STATUS: ACTIVE
PARLIAMENTARY RECORD SECTION 4242.9
MARK XZ-APO.G

ONE OF MANY SENTIENT (AND SOMEWHAT ANTHROPOMORPHIC) SPACECRAFTS FROM THE PLANET DETRUTOS – PREVIOUSLY REGARDED AS A GALACTIC JUNKYARD. WHEREAS SOME PLANETS GIVE EVENTUAL RISE TO ORGANIC LIFE, DETRUTOS IS CONSIDERED, BY MOST, TO BE THE FIRST WORLD TO PRODUCE MECHANICAL LIFE PRIOR TO THE SINGLE-CELLED ORGANISM.

MOBILIZED BY ROVING ELECTRICAL STORMS, EARLY DETRIDIANS DREW THEIR CONSCIOUSNESS FROM THE WRECKAGE OF KA'WEI NON, A GALACTIC PROBE DRIVEN BY A SELF-REPLICATING AI CORE. COMPRISED OF SPARE PARTS AND ABANDONED ALIEN SPACECRAFT, DETRIDIANS FIRST WORSHIPED THE PROBE AS A GOD, BEFORE EVENTUALLY DEVELOPING SUPERIOR FORMS OF ARTIFICIAL LIFE, AND THEREBY UPGRADING THEIR OWN SHIPBOARD COMPUTER CORES.

OFTEN REFERRED TO NEGATIVELY AS *SENTIENT SCRAP*, DETRIDIANS ARE PEACEFUL YET FORMIDABLE, MOST OF THEM CONTAINING MORE BUILT-IN FIREPOWER THAN EVEN THE NEWEST MELEE CLASS K'NIK WAR CRUISERS.

DRAMATIS PERSONÆ

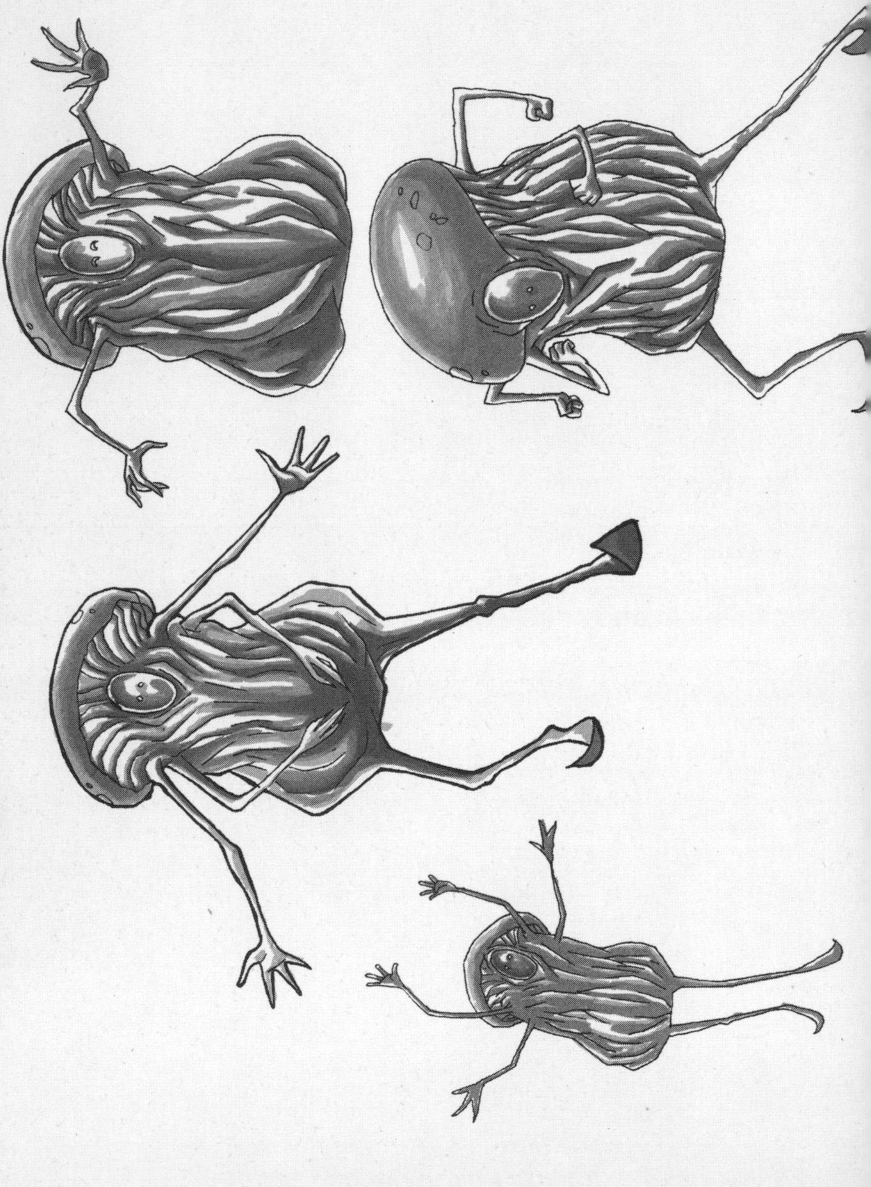

ZYG
AGE: IRRELEVANT
CLASSIFICATION: ZYG
STATUS: ACTIVE
PARLIAMENTARY RECORD SECTION 8619.8
MARK XU-ZYG.U

AS A RARE AND WHOLLY IMPROBABLE FORM OF INTERDIMENSIONAL
FUNGUS, ZYG HAS THE DUBIOUS ABILITY TO NOT ONLY SPAN MULTIPLE
DIMENSIONS, BUT TO SENSE EVENTS BEYOND PERCEIVABLE SPACE.
WHILE HIS OUTWARD FORM IS A VISUAL PROTRUSION INTO THREE-
DIMENSIONS, IT IS BUT AN INFINITESIMAL SLICE OF THE GREATER
BEING.

THE PRACTICAL SIDE EFFECT OF SPANNING SEVERAL DIMENSIONS
AT ONCE MANIFESTS ITSELF IN THE FORM OF A CHRONOLOGICALLY
DISTORTED SPEAKING PATTERN, OFTEN MAKING ZYG A CHALLENGING
CREATURE WITH WHICH TO CONVERSE.

IT IS POSTULATED THAT ZYG SPREADS ACROSS AND THRIVES UPON
THE VERY FABRIC OF THE UNIVERSE ITSELF; FEEDING ON OBSERVABLY
EMPTY SPACE AS MOST FUNGI WOULD ON DEAD MATTER, OR AS
SYMBIONTS OF PLANTS, ANIMALS, OR OTHER FUNGI.

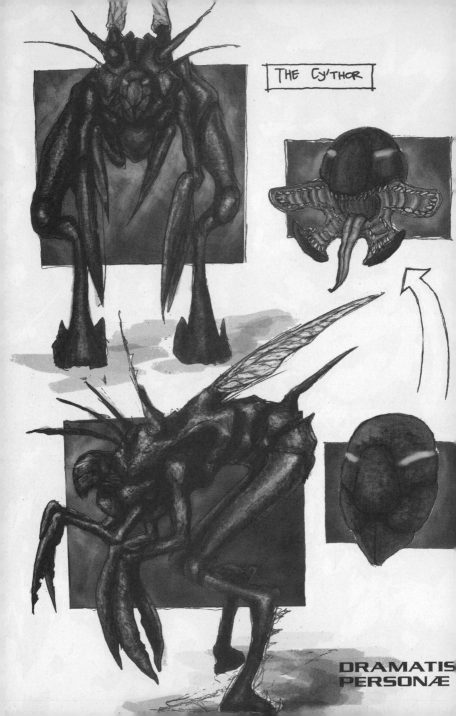

THE CY'THOR

DRAMATIS PERSONÆ

THE CY'THOR
STATUS: ACTIVE / HAZARDOUS
PARLIAMENTARY RECORD SECTION 0990.4
MARK XI-CTR.X

RECLUSIVE AND UNPLEASANT, THE CY'THOR ARE GENERALLY AVOIDED, AND OFTEN BLAMED FOR ANY RANDOM OR UNPROVOKED ATROCITY. THEIR HIVE MENTALITY, COUPLED WITH AN OUTWARDLY VICIOUS AND AGGRESSIVE DEMEANOR, MAKES THEM BOTH A LIABILITY AND A VERSATILE SCAPEGOAT.

WHILE OFFICIALLY UNCONNECTED TO ANY MAJOR DISASTER, THE CY'THOR ARE KNOWN TO BE FIERCELY TERRITORIAL, FREQUENTLY SEEN PATROLLING AMONGST THE RUINS OF NYU'TROS. FOR CENTURIES, THEIR INVOLVEMENT WITH THE NYU'TRALI WAS WELL DOCUMENTED, LEADING TO RAMPANT SPECULATION AS TO THEIR CONNECTION WITH NYU'TROS' DESTRUCTION.

A COORDINATED STRIKE ON THE PARLIAMENT ITSELF IS DEEMED INEVITABLE.

DRAMATIS PERSONÆ

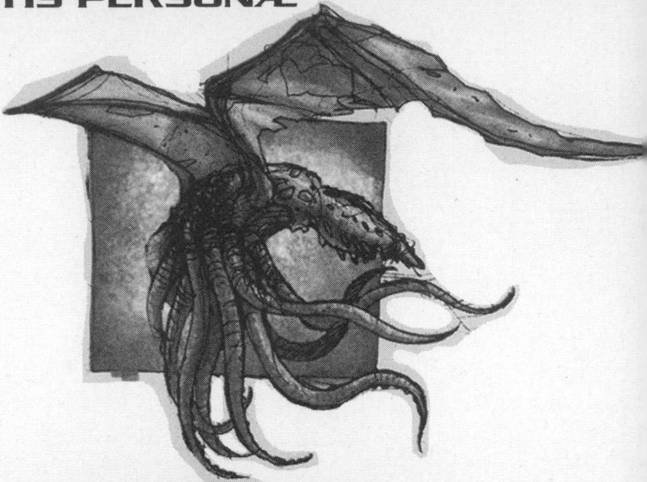

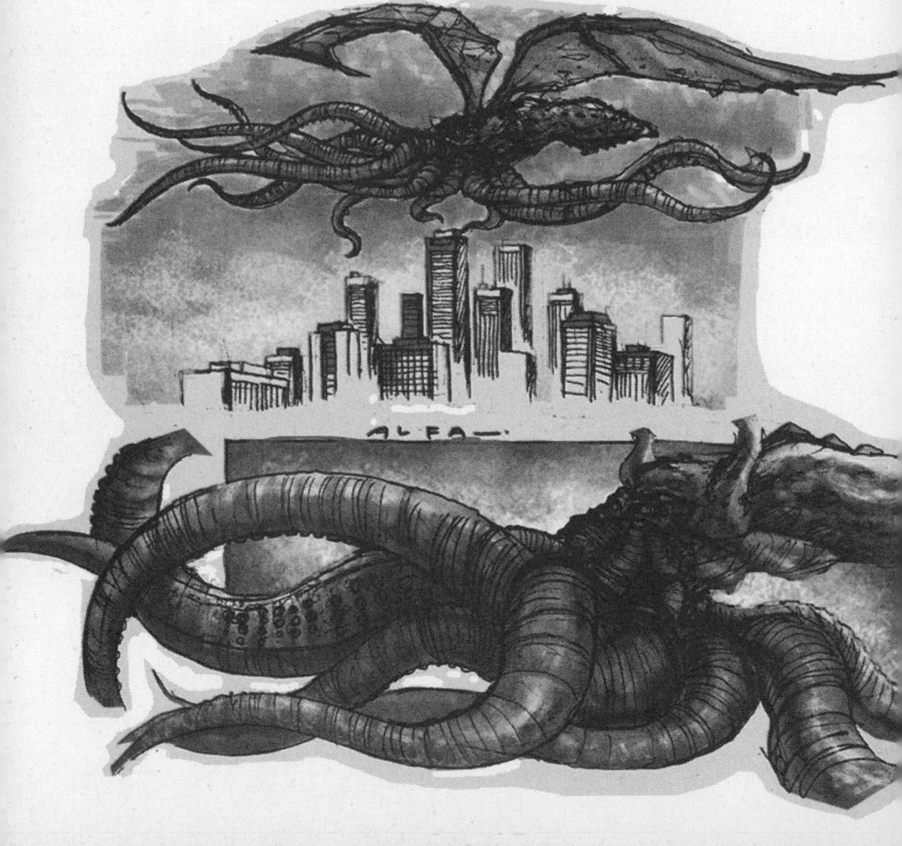

KU'THENDRIL THE DESTROYER
AGE: INFINITE
CLASSIFICATION: VOIDBRINGER
STATUS: UNKNOWN
PARLIAMENTARY RECORD SECTION 03417.0
MARK XX-KTH.A

FORGOTTEN BY MOST THROUGHOUT THE VASTNESS OF TIME, THE LEGEND OF KU'THENDRIL WAS GRADUALLY ABSORBED BY ANCIENT MYTH. WHISPERED TO BE OLDER THAN THE UNIVERSE ITSELF, AND WELL BEYOND THE BORDERS OF MORTAL UNDERSTANDING, THE DESTROYER EMBODIES ALL THAT IS DARK AND DESTRUCTIVE.

WHILE SOME CLAIM IT TO HAVE BEEN A NATURAL AND NECESSARY MITIGATING FORCE, OTHERS BELIEVE IT TO HAVE BEEN BORNE OF HUBRIS, FAITHLESSNESS, AND THE UNCHECKED EXPANSION OF GALACTIC CIVILIZATION. WHATEVER THE CASE, THE DESTROYER REMAINS ONE OF THE MOST COMMONLY INVOKED SPIRITS IN ALL THE COSMOS, LEANED UPON TO EXPLAIN NOT ONLY DEATH AND DISEASE, BUT TRAGEDY OF EVERY CONCEIVABLE VARIETY.

LEGEND HINTS THAT THE CREATURE WAS BOUND — LOCKED AWAY INDEFINITELY BEYOND THE WALL OF PERCEIVABLE SPACE. ONLY THE COMBINED WILL OF THE COSMOS, ITSELF, IS RUMORED TO BE CAPABLE OF RELEASING IT.

AFTERWORD

I KNOW I AM GOING TO SUFFER THE WRATH OF MANY READERS WHEN I SAY THAT, IN GENERAL, I JUST DON'T THINK THE WORLD NEEDS ANOTHER ZOMBIE STORY. SO I RESISTED SEVERAL REQUESTS FROM FRIENDS TO WATCH A WEB SERIES CALLED XOMBIFIED (WWW.XOMBIFIED.COM). BUT ON ONE OF THOSE VERY RARE DAYS WHEN I FOUND MYSELF WITH A LITTLE EXTRA TIME, I CAVED IN AND CLICKED ON THE LINK AND WAS SUCKED INTO ONE OF THE COOLEST STORIES -- ZOMBIE OR NOT! MY FEW SPARE MINUTES BECAME AN ENTIRE AFTERNOON. XOMBIFIED IS A UNIQUE STORY ABOUT A ZOMBIE NAMED DIRGE, WHO I LEARNED IS CONSIDERED A "QUASI-BATMAN OF THE UNDEAD" BY HIS TEEN AND ADULT FANS ALIKE. SINCE 2003, THE TEN ANIMATED XOMBIE EPISODES HAVE BEEN DOWNLOADED AND VIEWED OVER 13 MILLION TIMES! THESE GROUNDBREAKING WORKS HAVE SKYROCKETED TO POPULARITY AS A STAPLE OF NEWGROUNDS.COM, WHERE XOMBIE EPISODES CONSISTENTLY STEAL THE #1 SPOT FOR WEEKS, EVEN MONTHS, AT A TIME.

AS SOMEONE WHO CONSUMES WAY TOO MUCH MEDIA (FILM, TELEVISION, VIDEO GAMES, GRAPHIC NOVELS -- THE LIST GOES ON AND ON) IT WAS AMAZING TO BE SWEPT AWAY INTO A NEW WORLD CREATED BY AN ARTIST I HAVE BEGUN TO CALL THE "TORNADO OF TULSA." ONCE YOU GET CAUGHT UP IN JAMES FARR'S IMAGINATION THERE IS NO TELLING WHERE YOU'LL TOUCH DOWN. WHETHER IT'S AN ARMY OF TALKING SILVERWARE, A HOARD OF ZOMBIES OR OUR MAIN CHARACTER ARGUING WITH A VISUAL MANIFESTATION OF HER SUBCONSCIOUS, JAMES HAS A KNACK FOR BRINGING LIFE TO UNIQUE CHARACTERS.

AS A CREATOR, IT IS ALWAYS HARD TO HAND OVER YOUR BABY TO SOMEONE ELSE, BUT JAMES FARR WAS DESTINED TO RAISE THIS CHILD! BY THE END OF THE STORY, I NO LONGER REMEMBERED WHERE THE STORY CAME FROM AS JAMES JUMPED INTO THE WORLD (UMM... UNIVERSE) OF eV AND MADE IT HIS OWN. I THINK READERS OF eV WILL LOVE EVERYTHING IN THIS STORY, FROM EVIE'S BRIGHT RED HAIR, TO THE GIANT ALIENS, TO MY PERSONAL FAVORITE, THE ONGOING REPARTEE BETWEEN EVIE AND CRICKET. WE HOPE YOU'VE BEEN SUCKED INTO JAMES FARR'S VISION OF eV AS MUCH AS I HAVE.

ROGER MINCHEFF
PRESIDENT AND CEO OF SPACEDOG ENTERTAINMENT

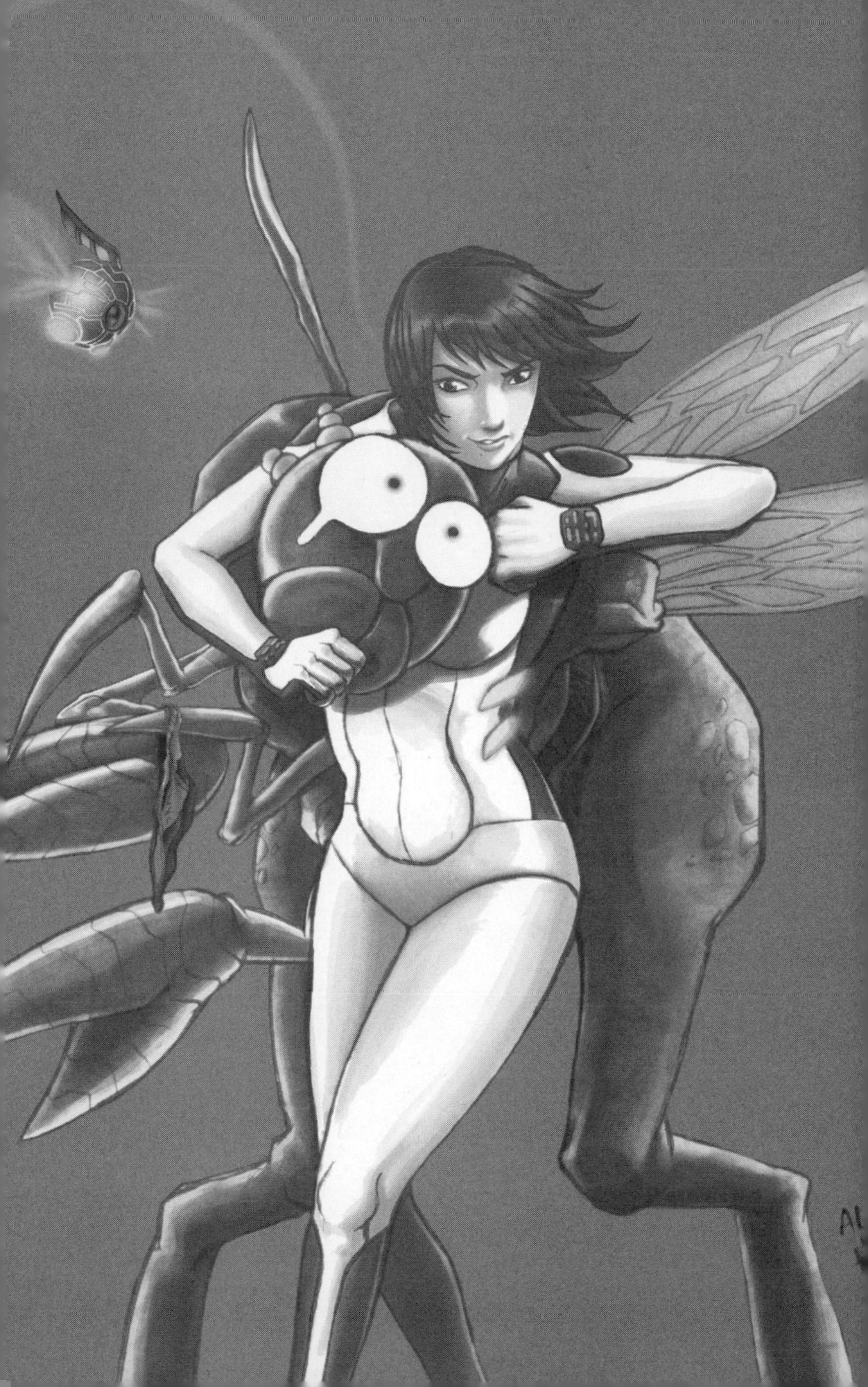

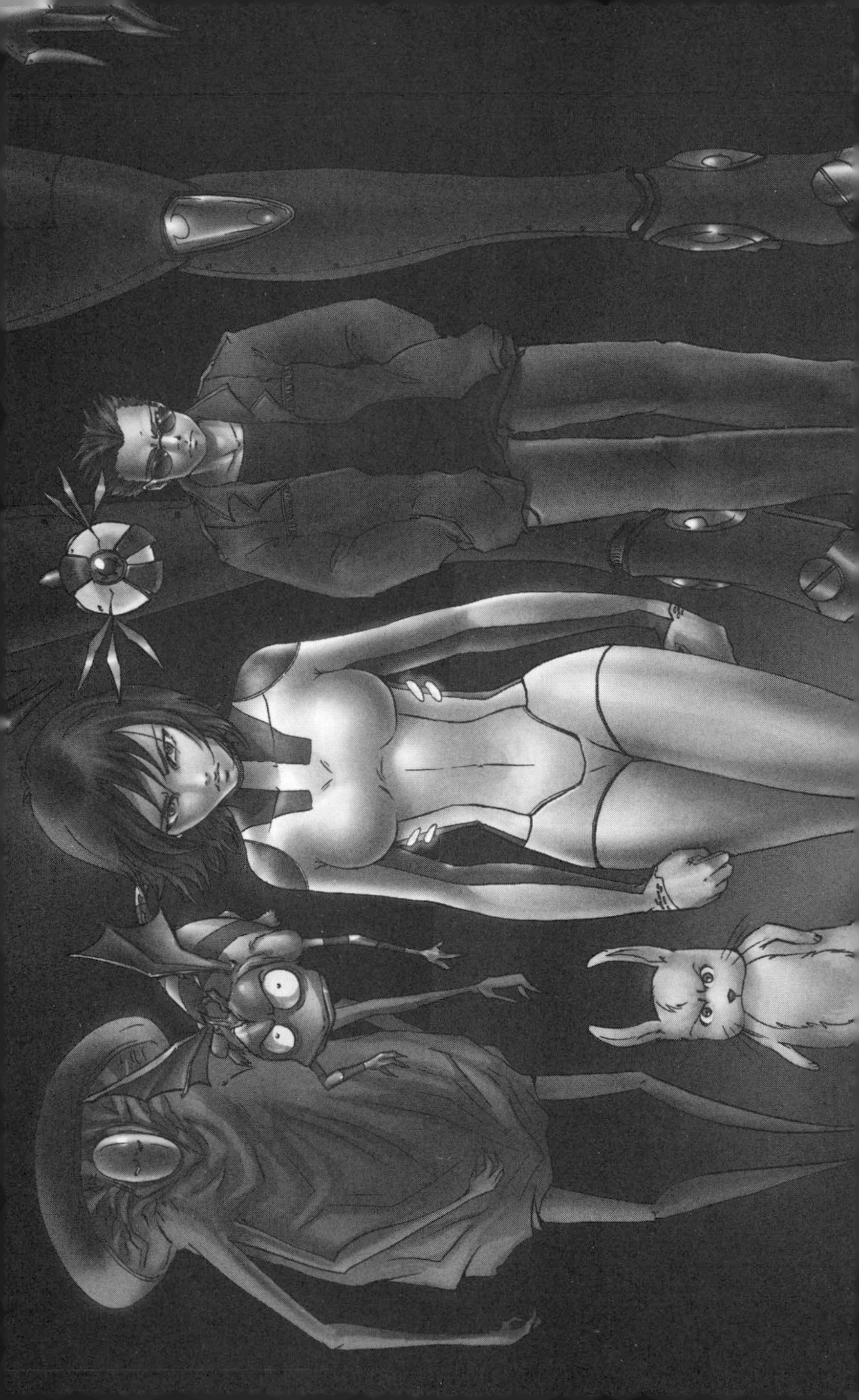